Directions for Pedagogical Construction Grammar

Applications of Cognitive Linguistics

Editors
Gitte Kristiansen
Francisco J. Ruiz de Mendoza Ibáñez

Honorary editor
René Dirven

Volume 49

Directions for Pedagogical Construction Grammar

Learning and Teaching (with) Constructions

Edited by
Hans C. Boas

DE GRUYTER
MOUTON

ISBN 978-3-11-135848-2
e-ISBN (PDF) 978-3-11-074672-3
e-ISBN (EPUB) 978-3-11-074677-8
ISSN 1861-4078

Library of Congress Control Number: 2021952144

Bibliographic information published by the Deutsche Nationalbibliothek
The Deutsche Nationalbibliothek lists this publication in the Deutsche Nationalbibliografie;
detailed bibliographic data are available on the Internet at http://dnb.dnb.de.

© 2023 Walter de Gruyter GmbH, Berlin/Boston
This volume is text- and page-identical with the hardback published in 2022.
Typesetting: Integra Software Services Pvt. Ltd.
Printing and binding: CPI books GmbH, Leck

www.degruyter.com

This volume is dedicated to the memory of my beloved father
Hans Ulrich Boas (1940–2020),
whose love, wit, curiosity, humor, and love of linguistics
continue to inspire me.

Preface

The past three decades have seen an ever-increasing interest in Construction Grammar (CxG), a theory of language that originated at UC Berkeley in the 1980s, together with its sister theory Frame Semantics. While the constructional research of Charles Fillmore and his associates at UC Berkeley ("Berkeley CxG") was initially focused primarily on English, a growing number of researchers during the 1990s also became interested in applying constructional insights to the analysis of other languages such as Finnish, French, German, Japanese, and Spanish.

During the 2000s, constructional research grew at an increasing pace, covering more linguistic phenomena in more languages, couched in a growing number of so-called "flavors" of Construction Grammar, including Cognitive CxG, Embodied CxG, Fluid CxG, Radical CxG, and Sign-based CxG. Most constructional research employs usage-based data to arrive at insights about how language "works" and how this knowledge can be modeled using a variety of notation systems. However, except for Embodied CxG and Fluid CxG, which both aim for a formalized implementation in a computational system that allows researchers to test hypotheses about language simulation, parsing, production, and learning, there has been relatively little research on how the "theory" of CxG can be applied to a variety of "real-world applications" such as foreign language teaching and learning.

Enter the first *Constructionist Approaches to Language Pedagogy* (CALP) conference, organized by Sabine de Knop and Gaëtanelle Gilquin in Brussels in November of 2013. The international conference drew about 70 participants with an interest in CxG coupled with a wide range of interests in language teaching and learning. The successful conference provided a first glimpse of what many colleagues had suspected for years, namely that there had been a significant interest in applying the results of constructional research to improving language teaching and learning. Some of the papers presented at the Brussels conference formed the basis for an edited volume by De Knop and Gilquin, which, for the first time, brought together in a coherent format the results of state-of-the-art constructional research as applied to language pedagogy.[1]

Subsequently, Heike Behrens and her team organized the second CALP conference in Basel in 2016. CALP-2 had a focus on usage-based foundations of L2 pedagogy, that is, on the intersections of usage-based (second) language acquisition research and constructionist approaches to (second) language learning,

---

[1] Sabine De Knop & Gaëtanelle Gilquin (eds.) (2016). *Applied Construction Grammar*. Berlin/New York: Mouton De Gruyter.

teaching, and assessment. This conference, too, was a great success, because it offered a variety of different theoretical and empirical perspectives on (1) input and interaction, (2) implicit and explicit (second) language learning and teaching, and (3) individual differences, as well as implications for (second) language assessment.

After the first two CALP conferences in Brussels and Basel, I decided to organize CALP-3 at the University of Texas at Austin in February of 2018. UT Austin is an exciting place for constructional research and language pedagogy specifically, and for linguistics more generally. There are about 50 linguistics faculty on campus in a variety of departments including Anthropology, Asian Studies, Bilingual Education, English, French and Italian, Germanic Studies, Linguistics, Psychology, Slavic Studies and Spanish and Portuguese. Several research centers, including the Center for Open Educational Resources and Language Learning, the Linguistics Research Center, and the Texas Language Center bring together faculty form across campus to promote research and teaching of languages. Some of the papers presented at CALP-3 in Austin form the basis of this edited volume, with a special focus on Pedagogical Construction Grammar.

My warmest thanks go to the many friends and colleagues who helped me with the reviewing process: Bert Cappelle, Oana David, Sabine De Knop, Tom Garza, Francisco Gonzálvez-García, Ben Lyngfelt, Miriam Petruck, Ute Römer, Josef Ruppenhofer, Paul Sambre, Roman Schneider, Peter Uhrig, Arne Zeschel, and Alexander Ziem. I would also like to thank the series editors of the *Applications of Cognitive Linguistics* series Gitte Kristiansen and Francisco J. Ruiz de Mendoza Ibáñes as well as an anonymous reviewer for their very valuable feedback. It has been a pleasure to work with the de Gruyter team Birgit Sievert and Kirstin Boergen on the various administrative and technical issues that go into the production of an edited volume. Finally, I want to thank my family (Claire, Lena, and Sophia) and my parents, Hans U. Boas and Ursula Boas, for their constant love and support.

This book is dedicated to the memory of my father, Hans Ulrich Boas, who passed away in September of 2020, while I was in the process of editing this book. Besides being a loving, caring, generous, funny, patient, and supportive father, he was also a great inspiration for me. Growing up, he instilled his love of languages, cultures, and linguistics in me, without which I might have never become a linguist myself. *Danke Papa!*

Austin, Texas, October 2021
Hans Christian Boas

Contents

Preface —— VII

I Introduction

Hans C. Boas
From Construction Grammar(s) to Pedagogical Construction Grammar —— 3

II Data and methodology in Pedagogical Construction Grammar

Stefan Th. Gries
On, or against?, (just) frequency —— 47

Gaëtanelle Gilquin
Constructing learner speech: On the use of spoken data in Applied Construction Grammar —— 73

Peter Uhrig, Susen Faulhaber, Ewa Dąbrowska, Thomas Herbst
L2-words that go together – more on collocation and learner language —— 97

III Learning and teaching constructions

Sabine De Knop, Fabio Mollica
Construction-based teaching of German verbless directives to Italian-speaking learners —— 123

Tore Nesset, Laura A. Janda
Securing strategic input for L2 learners: Constructions with Russian motion verbs —— 161

Amanda L. Patten, Florent Perek
Pedagogic applications of the English Constructicon —— 179

Karin Madlener-Charpentier
Learned attention beyond typological bootstrapping: Constructional repertoires and constructional complexity in the spatial language domain —— 217

IV Frame-based teaching and learning

Maggie Gemmell Hudson
Teaching second year German using frames and constructions —— 265

James Law
Frame-based metonymy in teaching L2 vocabulary —— 305

Alexander Ziem, Anastasia Neumann-Schneider
Towards a FrameNet for linguistic terminology: Theoretical foundations, lexicographic practice, didactic potential —— 333

Author Index —— 359

Subject Index —— 361

Introduction

Hans C. Boas
From Construction Grammar(s) to Pedagogical Construction Grammar

1 Introduction

The question of how insights from linguistic theory can be applied to solving problems involving language is an important one.[1] In times of shrinking budgets and a growing interest in testing theoretical insights in real life applications, more and more linguists have become interested in applying their insights in a variety of sub-disciplines, including foreign language learning (FLL) and foreign language teaching (FLT).[2] The chapters in this volume show how insights from Construction Grammar (CxG) can be applied to solve a number of issues in FLL and FLT.[3]

As such, this volume seeks to address a problem identified by Holme more than a decade ago, who pointed out that while construction grammars "are changing our perception of Second Language Acquisition (...) their impact on instruction has been muted." (Holme 2010a: 355) According to Holme, who adopts Ellis' (2001) proposal that second language learning is essentially construction learning, it should be possible to "let teachers derive an approach to grammar that is both descriptively accessible and psychologically plausible." (2010a: 356) On this view, grammatical form should be regarded as "symbolic, seeing its teaching as essential to language pedagogy, and closely bound up with the mastery of lexis and text-type." (Holme 2010a: 373)[4]

The ideas put forward by Holme and other researchers such as Queller (2001), Liang (2002), Gries and Wulff (2005), Littlemore (2009), and Eddington and Ruiz de Mendoza (2010) have provided the idea for a set of biannual conferences entitled "Constructional Approaches to Language Pedagogy" (CALP). Since 2014, these conferences have tackled, from several perspectives, the issues surrounding pedagogical applications of constructional insights in greater detail, leading to a

---

[1] Thanks to Francisco Gonzálvez-García and Marc Pierce for comments and feedback on an earlier version of this chapter. I am also thankful for the helpful comments from an anonymous reviewer. The usual disclaimers apply.
[2] For a discussion of different traditions within Applied Linguistics and how they relate to theoretical linguistics in North America and Europe, see, for example, Widdowson (2000), Angelis (2001), and Davies and Elder (2004).
[3] There are different strands of Construction Grammar, see Section 2.1.
[4] See also Holme (2010b).

converging interest in defining and developing a more unified applied version of CxG for pedagogical purposes.[5]

One of the more concrete visions of what an applied constructional paradigm to teaching and learning languages could look like is articulated by Herbst (2016), who coined the name *Pedagogical Construction Grammar*, which is a pedagogically inspired version of Applied Construction Grammar (De Knop and Gilquin 2016, Ruiz de Mendoza and Agustin Llach 2016). Building on prior research on the application of Cognitive Linguistics to FLL and FLT (see De Knop and De Rycker 2008), Herbst argues that combining usage-based and constructionist approaches with corpus linguistic analyses could result in more adequate and much simpler descriptions of the linguistic facts for the language classroom. The chapters in this volume each touch on several proposals put forward by Herbst (2016), thereby contributing towards a more fleshed-out vision of what a *Pedagogical Construction Grammar* could look like. The chapters contribute answers to the following questions:

- What different options are there to introduce the basic principles of CxG, e.g. non-modularity, form-meaning pairing, entrenchment, etc. to foreign language teaching, foreign language learning and second language acquisition (see Gries and Wulff 2005/2009, Holme 2010a/2010b, Gilquin 2012, Gilquin and De Knop 2016, Achard 2018, Gonzálvez-García 2019)?
- How should constructions (pairings of form with meaning/function) in the foreign language classroom be introduced (Boas/Ziem/Dux 2016, Bernolet and Hartsuiker 2018, De Knop and Mollica 2018, Garibyan et al. 2019)?
- What types of strategies does CxG offer to facilitate the acquisition of a second language? In particular, does it help when learners are confronted with constructions that are not present in their L1 (see Martínez Vázquez 2004, Wee 2007, Guilquin 2015, De Knop & Mollica 2016, Herbst 2016)?
- What do new constructional approaches to teaching and learning foreign language look like that take the insights of CxG seriously? Specifically, how must teaching materials be reconceptualized that give up the distinction between a vocabulary part and a grammar part in textbooks (see Boas and Dux 2013, Holme 2015, Gilquin 2018, Lorenz et al. 2020)?
- What should electronic resources using constructions and semantic frames for foreign language instruction look like (see Herbst 2016, Boas 2017a, Loenheim et al. 2016, Perek and Patten 2019)?

---

5 The first CALP conferences were held in Brussels (2014), Basel (2016), and Austin (2018). The fourth CALP conference did not take place in 2020 because of the COVID-19 pandemic. The contributions in De Knop and Gilquin (2016) are based on presentations given at the first CALP conference in Brussels.

- Are constructions acquired in the same way by foreign language learners as by native speakers? Are L2 constructions acquired differently by foreign language learners from different mother tongue backgrounds (see Martínez Vázquez 2008, Valenzuela and Rojo 2008, Ellis 2013, Guilquin 2016, Ellis et al. 2016, Herbst 2016, Glass 2019)?
- What role does frequency play in learning constructions in the language classroom (see Madlener 2015, Cappelle and Grabar 2016, Gries 2018, Herbst 2020)?

This chapter sets the stage for the remaining chapters in this volume. Section 2 provides the theoretical background of Construction Grammar and its sister theory Frame Semantics. It first gives an overview of how CxG evolved in the 1980s and 1990s as an alternative framework to the then prevalent Chomskyan paradigm. Then, it briefly reviews how during the 2000s, CxG evolved into different but compatible theoretical strands which all share the basic idea that constructions (pairings of form with meaning/function) are the basic units of language and that many meaning aspects of constructions can be modelled with Frame Semantics (Fillmore 1982). Then, Section 2 shows how key insights from CxG and Frame Semantics have been applied to the design, development, and implementation of constructional online resources, including FrameNets and constructicons.

Section 3 discusses Herbst's (2016) seven principles of Pedagogical Construction Grammar (PCxG), which is inspired by research in CxG, L2 acquisition, FLT, and FLL. To illustrate how Herbst's seven principles have been applied to overcome issues in FLT and FLL, I discuss their implementation in an online learners' dictionary based on semantic frames. Moreover, Section 3 highlights how the chapters in this volume each expand on Herbst's (2016) programmatic principles of PCxG, thereby opening avenues for further research. Finally, Section 4 provides a more general overview of each of the chapters in this volume.

2 Construction Grammar and Frame Semantics: From theory to application

2.1 Constructional approaches and principles

Construction Grammar (CxG) evolved in the 1980s at the University of California, Berkeley, as an alternative approach to language that sought to investigate the entirety of language, not only specific aspects. More specifically, CxG aims to account for both peripheral intransparent grammatical phenomena and fully regular semantic and syntactic structures. On the constructional view, the entirety of language consists of an ordered network of constructions (see Goldberg 1995, Langacker 2000, Boas 2011a, Diessel 2019).[6]

What first became known as CxG was later termed Berkeley Construction Grammar (Fillmore et al. 1998, Fillmore and Kay 1993, Fillmore 2013) as well as Cognitive Construction Grammar (Lakoff 1987, Goldberg 1995, Boas 2013). During the 1990s and beyond, different strands of CxG evolved, including Sign-based Construction Grammar (SBCG; Sag 2010, Boas and Sag 2012, Michaelis 2013), Radical Construction Grammar (Croft 2001, 2013), and Diasystematic Construction Grammar (Höder 2016/18, Boas and Höder 2018) (for an overview see Hoffmann and Trousdale 2013).[7] While the various strands of CxG differ not only in methodological terms but also with respect to the types of linguistic phenomena addressed and the conception of semantics invoked, they all embrace the view that both lexicon and grammar essentially consist of constructions, i.e. non-compositional (and compositional) form-meaning pairings of varying abstractness and syntagmatic complexity that must be learned.[8] The family of constructionist usage-based approaches (Goldberg 2013) aims at modeling what a language user knows in order to fully understand any linguistic expression. This is in contrast to other approaches (see, e.g., Chomsky 1981) that focus on an idealized speaker/hearer and that are primarily interested in a speaker's competence and not so much on performance (see Boas and Ziem 2018).[9]

Other constructional principles shared by the various strands of CxG include the following: First, the construction, a pairing of form with meaning/function, is the basic unit of language. Figure 1 illustrates the various types of information

---

[6] Goldberg (2006: 5) defines constructions as follows: "Any linguistic pattern is recognized as a construction as long as some aspect of its form or function is not strictly predictable from its component parts or form other constructions recognized to exist. In addition, patterns are stored as constructions even if they are fully predictable as long as they occur with sufficient frequency."
[7] See Boas and Dux (2017) and Boas (2021) for an overview of how CxG and Frame Semantics evolved out of Fillmore's (1968) research on Case Grammar.
[8] This view is in stark contrast to the Chomskyan framework, which claims that children growing up are not exposed to rich enough data to acquire every feature of their language ("poverty of the stimulus") (Chomsky 1988).
[9] There is another closely aligned framework that shares many of the principles of CxG and Frame Semantics and their application to FLL and FLT, namely Valency Theory (see Herbst 2014, 2015). For a discussion of the similarities and differences between CxG and Valency Theory, see Gonzálvez-García and Butler 2018.

encoded in a construction. Note that most constructions do not require specifications of all information types.

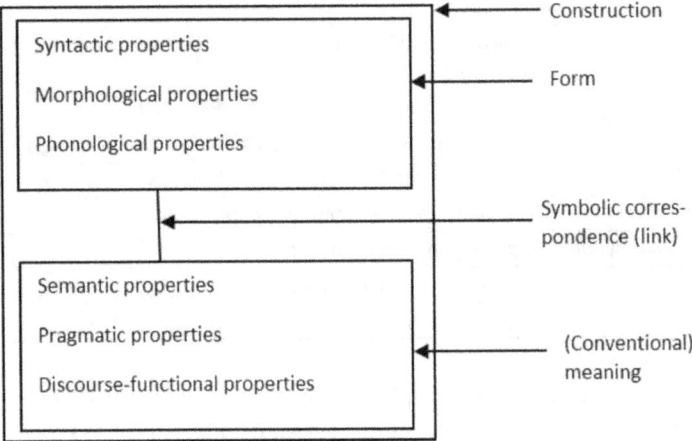

Figure 1: Types of information in constructions (Croft 2001: 18).

Second, form and meaning can typically not be separated from one another as they together constitute the linguistic sign (Goldberg 1995). Third, CxG does not make a difference between mechanisms that are at work in seemingly irregular grammatical instances as this has a critical impact on approaching more regular grammatical phenomena. By starting at the periphery, rather than at the core, where we find transparent structures, CxG aims at developing a "maximalist" approach covering both peripheral and core linguistic phenomena alike (see Boas and Ziem 2018). Fourth, CxG does not make a principled distinction between a so-called "lexicon" and "syntax." Instead, there is a continuum of grammatical constructions that differ in their complexity and level of schematicity/abstraction.[10] These constructions are basically the same type of declaratively represented data structure that pair form with meaning (see Goldberg 1995: 7). As Goldberg (2006: 18) puts it: "It's constructions all the way down." Table 1 provides an overview of constructions of various levels of size, complexitiy, and abstraction.

---

[10] Boas (2008) argues that in Goldberg's (1995) approach there still is a *de facto* separation of the lexicon and syntax, because lexical entries as separate entities fuse with ASCs, which are technically a different type of data structure.

Table 1: Constructions at various levels of size and abstraction (cf. Goldberg 2006).[11]

Subject-predicate agreement	NP VP-s (e.g. Kim walks)
Imperative	VP! (e.g. *Go home!, Buy that book!*)
Passive	Subj AUX V_{PP} (PP_{by}) (e.g. *The chocolate was eaten by the neighbors*)
Ditransitive	e.g. Subj V Obj_1 Obj_2 (e.g. *Lena baked Sophia a pizza*)
Covariational Conditional	e.g. The Xer the Yer (e.g. *the more you run the fitter you get*)
Idiom (partially filled)	e.g. *Pat doesn't like cake, let alone brownies*
Idiom (filled)	e.g. *hit the road, a penny for your thoughts*
Complex word (partially filled)	e.g. [N-s] (for regular plurals)
Word	e.g. *pizza, to walk, icy, but*
Morpheme	e.g. *un-, -able, -ment*

The constructions in Table 1 only display the form side of constructions, but not the meaning/function side. The meaning of most words, which in Table 1 are located at the lexical end of the syntax-lexicon continuum (at the bottom of Table 1), can be modelled with semantic frames (Fillmore 1982) as Section 2.2 below shows. Many constructions that are more abstract than morphemes and words, such as argument structure constructions, voice constructions, or word order constructions, to be found in the middle of the syntax-lexicon continuum in Table 1, may also evoke semantic frames. For example, the ditransitive construction evokes the Giving frame and the *way*-construction evokes the Self_motion frame. There is disagreement over whether all constructions have meaning (see Fillmore (1999) and Goldberg (2006) on the meaning of the subject auxiliary inversion construction), and whether the meaning side of all types of constructions can be represented using semantic frames (see Boas et al. 2019 and Boas 2021).

The fifth concept shared by different strands of CxG is that productivity plays an important role in shaping language. On this view, a construction's productivity can vary based on its syntactic, semantic, and pragmatic restrictions and therefore it can be located on a continuum, ranging from fully productive constructions to semi- and non-productive constructions. For example, the English subject-predicate construction is one of the most productive and regular constructions as it comes with very few restrictions. Other constructions are less productive: Due to its more numerous restrictions, the English double-object

---

11 Note that there is some disagreement on whether morphemes are the smallest constructional units. While Goldberg (2006: 5) assigns morphemes the status of constructions, Booij (2010: 15) argues that morphemes should not be assigned constructional status. See Booij (2013) for details.

construction is less productive than the *way*-construction (see Goldberg 1995: 141–151, 199–218). For more details on constructional productivity, see Clausner and Croft (1997), Stefanowitsch and Gries (2003), Barðdal (2012), and Diessel (2019).

With this brief overview of CxG we now turn to the main concepts underlying its sister theory, Frame Semantics, before discussing its application to the design and implementation of a lexicographic database of English. In Section 3 below I discuss how lexicographic resources based on FrameNet can be used for the teaching and learning of languages, thereby fleshing out some of Herbst's (2016: 41–45) principles regarding PCxG, including: (1) The principle of presenting constructions as form-meaning pairings; (2) The principle of one sense at a time; and (3) The principle of authenticity.

2.2 Lexicography: From theory (Frame Semantics) to application (FrameNet)

Frame Semantics (Fillmore 1982), which evolved out of Fillmore's earlier research on Case Grammar (Fillmore 1968), models knowledge about word meanings (as well as other linguistic units) with semantic frames, which characterize the types of underlying knowledge required to understand the meaning of a word.[12] According to Fillmore and Atkins (1992: 76–77), semantic frames can be characterized as follows.

> A word's meaning can be understood only with reference to a structured background of experience, beliefs, or practices, constituting a kind of conceptual prerequisite for understanding the meaning. Speakers can be said to know the meaning of the word only by first understanding the background frames that motivate the concept that the word encodes. Within such an approach, words or word senses are not related to each other directly, word to word, but only by way of their links to common background frames and indications of the manner in which their meanings highlight particular elements of such frames.

One of Fillmore's examples illustrating the central role played by semantic frames concerns the so-called `Commercial_transaction` frame, in which a BUYER buys GOODS from a SELLER in exchange for MONEY. The participants of such a commercial transaction scenario are so-called frame elements (FEs), which are situation-specific semantic roles. The semantic frame can be evoked by a number of different types of lexical units (a lexical unit is a word in one of its senses),

---

[12] Fillmore's use of the term "frame" is somewhat related to work in artificial intelligence as found in Minsky (1975) and psychology (Schank and Abelson 1975). For an extensive discussion of the use and various meanings of the term "frame", see Ziem (2008), Busse (2012), and Boas (2017a).

including verbs (e.g. *to buy, to sell, to pay*), nouns (e.g. *payment, buyer, receipt*), and adjectives (e.g. *cheap, expensive*).[13]

The 1980s and early 1990s saw an increased interest in Frame Semantics, which, for the most part remained theoretical (for an overview see Petruck 1996). This changed, however, when, in 1997, Fillmore founded the FrameNet project (Fillmore et al. 2003, Fillmore and Baker 2010, Ruppenhofer et al. 2013) at the International Computer Science Institute in Berkeley, California, with the goal of applying semantic frames to the creation of an online lexical database documenting a variety of frame-semantic and syntactic information for the English lexicon (see Boas 2017a, Ruppenhofer et al. 2017).[14] FrameNet (https://framenet.icsi.berkeley.edu) differs from other lexical databases such as WordNet (Fellbaum 1998), which relies primarily on lexical relations, in that it uses semantic frames to systematically structure the lexicon of English with frame-semantic criteria (see Boas 2005).

FrameNet is important for the emerging framework of PCxG for at least two main reasons. First, it shows how a linguistic theory has been successfully applied to develop a lexicographic resource for research that can be adopted for teaching and learning purposes (see Section 3.2 below). Second, FrameNet is based on usage-based data, extracted from the British National Corpus (BNC) as well as, more recently, the American National Corpus (ANC), thereby providing its users with authentic data instead of invented example sentences.

At the same time, however, there are a number of issues with FrameNet that make it problematic when considering its usefulness in the language classroom. In what follows, I first give a brief overview of the types of information contained in FrameNet to show that even though it is an extensive lexical database useful for linguistic research it is not very helpful for FLL and FLT, specifically at the beginning and intermediate levels. Then, in the next subsection, I will make the same point regarding a complimentary online repository of construction entries, the so-called constructicon, before turning to the question of how existing linguistic resources intended for linguistic research can be adopted and modified for language teaching and learning (see Section 3.3 below).

The FrameNet database is the result of a workflow of various steps during which lexicographers first identify semantically related lexical units to define semantic frames (according to the theory of Frame Semantics (Fillmore 1982, 1985)) that are evoked by these lexical units (LUs). This step is based on both

---

[13] LUs are specific senses of words or multi-word expressions that evoke a specific frame. Frame Semantics and FrameNet take a splitting approach to word meanings. On this view, a word may consist of various LUs (each representing a separate sense) that each evoke a separate frame. For details, see Fillmore and Atkins (2000) and Boas (2003/2011a/b).
[14] Parts of Section 2 are based on Boas (2017a/2020/2021).

corpus data as well as linguistic intuition by a group of lexicographers who have to come to a consensus about frame definitions. The second step involves extraction of corpus examples from the BNC and the ANC. Then, human annotators use a software annotation tool to annotate frame elements in the extracted corpus sentences. Finally, the lexical entries are compiled and stored in the database together with the frame description, the frame element definitions, and the annotated example sentences (see Fillmore and Baker 2010 and Boas 2017a for details). Users can search FrameNet by typing in a word such as *to wash*, which evokes the Grooming frame (as in the example sentence in Figure 2, *She washed the baby*).[15] Clicking on the name of a frame such as Grooming leads the user to a new page which presents a definition of the frame as in Figure 2.[16]

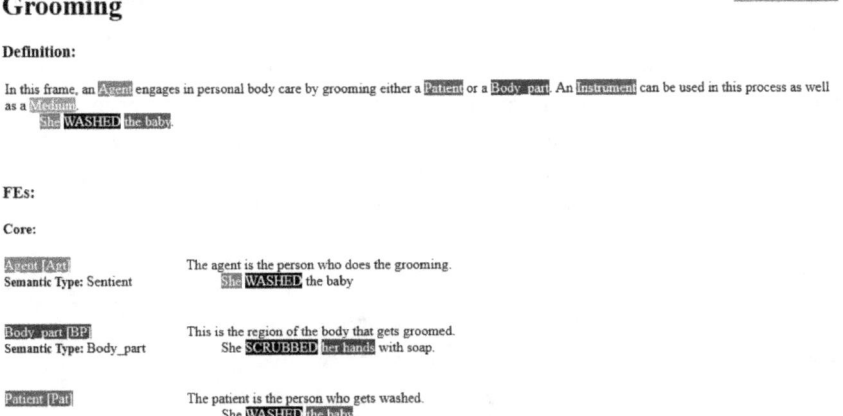

Figure 2: Frame and Frame Element Definitions of the Grooming frame in FrameNet.[17]

The frame description of the Grooming frame begins with a prose description of the frame, including its Frame Elements (FEs), highlighted in different colors, together with example sentences. The definitions of the core FEs of the Grooming frame, AGENT, BODY_PART, and PATIENT, appear below the prose description of the example sentence. The FE AGENT is defined as "the person who does the grooming,"

---

[15] Following FrameNet practice, frame labels are in Courier New font and FE labels are in small capital font.
[16] See https://framenet2.icsi.berkeley.edu/fnReports/data/frameIndex.xml?frame=Grooming for the GROOMING frame in FrameNet.
[17] FN makes a distinction between so-called core FEs that are crucial for the understanding of the frame itself and non-core FEs that do not define the frame but provide additional information such as TIME, PLACE, and MANNER. Here, we focus only on the core FEs.

the FE Body_Part is defined as "the region of the body that gets groomed," and the FE Patient is defined as "the person who gets washed." Following the frame description and the definition of the FEs, users can access information about frame-to-frame relations to see how a specific frame is related to other frames in the frame hierarchy (for details see Petruck et al. 2004 and Ruppenhofer et al. 2016). For example, the Grooming frame inherits frame-semantic information from the Intentionally_affect frame and it uses the Desirability frame.[18]

The frame description and FE definitions are followed by a list of different LUs that evoke the frame, including verbs such as *to bathe*, *to floss*, and *to shower* and nouns such as *facial* and *manicure*. Users can click on a specific link of an LU to get to their lexical entry reports and annotation reports (annotated corpus data that form the basis of the lexical entries, see Boas 2017a, Ruppenhofer et al. 2017). For examples, clicking on the lexical entry report for the verb *to shower* displays a definition of the verb (*to wash oneself in a shower*), followed by a list of FEs and their various syntactic realizations in terms of grammatical functions and phrase types. This information is followed by the valence table listing the valence patterns that show how the semantics of the Grooming frame are realized syntactically in various FE configurations (the valence patterns are the result of the manually annotated corpus examples extracted from the BNC and the ANC).

Valence Patterns:

These frame elements occur in the following syntactic patterns:

Number Annotated	Patterns			
1 TOTAL	Agent	Frequency	Frequency	Patient
(1)	NP Ext	NP Dep	PP[for] Dep	INI --
4 TOTAL	Agent	Manner	Patient	
(4)	NP Ext	AVP Dep	INI --	
3 TOTAL	Agent	Patient		
(3)	NP Ext	INI --		

Clear Sentences   Turn Colors Off

[X] I shaved and SHOWERED quickly , trying to think as I went along .INI

Figure 3: Valence patterns of the LU *to shower* in the Grooming frame.

---

[18] See https://framenet2.icsi.berkeley.edu/fnReports/data/frameIndex.xml?frame=Grooming for the Intentionally_affect frame and https://framenet2.icsi.berkeley.edu/fnReports/data/frameIndex.xml?frame=Grooming for the Desirability frame.

Figure 3 illustrates the valence patterns of the LU *to shower* in the `Grooming` frame. Each line with combinations of FEs is known as a frame element configuration (FEC). For example, the second line in Figure 3 lists the FEC AGENT, MANNER, and PATIENT. Clicking on the number 4 in Figure 3 lists all four annotated example sentences that serve as the basis for the FEC in the second line in the valence table of *to shower*. One of the sentences, *I shaved and showered quickly, trying to think as I went along* below the valence table, is displayed at the bottom of Figure 3 (the other three have been omitted for the purpose of this discussion). The example sentence shows that the FE AGENT is realized syntactically as an external NP, the FE MANNER is realized as a dependent ADVP, and the FE PATIENT is null-instantiated, i.e. it is not realized overtly at the syntactic level (it is understood from the context).[19]

In addition to the information on semantic frames evoked by specific LUs and the lexical entries of these LUs, FrameNet also contains for each LU a list of annotated example sentences illustrating the distribution of frame elements in corpus sentences from the BNC and the ANC. Figure 4 shows some of the annotated corpus sentences that form the basis for the information contained in lexical entries, including the valence patterns shown in Figure 3.

In its more than 20 years, the Berkeley FrameNet has worked on over 13,000 LUs in more than 1,200 frames.[20] This demonstrates that a linguistic theory can be successfully applied to the creation of linguistic resources, in this case a lexicographic database of English, which contributes to the broader (applied linguistics) field of lexicography. Since 2003, several research terms have re-used English FrameNet frames to create FrameNets for other languages, including German, Japanese, Swedish, French, Spanish, and Brazilian Portuguese (see Boas 2009, Boas et al. 2019, and Torrent et al. 2020 for details).[21]

However, when it comes to applying the FrameNet database to language teaching and learning, a few problematic issues arise.[22] First, using the database

---

[19] FN also documents null instantiated FEs, i.e. FEs that are not overtly realized in a sentence but that are conceptually understood as a part of the frame evoked by the relevant LU. There are three types of null instantiation recognized by FN: DNI (definite null instantiation), INI (indefinite null instantiation), and CNI (constructional null instantiation). For details, see Fillmore (1986), Ruppenhofer et al. (2016), and Boas (2017b).
[20] As of January 30, 2021. For updated information on the progress of FrameNet, see https://framenet.icsi.berkeley.edu/fndrupal/current_status.
[21] There are also a number of domain-specific FrameNets, such as one for soccer language (Schmidt 2009), biomedical language (Dolbey 2009), and legal language (Bertoldi et al. 2011).
[22] Note that the reference to extrinsic knowledge structured in terms of semantic frames can be of various sorts and levels of complexities. For example, they may refer to complex events (e.g. `Giving_birth` (*to birth, to bear*) or `death` (*to croak, to die, death*)), relations (e.g. `Personal_relationship`

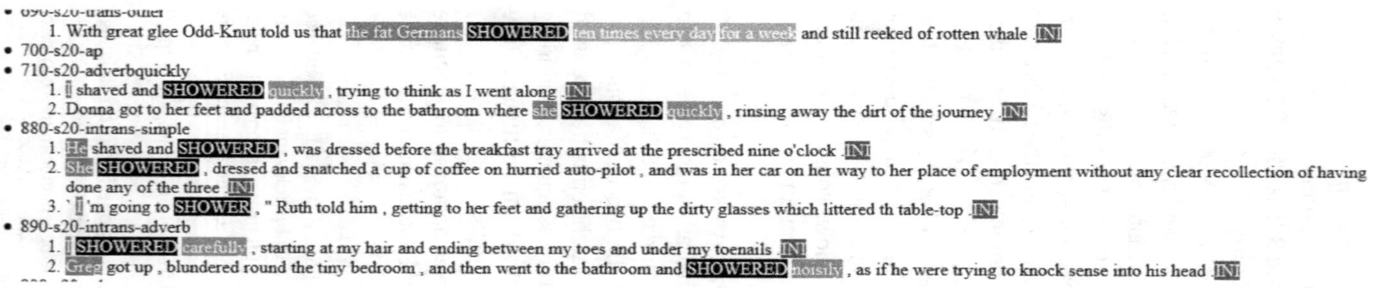

- 690-s20-trans-other
  1. With great glee Odd-Knut told us that the fat Germans SHOWERED ten times every day for a week and still reeked of rotten whale [N].
- 700-s20-ap
- 710-s20-adverbquickly
  1. I shaved and SHOWERED quickly, trying to think as I went along [N].
  2. Donna got to her feet and padded across to the bathroom where she SHOWERED quickly, rinsing away the dirt of the journey [N].
- 880-s20-intrans-simple
  1. He shaved and SHOWERED, was dressed before the breakfast tray arrived at the prescribed nine o'clock [N].
  2. She SHOWERED, dressed and snatched a cup of coffee on hurried auto-pilot, and was in her car on her way to her place of employment without any clear recollection of having done any of the three [N].
  3. 'I'm going to SHOWER," Ruth told him, getting to her feet and gathering up the dirty glasses which littered th table-top [N].
- 890-s20-intrans-adverb
  1. I SHOWERED carefully, starting at my hair and ending between my toes and under my toenails [N].
  2. Greg got up, blundered round the tiny bedroom, and then went to the bathroom and SHOWERED noisily, as if he were trying to knock sense into his head [N].

Figure 4: Annotated example sentences for to shower in the Grooming frame.

appropriately requires a significant amount of prior linguistic knowledge. Second, the amount of information contained in lexical entries is too much for language learners. Third, the corpus examples illustrating the use of LUs in context are often too long and complex, i.e. they make it difficult for the learner to understand which parts of an example are more relevant than others. Finally, FrameNet does not include frequency information about the distribution of LUs, which makes it difficult to decide a systematic program for progressive vocabulary learning.

In Section 3 I discuss a variety of ways in which the Berkeley FrameNet frames have been used as the basis for learners' dictionaries, thereby fulfilling several of Herbst's (2016) seven principles for PCxG. Before doing so, I briefly review how the expansion of lexical FrameNet was achieved in order to also cover constructions, resulting in a repository of construction entries, called a constructicon (Fillmore 2008). This discussion, too, forms the basis for our discussion of Herbst's (2016) principles of PCxG in Section 3.

2.3 Construction Grammar applied to Grammaticography: The constructicon

With a broad basis of frames and lexical entries in place, Fillmore became interested in expanding the lexicographic work of FrameNet to also describe and analyse grammatical constructions. One of the goals behind extending FrameNet's lexicographic work to grammaticography was to build a repository of grammatical constructions, a constructicon (Fillmore 2008), by using the same data structures, annotation techniques, and workflow that FrameNet employs in its lexicographic work.[23] Another goal was to determine how well the principles of CxG, the sister theory of Frame Semantics, can be applied to the description and analysis of grammatical constructions.[24] Fillmore et al. (2012) pin down the role of a constructicon, its relation to CxG, and its importance for language teaching as follows:

(*friend*, *bachelor*)), states (Being_located (*to find*, *situated*)), entities (Gizmo (*appliance*, *device*, *machine*)), scales (Temperature (*hot*, *freezing*)), and person and spatial deixis.
23 Recall from Section 2.1 that in CxG there is no strict separation between the lexicon and syntax and that language is thought to consist of a large, structured inventory of constructions, which vary in size and complexity.
24 This section builds on Boas (2017a/2020).

> While building a Constructicon has different goals from those of designing a construction based grammar of the language, the intention is that each construction will be represented in a way compatible with the development of a full grammar of the language (...). In some cases, we offer precise proposals for the treatment of a construction as it would appear in the grammar; in other cases the descriptions we present should be seen at least as organized observations about individual constructions, observations that need to be accounted for in a future complete grammar. In all cases we expect that the constructicon will contain useful information for advanced language pedagogy (...).[25]
>
> (Fillmore et al. 2012: 310)

Extending FrameNet's analytical and technical apparatus for lexical analysis to also cover non-lexical constructions, the FrameNet team began identifying, analysing, and annotating constructions in a very similar way as LUs. Building on a substantial amount of existing descriptions and analyses of constructions in the literature, FN researchers formulate a prose description of a construction, together with a definition of construct elements (CEs), parallel to that of frames and their corresponding FEs. A subsequent corpus search extracts relevant example sentences for annotation, a process very similar to that of annotating LUs (see Fillmore et al. 2012, Boas 2017a).[26] When annotating constructions, annotators may look for a so-called construction-evoking element (CEE), which is typically specific lexical material central for evoking the construction, such as the phrase *let alone* (see Fillmore et al. 1988 and Fillmore et al. 2012) in a sentence such as *Kim doesn't like citrus fruit, let alone grapefruit*.[27]

Annotators identify and mark CEs such as, in the case of the *Let-alone* construction, FIRST_CONJUNCT (*citrus fruit*) and SECOND_CONJUNCT (*grapefruit*), which are constituent parts of a construction. However, there are also constructions without any CEE such as *Subject_Predicate*, *Gapping*, and *Right_Node_Raising*, which have no overt lexical material signaling the presence of a construction. In such cases, annotators only employ the CE labels to identify the different parts of the construction. Besides the identification of CEs, annotations on different layers may also include information about grammatical functions and phrase types, parallel to FN's lexical annotation (for details see Fillmore et al. 2012, Boas 2017a, Lee-Goldman and Petruck 2018).

---

25 For more details on the relationship between grammatical theory and grammaticography, see Lyngfelt (2018) and the contributions in Fuss and Wöllstein (2018).
26 For details on how to systematically identify and describe constructions, see Fillmore et al. (2012), Lee-Goldman and Petruck (2018) and Boas (2019).
27 See http://sato.fm.senshu-u.ac.jp/frameSQL/cxn/CxNeng/cxn00/21colorTag/index.html-

Way_manner [NoColor] [NoTag] [ColorTag] [summary]
Evokes the Motion frame.
Inherits Way_neutral.

- A verb exceptionally takes *one's way* (the CEE) as a direct object, where *one's* is a possessive pronoun coindexed with the external argument of the verb. Together, they indicate that some entity moves while performing the action indicated by the manner verb. The manner verb is either transitive or intransitive, and thus labeled either Transitive_manner_verb or Intransitive_manner_verb). Following *one's way* is an obligatory frame element indicating some core aspect of motion (Source, Path, Goal, Direction).
- The semantics of this construction is identical (or at least very close to) that of the frame Motion: A Theme moves under its own power from a Source, in a Direction, along a Path, to a Goal, by a particular means. In many cases the path traversed by the Self mover is also created by them as they go, in a particular manner (i.e., while performing some temporally coextensive action) (as in *he whistled his way through the plaza*).
- [the She] [t_man whistled] [cee her way] [Path down the lane] [goal to the silo].
- References:
- Goldberg, Adele E. 1995. Constructions: A Construction Grammar Approach to Argument Structure. Chicago: Chicago University Press.
- Kuno, Susumu and Takami Ken-ichi. 2004. Functional Constraints in Grammar: On the Unergative-Unaccusative Distinction. Amsterdam: John Benjamins Publishing Company.

Figure 5: First part of *Way_manner* construction entry.

Figure 5 shows the first part of the construction entry of the `Way_manner` construction. The first line shows that it evokes the `Motion` frame, and it inherits from the `Way_neutral` construction. Below that we find the general prose description, including the semantics of the construction as well as references to publications on the *Way_manner* construction. The second part of the *Way_manner* construction in Figure 6 lists the definitions of CEE(s) and CEs. Recall that non-lexical constructions without meaning such as the `Subject_Predicate` construction are not evoked by a CEE. In contrast, lexical constructions (the LU entries found in FrameNet), semi-idiomatic constructions, argument structure constructions, and other meaningful constructions will typically list a specific CEE as one's way in the *Way_manner* construction, where *one's way* is co-indexed with the `Theme`. The third part of a construction entry is based on annotated example sentences illustrating the use of the construction in context.

In Figure 7 we see how the construction elements of the *Way_manner* construction are realized syntactically, similar to the valence tables in lexical FrameNet that illustrate how the FEs of the semantic frame evoked by an LU are realized syntactically. For example, the first line in Figure 7 shows one configuration of the semantics of the *Way_manner* construction, namely the THEME, followed by the Intransitive_manner_verb, the CEE, and the DIRECTION. Beneath the semantic configuration we find the various syntactic realizations (i.e. the form side of the construction). The second line below the semantic configuration lists one of the three possible syntactic realizations of the semantic configuration as [NP.Ext, VPbrst, NP._, PP.Dep], which licenses sentences such as *Kim elbowed her way through the room*.[28] The final part of the construction entry presents the annotated corpus examples that form the basis for the construction entry.

This brief overview of the constructicon has shown that it employs a similar architecture and data structure as lexical FrameNet, thereby effectively blurring the line between what has traditionally been called "the lexicon" and "syntax". However, this section has also shown that, despite its usefulness for linguistic research,[29] the constructicon in its present form exhibits some of the same issues as lexical FrameNet that make it less than ideal for using it in the foreign language classroom. In other words, the constructicon in its present form requires significant pre-existing knowledge of linguistic terminology and its constructions entries are difficult to access because they contain too much information for FLT

---

[28] "VPbrst" stands for "bare stem verb phrase".
[29] For details on how the constructicon has been used for linguistic research see Fillmore et al. (2012), Boas (2017a), and the contributions in Lyngfelt et al. (2018). Note that there are now several research groups working on constructicons for other languages, including Swedish, German, Japanese, and Brazilian Portuguese. For more information, see https://www.globalframenet.org/.

- **CEE**(cee): The construction-evoking element is the noun phrase *one's way*, where *one's* is coindexed to the [Theme].
  ex.: She whistled [cee her way] down the lane to the silo. TRANSLATIONS [1] [2]
- **Direction**(dir): The direction that the [Theme] heads in during the motion.
  ex.: She whistled her way down the lane [dir towards the silo]. TRANSLATIONS [1] [2]
- **Goal**(goa): [Goal] is used for any expression which tells where the [Theme] ends up as a result of the motion.
  ex.: She whistled her way down the lane [goa to the silo]. TRANSLATIONS [1] [2]
- **Intransitive_manner_verb**(i_man): The Intransitive_manner_verb takes the CEE as its object, and indicates the action performed by the [Theme] while it moves.
  ex.: She [i_man whistled] her way down the lane to the silo. TRANSLATIONS [1] [2]
- **Manner**(man): Any expression which describes a property of motion which is not directly related to the trajectory or rate of motion expresses the frame element Manner. Descriptions of steadiness, grace, means of motion, and other things count as Manner expressions.
  ex.: She [man gracefully] whistled her way down the lane to the silo. TRANSLATIONS [1] [2]
- **Means**(mea): An action which enables the [Theme] to move.
  ex.: She laughed her way home [mea by not thinking about all the horrible things that had happened]. TRANSLATIONS [1] [2]
- **Modifier**(mod): The *way* in the [CEE] may be modified by an adjective. It often depicts a state of the [Theme] related to or resulting from their motion, but in some cases it modifies the path taken, motion event itself, or (rarely) a trait of the [Theme] unrelated to the fact that it is in motion. The [Modifier] is always indicated on the second layer.
  ex.: She whistled her [mod cheerful] way down the lane to the silo. TRANSLATIONS [1] [2]
- **Path**(pat): The space traversed by the [Theme] between the [Source] and [Goal].
  ex.: She whistled her way [pat down the lane] to the silo. TRANSLATIONS [1] [2]
- **Source**(sou): [Source] is used for any expression which implies a definite starting-point of motion. In prepositional phrases, the prepositional object expresses the starting point of motion. With particles, the starting point of motion is understood from context.
  ex.: She whistled her way [sou from the schoolhouse] down the lane. TRANSLATIONS [1] [2]

Figure 6: Second part of *Way_manner* construction entry (partial).

and FLL.[30] In the following section, I review Herbst's (2016) proposals regarding PCxG and I show how existing linguistic resources such as the Berkeley FrameNet and Constructicon can be adopted for FLT and FLL.

04	Theme	Intransitive_manner_verb	CEE		Direction	
01	NP.Ext	VPbrst._	NP._		AVP.Dep	
01	NP.Ext	VPbrst._	NP._		PP.Dep	
02	NP.Ext	VPing._	NP._		PP.Dep	
01	Theme	Intransitive_manner_verb	CEE		Direction	Path
01	NP.Ext	VPfin._	NP._		AVP.Dep	PP.Dep
07	Theme	Intransitive_manner_verb	CEE		Path	
01	NP.Ext	VPbrst._	NP._		PP.Dep	
03	NP.Ext	VPfin._	NP._		PP.Dep	
03	NP.Ext	VPing._	NP._		PP.Dep	
01	Theme	Intransitive_manner_verb	CEE		Source	
01	NP.Ext	VPfin._	NP._		PP.Dep	
05	Theme	Intransitive_manner_verb	CEE		Goal	
01	NP.Ext	VPbrst._	NP._		PP.Dep	
03	NP.Ext	VPfin._	NP._		PP.Dep	
01	NP.Ext	VPing._	NP._		PP.Dep	
01	Theme	Intransitive_manner_verb	CEE		Goal	Goal
01	NP.Ext	VPfin._	NP._		AVP.Dep	PP.Dep
01	Theme	Intransitive_manner_verb	CEE		Manner	Path
01	NP.Ext	VPing._	NP._		AVP.Dep	PP.Dep

Figure 7: Third part of *Way_manner* construction entry: Partial summary.

3 Pedagogical Construction Grammar (PCxG)

Herbst (2016: 21) points out that many "categories of traditional grammar are employed in an unreflected and unhelpful way" in the foreign language classroom. Based on a review of how a variety of different grammatical concepts such as English tense, gerunds and participles, prepositions, conjunctions, and adverbs are taught to native speakers of German, Herbst comes to the conclusion that "something is rotten with the state of language teaching – at least in some areas." According to Herbst, "the teaching of grammar seems to be rather unsys-

---

[30] For a more general discussion of how constructional insights inform issues in second language acquisition, FLT, and FLL, see Gilquin and De Knop (2016) and Achard (2018).

tematic and to focus on a few selected problems, where some features happen to be mentioned (...), where others are not." (Herbst 2016: 32) To overcome these issues, Herbst proposes a usage-based Construction Grammar approach for the foreign language classroom. He points out that CxG has already been shown to be useful for analysing first language acquisition (Tomasello 2003, Lieven 2014) and explains his reasoning as follows:

> Many issues that are central in the field of foreign language learning such as valency and collocation are also at the centre of the Construction Grammar approach, and this is why one may have reason to believe that Construction Grammar has more to offer to language teaching than theories for which these issues belong to the periphery.   (Herbst 2016: 33)

Based on an overview of some of the basic principles of CxG, Herbst (2016: 37) points out that CxG without "doubt addresses many questions that are central to the teaching and learning of (foreign) languages." At the same time, however, Herbst also cautions that not all insights from constructional accounts of first language acquisition can be easily transferred to second language acquisition because the "relatively small amount of input presumably makes it much more difficult to arrive at generalizations" (see also Griess and Wulff 2005, Gilquin 2010, De Knop 2020). Nevertheless, Herbst (2016) makes a number of concrete proposals for how foreign language textbooks and pedagogical grammars could be considerably improved by adopting some of the key insights from constructional research.

In each of the following seven sub-sections I will first summarize one of Herbst's programmatic proposals labelled "Seven principles for Pedagogical Construction Grammar," then I will show how each of his principles has been applied to the design of an online learner's dictionary of German for speakers of English (implementing constructional and frame-semantic principles), and finally I will point to how each of the chapters in this volume contributes to elaborating on each of Herbst's seven principles, thereby laying the ground for future research.

3.1 Principle 1: The basic principle of PCxG

Adopting Goldberg's (2006: 18) claim that "It's constructions all the way down," Herbst (2016: 41) proposes that "language learning consists of the learning of constructions" and therefore "language teaching should consist of the teaching of constructions." With respect to the design of teaching materials for vocabulary learning, Herbst suggests that "it must be clear that this "vocabulary section" also contains a lot of grammatical information, namely all the (in the sense of most important) item-specific properties of the vocabulary items introduced"

(2016: 41). To show how Herbst's first principle has been applied to the design of teaching materials for FLT and FLL, I first give a brief overview of the German Frame-based Online Lexicon (G-FOL) (www.coerll.utexas.edu/frames/), a beginning learner's dictionary of German for speakers of English.[31] Then, I discuss how Herbst's first principle has been implemented in the design of G-FOL to demonstrate how constructional and frame-semantic insights can be applied to improve FLT and FLL.

The G-FOL is based on the original semantic frames from the English FrameNet database that have been mapped onto the vocabulary of the University of Texas at Austin's first-year German online textbook *Deutsch im Blick*.[32] 97% of the roughly 2,000 words in *Deutsch im Blick* are covered by existing English frames. Working with the original semantic frames from FrameNet, a group of faculty and graduate students at UT Austin uses corpus data from the *Digitales Wörterbuch der Deutschen Sprache* ('Digital Dictionary of the German Language'; http://www.dwds.de) and data from other corpora (together with native speaker intuitions) to compile a freely available frame-based learners' dictionary for first-year German students (for details see Boas and Dux 2013 and Boas et al. 2016). A crucial step in the G-FOL workflow involves simplifying Berkeley FrameNet frames to avoid linguistic jargon that might be too technical for beginning language learners. G-FOL users typically access information about words via the semantic frame they evoke. For example, *sich duschen* ('to shower') in G-FOL evokes the `Grooming` frame as in Figure 8.

Each frame in G-FOL has its own web page. The top of each page lists the frame description together with definitions of the FEs followed by a list of German LUs with their English translation equivalents that evoke the frame. For each LU, learners can access further information about (1) the "Details" (brief instructions about how the LU may differ in use from its English translation equivalent), (2) simple annotated example sentences together with their English translations, (3) grammar notes, (4) contrastive sentence templates, and (5) alternate forms (typically irregular word forms such as principle parts of the verb).

G-FOL shows how Herbst's (2016) first principle of PCxG ("language teaching should consist of the teaching of constructions") can be implemented in the design of teaching and learning materials. For example, when beginning learners of German want to find out about the basic types of constructions instanti-

---

[31] The G-FOL project was developed in collaboration with the Center for Open Educational Resources and Language Learning (COERLL) at the University of Texas at Austin and supported by funds from Title VI grants P229A140005 and P229A180003 from the U.S. Department of Education.
[32] See https://coerll.utexas.edu/dib/.

Frame description

In this frame, an Agent engages in personal body care. An Instrument (e.g. a wash cloth) can be used in this process as well as a Medium (e.g. soap and water).

Frame Elements

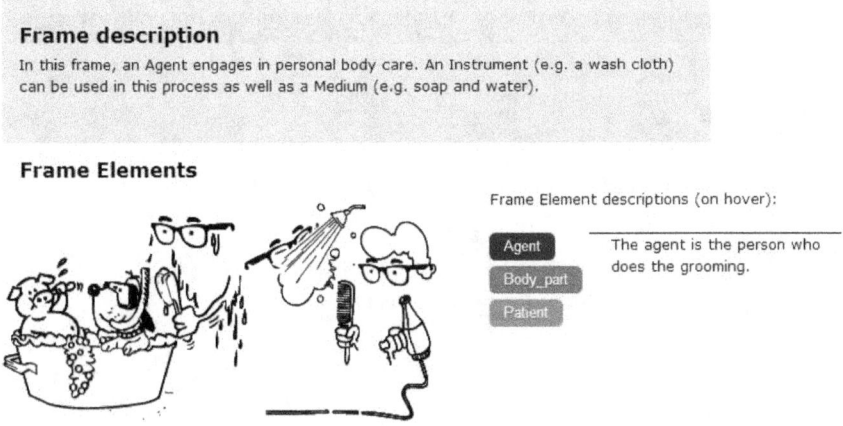

Frame Element descriptions (on hover):

Agent	The agent is the person who does the grooming.
Body_part	
Patient	

Figure 8: Frame Description for the Grooming frame in G-FOL.

| die Seife | noun | soap, body wash | ○ | ○ | | ○ | ○ | ○ | □ |
| duschen | verb | to shower | ● | ● | ● | ○ | ● | ● | ■ |

Templates with Frame Elements:

1. AGENT duscht.
2. AGENT duscht PATIENT.

1. AGENT takes a shower.
2. AGENT showers PATIENT.

TOP OF PAGE | COLLAPSE ALL

| kämmen (die Haare kämmen) | verb | to comb | ○ | ○ | ○ | ○ | ○ | ○ | □ |

Figure 9: Sentence templates with *duschen* ('to shower').

ated by *duschen*, they click on the "Sentence Template" button, which displays the information in Figure 9. Note that the two sentence templates occurring with *duschen* in Figure 9 only display the realization of the FEs AGENT and PATIENT. Even though the sentence templates do not explicitly list the form side (phrase type(s) and grammatical function(s)), learners implicitly learn this crucial information when they access a different part of the LU entry of *duschen*, such as the contrastive example sentences as in Figure 10.

In this part of an LU's entry, learners discover the various (simple) ways in which the FEs are realized syntactically without any implicit mentioning of phrase types and grammatical functions. This information, together with an explicit description of the differences between German and English, see Figure 10, allow the learner to associate the meaning side (represented in terms of FEs) of a mini-construction of *duschen* (e.g., [Agent$_i$ V Patient$_j$]) with its corresponding form side (e.g. [NP/Subj$_i$ V NP/D.Obj$_j$]). In other words, the G-FOL

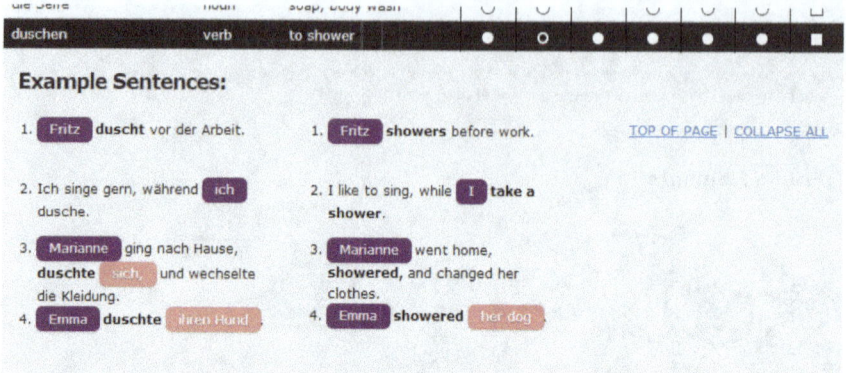

Figure 10: Contrastive example sentences German-English for *duschen* ('to shower').

entries, parallel to entries in FrameNet, can be thought of as mini-constructions (see Boas 2003), where each sense of a word evokes a particular semantic frame (the meaning side of a construction) and the semantics of the frame is realized in various ways syntactically (the form side of a construction). More specifically, in the case of *duschen* we are dealing with two mini-constructions (intransitive and transitive).[33]

In addition to the information discussed above, each LU entry in G-FOL also includes extensive grammar notes containing "a lot of grammatical information, namely all the (in the sense of the most important) item-specific properties of the vocabulary items introduced" (Herbst 2016: 41). We will discuss this point in detail in Section 3.6 below. Finally, Herbst (2016: 41) proposes that frequency should play a role in PCxG (see also Herbst 2017). This applied pedagogical goal is implicitly encoded in G-FOL as it covers the vocabulary of first-year German instruction, which, for the most part, consists of high-frequency words.

Frequency in PCxG also plays a role in a number of chapters in this volume. Gries (this volume) argues that even though frequency has been shown to play an important role in usage-based approaches to language such as CxG, its role should be reconsidered. Based on a discussion of a number of underexplored constructions in various corpora, Gries shows, among other things, that the role of frequency has been overestimated considerably. Law (this volume) argues that the presentation of unrelated vocabulary based on frequency alone is not always

---

[33] It is important to remember that G-FOL, in its current state, is designed for first-year learners of German. As such, the amount of sentence templates is relatively small. Once the first-year German vocabulary is covered, G-FOL will move on to the vocabulary of second-year German, which will yield additional sentence templates (i.e. mini-constructions) for most LUs.

a good solution in FLT and FLL. Instead, he argues, language learners appear to be more successful at learning words when using a frame-based organization of vocabulary that helps them to create lexical associations between related words. Nesset and Janda (this volume) also highlight the importance of frequency in FLL. Investigating how L2 learners acquire constructions with Russian motion verbs, they develop a methodology combining constructional and grammatical profiles that make it possible to pinpoint the most relevant morphological and syntactic constructions, based on frequency. Finally, Patten and Perek (this volume), following the practice of the COBUILD Grammar Patterns, propose to include two types of information about frequency as a part of their Lexical Index: (1) relative frequency of lexical items across constructions and (2) type frequency of constructions.

3.2 Principle 2. The principle of presenting constructions as form-meaning pairings

Herbst (2016: 41) proposes that "since constructions are form-meaning pairings, they should be presented as such." This strategy, according to Herbst (2016: 42) should overcome the problems of many traditional grammars which "introduce the form of a construction and explain its use rather indirectly as being equivalent or as shortening another construction without actually stating the communicative impact of the construction as such."

In G-FOL, words are represented explicitly as pairings of form (the base form of a word) with meaning (a specific definition, together with the semantic frame (and its FEs) and an English translation)). As already pointed out above, lexical entries in G-FOL can be regarded as (lexical) mini-constructions in the sense of Boas (2003). Even though G-FOL aims to cover words and not higher-level abstract constructions, it provides specific information about regular grammatical constructions as form-meaning pairings whenever it is possible to state specific generalizations over semantic classes of words (typically verbs). For example, all German verbs evoking the Grooming frame occur in the accusative or dative reflexive construction, depending on whether the FE BODY_PART is mentioned or not. G-FOL explicitly presents this important information about the use of the two reflexive constructions (in prose) as a part of each verb's lexical entry in the Grooming frame, as illustrated by Figure 11 below.

Since G-FOL is conceptualized for beginning students of German without much prior knowledge of grammatical terminology, the connection between form and meaning is represented implicitly (via the examples in which the FEs of the frame are highlighted). Future work on G-FOL aims to identify other low-level grammatical regularities that can be accounted for by frame-specific constructions (see Dux 2020) that can be listed in lexical entries.

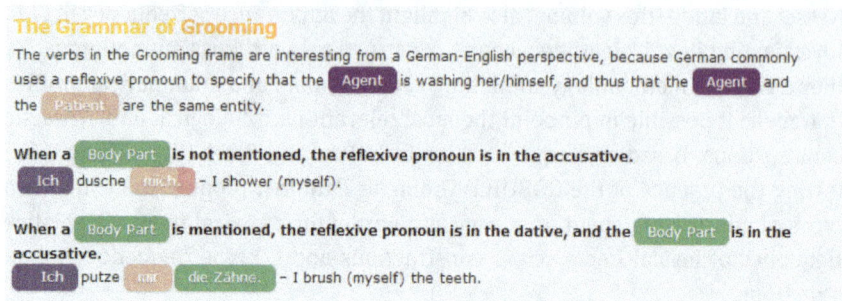

Figure 11: Partial grammatical information for grooming verbs.

Several chapters in this volume also address the teaching of constructions as form-meaning pairings. In their case study of teaching Russian verbs of motion Nesset and Janda (this volume) propose a combination of constructional and grammatical profiles that make it possible to specify the syntactic environments of each verb, thereby showing which grammatical forms appear in each construction. In addition, Nesset and Janda show how their verb-centered approach combined with constructional profiles allows for a more strategic input for L2 learners. Gemmell Hudson (this volume) discusses how constructions and frames can be employed in a second year German curriculum. With respect to Herbst's (2016) second principle of PCxG, she shows how different types of student activities in various thematic units make explicit use of form-meaning pairings. For example, students have to identify specific cases in sentences (matching a form to a specific meaning), they have to create sentences based on specific images (mapping a meaning to a specific form), and they have to produce specific words that realize the meaning of a semantic frame.

Madlener-Charpentier (this volume) also sheds light on how Herbst's (2016) principle can be applied in a PCxG approach. In her investigation of constructional repertoires in the spatial language domain in L1 German speakers and L2 users of English, she suggests that the teaching of L2 spatial language should go beyond vocabulary teaching and provide explicit meaningful contexts for negotiating different form-meaning mappings. Finally, De Knop and Mollica (this volume) make a related point in their chapter on teaching German verbless directives to speakers of Italian. Because of the typological differences between German and Italian they propose a teaching methodology based on structural priming with comic strips, whose explicit visual information are a crucial clue on the meaning side of German constructions and their Italian counterparts.

3.3 Principle 3: The principle of one sense at a time

Herbst's third principle of PCxG suggests that "[l]exical constructions should be presented in textbooks as units of lexical form and a single sense" (2016: 42). G-FOL implements Herbst's third principle by adhering to the splitting approach taken by Frame Semantics (Fillmore 1982). On this view, each word consists of different LUs, with each LU evoking a different semantic frame covering a distinct sense of that word (see Fillmore and Atkins 2000). To illustrate, consider the verb *to run*, which evokes several senses in FrameNet including the Self_motion frame (e.g. *Jill ran up the hill*), the Leadership frame (e.g. *The nursery is run by trained staff*), the Cause_impact frame (e.g. *He ran his head into a hornet's nest*), the Cause_motion frame (e.g. *Pat ran Kim off the street*), and the Path_shape frame (e.g. *Two streets through the woods*). Since G-FOL implements the principles of FrameNet, it, too, follows Herbst's third principle of PCxG.[34] Structuring G-FOL based on semantic frames and grouping semantically related words with each other make it easier for learners to approach vocabulary in a more systematic way (see Lorenz et al. 2020).[35]

Several chapters in this volume demonstrate how Herbst's third principle of PCxG has been applied to the teaching of language. Patten and Perek's (this volume) discussion of English verb complementation patterns shows how semantic frames make it possible to describe specific meaning patterns in the COBUILD grammar patterns. This approach allows Patten and Perek to devise specific groups of constructions that each go with specific types of verbs that evoke specific frames such as Experiencer_focused_emotion, Choosing, Commitment, Desiring, and Deciding. Ziem and Neumann-Schneider's (this volume) chapter also shows how the implementation of Herbst's third principle of PCxG enables learners of linguistic terminology to gain a better understanding of word meanings based on semantic frames. Law (this volume), in his discussion of teaching L2 vocabulary, also points to the usefulness of semantic frames for teaching metonymy to learners of French.

---

34 Since G-FOL currently only aims to cover the vocabulary of a first-year German curriculum we have so far not encountered any polysemous words whose various LUs evoke separate frames. This issue will become more relevant as G-FOL seeks to account for the vocabulary of more advanced levels of German.
35 See also Gonzálvez-García (2019) for an application of Herbst's third principle of PCxG to the teaching of different senses of the family of subjective-transitive constructions to advanced learners of Spanish as a foreign language.

3.4 Principle 4: The principle of indicating chunks

Herbst (2016: 42) suggests that in "the vocabulary sections of textbooks, important collocations and phrases should be listed explicitly." To date, G-FOL has not implemented Herbst's fourth principle of PCxG, but it aims to do so at a later point in time. Two chapters in this volume, however, show how Herbst's fourth principle can be applied in FLT and FLL. For example, Gemmell Hudson (this volume) discusses student-centered activities that help students discover cross-linguistic similarities and differences between English and German. Discussing several words evoking the Exercise frame, Gemmell Hudson discusses the various contexts in which *machen* ('to do') is used with expressions denoting sports and non-game sports activities (as opposed to *spielen* ('to play')): *Yoga machen* ('to do yoga') vs. **Yoga spielen* ('to play yoga'). With respect to indicating chunks in learning materials, Uhrig et al. (this volume) highlight the importance of collocations, which are often difficult for language learners because they are unpredictable. The authors argue that one should think about shifting attention from the issue of combining words to that of expressing meaning (as chunks/collocations). On this view, explicit teaching of collocations in textbooks and other teaching materials is an important objective for materials development: "This is why we can do no more than to underscore the importance of giving prominence to the phenomenon of collocation in textbooks and teaching materials."

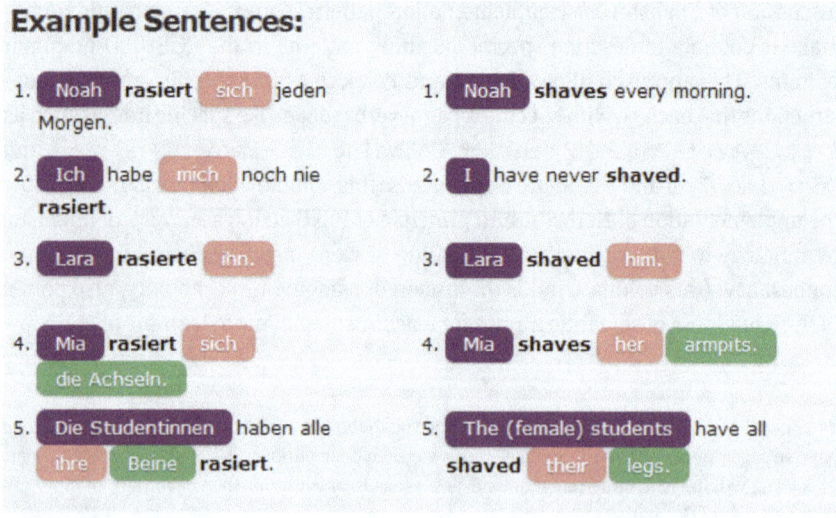

Figure 12: Valency constructions encoded in contrastive example sentence for *rasieren* ('to shave') in the Grooming frame.

Uhrig et al. (this volume) address the importance of valency constructions in textbooks and dictionaries. They point out that, if vocabulary parts of textbooks contained an increased number of valency patterns and collocations, then students would gain a more advanced level of fluency in the language. Patten and Perek (this volume) make a similar point with respect to the construction entries in their English constructicon. Pairing the valency constructions contained in the lexical entries in FrameNet with the COBUILD Grammar Patterns allows Patten and Perek to compile new construction entries that can be integrated into existing grammar instruction, thereby supporting a constructional approach to language learning.

3.6 Principle 6: The principle of moderate and meaningful use of grammatical terminology

Herbst (2016) suggests that "the use of grammatical terminology should be restricted to a useful minimum, i.e. to cases in which the terminology contributes to language learning. In particular, the terminology used should be employed consistently, be appropriate for the language in question and not be based on the teaching traditions of another language." G-FOL has implemented Herbst's sixth principle by using only very minimal grammatical terminology. It employs categories for parts of speech, names of grammatical functions, and names of cases.

In addition, it provides links to another UT Austin web resource, *Grimm Grammar*, which defines grammatical terminology in simple terms. For example, learners can click on the term "reflexive verbs" and are led to a page on the *Grimm Grammar* web site that defines reflexive verbs with contrastive English and German examples, together with specific usage instructions for particular contexts.[36] The section on reflexive verbs contains further simple grammatical terminology such as subject and object, which are linked to additional pages so that learners can access information about the meaning of these terms.

Beyond that, G-FOL offers specific simple definitions of semantic frames in prose as well as the FEs of each frame (see Figure 8 above). For example, in the `Grooming` frame, G-FOL defines the FE AGENT as the person who does the grooming, the BODY_PART as the region of the body that gets groomed, and the PATIENT as the person who gets washed.

Two chapters in this volume specifically address the use of grammatical terminology, thereby elaborating on Herbst's sixth principle of PCxG. Ziem and Neumann-Schneider (this volume) present the motivation behind and architecture

---

[36] For details see https://coerll.utexas.edu/gg/gr/vrf_01.html.

of LingTermNet, an online repository of linguistic terminology that is methodologically related to FrameNet. The goal of this online lexical resource is to provide students in linguistics courses with accessible explanations of technical terms in linguistics, which will help them with a better understanding of texts regarding FLT and FLL. Gemmell Hudson's (this volume) chapter shows how Herbst's sixth principle of PCxG is implemented in teaching materials used in a second year German curriculum. For example, based on the information in G-FOL, Gemmell Hudson discusses how different in-class activities entice students to employ the basic grammatical terminology used in G-FOL to identify cases of noun phrases in the Eating and Drinking frame. Other in-class activities ask students to identify FEs in texts and to write sentences based on prose descriptions of semantic frames in G-FOL.

3.7 Principle 7: The principle of authenticity

Herbst's (2016: 44) seventh principle calls for teaching materials to "be based on the analysis of corpora or on reference works based on corpus analysis and the frequency of constructions should be reflected in the design of teaching materials." G-FOL implemented Herbst's seventh principle by basing its corpus examples on the *Digitales Wörterbuch der Deutschen Sprache* ('Digital Dictionary of the German Language'; www.dwds.de), which itself is based on a number of different German text corpora. Since G-FOL is aimed at beginning learners of German, most corpus examples from DWDS have been shortened or simplified so that the relevant valency constructions and FEs can be more easily identified by beginning learners of German in the LU entries.

Several chapters in this volume explicitly address the use of authentic teaching materials. Gemmell Hudson (this volume) discusses how authentic texts from German media can be used in connection with semantic frames and LU entries from G-FOL in the classroom to teach vocabulary, grammar, and usage concurrently. Ziem and Neumann-Schneider (this volume) also employ authentic texts for the creation of LingTermNet, their online frame-based database of linguistic terminology. In contrast to general language domain corpora typically used in FLT and FLL, LingTermNet relies on a corpus of linguistics text containing the relevant LUs under discussion. Tackling the question of authenticity from a different perspective, Gilquin (this volume) argues for including spoken data in FLL, because it allows for a more elaborate and different view of construction learning. One of the advantages of including spoken data in FLL, according to Gilquin, is that language learners become more aware of the differences between spoken and written language. Another advantage of using spoken data is that researchers can more easily determine how learners build their spoken learner constructicons.

3.8 Pedagogical Construction Grammar: Quo Vadis?

Based on the review of how CxG and its sister theory Frame Semantics developed over the past three decades I showed in Section 2 how the theoretical insights from both theories were applied to the design and implementation of the FrameNet and the Constructicon databases. I argued that even though both usage-based online resources offer an unprecedented wealth of linguistic information in the form of LU entries, the semantic frames they evoke, and the construction entries, they are not suitable for language learners.

The goal of Section 3 was to show how insights from constructional research more generally has been applied to the teaching and learning of languages. In this context I reviewed the seven principles of PCxG as outlined by Herbst (2016) and I have shown how they have been implemented in a frame-based online learners' dictionary for beginning learners of German. This review served as the basis for discussing how the chapters in this volume contribute to our understanding of each of Herbst's (2016) seven principles of PCxG. The various strands of applied constructional research presented in this volume cover a wide range of different topics, each contributing to the elaboration of Herbst's seven principles in different ways.

Obviously, much future research is required to contribute additional insights into how each of Herbst's seven principles of PCxG can be implemented more effectively, thereby demonstrating the applicability of constructional insights to FLT and FLL. The goals of this introductory chapter have been more modest: to illustrate how Herbst's seven principles have been implemented to various degrees in an online frame-based learners' dictionary and to highlight the various ways in which each of the chapters in this volume contribute to a greater understanding of Herbst's seven principles of PCxG. This introductory chapter concludes with an overview of each of the chapters in this volume, grouped by thematic areas.

4 The papers in this volume

4.1 Data and methodology in Pedagogical Construction Grammar

In his chapter *On, or against?, (just) frequency*, Stefan Th. Gries explores the role of frequency (of use) as one of the central theoretical notions in usage-based approaches. Since the 1980s, researchers have used frequency as a central factor to explain or operationalize entrenchment, productivity, and many other matters concerning language acquisition/learning, use, processing, and change. Despite the widespread acceptance of the role of frequency, Gries argues in his paper that (i) the role of frequency as a cause (conceptually speaking) and as a predictor (statistically speaking) has been overestimated considerably and that (ii) usage-based construction grammarians need to explore their observational data with a much higher degree of resolution. To support this view, Gries discusses a variety of distributional characteristics of constructions in corpora that are routinely underexplored. These include paradigmatic and syntagmatic variability, dispersion, and contingency. Gries shows how they are important and he relates them to relevant research that not only the cognitive commitment requires us to consider, but that also provides fundamental support of many constructionist/usage-based tenets.

The chapter *Constructing learner speech: On the use of spoken data in Applied Construction Grammar* by Gaëtanelle Gilquin addresses the bias in Applied Construction Grammar towards the study of written, rather than spoken, language. Gilquin adopts a three-fold perspective that is aimed to foster further research on speech in Applied Construction Grammar. First, the chapter argues that, from a descriptive point of view, we cannot dispense with the investigation of constructions (and constructicons) in speech and in learner speech in particular. Second, turning to applications among foreign language learners, it highlights the potential benefits of the study of spoken language for the learning and teaching of constructions. Finally, it considers more theoretical issues, showing how the recognition of speech can help refine the (Applied) Construction Grammar model. Gilquin's chapter argues that we need better descriptions of spoken learner constructions, which may differ from written learner constructions or spoken native constructions, and which can help approach the spoken learner constructicon. Spoken language research can also offer insights into the cognitive mechanisms underlying L2 acquisition, answering questions such as "how do learners build their constructicon?" or "how do they process constructions?"

In their chapter *L2-words that go together – more on collocation and learner language* Peter Uhrig, Susen Faulhaber, Ewa Dąbrowska, and Thomas Herbst address the status of collocations in the learning of a foreign language. More specifically, the authors are interested in differences between speakers of English as a foreign language and native speakers of English and differences between individuals within these groups. Based on a replication of Dąbrowska's *words-that-go-together* test with 97 advanced foreign learners of English, all of whom were students of English at the Friedrich-Alexander-Universität Erlangen-Nürnberg in 2016, the authors investigate the influence of foreign language instruction (overall exposure, input-related factors, motivational factors, dictionary use, and grades they received in school) on the ability of foreign language students to produce collocations appropriately. Central to their analysis is the idea that collocations are constructions which are characterized by a close affinity between two words which can be determined by frequency and/or unpredictability. Based on the results of their test, the authors argue (1) that students should be made aware of the central role played by phraseological units (including collocations) and (2) that students should be taught the most important collocations of the words that they (are supposed to) learn.

4.2 Learning and teaching constructions

In *Construction-based teaching of German verbless directives to Italian-speaking learners*, Sabine de Knop and Fabio Mollica investigate how at an intermediate or advanced level, language teaching should focus on various differentiated structures that represent authentic ways of expression in the foreign language. At the center of their chapter are German verbless directives, which are constructions according to Goldberg (2006), i.e. form-meaning pairs which are productive and frequent in German and cognitively well-entrenched. German as a satellite-framed language (Talmy 2000) favors the expression of the motion path with so-called satellites. Therefore, it does not surprise that short verbless constructions consisting only of a directional prepositional phrase are common in German and the authors first introduce the source of data for their study, namely a collection of comic strips in German and Italian. De Knop and Mollica describe the semantic, pragmatic (illocutionary potential), syntactic and morpho-syntactic (German cases) constraints of such 'verb-free' examples within a constructionist framework. Then, the authors show how for Italian-speaking learners of German, verbless directives constitute a challenge. Because Romance languages express the path of motion mainly with full verbs, learners tend to use a full verb also in German, which does not necessarily reflect the authentic expressions of motion. De Knop and Mollica propose a teaching methodology based on structural priming (Gries 2005). The efficiency of this methodology is tested with picture-depicting tasks designed for Italian master students of German as a foreign language (proficiency level B2+/C1).

The chapter *Securing strategic input for L2 learners: Constructions with Russian motion verbs* by Tore Nesset and Laura A. Janda investigates how constructional and usage-based approaches to linguistics can be used to identify strategic input for L2 learners, i.e. input that reflects high frequency patterns in the target language. The authors suggest a methodology using linguistic profiles (statistical distribution of features related to a linguistic unit), and argue that this methodology enables us to identify the most relevant morphological and syntactic constructions, and in addition makes it possible to pinpoint the grammatical forms that are most characteristic of each construction. This research builds on Divjak and Gries (2006), whose "behavioral profiles" summarized the statistical distribution of a large number of properties of linguistic units. In their study of Russian motion verbs, Nesset and Janda are concerned with two kinds of linguistic profiles: constructional profiles and grammatical profiles. Their argument is based on a case study of Russian verbs of motion, so in addition to implications for L2 instruction in general, the study also has consequences for how one teaches Russian motion verbs. Nesset and Janda show that their methodology involving the combination of constructional and grammatical profiles is capable of pinpointing patterns that are of particular relevance for L2 learners.

In their chapter *Pedagogic applications of the English Constructicon*, Amanda Patten and Florent Perek outline a proposal for a new type of constructicon of English before examining its potential as a pedagogic resource. Constructicon research is an emerging field of applied linguistics (see Lyngfelt et al. 2018) that relates to a practical application of the central theoretical tenets of Construction Grammar: that language is not a system of rules that govern how we combine words to make sentences, but it is a network of symbolic units (form-meaning pairings) of varying size and complexity (see e.g. Fillmore, Kay, and O'Connor 1988). The linguistic network of the mind has been referred to as a constructicon. The authors discuss the uses of constructicons as descriptive resources, because they are structured repositories of the lexicogrammatical constructions of a particular language, typically in electronic form. This discussion leads Patten and Perek to show how the development of such resources involves the application of lexicographic practices to construction grammar theories (a method labelled *constructicography* by Lyngfelt et al. 2018). More specifically, the authors discuss their project of combining the existing electronic resources of FrameNet and the COBUILD Grammar Patterns in order to create a new electronic resource for English language learning and teaching. The final part of the paper highlights the additional value of such a resource for language pedagogy, illustrating and enriching this discussion through a case study that compares a test case for the proposed constructicon with existing pedagogic works designed to support teachers and learners in English grammar.

In the chapter *Learned attention beyond typological bootstrapping: Constructional repertoires and constructional complexity in the spatial language domain*, Karin Madlener-Charpentier addresses two main research questions: First, how do L2 constructional repertoires, constructional variability, and constructional complexity unfold in the spatial language domain in English and German? Second, to what extent do we find evidence for and effects of learned attention beyond basic lexicalization patterns? Madlener-Chaprentier's chapter begins with an overview of the theoretical background and empirical findings concerning spatial language use and acquisition from the L1 and L2 perspectives. More specifically, she discusses cross-linguistic differences regarding information focus and information locus, as well as typological bootstrapping. Madlener-Charpentier then presents the methodology and data of the study (retellings of cartoon sequences and wordless picture books) and discusses selected findings regarding constructional repertoires, preferences, and complexity in the spatial language domain in English as compared to German and in first as compared to second language use. Madlener-Charpentier outlines specific implications for construction-based second language teaching in the final section of her paper.

4.3 Frame-based teaching and learning

Maggie Gemmell Hudson's chapter *Teaching Second Year German using Frames and Constructions* presents a frame-semantic and constructional approach to organizing a second-year German curriculum. The tenets of her approach are (1) lexicon and grammar are united in a continuum of meaningful linguistic forms, (2) contextualized language use is critical, (3) cross-linguistic differences between German and American English must be identified and dealt with for students to fully grasp and meaningfully use the linguistic forms covered, and (4) constructions with a high frequency should be reinforced through repetition in a variety of contexts to allow entrenchment of those concepts. Gemmell Hudson argues that explicit vocabulary instruction is necessary in the foreign language classroom and she proposes a frame-based approach using on-line learner's dictionaries such as the German Frame-Semantic Online Lexicon (G-FOL, https://www.coerll.utexas.edu/frames/) is advantageous for learners, because they develop a richer understanding of all linguistic forms they learn (from vocabulary to grammatical structures). In addition, learners have the opportunity to build on their understanding of constructions by observing how each relates to the various frames they study in terms of frame elements. The specificity of meaning analysis allowed by the frames provides the means to more fully understand how constructions function.

The chapter *Frame-based metonymy in teaching L2 vocabulary*, by Jim Law, discusses new opportunities to develop a rich understanding of the semantics of L2 vocabulary, thereby enhancing foreign language teaching and learning. Using data from FrameNet (http://framenet.icsi.berkeley.edu), which is based on Fillmore's (1982) Frame Semantics, Law shows how many frames allow for any one of a set of frame elements, known as a CoreSet, to satisfy the same valence requirement (Ruppenhofer et al. 2016). In some cases, Law argues, CoreSets involve metonymic substitution among these related frame elements. Versions of the CoreSet {Medium, Speaker} are found throughout frames related to communication, where the same constructional slot can be occupied by the Speaker or the Medium. Law proposes a frame-centered approach to vocabulary instruction that addresses this type of variability and illustrates this approach with a sample beginning French lesson on the verb *dire* ('to say'). Rather than the traditional approach which introduces *dire* alongside other verbs of the same inflectional class, Law's lesson introduces *dire* within the context of Communication frames. Vocabulary is presented within a semantically integrated and functionally oriented context, while exposing learners to a wide range of authentic examples adapted from FrameNet data which include metonymic substitutions. This lesson serves as a concrete example of frame-centered approaches to language teaching which empower learners with greater flexibility in their language use.

In *Towards a FrameNet for linguistic terminology: Theoretical foundations, lexicographic practice, didactic potential*, Alexander Ziem and Anastasia Neumann-Schneider present an online repository of linguistic terminology based on the Berkeley FrameNet. The authors first introduce the theortical foundations underlying the design and use of LingTermNet ("Linguistic Terminology Net"; http://www.lingterm.net), namely Frame Semantics (Fillmore 1982). For illustration, they present the Communication frame, which they employ for their sample analysis of technical linguistic terms in the remainder of the chapter. Next, the authors argue that meanings of technical terms can be taught and learned more efficiently with reference to (a) the frame evoked by the term and (b) the network structure of frames into which it is tied. To validate this hypothesis, Ziem and Neumann-Schneider use linguistic terms from the domain of conversation analysis. Specifically, they show to what extent the Speaker_signal and the Hearer_signal frames hook into the Signal_scenario frame. Given that meanings of technical terms are determined by the frames they evoke, the authors discuss the structure of frame entries as well as dictionary entries for each technical term. The definitions are compiled in recourse to the frames the technical terms evoke. Finally, Ziem and Neumann-Schneider summarize the results and give an outlook on future research.

References

Achard, Michel (2018). Teaching usage and concepts: Toward a cognitive pedagogical grammar. In A. Tyler, L. Huang & H. Jan (eds.), *What is applied cognitive linguistics?*, 37–62. Berlin/Boston: De Gruyter.

Angelis, Paul (2001). *The roots of Applied Linguistics in North America*. Colloquium on the Roots of Applied Linguistics in Different Contexts. St. Louis: AAAL.

Baker, Collin, Ellsworth, Michael & Katrin Erk (2007). SemEval-2007 Task 19: Frame semantic structure extraction. *Proceedings of the Fourth International Workshop on Semantic Evaluations (SemEval-2007)*, 99–104.
Barðdal, Johanna (2012). Predicting the productivity of argument structure constructions. *Proceedings of the Annual Meeting of the Berkeley Linguistics Society* 32, 467–478.
Bernolet, Sarah & Robert J. Hartsuiker (2018). Syntactic representations in late learners of a second language. A learning trajectory. In David Miller, Fatih Bayram, Jason Rothman & Ludovica Serratrice (eds.), *Bilingual Cognition and Language: The state of the science across its subfields*, 205–224. Amsterdam: John Benjamins.
Bertoldi, Anderson & Rove Luiza de Oliveira Chishman (2011). Developing a frame-based lexicon for the Brazilian legal language: the case of the criminal_process frame. In *International Workshop on AI Approaches to the Complexity of Legal Systems*, 256–270. Berlin/Heidelberg: Springer.
Boas, Hans C. (2003). *A constructional approach to resultatives*. Stanford: CSLI Publications.
Boas, Hans C. (2005). From Theory to Practice: Frame Semantics and the Design of FrameNet. In S. Langer & D. Schnorbusch (eds.), *Semantik im Lexikon*, 129–160. Tübingen: Narr.
Boas, Hans C. (2008). Determining the structure of lexical entries and grammatical constructions in Construction Grammar. *Annual Review of Cognitive Linguistics* 6, 113–144.
Boas, Hans C. (ed.) (2009). *Multilingual FrameNets in Computational Lexicography: Methods and Applications*. Berlin/New York: De Gruyter.
Boas, Hans (ed.) (2010). *Contrastive Studies in Construction Grammar*. Amsterdam/Philadelphia: John Benjamins.
Boas, Hans C. (2011a). Zum Abstraktionsgrad von Resultativkonstruktionen. In S. Engelberg, K. Proost, and A. Holler (eds.), *Sprachliches Wissen zwischen Lexikon und Grammatik*, 37–69. Berlin/New York: Mouton de Gruyter.
Boas, Hans C. (2011b). A frame-semantic approach to syntactic alternations with *build*-verbs. In P. Guerrero Medina (ed.), *Morphosyntactic alternations in English*, 207–234. London: Equinox.
Boas, Hans C. (2013). Cognitive Construction Grammar. In T. Hoffmann & G. Trousdale (eds.), *The Oxford Handbook of Construction Grammar*, 233–254. Oxford: Oxford University Press.
Boas, Hans C. (2017a). Computational Resources: FrameNet and Constructicon. In B. Dancygier (ed.), *The Cambridge Handbook of Cognitive Linguistics*, 549–573. Cambridge: Cambridge University Press.
Boas, Hans C. (2017b). What you see is not what you get: Capturing the meaning of missing words with Frame Semantics. In *Proceedings of the Chicago Linguistics Society* 52, 53–70.
Boas, Hans C. (2019). Zur methodologischen Grundlage der empirischen Konstruktikographie. In D. Czicza, V. Dekalo, & G. Diewald (eds.), *Konstruktionsgrammatik VI. Varianz in der konstruktionalen Schematizität*, 237–263. Tübingen: Stauffenburg.
Boas, Hans C. (2020). Constructions in English Grammar. In B. Aarts, A. McMahon & L. Hinrichs (eds.), *The Handbook of English Linguistics*, 277–297. Oxford: Wiley.
Boas, Hans C. (2021). Construction Grammar and Frame Semantics. In X. Wen & J. Taylor (eds.), *The Routledge Handbook of Cognitive Linguistics*. New York/London: Routledge.
Boas, Hans C. and Ryan Dux (2013). Semantic frames for foreign-language education: Towards a German frame-based dictionary. *Veridas On-Line* 1/2013, 81–100.
Boas, Hans C. and Ryan Dux (2017). From the past into the present: From case frames to semantic frames. In *Linguistics Vanguard* 2017. 1–14. DOI: 10.1515/lingvan-2016-0003.

Boas, Hans C. and Steffen Höder (eds.) (2018). *Constructions in Contact*. Amsterdam/Philadelphia: John Benjamins.
Boas, Hans C., Lyngfelt, Benjamin, and Tiago Timponi Torrent (2019). Framing Constructicography. In *Lexicographica* 35(1), 41–95.
Boas, Hans C. & Ivan Sag (eds.) (2012). *Sign-based Construction Grammar*. Stanford: CSLI Publications.
Boas, Hans C. & Alexander Ziem (eds.) (2018). *Constructional Approaches to Syntactic Structures in German*. Berlin/Boston: De Gruyter Mouton.
Boas, Hans C., Ziem, Alexander, & Ryan Dux (2016). Frames and constructions in an online learner's dictionary of German. In S. De Knop & G. Gilquin (eds.), *Applied Construction Grammar*, 303–326. Berlin/Boston: De Gruyter.
Booij, Geert (2010). *Construction Morphology*. Oxford: Oxford University Press.
Booij, Geert (2013). Morphology in Construction Grammar. In T. Hoffmann & G. Trousdale (eds.), *The Oxford Handbook of Construction Grammar*, 255–273. Oxford: Oxford University Press.
Busse, Dietrich (2012). *Frame-Semantik. Ein Kompendium*. Berlin/Boston: De Gruyter.
Cappelle, Bert & Natalia Grabar (2016). Towards an n-grammar of English. In S. De Knop & G. Gilquin (eds.), *Applied Construction Grammar*, 271–302. Berlin/Boston: De Gruyter.
Chomsky, Noam (1965). *Aspects of the Theory of Syntax*. Cambridge, Mass.: MIT Press.
Chomsky, Noam (1981). *Lectures in Government and Binding*. Dordrecht: Foris Publications.
Chomsky, Noam (1988). *Language and the problems of knowledge*. Cambridge: MIT Press.
Clausner, Timothy C. & William Croft (1997). Productivity and Schematicity in Metaphors. *Cognitive Science* 21(3), 247–82.
Croft, William (2001). *Radical Construction Grammar*. Oxford: Oxford University Press.
Croft, William (2013). Radical Construction Grammar. In T. Hoffmann & G. Trousdale (Eds.), *The Oxford Handbook of Construction Grammar*, 211–232. Oxford: Oxford University Press.
De Knop, Sabine & Teun De Rycker (eds.) (2008). *Cognitive approaches to Pedagogical Grammar: A volume in honour of René Dirven*. Berlin & New York: Mouton De Gruyter.
Davies, Alan & Catherine Elder (eds.) (2004). *The Handbook of Applied Linguistics*. Oxford: Blackwell.
De Knop, Sabine (2020). The embodied teaching of complex verbal constructions with German placement verbs and spatial prepositions. *Annual Review of Cognitive Linguistics* 18(1), 131–161.
De Knop, Sabine & Gaetanelle Gilquin (eds.) (2016). *Applied Construction Grammar*. Berlin/New York: Mouton De Gruyter.
De Knop, Sabine & Fabio Mollica (2016). A construction-based analysis of German ditransitive phraseologisms for language pedagogy. In S. De Knop & G. Gilquin (eds.), *Applied Construction Grammar*, 53–88. Berlin/Boston: De Gruyter.
De Knop, Sabine & Fabio Mollica (2018). Verblose Direktiva als Konstruktionen: ein kontrastiver Vergleich zwischen Deutsch, Französisch und Italienisch. In Jürgen Erfurt & Sabine De Knop (eds.), *Konstruktionsgrammatik und Mehrsprachigkeit*, 127–148. Universität Duisburg-Essen: Universitätsverlag Rhein-Ruhr OHG.
De Knop, Sabine & Fabio Mollica (this volume). Construction-based teaching of German verbless directives to Italian-speaking learners.
Diessel, Holger (2019). *The grammar network*. Cambridge: Cambridge University Press.
Divjak, Dagmar & Stefan Th. Gries (2006). Ways of trying in Russian: Clustering behavioral profiles. *Corpus linguistics and linguistic theory* 2(1), 23–60.

Dolbey, Andrew (2009). Bioframenet: a framenet extension to the domain of molecular biology. Unpublished Ph.D. dissertation, UC Berkeley.

Dux, Ryan (2020). *Frame-constructional verb classes*. Amsterdam/Philadelphia: John Benjamins.

Eddington, David & Francisco J. Ruiz de Mendoza (2010). Argument constructions and language processing: Evidence from a priming experiment and pedagogical implications. *Fostering language teaching efficiency through cognitive linguistics* 17, 213.

Ellis, Nick (2001). Memory for language. In R. Robinson (ed.), *Cognition and Second Language Instruction*, 33–68, Cambridge: Cambridge University Press.

Ellis, Nick (2013). Construction Grammar and Second Language Acquisition. In T. Hoffmann & G. Trousdale (eds.), *The Oxford Handbook of Construction Grammar*, 365–368. Oxford: Oxford University Press.

Ellis, Nick & Teresa Cadierno (eds.) (2009). Constructing a second language, special section of *Annual Review of Cognitive Linguistics* 7, 111–290.

Ellis, Nick, Römer, Ute, & Matthew O'Donnell (2016). *Usage-based Approaches to Language Acquisition and Processing: Cognitive and Corpus Investigations of Construction Grammar*. Malden, MA: Wiley.

Fellbaum, Christiane (eds.) (1998). *WordNet*. Cambridge: MIT Press.

Fillmore, Charles J. (1968). The case for case. In E. Bach & R.T. Harms (eds.), *Universals in Linguistic Theory*, 1–88. New York: Holt, Rinehart and Winston.

Fillmore, Charles J. (1982). Frame Semantics. In Linguistic Society of Korea (eds.), *Linguistics in the Morning Calm.*, 111–138. Seoul: Hanshin.

Fillmore, Charles J. (1985). Frames and the Semantics of Understanding. *Quaderni di Semantica* 6(2),222–254.

Fillmore, Charles J. (1986). Pragmatically controlled zero anaphora. *Proceedings of the 12th annual meeting of the Berkeley Linguistics Society*, 95–107.

Fillmore, Charles J. (1999). Inversion and constructional inheritance. In G. Webelhuth, J.-P. Koenig & A. Kathol (eds.), *Lexical and Constructional Aspects of Linguistic Explanation*, 113–128. Stanford: CSLI Publications.

Fillmore, Charles J. (2008). Border Conflicts: FrameNet meets Construction Grammar. *Proceedings of the XIII EURALEX International Congress* (Barcelona, 15–19 July 2008), 49–68.

Fillmore, Charles J. (2013). Berkeley Construction Grammar. In T. Hoffmann & G. Trousdale (eds.), *The Oxford Handbook of Construction Grammar*, 111–132. Oxford: Oxford University Press.

Fillmore, Charles J. & B.T.S. Atkins (1992). Toward a Frame-based Lexicon: The Semantics of RISK and its Neighbors. In A. Lehrer & E. Kittay (eds.), *Frames, Fields and Contrasts: New Essays in Semantic and Lexical Organization*, 75–102. Hillsdale: Erlbaum.

Fillmore, Charles J. & B.T.S. Atkins (2000). Describing polysemy: The case of crawly. In Y. Ravin & C. Laecock (eds.), *Polysemy*, 91–110. Oxford: Oxford University Press.

Fillmore, Charles J. & Collin Baker (2010). A frames approach to semantic analysis. In B. Heine & H. Narrog (eds.), *The Oxford Handbook of Linguistic Analysis*, 13–340. Oxford: Oxford University Press.

Fillmore, Charles J., Johnson, Chris R., & Miriam R.L. Petruck (2003). *Background to FrameNet*. International Journal of Lexicography 16(3),235–250.

Fillmore, C. J., Lee-Goldman, Russell., & Russell Rhodes (2012). The framenet constructicon. In H.C. Boas & I. Sag (eds.), *Sign-based construction grammar*, 309–372. Stanford: CSLI Publications.

Fillmore, Charles J. & Paul Kay (1993). *Construction Grammar Course Book*. Manuscript. UC Berkeley.
Fillmore, Charles J., Paul Kay & Mary Catherine O'Connor (1988). Regularity and idiomaticity in grammatical constructions: The case of 'let alone'. *Language* 6(3),501–538.
Fuss, Eric & Angelika Wöllstein (eds.) (2018). *Grammatiktheorie und Grammatikographie*. Tübingen: Narr.
Garibyan, Armine, Balog, Evelin, & Thomas Herbst (2020). L2-constructions that go together – more on valency constructions and learner language. In C. Juchem-Grundmann, M. Pleyer & M. Pleyer (eds.), *Yearbook of the German Cognitive Linguistics Association*, 9–30. Berlin/Boston: De Gruyter Mouton.
Gemmell Hudson, Maggie (this volume). Teaching second year German using frames and constructions.
Gilquin, Gaëtanelle (2012). Lexical infelicity in English causative constructions. Comparing native and learner collostructions. In J. Leino & R. von Waldenfels (eds.) *Analytical Causatives. From 'give' and 'come' to 'let' and 'make'*, 41–63. München: Lincom Europa.
Gilquin, Gaëtanelle (2015). The use of phrasal verbs by French-speaking EFL learners. A constructional and collostructional corpus-based approach. *Corpus Linguistics and Linguistic Theory* 11(1),51–88.
Gilquin, Gaëtanelle (2016). Discourse markers in L2 English: From classroom to naturalistic input. In Olga Timofeeva, Anne-Christine Gardner, Alpo Honkapohja & Sarah Chevalier (eds.), *New approaches to English linguistics: Building bridges*, 213–249. Amsterdam / Philadelphia: John Benjamins.
Gilquin, Gaëtanelle (2018). Exploring the spoken learner English constructicon: A corpus-driven approach. In R.Alonso Alonso (ed.), *Speaking in a second language*, 127–152. Amsterdam/ Philadelphia: John Benjamins.
Gilquin, Gaëtanelle (this volume). Constructing learner speech: On the use of spoken data in Applied Construction Grammar.
Gilquin, Gaëtanelle & Sabine De Knop (2016). Exploring L2 constructionist approaches. In S. De Knop & G. Gilquin (eds.), *Applied Construction Grammar*, 3–17. Berlin: De Gruyter.
Glass, Cordula (2019). *Collocations, creativity and constructions*. Tübingen: Narr.
Goldberg, Adele E. (1995). *Constructions. A Construction Grammar Approach to Argument Structure*. Chicago & London: The University of Chicago Press.
Goldberg, Adele E. (2006), *Constructions at Work. The Nature of Generalization in Language*. Oxford: Oxford University Press.
Goldberg, Adele E. (2013). Constructionist approaches. In T. Hoffmann & G. Trousdale (eds.), *The Oxford Handbook of Construction Grammar*, 15–31. Oxford: OUP.
Gonzálvez-García, Francisco (2019). Exploring the pedagogical potential of vertical and horizontal relations in the constructicon: The case of the family of subjective-transitive constructions with decir in Spanish. *International Review of Applied Linguistics in Language Teaching*, 57(1),121–145.
Gonzálvez-García, Franciso & Chris Butler (2018). Situating Valency Theory within functional-cognitive space. *Review of Cognitive Linguistics* 16(2),348–398.
Gries, Stefan Th. (2005). Syntactic priming: A corpus-based approach. *Journal of Psycholinguistic Research* 34(4),365–399.
Gries, Stefan Th. (2018). On over- and underuse in learner corpus research and multifactoriality in corpus linguistics more generally. *Journal of Second Language Studies* 1(2),276–308.

Gries, Stefan Th. (this volume). On, or against?, (just) frequency.
Gries, Stefan Th. & Stefanie Wulff (2005). Do foreign language learners also have constructions? Evidence from priming, sorting, and corpora. *Annual Review of Cognitive Linguistics* 3, 182–200.
Gries, Stefan Th. & Stefanie Wulff (2009). Psycholinguistic and corpus-linguistic evidence for L2 constructions. *Annual Review of Cognitive Linguistics* 7, 163–186.
Herbst, Thomas (2014). The valency approach to argument structure constructions. In T. Herbst, H. J. Schmid, & S. Faulhaber (Eds.), *Constructions – collocations – patterns*, 167–216. Berlin: Mouton de Gruyter.
Herbst, Thomas (2015). Why Construction Grammar catches the worm and corpus data can drive you crazy: Accounting for idiomatic and nonidiomatic idiomaticity. *Journal of Social Sciences*, 11(3),91–110.
Herbst, Thomas (2016). Foreign language learning is construction learning – what else? Moving towards Pedagogical Construction Grammar. In S. De Knop & G. Gilquin (eds.), *Applied Construction Grammar*, 21–52. Berlin/Boston: De Gruyter.
Herbst, Thomas (2017). "Grünes Licht für pädagogische Konstruktionsgrammatik – Denn: Linguistik ist nicht (mehr) nur Chomsky." *Fremdsprachen Lehren und Lernen* 46(2), 119–135.
Herbst, Thomas (2020). Constructions, generalizations, and the unpredictability of language: Moving towards colloconstruction grammar. *Constructions and Frames* 12(1),56–96.
Herbst, Thomas & Michael Klotz (2003). *Lexikografie*. Paderborn: Schöningh.
Höder, Steffen (2016). Niederdeutsche Form, unspezifische Struktur. Diasystematische Konstruktionen in der deutsch-dänischen Kontaktzone. In H. Spiekermann et al. (eds.), *Niederdeutsch: Grenzen, Strukturen, Variation*, 293–309. Wien/Köln/Weimar: Böhlau.
Höder, Steffen (2018). Grammar is community-specific: Background and basic concepts of Diasystematic Construction Grammar. In H.C. Boas & S. Höder (eds.), *Constructions in contact*, 37–70. Amsterdam/Philadelphia: John Benjamins.
Hoffmann, Thomas & Graeme Trousdale (eds.) (2013). *The Oxford Handbook of Construction Grammar*. Oxford: Oxford University Press.
Holme, Randal (2010a). A construction grammar for the classroom. *IRAL* 48, 355–377.
Holme, Randal (2010b). Construction grammars: Towards a pedagogical model. *AILA Review* 23, 115–133.
Holme, Randal (2015). 'Someone to open each and every door': Construction Grammar as a learner grammar: The case of English indefinite pronouns. *Journal of Social Sciences* 11(3),352–362.
Jurafsky, D. (1991). *An on-line computational model of human sentence interpretation: A theory of the representation and use of linguistic knowledge*. Ph.D. dissertation, University of California, Berkeley.
Lakoff, George (1987). *Women, fire, and dangerous things*. Chicago: Chicago University Press.
Langacker, Ronald (2000). A dynamic usage-based model. In M. Barlow & S. Kemmer (eds.), *Usage based models of language*, 1–64. Stanford: CSLI Publications.
Law, James (this volume). Frame-based metonymy in teaching L2 vocabulary.
Lee-Goldman, Russell & Miriam R.L. Petruck (2018). The FrameNet constructicon in action. In B. Lyngfelt, L. Borin, K. Ohara, T. T. Torrent (eds.), *Constructicography: Constructicon development across languages*, 19–40. Amsterdam/Philadelphia: John Benjamins.
Liang, Junying (2002). *How do Chinese ESL learners construct sentence meaning: Verb-centered or construction-based?* M.A. thesis, Guangdong University of Foreign Studies.

Lieven, Elena (2014). First language learning from a usage-based approach. In T. Herbst, H.-J. Schmidt, & Susen Faulhaber (eds.), *Constructions, collocations, patterns*, 1–24. Berlin/Boston: De Gruyter.

Littlemore, Jeanette (2009). *Applying Cognitive Linguistics to second language learning and teaching*. Basingstoke: Palgrave Macmillan.

Loenheim, Lisa, Lyngfelt, Benjamin, Olofsson, Joel, Prentice, Julia, & Sofia Tingsell (2016). Constructicography meets (second) language education: On constructions in teaching aids and the usefulness of a Swedish constructicon. In S. De Knop & G. Gilquin (eds.), *Applied Construction Grammar*, 327–356. Berlin/Boston: De Gruyter.

Lorenz, Alexander, Crane, Cori, Benjamins, John, and Hans C. Boas (2020). L2 German Learners' Perceptions and Use of an Online Semantic Frame-Based Dictionary. *Die Unterrichtspraxis/ Teaching German* 53(2), 191–209.

Lyngfelt, Benjamin (2018). Introduction: Constructions and constructicography. In B. Lyngfelt, L. Borin, K. Ohara, & T.T. Torrent (eds.), *Constructicography. Constructicon development across languages*, 1–18. Amsterdam/Philadelphia: John Benjamins.

Lyngfelt, Benjamin, Borin, Lars, Ohara, Kyoko & Tiago T. Torrent (eds.) (2018). *Constructicography: Constructicon development across languages*. Amsterdam/ Philadelphia: John Benjamins.

Madlener, Karin (2015). *Frequency effects in instructed second language acquisition*. Berlin/ Boston: De Gruyter/Mouton.

Madlener-Charpentier, Karin (this volume). Learned attention beyond typological bootstrapping: Constructional repertoires and constructional complexity in the spatial language domain.

Martínez Vázquez, M. (2008). Constructions in learner language. Círculo de lingüística aplicada a la comunicación, N°. 36. http://webs.ucm.es/info/circulo/no36/marvaz.pdf

Michaelis, Laura (2013). Sign-Based Construction Grammar. In T. Hoffman & G. Trousdale (eds.), *The Oxford Handbook of Construction Grammar*, 133–152. Oxford: Oxford University Press.

Minsky, Marvin (1975). Minsky's frame system theory. *TINLAP* 75,104–116.

Nesset, Tore & Laura Janda (this volume). Securing strategic input for L2 learners: Constructions with Russian motion verbs.

Patten, Amanda & Florent Perek (this volume). Pedagogic applications of the English Constructicon.

Perek, Florent & Amanda L. Patten (2019). Towards an English Constructicon using patterns and frames. *International Journal of Corpus Linguistics* 24(3),354–384.

Petruck, Miriam R.L. (1996). Frame Semantics. In J. Verschueren, J-O Östman, J. Blommaert & C. Bulcaen (eds.), *Handbook of Pragmatics*, 1–13. Amsterdam: John Benjamins.

Petruck, Miriam R. L., Fillmore, Charles J., Baker, Collin, Ellsworth, Michael & Josef Ruppenhofer (2004). Reframing FrameNet data. *Proceedings of the 11th EURALEX International Congress, Lorient, France*, 405–416.

Queller, Kurt (2001). A usage-based approach to modeling and teaching the phrasal lexicon. *Applied Cognitive Linguistics* 2, 55–83.

Roehr-Brackin, Karen (2014). Explicit knowledge and processes from a usage-based perspective: The developmental trajectory of an instructed L2 learner. *Language Learning* 64(4),771–808.

Ruiz de Mendoza Ibáñez, Francisco J. & María del Pilar Agustín Llach (2016). Cognitive Pedagogical Grammar and meaning construction in L2. In Gaetanelle Gilquin & Sabine De Knop (eds.), *Applied Construction Grammar*, 149–184. Berlin & New York: Mouton De Gruyter.

Ruppenhofer, Josef, Boas, Hans C. & Collin Baker (2013). The FrameNet approach to relating syntax and semantics. In R.H. Gouws, U. Heid, W. Schweickard, & H.E. Wiegand (eds.), *Dictionaries. An International Encyclopedia of Lexicography*, 1320–1329. Berlin/New York: De Gruyter/Mouton.

Ruppenhofer, Josef, Ellsworth, Michael, Petruck, Miriam R.L., Johnson, Christopher R. & Jan Scheffczyk (2016). *FrameNet II: Extended Theory and Practice*. Manuscript, International Computer Science Institute, Berkeley, CA.

Ruppenhofer, Josef, Boas, Hans C. & Collin Baker (2017). FrameNet. In P. A. Fuertes-Olivera (Ed.), *The Routledge Handbook of Lexicography*, 183–398. New York: Routledge.

Sag, Ivan (2010). English Filler-Gap Constructions. *Language* 86(3),486–545.

Schank, Roger & Robert Abelson (1975). Scripts, plans, and knowledge. *IJCAI* 75, 151–157.

Schmidt, Thomas (2009). The Kicktionary – A multilingual lexical resource of football language. In H.C. Boas (ed.), *Multilingual FrameNets in Computational Lexicography*, 59–100. Berlin/New York: Mouton de Gruyter.

Stefanowitsch, Anatol & Stefan Th. Gries (2003). Collostructions: Investigating the interaction of words and constructions. *International journal of corpus linguistics*, 8(2), 209–243.

Talmy, Leonard (2000). *Toward a Cognitive Semantics*. Cambridge, MA: MIT Press.

Tomasello, Michael (2003). *Constructing a language*. Cambridge, Mass.: Harvard University Press.

Torrent, Tiago T., Baker, Collin F., Czulo, Oliver, Ohara, Kyoko, & Petruck, Miriam R.L. (eds.) (2020). *Proceedings of the International FrameNet Workshop 2020: Towards a Global, Multilingual FrameNet*.

Uhrig, Peter, Faulhaber, Susen, Dabrowska, Ewa, & Thomas Herbst (this volume). L2-words that go together – more on collocation and learner language.

Valenzuela Manzanares, Javier & Ana María Rojo López (2008). What can language learners tell us about constructions? In Sabine De Knop & Teun De Rycker (eds.), *Cognitive Approaches to Pedagogical Grammar: A Volume in Honour of René Dirven*, 197–230. Berlin: Mouton de Gruyter.

Wee, Lionel (2007). Construction grammar and English language teaching. *Indonesian Journal of English Language Teaching* 3(1),20–32.

Widdowson, Henry (2000). On the limitations of linguistics applied. *Applied Linguistics* 21(1), 3–25.

Ziem, Alexander (2008). *Frames und sprachliches Wissen*. Berlin: Walter de Gruyter.

Ziem, Alexander & Anastasia Neumann-Schneider (this volume). Towards a FrameNet for linguistic terminology: Theoretical foundations, lexicographic practice, didactic potential.

II Data and methodology in Pedagogical Construction Grammar

Stefan Th. Gries
On, or against?, (just) frequency

1 Introduction

Over the past 20 years or so, it seems as if the field of cognitive linguistics has changed quite a bit. While much work during the 1980s and 1990s followed many suggestions by Lakoff, Langacker, Talmy, and others and studied polysemy, metaphor, subjectification, etc., cognitive linguistics now seems to have evolved into a field that is largely construction-based and nearly completely usage-based (see in particular Bybee 2006, 2010, Goldberg 2006). On the whole, I welcome this evolution, but I also sometimes feel that the usage-based part of what cognitive linguistics now is is lacking to a degree that is becoming more and more problematic. The most important problem I see is concerned with the role, maybe since Langacker 1987, of the *f*-word in usage-based linguistics and its relation to Lakoff's (1991) hugely influential cognitive commitment. More specifically, usage-based linguists
- are using the *f*-word too much;
- are using the *f*-word too simplistically; and
- are not considering alternatives to the *f*-word enough,

the *f*-word being, obviously, *frequency*, specifically *token frequency*. In this paper, I want to (i) discuss a few ways in which the heavy reliance on a simplistic notion of frequency is problematic as well as (ii) point to notions that should replace or complement frequency much more in future cognitive-linguistic research if the field wants to do more than merely paying lip service to Lakoff's cognitive commitment.

2 On (token) frequencies

2.1 How (token) frequencies vary

The first major issue with token frequency data (on morphemes, words, (syntactic) constructions, . . .) as they are mostly used in cognitive linguistics is that they are usually based on corpora with too little regard to between- and

Stefan Th. Gries, Department of Linguistics, University of California, Santa Barbara

https://doi.org/10.1515/9783110746723-002

within-corpus variability. *Between-corpora variability* refers to the fact that frequencies for the same elements can vary drastically even between corpora that are (supposed to be) representative of similar speakers, registers, and/or time periods. For instance, Schlüter (2005) showed that frequencies of present perfects differ hugely between corpora representing similar as well as different registers of English. Consider also as a much more comprehensive example, Roland, Elman, & Dick's (2007) data, which show that the relative frequencies of argument structure and syntactic constructions are, while certainly correlated across corpora, also considerably different across the five corpora they analyzed: Figure 1 shows how the (square roots of the) relative frequencies of

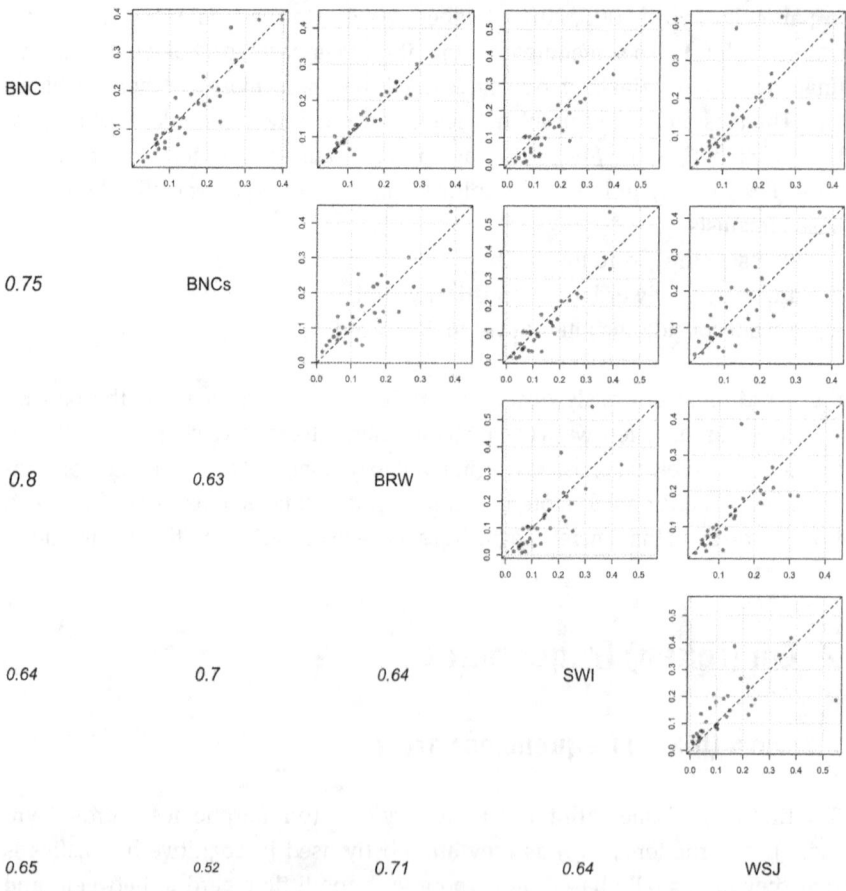

Figure 1: Correlations of frequencies of constructions in the British National Corpus (BNC), the spoken part of the British National Corpus (BNCs), the Brown corpus (BRW), the Switchboard corpus (SWI), and the Wall Street Journal Corpus (WSJ), all data from Roland, Elman, & Dick (2007).

their 32 constructions are distributed in the five corpora: the *x*-axis always represents the relative frequency of constructions in the corpus mentioned in the row of the main diagonal, the *y*-axis always represents the relative frequency of the same constructions in the corpus mentioned in the column of the main diagonal, and the dashed line indicates where all points would be if the constructions were equally frequent in both corpora. Even though there is often a sizable correlation (indicated in the diagonally opposite cells), it is clear that there are often multiple outliers.

Even more striking can be a look at *within-corpus variability*, which can be unexpectedly high. For instance, in a follow-up study on Schlüter (2005), Gries (2006) showed that the present perfect's frequency in a single corpus, the British Component of the International Corpus of English (ICE-GB) varies extremely widely, as shown in Figure 2: While the overall mean is around 3%, it comes with a wide degree of variability between the extreme values of 0 and 9.79%.

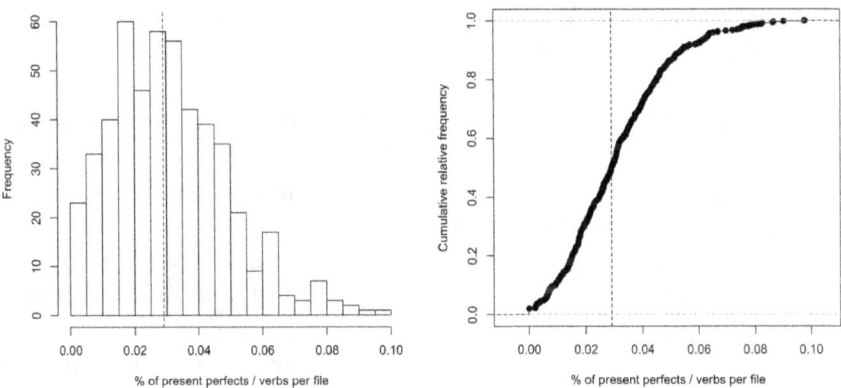

Figure 2: (Relative) Frequencies of present perfects in the 500 files of the ICE-GB.

These are not isolated and/or exaggerated findings: For instance, anyone who has ever worked on first language acquisition of English will probably know that, in the Brown (1973) corpus, Eve's data are quite different from Adam's and Sarah's, or in the Manchester Corpus (Theakston et al. 2001), Ruth's data can look extremely differently from those of the other 11 children. The same is true in second/foreign language acquisition/learning data: Callies (2013) finds a lot of variability in first person pronoun use in MICUSP and CALE, Gablasova, Brezina, & McEnery (2017) show that learner as well as native-speaker data also exhibit a wide spread of frequencies of *I think*, Gries (2018) shows huge individual differences in the use of *quite* in learner and native speaker data, and Wulff & Gries (2019) show that the use of verb-particle constructions can be very different across different learners.

In cognitive linguistics, however, there is much too little work that takes both between- and within-corpus variability seriously. Of the little work that there is on individual differences in cognitive linguistics, that of Dąbrowska and colleagues is probably most relevant. For instance, Street & Dąbrowska (2010) show that there are "considerable differences in native language attainment" that are correlated with the frequencies of constructions; similarly, Dąbrowska (2018) studies native-speaker attainment of a language and its correlations with both linguistic and non-linguistic predictors. There are other studies that try to consider differences between group and speaker behaviors (e.g., Divjak, Dąbrowska, & Arppe 2016 for another recent example), but on the whole many discussions of frequency effects settle for whole-corpus token frequencies that, at best, approximate a rather crude average of a speaker's input, but no more; cf. Dąbrowska's (2016) discussion of Cognitive Linguistics' 'fourth deadly sin' for a similar view of the field's state-of-the-art.

2.2 How we can deal with this? By increasing the resolution of our corpus studies

The main remedy to this issue is to always increase the resolution on the frequency data: Simple overall corpus frequencies of, say, words or other constructions, are always going to be too much of an imprecise conflation; just like one should never provide a measure of central tendency (e.g., a mean) without a measure of dispersion (e.g., a standard deviation), one should also never provide any overall corpus frequencies without, minimally, a summary indication of their variation in the corpus (e.g. an interquartile range of the frequencies of the construction in question in each part of the corpus, however defined (in terms of meaningful units such as speakers/files, registers, . . .)) or, better, an index of the dispersion of the construction in question (Gries 2008). Crucially, this means that a lot of work that is now done only on mostly web-based corpora will need to be done better. Corpora such as COCA, when accessed only in a browser, make it hard to compute such statistics, whereas computing such statistics on corpora whose full text one can access from a hard drive is very straightforward. Cognitive linguistics may need to begin to eschew the convenience of web-access corpora to get higher-quality results.

2.3 What token frequencies correlate with and how much

The next question is how much the notion of frequency actually explains. In much corpus-linguistically informed cognitive or psycholinguistic work, frequency is a significant predictor of acquisition (e.g., in how frequent verbs drive the recognition of constructional semantics), constructionalization/grammaticalization (e.g., *gonna* or *wanna*), or processing (e.g. in the form of reaction times in lexical decision tasks); the central role that frequency assumes in much psycholinguistic work is neatly summarized by, for instance, Christiansen & Chater (2016:175): "contemporary theories of perception and action have proposed that the cognitive system aims to build a probabilistic model, which captures the statistical structure of the external world". Especially earlier cognitive-linguistic work has also placed a great degree of importance on frequency of occurrence, which has been argued to be an operationalization of the notion of cognitive entrenchment:

> Linguistic structures are more realistically conceived as falling along a continuous scale of entrenchment in cognitive organization. Every use of a structure has a positive impact on its degree of entrenchment, whereas extended periods of disuse have a negative impact. With repeated use, a novel structure becomes progressively entrenched, to the point of becoming a unit; moreover, units are variably entrenched depending on the frequency of their occurrence. (Langacker 1987:59)

However, from a statistical perspective, attempting to support the relevance of frequency with largely monofactorial studies is problematic in a way that is as straightforward as it is often ignored. It is easy to obtain significant correlations between frequency as a predictor and some dependent variable because such a test tests the role of frequency against a null hypothesis that frequency plays no role while controlling for nothing else. However, this kind of testing and similar kinds amount to pretending we do not know anything else already about the phenomenon in question whereas what would really be required is to show that frequency can
- either *complement* what we already know (with controls),
- or *replace* what we already know (but with controls).

This problem is similar to that found in quite a number of studies in learner corpus research (LCR). In many such studies, the frequency of occurrence is actually the response/dependent variable rather than the predictor/independent variable that it is in many cognitive-linguistic/usage-based studies, but the problem is similar in that in many such LCR studies are also monofactorial and consider only one predictor, namely the L1 of the speakers (native speakers vs. different learners). Not only are many of these studies averaging across speakers and even ignoring the sometimes huge percentages of speakers who do not use a certain expression at all (Gries 2018), they also often proceed without regard to any other linguistic/contextual factors that affect the use of the constructions in question.

Thus, many (i) cognitive-linguistic studies that rely on frequency as the main predictor, or even the only one, and many (ii) LCR studies that rely on L1 as the main predictor, or even the only one, share the problem that both leave all the variability that could be explained by many other linguistic, contextual, or psycholinguistic factors one should have included 'up for grabs' by the factors frequency and L1 respectively, leading to anti-conservative overly optimistic estimates of the role of their pet predictors (see Gries 2018 for discussion of this in an LCR context). This, obviously, points to an urgent need for multifactorial explorations of the role of frequency, which in turn requires that we develop accounts of entrenchment or the role of frequency that are more comprehensive in, for instance, including a broader range of predictors (potentially correlated with frequency).

This argument, however raises two questions: (i) is this really necessary? Is there any evidence that calls into question the so widely-attested and seemingly so robust effect of frequency? And (ii) what 'other factors' might those be? Whatever they are, they need to be correlated enough with frequency to explain that frequency has for such a long time been assumed to be so powerful, but at the same time they may be more strongly and even causally related to the phenomena we have so far been explaining with frequency? As it turns out, exploring the former question will begin to address the latter . . .

3 Why token frequency might be less important than is believed

Over the last few years, a variety of studies has indicated that token frequency might not play as much a causal role as has been assumed now for decades. These studies have particularly been concerned with one of the most widely-discussed and robust manifestations of the frequency effect, namely response time latencies or reaction times in lexical decision tasks. This is relevant here because, while there is probably not much prototypical cognitive-linguistic research on such latencies, the kind of frequency effect cognitive linguists have nonetheless been assuming is one that is ultimately grounded in psycholinguistic studies of naming and response latencies. This kind of frequency effects essentially corresponds to a frequency-as-repetition counter along the lines of the above Langacker (1987) quote, or quotes such as "each instance redefines the system, however infinitesimally, maintaining its present state or shifting its probabilities in one direction or the other" (Halliday 1991/2005:67) or "it is usual that each learning event updates a statistical representation of a category independently of other learning events." (Ellis 2002:147). On top of that, the way this frequency effect is supposed to 'work' is in cognitive linguistics often characterized in terms of (interactive) activation models (also borrowed from psycholinguistics) where more frequent activation of a node is hypothesized to lead to, say, an increase of that node's resting level of activation, which makes it easier for that node to be activated again (after a brief refractory phase, that is) or to an increase in the strength of connections between nodes.

For two to three decades, this view of frequency effects from psycholinguistics has been more or less completely adopted in cognitive linguistics, but in this section, I will discuss a few studies that begin to question the central role of frequency in general or of frequency-as-repetition in particular and then highlight their implications.

3.1 McDonald & Shillcock (2001)

McDonald & Shillcock (2001) discuss a variety of dimensions of lexical variation – frequency of occurrence, concreteness, context availability, age of acquisition, ambiguity – and their correlation with response time latencies. Most importantly, however, they propose a new dimension of lexical variation, one that is correlated with many of the above-mentioned ones, but one that also contains additional information, in particular because, unlike all others, it involves contextual information about words; this, they argue, is necessary because

> [p]sycholinguistic theory has advanced considerably by adopting the convention that lexical representations are discrete entities, and that the meaning of a word can be represented by a simple local representation or by a particular listing of semantic features. In reality it is not possible to provide discrete, necessary, and sufficient representations for the meanings of words; [...] It is possible to conclude that the meanings of words are determined by their contexts of usage. (McDonald & Shillcock 2001:300)

The measure they propose is based on co-occurrence information and is called *contextual distinctiveness*; measuring it for a word or a lemma l involves
- retrieving all instances of l within its context;
- computing the relative frequencies of a set of n collocates within a context window around l (e.g., ±5 words); this is the so-called *posterior distribution*, essentially the list of conditional probabilities $p(collocate|l)$;
- computing the relative frequencies of those n collocates in the corpus in general; this is the so-called *prior distribution*, essentially the list of probabilities $p(collocate)$;
- compute the relative entropy / Kullback-Leibler divergence from the prior to the posterior distribution as in (1).

(1) $\quad\text{Contextual Distinctiveness} = \sum_{i=1}^{n} p(coll_i|lemma) \cdot \log_2 \frac{p(coll_i|lemma)}{p(coll_i)}$

Thus, contextual distinctiveness "measures the amount of information conveyed by a word about its contexts of use" (p. 303) and is "derived from the distribution of words co-occurring with the word of interest, whereas Word Frequency (WF) is measured independently of this distribution" (p. 307). Contextual distinctiveness is correlated with observed log-transformed word frequency (r=−0.82), but its computation does not involve it *directly* because it is based on co-occurrence percentages; in addition, contextual distinctiveness incorporates prior knowledge (in the form of the probabilities of collocates in the corpus at large).

More important than the theoretical advantages are McDonald & Shillcock's empirical results. In their experiment 1, they find that contextual distinctiveness accounts (marginally significantly) for variance in reaction times in a lexical decision task even when word frequency and length are statistically controlled for (r_{part}=0.2), whereas frequency did not when word length and *CD* were statistically controlled (r_{part}=−0.03). They conclude "[w]ords that appear in relatively constrained (or distinctive) linguistic contexts have high contextual distinctiveness scores and tend to attract longer lexical decision latencies" (McDonald & Shillcock 2011:312). A similar result with regard to partial correlations was then also obtained for data from the lexical decision study carried out by Balota, Cortese, & Pilotti (1999); note in passing that Recchia, Johns, & Jones (2008:271f.) arrive at very similar conclusions:

> lexical processing is optimized for precisely those words that are most likely to be required in any given situation. [...] context variability is potentially a more important variable than is frequency in word recognition and memory access.

McDonald & Shillcock then proceed to explore contextual distinctiveness's correlations with the other dimensions of variation and find that it is not derivative from any of the other dimensions but does add something new to the mix since it "has theoretical and empirical advantages over simple word frequency which need to be considered in future research into meaning-based lexical processing behavior" (p. 319).

3.2 Adelman, Brown, & Quesada (2006)

Adelman, Brown, & Quesada (2006) start out from the observation (not often considered in cognitive linguistics at all) that, while psycholinguistic models of lexical access and reading assume that each encounter of a word allows the word to be processed more quickly later,

> [r]esearch on memory, however, has found that the extent to which the number of repeated exposures to a particular item affects that item's later retrieval depends on the separation of the exposures in time and context (Glenberg, 1976, 1979). Indeed, under some conditions, if neither time nor context changes substantially, there may be no benefit of repetition at all (Verkoeijen, Rikers, & Schmidt, 2004). (p. 814)

From that, they infer that

> [i]f the memory for words that subserves word recognition operates in the same fashion, then the effect of repetitions (i.e., WF) will be diminished or eliminated when these repetitions occur in the same context. Accordingly, the number of contexts in which words are experienced, their contextual diversity (CD), should determine their accessibility and hence response times (RTs) in word naming and lexical decision. A normative measure of a word's CD may be obtained by counting the number of passages (documents) in a corpus that contain that word. (p. 814f.)

It was necessary to quote these passages at length because their argumentation can actually not be left uncommented. This is because, while the empirical studies they report on per se are instructive, the above passage is fraught with some terminological confusion and one critical oversight. First, referring to the "number of contexts in which words are experienced" as *contextual diversity* is not ideal: Just because a "number of contexts" increases does not mean that the diversity of the contexts increases as well. No matter how often *hermetically* is seen in a corpus, the next word will virtually always be *sealed*; no matter how often the expression *was regarded* is seen in a corpus, the next words will virtually always either be *as* or *by*. Yes, given the Zipfian frequency distribution of words in general or in constructionally-defined slots, if one looks at more occurrences of a word, one will ultimately see more different contexts, but this relationship is far from deterministic, and diversity is more usefully operationalized as type frequency in many (cognitive-)linguistic applications.

Second, the proposal to measure contextual diversity in terms of document frequency is surprising for several reasons. On the one hand, finding a certain word in a variety of documents does not at all guarantee that the actual usage contexts of the word will be different (see *hermetically* and *was regarded* above). On the other hand, Adelman, Brown, & Quesada (2006) do not seem to be aware of the fact that (i) they are suggesting to use what in corpus linguistics has for many decades been referred to as *dispersion*, the degree to which an element is distributed evenly across the parts/documents of a corpus, and that (ii) compared to many of the dispersion measures that have been proposed (see Gries 2008 for the currently most comprehensive overview), the measure they are proposing – called *range* in corpus linguistics – is probably the crudest one, because it either presupposes that the documents are equally large or it neglects document/corpus part sizes, which will skew the results to some degree.

In their empirical evaluations, they use,
- as dependent variables (responses), reaction time data from six different data bases;
- as independent variables (predictors), log-transformed range and frequency information from three corpora: (i) the Brown corpus (1m words of written American English from the 1960s), (ii) the LSA/TASA corpus of approx. 8.26m words aimed at representing lexical knowledge of 12th-grade high school students, and (iii) the written part of the British National Corpus (90m words of written British English from the 1990s);
- as controls, word lengths, orthographic neighborhood size, rime consistency, number of syllables, and initial phoneme.

Their statistical analysis is based on 18 different regressions on the combinations of six reaction-time data bases and three corpora. They find that, while both word frequency and range add significantly to the explanatory power of regression models already containing the controls, "the improvement in prediction was always greater for [range] than for [frequency]" (p. 815).

Adelman, Brown, & Quesada then speculate on whether range is influenced by semantic variables such as ambiguity "as words with multiple meanings should be used in multiple contexts", but I do not consider this too fruitful because, first, as discussed above, occurring in multiple documents/files of a corpus does not guarantee at all that the different occurrences are in actually different contexts and, second, the number of meanings of words is correlated with the frequency of words, another one of Zipf's laws. They do show, however, that range is positively correlated with faster response times "regardless of imageability, concreteness, ambiguity, and other lexical measures" (p. 818) whereas high word frequency is not. The authors conclude that "[l]earning-based models of reading cannot accommodate these results unless they are modified so that learning mechanisms are sensitive to context, not frequency" (p. 822), an interesting conclusion in how it, just like the findings from McDonald & Shillcock (2001), does not really support the frequency-as-repetition counter view that underlies much cognitive-linguistic work using the notion of entrenchment (see Jones, Johns, & Recchia 2012 or Johns, Dye, & Jones 2016 for similar findings regarding the processing of novel words and their distribution over discourse contexts).

3.3 Gries (2010) and more recent work

Gries (2008) surveyed and critiqued approximately two dozen dispersion measures and adjusted frequencies (frequencies of words that are adjusted downwards if a word's distribution is very uneven). Gries (2010) is a follow-up paper to this publication and is relevant in how it explores more and better dispersion measures than Adelman, Brown, & Quesada. The first part of Gries (2010) is not that relevant to the current discussion because it explores intercorrelations between different dispersion measures to determine to what degree the 16 measures included in the study fall into clusters/components that are internally homogeneous but differ a lot from each other.

The more interesting part is the second, in which Gries computes rank correlations (Kendall's τ) of frequencies with more than two dozen dispersion measures and adjusted frequencies from the 10m words spoken component of the British National Corpus with (i) two of the databases also studied in Adelman, Brown, & Quesada – Spieler & Balota (1997) and Balota & Spieler (1998) – and (ii) reaction time data from Baayen (2008).

The results for the reaction times data from Balota and Spieler show that Gries's own dispersion measure – DP/DP_{norm} – is among those most highly correlated with the reaction time data, but, on the whole, all measures exhibit rather similar correlations: none or no small group is *clearly* superior to the others. This changes with the reaction time data from Baayen (2008), because here there is a clear difference in predictive power between the measures included in the analysis. Gries's DP fares well again, but so do some other measures, most of which are measures that – unlike Adelman, Brown, & Quesada's range – correct for differently-sized corpus parts. In fact, frequency is outperformed slightly by range, but range in turn is outperformed considerably by, for instance, the variation coefficient, D, and DP.

Gries (2019a) is a further application of dispersion measures by (i) using a few more corpora and (ii) measuring correlation in a more flexible way that all studies reported on so far, namely by not using simple linear regression models on the data. As for (i), Gries correlates Balota and Spieler's reaction time data with frequencies and DP-values based on the whole BNC, the spoken component of the BNC, the BNC Baby, the BNC Sampler, the Brown corpus, and the British component of the International Corpus of English (ICE-GB). As for (ii), rather than using linear regression modeling (and hoping that log transformations capture all of the non-linearity in the data), he instead uses generalized additive models, i.e. a kind of regression model that can accommodate multiple degrees of curvature in correlation data. The results of separate analyses (for the sake of a rough comparison to Adelman, Brown, & Quesada) are shown in Table 1 and they are as clear as they can be: For every comparison of *DP* to frequency for each of the corpora and speaker groups, *DP* outperforms frequency, sometimes by more than doubling the amount of deviance accounted for.

Table 1: Percentage of deviance of the reaction time data each explained by a GAM.

	Young speakers		Older speakers	
	DP	Frequency	DP	Frequency
BNC	9.26	5.06	17.3	7.57
BNC spoken	8.64	4.26	14.3	5.88
BNC Baby	8.48	4.96	14.9	7.06
BNC Sampler	9.07	5.22	13	6.44
Brown	7.85	4.78	13.2	6.77
ICE-GB	6.1	3.79	9.3	4.78

In other words, despite its ubiquity, frequency is never the best predictor, lending support to the works discussed above.

3.4 Baayen (2010)

The most impressive study on the effect, or lack of effect, of frequency is Baayen (2010), a study explicitly designed to test, among other things, the results of McDonald & Shillcock (2001) discussed above. This study is based on lexical decision latencies for 1042 monomorphemic and monosyllabic words from the English Lexicon Project; here, we will be concerned with two parts of the study, one that determines which predictors (including a token frequency predictor) are correlated with the dependent variable, lexical decision latencies how strongly, and one that determines what the role of of the frequency predictor is vis-à-vis the other predictors. What are these other predictors? In part one of the study they consist of a variety of local and contextual features of words w_{1-n}:

- their contextual diversity and range from above based on measurements from the British National Corpus;
- their textual microcontext based on (i) the type frequency of the immediately preceding word slot, (ii) the entropy H of the w's left syntactic family, (iii) the KL-divergence of the probability distribution of adjectives preceding w and those adjectives' probability distribution in the corpus as a whole, and (iv) the KL-divergence of the probability distribution of prepositions plus

indefinite articles preceding *w* and those prepositions and indefinite articles' probability distribution in the corpus as a whole;
- morphological predictors: (i) the entropy H of *w*'s inflectional paradigm, (ii) the noun-verb ratio of the *w*, (iii) *w*'s morphological family size, and (iv) the number of complex words that are synonyms of *w* (according to WordNet);
- word-level predictors: (i) *w*'s neighborhood density, (ii) *w*'s orthographic Levenshtein distance, (iii) *w*'s length (in characters), and (iv) *w*'s letter pair familiarity.

A variety of single-predictor models indicate that the frequency predictor scores the highest R^2-value of all predictors when it comes to accounting for the decision latencies, followed by dispersion (even when only measured by range) and contextual diversity.

However, the more important part of the study for our present purposes is the second one, which explores how predictable the frequency predictor is from the other predictors. This is not only to determine how collinear frequency is with everything else, but also to see what, if any, effect frequency has when all other predictors are residualized out of frequency. As it turns out, all significant predictors account for 91% of the variability of the frequency predictor; one of the strongest predictors is in fact range/dispersion. The most important finding, however, is that, once all other predictors are residualized out of frequency, yielding a bare-bones version of frequency that really only incorporates frequency-as-repetition, that version of frequency
- is still significantly correlated with the original 'regular' frequency predictor, but
- has a very small amount of explanatory power.

In other words, "frequency of occurrence, in the sense of pure repetition, turns out not to be a particularly important predictor" (p. 437). Rather, as further analysis reveals,

> [s]yntactic and morphological family size, dispersion, and syntactic (relative) entropy measures are jointly most predictive, accounting for some 36.7% of the variance. Repetition Frequency does contribute, but [...] only 8.8% of the variance is accounted for. This finding replicates the results obtained by. (McDonald & Shillcock 2001)

In sum, Baayen's impressive study, while conducted in a psycholinguistic context and focusing on a psycholinguistic concept that, per se, has not been a central issue in cognitive linguistics – lexical access – is one of the earliest comprehensive studies that should have important implications for cognitive linguistics, some of which will be discussed in what follows.

> So far we have understood neither the nature of frequency itself nor its relation to entrenchment, let alone come up with a convincing way of capturing either one of them or the relation between them in quantitative terms. (Schmid 2010:125)

3.5 Interim conclusions

Cognitive linguistics has for decades now used frequency as the main determinant of cognitive entrenchment, relying on psycholinguistic models largely informed by issues of lexical access and processing (even if cognitive linguists have not always been concerned with lexical access per se themselves). However, given the previous sections, there is strong evidence that at least two other simple factors – contextual distinctiveness and dispersion – outperform cognitive linguistics' pet *explanans* even when it comes to explaining the very kind of phenomenon – lexical access – on which cognitive linguistics have based their reliance on frequencies as an explanation of many many phenomena. And the above studies are not alone; there is a growing body of research that either qualifies the effect of frequency by showing how it interacts with other predictors not often discussed in cognitive linguistics or argues that frequency is generally just less important than is often assumed:

– Diependaele, Lemhöfer, & Brysbaert (2013) demonstrate that the magnitude of the word frequency effect interacts with speakers' vocabulary size, with weaker effects for those with larger vocabularies (see Preston 1935 for a very early discussion of this interaction);
– Rayner et al. (2006) find an interaction between frequency and age such that older readers are slower than younger readers, but show a stronger effect of frequency on, e.g., lexical decision and naming latencies;
– Balota et al.'s (2001) mega study shows that subjective frequency estimates from norming data explain unique variability in lexical decision and naming latencies above and beyond apart from objective corpus frequency (see also Williams & Morris's 2004 results from eye movement latencies). Additionally, Kuperman & Van Dyke (2013) discuss the interaction of frequency and (reading) skill in a variety of processing tasks and show that "corpus-based frequency estimates are not at all reflective of poor readers' true experience with a word, nor can they bring forward the systematically different experiences with common and rare words that readers of varying experience may have", which coincides with Dąbrowska's (2016) deadly sin number 4 again, 'ignoring individual differences'.

In addition to the role of the two factors above and other ones that word frequency at least interacts with, there is also strong evidence that frequency-as-repetition, precisely the notion that is so predominant in cognitive and usage-based linguistics, really does not explain much, at least not in a cognitively/psycholinguistically relevant way. These findings of Baayen's analysis are supported by other similar analyses such as a recent megastudy by Brysbaert et al, which also finds that "when the effects of all other variables are partialed out, there is still a robust word frequency effect (although its impact is diminished to some 5–10% of the variance explained)" (Brysbaert, Mandera, & Keulers 2018:47).

Given all of this, one cannot help but think that the rigor that these studies exhibit and the care with which many psycholinguists try to define and delineate the true causal nature of frequency vs. other factors stand in stark contrast to the often somewhat loose talk about frequency effects in cognitive and usage-based linguistics. It has been quite common and very easy to (i) equate frequency with entrenchment or, more formally, simply operationalize entrenchment using frequency and then (ii) discuss frequency effects with some loose connection to psycholinguistic models whose exact details usually remain unspecified (see Dąbrowska's 2016 deadly sin 2, 'not enough serious hypothesis-testing'). I challenge the reader to read up on cognitive-linguistic studies and compare the number of studies that discuss a frequency effect but remain agnostic about its cognitive/psycholinguistic foundation to those that commit to a testable psycholinguistic model. Thus, while staying at the level of 'general frequency effects' may sometimes be a good-enough work-around to arrive at some first understanding of some data, it falls short of honoring Lakoff's cognitive commitment, which requires much more than the above, namely to be more explicit about the true cognitive (!) underpinnings of frequency and how our knowledge can be informed from other disciplines, here psycholinguistics and corpus linguistics; recall Dąbrowska's (2016) deadly sins number 3, 'not treating the cognitive commitment seriously'.

What needs to be done in order to take the cognitive commitment more seriously? One answer has been the topic of the preceding sections: we need to be more careful in how we deal with frequency in our theory/theories. Here is an admittedly pedantic example of a quotation that highlights at least one problem (but also a first underutilized solution with its mention of recency):

> [t]his seems highly convincing, not least in view of the considerable body of evidence from psycholinguistic experiments suggesting that frequency is one major determinant of the ease and speed of lexical access and retrieval, alongside recency of mention in discourse [...]. As speed of access in, and retrieval from, the mental lexicon is the closest behavioural correlate to routinization, this indeed supports the idea that frequency and entrenchment co-vary. (Schmid 2010:115f.)

This quotation includes both causal language (*determinant*) and merely correlational language (*co-vary*) and, thus, makes it harder to infer what mechanism is exactly is envisioned. We need a better understanding of what the variable of frequency does and does not do, we need to determine (better) whether it, or how much of it, is an actual cause or whether it is just correlated with the 'real' causes, we need to get a better idea of what all the things are that frequency is related to how and how much – this also means we may need to consider different versions of frequency to tease apart its components, so to speak – and we need to be clear(er) in what psycholinguistic model we are having in mind or are committing to when we talk about the frequency effect: resting activation levels as a result of repetition, resting activation levels as a result of converging activation from nodes in contexts, profiles of strengths of connections to a node, . . .

However, the other main way in which to take the cognitive commitment more seriously is to explore factors above and beyond frequency. Pertinent suggestions what to look at are already mentioned in places, in fact even in Schmid's quote above: "frequency is one major determinant of the ease and speed of lexical access and retrieval, alongside *recency of mention in discourse*" (my emphasis). Similarly, we find the statement that "[l]earning, memory and perception are all affected by *frequency, recency, and context of usage*" (Ellis, Römer, & O'Donnell 2016:45, my emphasis). Thus, it is no coincidence that the measures discussed above are as powerful and important as they turned out to be: contextual distinctiveness as a measure of how much a word 'warps' the frequency distribution of the collocates (or also more abstract constructions) in its context, and dispersion as one of two manifestations of recency. More specifically, I consider priming the short-term manifestation of recency (because of how priming is related to what a speaker recently processed) and dispersion the long-term manifestation of recency (because, if a corpus is seen as an (obviously) imperfect approximation of what a speaker is exposed to, then dispersion is relatable to what a speaker experienced in the not so recent past). However, despite such statements in theoretical discussions, these factors have received much less attention in empirical cognitive-linguistic studies or even position papers such as those in the special issue of *Cognitive Linguistics* in 2016. This absence is particularly surprising especially for the dispersion component of recency, since one central area in cognitive linguistics has always been the developments of plausible usage-based accounts of language acquisition (i.e. a process fundamentally involving learning, forgetting, and categorization) and processing and previous studies have commented on it explicitly:

> Given a certain number of exposures to a stimulus, or a certain amount of training, learning is always better when exposures or training trials are distributed over several sessions than when they are massed into one session. This finding is extremely robust in many domains of human cognition. (Ambridge et al. 2006:175)

Schooler & Anderson (1997) also demonstrated that there is a power (i.e., log-log linear) function relating probability of a word occurring in the headline in the NYT on day n to how long it has been since the word previously occurred in that context. The human forgetting curve (Ebbinghaus, 1885) is rational in that it follows this trend.

(Ellis, Römer, & O'Donnell 2016:37f.)

plus recall the above quotes from Adelman, Brown, & Quesada themselves.

It is therefore time that cognitive linguistics at least becomes more aware of how these kinds of studies relativize, or contextualize, our view of frequency and its exact workings and that it explores other dimensions of information. In the following section, I briefly survey a few other dimensions that psycholinguistic work, and at least some cognitive-linguistic work, has found to be important and how they might inform a more comprehensive view of (corpus-based) frequency for cognitive linguistics.

4 What else is there and where does this all (have to) lead?

Above I argued that the notion of frequency is central to cognitive usage-based linguistics, but that such counts do not go far enough. It is useful to reiterate here that my above discussion is critical about the role of frequency as operationalized by the number of corpus attestations of a construction in question and the corresponding view of frequency as a repetition counter – my discussion should not be misunderstood as a blanket attack against frequency data as a whole. This is because, as I have frequently argued elsewhere, of course basically all kinds of corpus-based statistics are ultimately frequency-based: even the computation of contextual distinctiveness or dispersion feature, at some step, the use of frequencies. Thus, my point is specifically that frequencies shouldn't be studied just as frequencies per se (with an accompanying frequency-as-repetition theory), but that they can and should of course also form the input to more sophisticated measures (such as contextual distinctiveness or dispersion). This view is essentially an attempt to take Christiansen & Chater (2016) seriously: if, as they argue, "the cognitive system aims to build a probabilistic model, which captures the statistical structure of the external world," then we should not only go with the simplest/most widely-used kinds of info corpora offer – absolute/relative frequencies of (co-)occurrence – because, are we really assuming that's all the cognitive system does? Of course not, so this section discusses briefly what other kinds of information corpus data have to offer and how they are obtained; I will focus on association/contingency as well as entropy and surprisal.

4.1 Association/contingency

The role of association/contingency can in fact hardly be overstated and Nick Ellis is one of the researchers who has put that notion forward most insightfully on a theoretical level and most forcefully on an empirical level. Ellis (2006) summarized previous work from the psychology of learning as "it [is] contingency, not temporal pairing, that generated conditioned responding in classical conditioning" (p. 10) and that

> human learning is to all intents and purposes perfectly calibrated with normative statistical measures of contingency like r, χ^2 and ΔP [. . .] and that probability theory and statistics provided a firm basis for psychological models that integrate and account for human performance in a wide range of inferential tasks. (Ellis 2006:7)

Thus, it is not just enough to consider how often something happens (e.g. the use of a construction, or the use of a construction with a certain item in one if its slots), but how predictive one (usage) event is of another one, for which one needs to 'normalize' a, say, frequency of co-occurrence against what, in the above example, the word does elsewhere or the construction does elsewhere (see Gries 2012, 2015, 2019b for much discussion for how to do this (best)). The simplest way in which this might be done is to to look at how frequencies of co-occurrence and association measures can return different results. For instance, if one sorts the verbs occurring in the imperative construction in the ICE-GB, then these are the top seven verbs: *be, see, let, have, look, fold*, and *worry*. This is interesting because several of those seem to intuitively make a lot of sense – *see, let, look, worry* – but (i) *be* and *have* are only in the top seven list because they are very frequent everywhere, but an approach that does not correct for that does not see that their observed frequencies in the imperative are actually less than their expected frequencies (*be* in particular has a high negative log odds ratio to the imperative (nearly –4) and (ii) *fold* is surprising because it only shows up in the imperative in a single file (i.e., it is very underdispersed, see Section 3.2 above) and therefore hardly representative of the imperative anywhere but in books on origami. Thus, we need to adopt more than just frequency: we need association and we need dispersion (all in one tuple, see Gries 2019b) – only then can we get a better resolution on everything that the language learner – L1, L2, FL, . . . – is exposed to and uses in acquisition.

4.2 Entropy and surprisal

Another relevant concept that cognitive linguists need to explore on top of token frequency is that of entropy. For a long time it has been recognized that type frequencies are relevant to (cognitive) linguists in how they are correlated with productivity (e.g. Bybee & Moder 1983, Goldberg 1995: Ch. 5, Bybee & Hopper 2001, Bybee 2010: Section 5.10) and therefore with grammaticalization/constructionalization (e.g. Bybee 2010: Section 6.3) and language learning and acquisition (e.g. Schwartz & Causarano 2007, Endress & Hauser 2011). However, type frequencies, and type-token ratios for that matter, are not all that is relevant because they are not comprehensive enough, especially from a cognitive-linguistic perspective.

For instance, consider Goldberg, Casenhiser, & Sethuraman's (2004) learning experiment: Subjects were exposed to a certain number of tokens (16) instantiated by the same number of types (5). However, the two conditions had different type-token distributions: there was a balanced condition of 4-4-4-2-2 (with an entropy of $H=2.25$) and a skewed lower-variance condition of 8-2-2-2-2 ($H=2$). The more skewed distribution was learned significantly better, but this cannot be explained by reference to the type-token ratios of both conditions (because those were identical, namely $5/_{16}$), but it *can* be explained with the distributions' entropies ($H=2.25$ for the balanced condition and $H=2$ for the skewed condition). But by now there are a lot of other studies that underscore the relevance entropy has for production/processing:

- Linzen & Jaeger (2015) find that the entropy reduction of potential parse completions is correlated with reading times of sentences involving the DO/SC alternation; e.g., *accept* in *Worf accepted Picard was right* has a lower entropy of possible complementation patterns compared to *forgot* in *Worf forgot Picard was right*, which is reflected in reading speeds.
- Blumenthal-Dramé (2016:500) reports that the entropy of verbs' subcategorization frames correlates with activity in the anterior temporal lobe 200–300 ms after the stimulus.
- Lester & Moscoso del Prado (2017) find that entropies of syntactic distributions affect response times of Ns in isolation and the ordering in coordinate NPs and conclude in a as-construction-grammar-as-it-gets kind of way that "words are finely articulated syntactic entities whose history of use partially determines how efficiently they are produced [...] Perhaps words and syntactic structures are much more tightly linked than is typically acknowledged".

Psycholinguistically, the connection between processing and entropy might be explainable in terms of the fan effect, which is "[s]imply put, the more things that are learned about a concept [the more factual associations fan out from the concept], the longer it takes to retrieve any one of those facts" (Radvansky 1999: 198) or within Anderson's ACT-R theory, where the strength of activation S_{ji} between a source of activation j and a fact i is dependent on the log of the fan: "activation [...] will decrease as a logarithmic function of the fan associated with the concept. [...] the strengths of associations decrease with fan because the probability of any fact, given the concept, decreases with fan" (Anderson & Reder 1999:188). For the association of a word to constructions, this would mean that the strength of the word's associations will be affected by the number of constructions to which it is connected.

An additional factor that is relevant in this information-theoretic connection is surprisal. Some contemporary learning theories hold that learning is driven by prediction errors: we learn more from the surprise that comes when our predictions are incorrect than when our predictions are confirmed (Rescorla & Wagner 1972). Surprisal is often operationalized as $-\log_2 p$, i.e. the less likely something is, the more we are surprised, and the other way around, where p is typically a conditional probability, e.g. p(verb|construction) or p(function|form) or p(form|function). As Ellis, Römer, & O'Donnell (2016:58) put it, "the surprisal of a word in a sentential context is the probability mass of the analyses not consistent with it". There is now increasing evidence for surprisal-driven language processing and acquisition (Demberg & Keller 2008, Jaeger & Snider 2013, Pickering & Garrod 2013) and it is probably not too far-fetched to consider the possibility that at least some of what surprisal measures will be correlated with another important but often elusive notion in (cognitive) linguistics, salience (Gries 2017:593); also see Gries (2012: Section 5.3) for a discussion of how entropy and surprisal are relevant to discussions of category/construction learning and Jaeger & Weatherholtz (2016) on salience and surprisal for sociolinguistics; however, it seems as if that discussion has only just begun and is fraught with terminological inconsistency (see Zarcone et al. 2016 for a start).

In sum, given both existing empirical findings and possible theoretical explanations for them that are compatible with a cognitive-linguistic framework, it is time that entropy and surprisal be considered and integrated more thoroughly in cognitive linguistics and maybe be afforded a status similarly important as frequency, entrenchment, and other notions.

4.3 Final comments

Let us now conclude and begin with a bit of a 'reminiscent warning'... It sometimes seems to me as if (too) much of usage-based linguistics is falling into the same kind of trap much of cognitive linguistics did in the 1990s until Sandra & Rice's seminal article demonstrated the dangers of how liberally notions such as polysemy and semantic networks were used. From a quantitative corpus linguist's point of view, we have now been doing something similar with uncritical assumptions of how frequency 'determines' entrenchment and how frequency is an important cause for everything . . . How many studies are there that use even one, let alone more, of the more complex kinds of data from above? And how many studies are there that adopt even more of the available methods such as corpus-based prototypicality and semantic-network measures (see Ellis, Römer, & O'Donnell 2016, which should be obligatory literature for any usage-based linguist working with corpora)?

All the above being said, I am *not* trying to say that frequency doesn't do anything or that frequency is not nicely and significantly correlated with many things of interest, so it is certainly very tempting and convenient to use it as an all-purpose tool, the Swiss Army predictor of cognitive/usage-based linguistics. However, if we take seriously Lakoff's cognitive commitment and Ellis's as well as Christiansen & Chater's view of the cognitive system – one that ascribes statistical learning to the cognitive, and thus linguistic, system(s) – then maybe it is time to not just be happy anymore that we found something that 'correlates somewhat well' – we should want more things that actually *cause* and stop pretending that all usage-based linguists need for that is the simplest of statistics, frequency counts. In other words, it is great if usage-based linguists can approximate things well (can we even?) – but it's not great if (i) we already actually know from statistical controls, other studies, . . . that frequency is not necessarily a cause and if (ii) many other factors are available for exploration that do already figure in other cognitive theories (e.g. Anderson's rational theory of learning and memory, e.g. Anderson 1990) or psycholinguistic theories (e.g., expectation-based theories of complexity, e.g. Levy 2008).

One final remark on what that means methodologically. As is clear from the above, the degree of statistical complexity increases once we do not just look at a single frequency list from a whole corpus. And apparently this is scary to many practitioners, as we can see in a recent overview article discussing current challenges, namely when Divjak, Levshina, & Klavan (2016) quote some scholars' views such as "concerns have been raised that the field may be becoming too empirical", "numbers just for numbers' sake", "number-crunching", and "empirical imperialism" . . . These kinds of statements are hugely problematic. It takes a truly interesting view of cognitive linguistics (especially when viewed with Lakoff's cognitive commitment in mind) that condemns the field for becoming too empirical: As if it was unproblematic that the field has been very theoretical for a long time during which unproven theories of various kinds of polysemy networks, metaphorical mappings, and different kinds of construals and scanning abounded . . . (see again also Dąbrowska 2016). As if cognitive linguists were interested in things that are so simple, linear, and accessible to armchair linguistics that one, obviously!, just needed to think about them and maybe eyeball some conveniently small data and/or frequency lists for obvious patterns.

Strangely enough, statements like that sound like they were made by exactly the kind of generative linguists in the 1970s and 1980s, in response to which cognitive linguistics emerged in the first place and, strangely enough, I have yet to see such statements in position papers from psycholinguistics, cognitive science, psychology of learning etc. – how many cognitive science papers do we know that lament that cognitive science is so empirical and is using more and more state-of-the-art statistical methods? If as cognitive linguists we are not just interested in good enough approximations and correlations, but truly interested in causality, then we need advanced statistical modeling of data, which, with its multifaceted kinds of analysis and its proper experimental and statistical controls, will further our understanding of our critical predictors and their causal relations. Avoiding the difficult issues and refusing to engage the line of research Lakoff's cognitive commitment laid out for us nearly 30 years ago is definitely *not* the way forward that the discipline needs to stay vibrant, innovative, but, let's face it, also relevant in an ever-changing scientific and theoretical environment.

References

Adelman, James S., Gordon D.A. Brown, & José F. Quesada. 2006. Contextual diversity, nor word frequency, determines word-naming and lexical decision times. *Psychological Science* 17(9). 814–423.

Ambridge, Ben, Anna L. Theakston, Elena V.M. Lieven, & Michael Tomasello. 2006. The distributed learning effect for children's acquisition of an abstract syntactic construction. *Cognitive Development* 21(2). 174–193.

Anderson, John R. 1990. *The adaptive character of thought*. Hillsdale, NJ: Lawrence Erlbaum.

Anderson, John R. & Lynne M. Reder. 1999. The fact effect: new results and new theories. *Journal of Experimental Psychology: General* 128(2). 186–197.

Baayen, R. Harald. 2008. *Analyzing linguistic data: a practical introduction to statistics with R*. Cambridge: Cambridge University Press.

Baayen, R. Harald. 2010. Demythologizing the word frequency effect: A discriminative learning perspective. *The Mental Lexicon* 5(3). 436–461.

Balota, David A., Maura Pilotti, & Michael J. Cortese. 2001. Subjective frequency estimates for 2,938 monosyllabic words. *Memory and Cognition* 20(4). 639–647.

Balota, David A. & Daniel H. Spieler. 1998. The utility of item level analyses in model evaluation: a reply to Seidenberg and Plaut. *Psychological Science* 9(3). 238–240.

Brown, Roger. 1973. *A first language: The early stages*. Cambridge, MA: Harvard University Press.

Brysbaert, Marc, Pawel Mandera, & Emmanual Keulers. 2018. The word frequency effect in word processing: an updated review. *Current Directions in Psychological Science* 27(1). 45–50.

Bybee, Joan. 2006. From usage to grammar: the mind's response to repetition. *Language* 82(4). 711–733.

Bybee, Joan. 2010. *Language, usage, and cognition*. Cambridge: Cambridge University Press.

Bybee, Joan & Carol Lynn Moder. 1983. Morphological classes as natural categories. *Language* 59(2). 251–270.
Bybee, Joan & Paul Hopper (eds). 2001. *Frequency and the emergence of linguistic structure*. Amsterdam & Philadelphia: John Benjamins.
Christiansen, Morten H. & Nick Chater. 2016. *Creating language: intergrating evolution, acquisition, and processing*. Cambridge, MA: The MIT Press.
Dąbrowska, Ewa. 2016. Cognitive Linguistics' seven deadly sins. *Cognitive Linguistics* 27(4). 479–491.
Dąbrowska, Ewa. 2018. Experience, aptitude and individual differences in native language ultimate attainment. *Cognition* 178. 222–235.
Demberg, Vera & Frank Keller. 2008. Data from eye-tracking corpora as evidence for theories of syntactic processing complexity. *Cognition* 109(2). 193–210.
Diependaele, Kevin, Kristin Lemhöfer, & Marc Brysbaert. 2013. The word frequency effect in first- and second-language word recognition: A lexical entrenchment account. *The Quarterly Journal of Experimental Psychology* 66(5). 843–863.
Divjak, Dagmar S., Ewa Dąbrowska, & Antti Arppe. 2016. Machine meets man: evaluating the psychological reality of corpus-based models. *Cognitive Linguistics* 27(1). 1–33.
Divjak, Dagmar S., Natalia Levshina, & Jane Klavan. 2016. Cognitive Linguistics: looking back, looking forward. *Cognitive Linguistics* 27(4). 447–463.
Ellis, Nick C. 2002. Frequency effects in language processing and acquisition. *Studies in Second Language Acquisition* 24(2). 143–188.
Ellis, Nick C. 2006. Language acquisition as rational contingency learning. *Applied Linguistics* 27(1). 1–24.
Ellis, Nick C., Ute Römer, & Matthew Brook O'Donnell. 2016. *Usage-based approaches to language acquisition and processing*. New York: Wiley-Blackwell.
Endress, Ansgar D. & Marc D. Hauser. 2011. The influence of type and token frequency on the acquisition of affixation patterns: implications for language processing. *Journal of Experimental Psychology: Learning, Memory, and Cognition* 37(1). 77–95.
Gablasova, Dana, Vaclav Brezina, & Tony McEnery. 2017. Exploring learner language through corpora: comparing and interpreting corpus frequency information. *Language Learning* 67(S1). 130–154.
Goldberg, Adele E. 1995. *Constructions: a construction grammar approach to argument structure*. Chicago, IL. The University of Chicago Press.
Goldberg, Adele E. 2006. *Constructions at work: The nature of generalization in language*. Oxford. Oxford University Press.
Goldberg, Adele E., Devin M. Casenhiser, & Nitya Sethuraman. 2004. Learning argument structure generalizations. *Cognitive Linguistics* 15(3). 289–316.
Gries, Stefan Th. 2008. Dispersions and adjusted frequencies in corpora. *International Journal of Corpus Linguistics* 13(4). 403–437.
Gries, Stefan Th. 2010. Dispersions and adjusted frequencies in corpora: further explorations. In Stefan Th. Gries, Stefanie Wulff, & Mark Davies (eds.), *Corpus linguistic applications: current studies, new directions*, 197–212. Amsterdam: Rodopi.
Gries, Stefan Th. 2012. Frequencies, probabilities, association measures in usage-/exemplar-based linguistics: some necessary clarifications. *Studies in Language* 36(3). 477–510.
Gries, Stefan Th. 2015. More (old and new) misunderstandings of collostructional analysis: on Schmid & Küchenhoff (2013). *Cognitive Linguistics* 26(3). 505–536.

Gries, Stefan Th. 2017. Corpus approaches. In Barbara Dancygier (eds.), *Cambridge Handbook of Cognitive Linguistics*, 590–606. Cambridge: Cambridge University Press.
Gries, Stefan Th. 2018. On over- and underuse in learner corpus research and multifactoriality in corpus linguistics more generally. *Journal of Second Language Studies* 1(2). 276–308.
Gries, Stefan Th. 2019a. *Ten lectures on corpus-linguistic approaches in cognitive linguistics*. Leiden & Boston: Brill.
Gries, Stefan Th. 2019b. 15 years of collostructions: some long overdue additions/corrections (to/of actually all sorts of corpus-linguistics measures). *International Journal of Corpus Linguistics* 24(3). 385–412.
Halliday, Michael A. K. 2005. *Computational and quantitative studies*. London & New York: Continuum.
Jaeger, T. Florian & Neal E. Snider. 2013. Alignment as a consequence of expectation adaptation: Syntactic priming is affected by the prime's prediction error given both prior and recent experience. *Cognition* 127(1). 57–83.
Jaeger, T. Florian & Kodi Weatherholtz. 2016. What the heck Is salience? How predictive language processing contributes to sociolinguistic perception. *Frontiers of Psychology* 7. 1115.
Jones, Michael N. Brendan T. Johns, & Gabriel Recchia. 2012. The role of semantic diversity on lexical organization. *Canadian Journal of Experimental Psychology* 66(2). 115–124.
Johns, Brendan T., Melody Dye, & Michael N. Jones. 2016. The influence of contextual diversity on word learning. *Psychonomic Bulletin & Review* 23(4). 1214–1220.
Kuperman, Victor & Julie A. Van Dyke. 2013. Reassessing word frequency as a determinant of word recognition for skilled and unskilled readers. *Journal of Experimental Psychology: Human Perception and Performance* 39(3). 802–823.
Lakoff, George. 1991. Cognitive versus generative linguistics: How commitments influence results. Language and Communication 11(1–2). 53–62.
Langacker, Ronald W. 1987. *Foundations of Cognitive Grammar I: Theoretical prerequisites*. Stanford. Stanford University Press.
Lester, Nicholas A. & Fermín Moscoso del Prado Martín. 2017. Syntactic flexibility in the noun: evidence from picture naming. *Proceedings of the 38th Annual Conference of the Cognitive Science Society*, 2585–2590.
Levy, Roger. 2008. Expectation-based syntactic comprehension. *Cognition* 106(3). 1126–1177.
Linzen, Tal & T. Florian Jaeger. 2015. Uncertainty and expectation in sentence processing: evidence From subcategorization distributions. *Cognitive Science* 40(6). 1382–1411.
McDonald, Scott A. & Richard C. Shillcock. 2001. Rethinking the word frequency effect: the neglected role of distributional information in lexical processing. *Language and Speech* 44(3). 295–323.
Pickering, Martin J., & Simon Garrod. 2013. An integrated theory of language production and comprehension. *Behavioral and Brain Sciences* 36(4). 329–347.
Preston, Katherine A. 1935. The speed of word perception and relation to reading ability. *The Journal of General Psychology* 13(1). 199–203.
Radvansky, Gabriel A. 1999. The Fan Effect: A tale of two theories. *Journal of Experimental Psychology: General* 128(2). 198–206.
Rayner, Keith, Erik D. Reichle, Michael J. Stroud, Carrick C. Williams, & Alexander Pollatsek. 2006. The effect of word frequency, word predictability, and font difficulty on the eye movements of young and older readers. *Psychology and Aging* 21(3). 448–465.

Recchia, Gabriel, Brendan T. Johns, & Michael N. Jones. 2008. Context repetition effects are dependent on context redundancy. *Proceedings of the Annual Conference of the Cognitive Science Society* 30. 267–272.

Rescorla, Robert A. & Allen R. Wagner. 1972. A theory of Pavlovian conditioning: Variations in the effectiveness of reinforcement and nonreinforcement. In Abraham H. Black & William F. Prokasy (eds.), *Classical conditioning II: Current theory and research*, 64–99. New York: Appleton-Century-Crofts.

Schmid, Hans-Jörg. 2010. Does frequency in the text instantiate entrenchment in the cognitive system? In Dylan Glynn & Kerstin Fischer (eds.), *Quantitative methods in cognitive semantics: corpus-driven approaches*, 101–133. Berlin & Boston: De Gruyter.

Schwartz, Michael & Pei-ni L. Causarano. 2007. The role of frequency in SLA: an analysis of gerunds and infinitives in ESL written discourse. *Arizona Working Papers in SLA & Teaching* 14. 43–57.

Spieler, Daniel H. & David A. Balota. 1997. Bringing computational models of word naming down to the item level. *Psychological Science* 8. 411–416.

Street, James A. & Ewa Dąbrowska. 2010. More individual differences in language attainment: How much do adult native speakers of English know about passives and quantifiers? *Lingua* 120(8). 2080–2094.

Theakston, Anna L. Elena V.M. Lieven, Julian M. Pine, & Catherine F. Rowland. 2001. The role of performance limitations in the acquisition of Verb-Argument structure: An alternative account. *Journal of Child Language* 28(1). 127–152.

Williams, Rihana & Robin Morris. 2004. Eye movements, word familiarity, and vocabulary acquisition. *European Journal of Cognitive Psychology* 16 (1–2). 312–339.

Wulff, Stefanie & Stefan Th. Gries. Particle placement in learner English: Measuring effects of context, first language, and individual variation. *Language Learning* 69(4). 873–910.

Zarcone, Alessandra, Marten van Schijndel, Jorrig Vogels, & Vera Demberg. 2016. Salience and attention in surprisal-based accounts of language processing. *Frontiers of Psychology* 7. 844.

Gaëtanelle Gilquin
Constructing learner speech: On the use of spoken data in Applied Construction Grammar

1 Introduction

The Latin proverb according to which spoken words fly away and written words remain (*verba volant, scripta manent*) emphasizes the ephemeral nature of speech. Thanks to technological advances, it has become possible to capture speech for linguistic purposes, most notably in the form of spoken corpora, and to make it permanent, just like writing. Once transcribed, spoken language can be analysed in a systematic way, using the same tools as those developed for the linguistic analysis of writing. As for the acoustic signal, it can be studied by means of special linguistic programs, which have been specifically designed to deal with audio files. Yet, for reasons that may range from the very practical (difficulty of collecting and analysing spoken data) to the very ideological (lack of consideration for spoken forms of communication), speech has, on the whole, received less scholarly attention than writing. While this is true of many linguistic frameworks, we will focus here on Construction Grammar, and more particularly Applied Construction Grammar, which is concerned with "the acquisitional and pedagogical implications of Construction Grammar in second/foreign language teaching and learning" (Gilquin and De Knop 2016: 8; see also the contributions in De Knop and Gilquin 2016).

Starting from the observation that the study of speech has been neglected in (Applied) Construction Grammar (Section 2), this paper pleads for more research on spoken language data in this framework, arguing that it can be beneficial from a descriptive, applied and theoretical perspective. From a descriptive point of view, we will consider the comparison of spoken and written constructions (Section 3.1), as well as the study of the spoken learner constructicon (Section 3.2). From a more directly applied point of view, we will see how spoken data can be used to better understand foreign language learning (Section 4.1) and to improve foreign language teaching (Section 4.2). From a theoretical point of view, it will be shown that the study of speech can help refine the Construction Grammar model (Section 5).

This overview of the benefits that Applied Construction Grammar can derive from spoken language research relies on the discussion of relevant works taken from the literature. Not all of these works are embedded within the theories of

Construction Grammar, but they are all deemed compatible with (some aspects of) these theories, and in particular with the tenets of Goldbergian Construction Grammar. Similarly, the studies that are cited are not necessarily related to learner language, but they are applicable to it. Most of them have to do with the English language, but the general principles emerging from these studies are believed to be potentially valid for other languages as well. It should also be pointed out that the perspective that is adopted in this paper is that of a foreign (not second) language learning context. As briefly shown in Section 4.1, the situation for second language learners may differ in certain respects.

2 A written bias in (Applied) Construction Grammar

Despite the greater ease with which spoken language can now be investigated (see Section 1), it is probably fair to say that, as claimed by Linell (2005), linguistics is still very much characterized by a "written language bias": not only are most theories of language developed with written language in mind, but the discipline of linguistics relies more on the investigation of writing than speech. This can be explained by two main reasons (see also Gilquin and De Cock 2011). The first one is that capturing speech for linguistic analysis is generally more complex, more time-consuming and more expensive than capturing writing (think of the laborious task of transcribing speech verbatim, for example). Attempts at collecting spoken data have therefore been less common, and publicly available databases of speech are less numerous. The second reason is that writing has often been considered as the most prestigious form of language, more worthy of linguistic investigation than speech, which has frequently been relegated to the status of "stepchild of descriptive linguistics" (Tottie 1991: 255).[1]

Within the framework of Construction Grammar, too, writing tends to take center stage, to the detriment of speech. This can be illustrated by means of examples (1) to (4), quoted in the introductory chapter of Goldberg (2006: 6) and all taken from written sources. Such examples have served to develop the model of Construction Grammar, by demonstrating that abstract constructions carry meaning – one of the essential theoretical tenets of Construction Grammar.

---

[1] Paradoxically, however, speech can be argued to be the primary form of language: it developed long before the first writing systems appeared, it is acquired by children before they learn to write, language changes tend to occur in speech first, etc. (see Algeo and Pyles 2010: 6).

Although the constructions they represent are not limited to writing, such creative uses of the constructions are much more likely to occur in writing than in speech.

(1) He sneezed his tooth right across town. (Robert Munsch, *Andrew's Loose Tooth*, Scholastic Canada Ltd., 2002)

(2) She smiled herself an upgrade. (Douglas Adams, *Hitchhiker's Guide to the Galaxy*, New York: Harmony Books, 1979)

(3) We laughed our conversation to an end. (J. Hart, *Sin*, New York: Ivy Books, 1992)

(4) They could easily co-pay a family to death. (*New York Times*, January 14, 2002)

Two of the constructions that were investigated very early on in Construction Grammar, the *let alone* construction (cf. Fillmore, Kay, and O'Connor 1988) and the *way*-construction (cf. Israel 1996), are also more characteristic of the written register. While the former has a relative frequency of 13.84 per million words (pmw) in the written section of the British National Corpus and 5.67 pmw in the spoken section, the latter (in the form "V POSS. PR. *way* PREP.") has a relative frequency of 46.57 pmw in writing and 12.01 pmw in speech.[2]

Several linguists have underlined the written bias in Construction Grammar. Linell (2005: 215) specifically mentions Construction Grammar when describing the written language bias in linguistics, noting that it "has so far not heeded the interactional aspects sufficiently". Fried and Östman (2005: 1753) refer to the "bias away from spoken language". More recently, Ginzburg and Poesio (2016: 1–2) claim the following, explicitly including Construction Grammar among contemporary linguistic theories:

> In practice contemporary theoretical linguistics is typically not interested or able to provide analyses for the rules governing language as it occurs in actual spoken interaction. Its analyses are developed for a cleaned up version of language [. . .], which omits the disfluencies, interjections, overlapping turns, non-sentential utterances, and *ad hoc* coinages which are ubiquitous in spoken language [. . .].

---

2 As pointed out by a reviewer, the figures for speech might actually be slightly higher, because of possible intervening disfluencies that might prevent the retrieval of the pattern. A search for *er* and *erm* between the different elements of the constructions, however, did not produce any hits at all.

Yet, as a theoretical framework, Construction Grammar is perfectly suited to accommodate spoken phenomena. As Fried and Östman (2005: 1753) emphasize, there is no "built-in limitation of Construction Grammar with respect to its applicability to the study of spoken data and to larger stretches of discourse as the domain of analysis". In fact, speech has been involved in Construction Grammar right from the start. For example, in Fillmore, Kay, and O'Connor's (1988) paper, attention is paid to the typical prosody associated with the *let alone* construction, as in *She doesn't get up for LUNCH, let alone BREAKFAST*, where the capital letters represent prosodic peaks. As shown in Goldberg (2006: 14), other studies have focused on constructions that are more typical of speech, like the 'What's X doing Y' construction (e.g. *What's that fly doing in my soup?!*) investigated in Kay and Fillmore (1999), the 'Nominal Extraposition' construction (e.g. *It's amazing the difference!*) studied by Michaelis and Lambrecht (1996), or the so-called 'Mad Magazine' construction (e.g. *Him, a doctor?!*) explored in Lambrecht (1990). There is also a small number of Construction Grammar studies dealing with distinctively spoken phenomena, such as Fried and Östman (2005), Fischer (2010) and Fischer and Alm (2013) on pragmatic markers.

As for studies on child language acquisition (e.g. Diessel and Tomasello 2001), they are, for obvious reasons, always based on spoken data. In addition, most constructions, like the transitive, ditransitive, or intransitive motion constructions, are common in both speech and writing, and many corpus-based Construction Grammar studies "are based on a mixture of spoken and written data that characterizes most contemporary corpora" (Gries 2013: 97). Speech thus has a place in Construction Grammar, but in comparison with writing, there are fewer studies in Construction Grammar that deal specifically with speech and with typically spoken features.

If we now turn to Applied Construction Grammar and its focus on learner language, we find the same "bias away from spoken language" (Fried and Östman 2005: 1753), with most studies being based on experimental data and/or written corpus data (see Gilquin 2018: 128). The few studies that have relied on spoken data tend to be characterized by a small set of data, representing only a few learners, usually less than ten, and sometimes even just a single one, cf. Ellis and Ferreira-Junior (2009) on English verb-argument constructions, Eskildsen (2012) on English negation constructions, Eskildsen (2014) on the emergence of utterance schemas and schematic constructions, or Roehr-Brackin (2014) on German Perfekt constructions with *gehen* and *fahren*. Sambre et al. (2018) rely on a corpus made up of spoken data from 20 learners to investigate constructions expressing futurity. While Gilquin (2015) looks at more learners (almost 350) for a study of phrasal verb constructions, it is not exclusively concerned with speech, but with a combination of speech and writing. Naturally, as a relatively recent field, with a limited amount of research carried out so far, Applied Construction Grammar cannot be blamed for not having explored all the aspects of language, including its different registers, but the above shows that it could do better justice to spoken phenomena. In what follows, we will consider several ways in which the study of speech can be beneficial to Applied Construction Grammar.

3 Descriptive perspective

This section examines how Applied Construction Grammar can benefit from the study of speech in terms of the description of constructions and of the constructicon. More precisely, it claims that we cannot dispense with the study of constructions in learner speech (Section 3.1) and that a comprehensive repertoire of spoken learner constructions (including disfluent and phonological constructions) is yet to be built (Section 3.2).

3.1 Comparison of spoken and written constructions

The stylistic sensitivity of constructions is a relatively well-established fact by now. Constructions in native language tend to vary according to register (cf. Nikiforidou and Fischer 2015). This variation can affect different aspects of the construction, such as its frequency or its behavior. Smith (2009), for example, has demonstrated that light verb constructions with *have* and *make* are generally more frequent in speech than in writing. Shank, Plevoets, and Van Bogaert (2016), who study constructions with an object clause, note that *understand* is mostly used with a *that* complementizer in writing, but no complementizer in speech. Constructions in writing are thus not necessarily the same as constructions in speech.

Because learners have been claimed to lack stylistic awareness (Altenberg and Tapper 1998, Gilquin and Paquot 2008) and to use spoken-like features in writing and written-like features in speech, we can expect them to use constructions inappropriately in terms of register. This can be illustrated by means of the phrasal verb construction with *up* ([V *up*]) in speech and writing. Figure 1 shows the relative frequency per 100,000 words of the construction in the Louvain International Database of Spoken English Interlanguage (learner speech), the International Corpus of Learner English (learner writing), the Louvain Corpus of Native English Conversation (native speech), and the Louvain Corpus of Native English Essays (native writing). It appears from the graph that learners of English use the [V *up*] construction more often in writing than in speech, which is the opposite of the situation in native English, where the [V *up*] construction is more frequent in speech than in writing. This example shows that constructions may be used differently in native and learner speech.

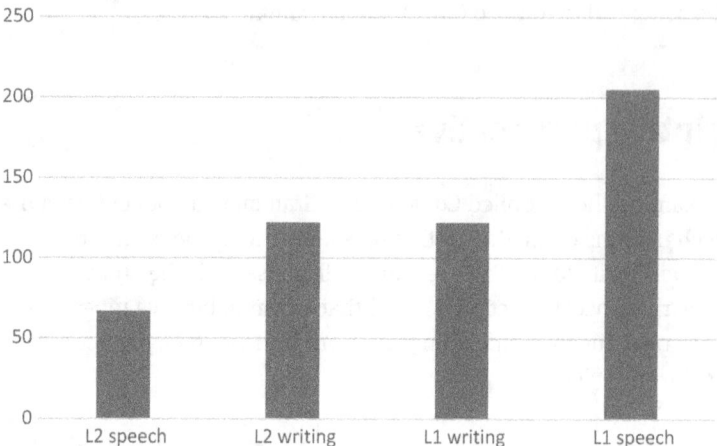

Figure 1: Relative frequency per 100,000 words of the [V *up*] construction in native (L1) and non-native (L2) speech and writing.

If constructions in native writing may differ from constructions in native speech, and if constructions in native speech may differ from constructions in learner speech, then no shortcut from one to the other is possible. We can therefore not dispense with the study and the description of constructions in speech and in learner speech in particular. More generally, it is important to be aware of the possible impact of register on constructions and to bear in mind that constructions in speech may have their own specificities. The next obvious step, therefore, is to get to know more about the spoken learner constructicon: What does it look like? What constructions is it made up of? How can these constructions be described? We address this issue in the next section.

3.2 The spoken learner constructicon

While several projects have been launched to describe the constructicon of different languages (cf. Lyngfelt et al. 2018), as far as I know, no similar efforts have been made for learner language, let alone learner speech. We do have information about the use of linguistic phenomena in learner speech, such as clausal complementation in Tizón-Couto (2014), epistemic adverbial markers in Gablasova and Brezina (2015), or formulaic language in Wood (2010), all of which qualify as constructions in the Construction Grammar sense (although these studies are not theoretically embedded within Construction Grammar). However, these are isolated findings, which do not make it possible to approach learner speech from a global perspective. The spoken learner constructicon is thus still largely unexplored in Applied Construction Grammar.

In an attempt to start exploring the spoken learner constructicon, Gilquin (2018) carried out a study inspired by Cappelle and Grabar (2016), who suggested using recurrent sequences of part-of-speech (POS) tags, or POS n-grams, as an approximation to constructions, on the grounds that "patterns are stored as constructions even if they are fully predictable as long as they occur with sufficient frequency" (Goldberg 2006: 5). Cappelle and Grabar (2016) applied this methodology to native English, extracting the most frequent sequences of five POS tags from the Corpus of Contemporary American English. In Gilquin (2018), the methodology was applied to a part-of-speech tagged version of the Louvain International Database of Spoken English Interlanguage (LINDSEI; Gilquin, De Cock, and Granger 2010), representing 11 mother tongue populations, 554 different learners, and almost 800,000 words of L2 English spoken production. Recurrent sequences of 2 to 10 part-of-speech tags were extracted from the corpus taken as a whole (i.e. without making any distinction between the different L1 populations).

The results suggest that learners' spoken constructicon relies, in the first place, on short and simple constructions (mainly bigrams) of the type [NP], [Subj V] and [PP], and that the internal structure of these constructions seems relatively basic. The most frequent POS n-gram in LINDSEI corresponds to an NP which is made up of a determiner and a noun (e.g. *my brother*); the second and third POS n-grams correspond to VPs in which the subject consists of a personal pronoun, and the verb is either a lexical verb (e.g. *he left*) or the verb *be* (e.g. *I was*). More complex constructions of the type most often discussed in Construction Grammar, like argument structure constructions, are only found much further down the list of POS n-grams, which indicates that they are comparatively not very common in learner speech.[3] The spoken learner constructicon also turns out to be characterized by a great deal of disfluency. This appears from the presence of tags for interjections (predominantly corresponding to filled pauses) and truncations (i.e.

---

3 The results in Gilquin (2018) include a comparison with the POS n-grams in the native counterpart of LINDSEI, the Louvain Corpus of Native English Conversation (LOCNEC; De Cock 2004). It appears from the comparison that the spoken learner and native constructicons overlap to a certain extent, with both of them relying more on relatively basic constructions than on complex argument structure constructions.

unfinished words), as well as from incomplete sequences of tags, some of which are due to the spontaneous and unrehearsed nature of speech (e.g. *in the* as we can see in the fourth picture).

While the analysis in Gilquin (2018) was based on written transcriptions of the spoken data and could therefore not take phonological aspects into account, it stands to reason that a comprehensive account of the spoken learner constructicon should also include what could be referred to as phonological constructions. In this respect, I would like to mention a study by Drummond (2011), which is not embedded within the framework of Construction Grammar and does not use the term construction, but which is perfectly compatible with the tenets of Construction Grammar. The study considers glottal replacement (i.e. the replacement of /t/ by a glottal stop, /ʔ/) among Polish learners of English. Drummond identifies what he calls different 'environments' for potential glottal replacement, for example word final /t/ preceded by a vowel and followed by a word starting with a stop consonant (V/t/#S) as in 'h_o_t _p_otato' or word medial intervocalic /t/ as in 'm_a_**tt**_e_r' (V/t/V). He then highlights some preferences among the learners in terms of glottal replacement in these different environments, such as the fact that it is almost inexistent in word medial position (V/t/V) or the fact that it represents only 17% in the V/t/#V (vowel + /t/ + word starting with a vowel, e.g. 'n_o_t _e_ven') and V/t/#P (vowel + /t/ + pause, e.g. 'did _it._') environments, to be compared with 40% and 36% respectively in native English. He also suggests that there might be a certain order of acquisition among learners, who seem to first use glottal replacement in the V/t/#V ('n_o_t _e_ven') environment, and only then in the V/t/#P ('did _it._') environment. The different environments identified by Drummond could be said to resemble constructions in the Construction Grammar sense, with a sequence of phones (vowel, stop consonant, etc.) corresponding to a certain meaning. The sequences with a /t/ vs /ʔ/ pronunciation are not unlike allostructions (Cappelle 2006), being two variants of a construction that share closely related semantics but produce different effects (e.g. in terms of formality). As for the preferences highlighted by Drummond, they could be systematized by means of a collostructional analysis, measuring the degree of attraction between phones (in this case, /t/ or /ʔ/) and a certain slot in the different constructions (or 'environments') identified.

Approaches such as those illustrated above can help build a map of the spoken learner constructicon, including disfluent constructions and phonological constructions. They also provide a useful basis to draw comparisons between spoken and written learner constructicons, as well as between spoken learner and native constructicons. The information thus collected makes it possible to fulfill a descriptive objective. In the next section, we consider the possible applications, among foreign language learners, of a Construction Grammar approach to speech.

4 Applied perspective

Studying learner speech from a Construction Grammar perspective can lead to useful applications. This section deals with the more cognitive/psycholinguistic aspects of foreign language learning (Section 4.1), as well as the pedagogical aspects of foreign language teaching (Section 4.2).

4.1 Understanding foreign language learning

Speech can help us understand the process of foreign language learning in ways that writing cannot, by providing better insights into the cognitive/psycholinguistic mechanisms that are at work during language production. The main reason for this is that written texts can be edited and redrafted a number of times, and that these changes are normally hidden from the final product. By contrast, speech is typically produced online, with no time to plan ahead. As a result, it may – and often does – include signs such as interruptions or restarts which show some of the processes that the speaker is going through when producing an utterance. Admittedly, even speech provides only a very partial window onto the psycholinguistic processes that characterize the production of language, as many things go on in the speaker's mind without being materialized by any actual language, but speech arguably gives a better understanding of these processes than writing.

The study of (spontaneous) learner speech can provide information about learners' degree of automaticity, a concept that is well-known in second language acquisition research and that describes the extent to which the application of rules has become automatic (cf. Segalowitz and Hulstijn 2005). Within the framework of Construction Grammar, automaticity can be said to correspond to the degree of entrenchment of a construction. If a construction is well entrenched, then the learner should be able to produce it automatically, in a rather smooth manner.

Examples (5) to (7) illustrate a gradual decrease in the degree of automaticity with which the learner applies the rule of the third person singular verb inflection. In (5), the learner seems to have internalized the rule and to apply it in a fully automatic manner; the construction is apparently well entrenched. In (6), the learner is able to correct herself thanks to attentional control, as indicated by the filled pause (*er*) followed by a restart; the application of the rule is not fully automatic and the construction is less entrenched. In (7), finally, the learner is either unaware of the rule or would need much more attentional control to be able to apply it; the entrenchment of the construction is non-existent or very limited.

(5) he's very successful cos **he works** hard in school (LINDSEI-CH)

(6) **he work** in a company (er) **he works** in a company (LINDSEI-CH)

(7) **he work** for the company for almost all his mature life (LINDSEI-CH)

Speech can also help identify constructions better, based, for example, on linguistic elements that are suggestive of language chunking. Thus, filled pauses have been said to be "indirect indicators of prefabricated language and holistic storage" (Dahlmann and Adolphs 2009: 126) – a description that is reminiscent of Goldberg's (2003: 219) definition of constructions as "*stored* pairings of form and function" (emphasis added). Filled pauses can therefore inform us about the constructions that are likely to be stored – or not – in the learner's mind.[4]

The POS n-gram-based exploration of the spoken learner constructicon in Gilquin (2018) revealed that filled pauses sometimes interrupt closely-knit structures in English as a foreign language. Table 1, based on the analysis of the Louvain Corpus of Native English Conversation (LOCNEC; De Cock 2004) for native speech (NS) and of LINDSEI for non-native speech (NNS), shows the distribution of a number of patterns centered around a prepositional phrase made up of a preposition (Prep), a determiner (Det) and a noun (N), and interrupted or not by a filled pause (UH). In a majority of cases in both native and non-native speech, the sequence is not interrupted by any pause and is not preceded nor followed by any pause either, which suggests that for most native and non-native speakers the prepositional phrase is a well-entrenched construction. The proportion of such cases, however, is much higher in NS (94.8%) than in NNS (79.2%). This is to be related to the fact that in NNS the prepositional phrase is regularly preceded, followed or interrupted by a pause.

Interruptions of the prepositional phrase by a pause are particularly interesting, because they suggest that among certain speakers, the PREP-DET-N sequence may not be stored as a construction, or at least may not be well entrenched in the mind. In NNS the interruption between the preposition and the determiner, as in *to er the lady*, accounts for more than 3%, to be compared with 0.6% in NS. The proportion of interruptions between the determiner and the noun, as in *to our erm bus*, is lower, but still higher in NNS (1.7%) than in NS (0.3%). This difference between the two interrupted patterns, incidentally, also suggests that there are

---

[4] Note that pauses can also be symptomatic of other problems, such as lexical retrieval difficulties, and that in some cases pauses may be intentional (e.g. to create rhetorical emphasis).

Table 1: Percentage of interrupted and uninterrupted uses of the prepositional phrase [Prep Det N] in LOCNEC (NS) and LINDSEI (NNS).

	Structure					Examples	NS	NNS
	Prep		Det		N	*about a book*	94.8%	79.2%
UH	Prep		Det		N	*eh in the film*	1.9%	8.6%
	Prep	UH	Det		N	*to er the lady*	0.6%	3.2%
	Prep		Det	UH	N	*to our erm bus*	0.3%	1.7%
	Prep		Det		N	UH *in a hotel er*	2.4%	7.3%

fewer learners for whom the noun phrase may not be stored as a construction, since the determiner and the noun are less often interrupted by means of a pause than the preposition and the noun phrase.

The same sort of phenomenon can be found with discourse markers, which also sometimes interrupt closely-knit structures and can be indicative of the (lack of) storage of certain constructions. Gilquin and Granger (2015: 434) found out that the discourse marker *you know* was overused by Polish learners of English in LINDSEI in comparison to native speakers in LOCNEC, and that the proportion of interrupted uses was much higher among the learners (60%) than among the native speakers (35%). The learners, for instance, used the discourse marker between a copula and the predicative (e.g. *he stopped being **you know** humorous*; *it was always **you know** a kind of foreigner*) or between a preposition and the rest of the prepositional phrase (e.g. *I changed my mind under the pressure of of **you know** society*; *that was some guy from **you know** the upper classes*). Such interruptions seem to indicate that constructions of a higher level like prepositional phrases may not be stored among some learners, and that their entrenchment is weaker than that of lower-level constructions like individual words.

The fact that foreign language learners may rely more on lower-level constructions than on higher-level constructions, and in particular more on words than on phrases, ties in with Wible's (2008: 166–167) claim about multiword expressions. He argues that learners who depend mainly on spoken input tend to go through a "whole to parts" process, which involves the segmentation of the speech stream into individual words. Learners who rely mainly on written input, on the other hand, are more likely to go through a "parts to whole" process, starting from individual words, clearly delineated from each other in writing, and building up multiword expressions on this basis. This may point to a difference in the way foreign language learners, on the one hand, and children and second language learners, on the other hand, build their constructicons.

In this view, foreign language learners, whose main input in the target language tends to be written (see Section 4.2), can be hypothesized to start from lower-level constructions (especially words) and to gradually build up higher-level constructions on this basis. Children and second language learners, by contrast, are primarily exposed to the target language in its spoken form, and can therefore be hypothesized to first acquire higher-level constructions, which they then have to segment into lower-level constructions. The so-called "emergent lexicon" (Bybee 1998: 434), according to which "[t]he smaller units [. . .] emerge from these larger stored units via a network of connections among them", may thus apply to children acquiring their mother tongue and to second learners of a language, but perhaps not to foreign language learners, whose primary input in the target language is usually written.

The phonetic aspects of speech can also provide insights into the processing of constructions, and more particularly into the ease with which constructions are processed, depending on their probability in the (learner) constructicon. Thus, Kuperman and Bresnan (2012: 590) point out that "low-level continuous phonetic variation is sensitive to high-level construction probabilities". This has been demonstrated for both elicited and spontaneous speech. In elicited speech based on a visual cue, it appears that when subjects produce a variant that, on the basis of the linguistic environment, is less likely, the voice initiation time, i.e. the time lag between the visual cue and the onset of speech, is longer (Francis and Michaelis 2017). In spontaneous speech, the production of a less probable variant, given a certain linguistic context, tends to correspond to longer acoustic duration (Kuperman and Bresnan 2012). Reduction effects in speech point in the same direction, since "words are pronounced in a more reduced fashion if they occur in a construction of which they are highly typical" (Hilpert 2014: 144); words that occur in a construction of which they are not typical, conversely, are less likely to display such reduction effects.

Longer voice initiation time in elicited speech and longer acoustic duration in spontaneous speech are indicative of processing effort, which itself depends on the probability (or rather, improbability) of the construction. Although these studies concern native speech, it seems reasonable to assume that, in learner speech, too, phonetic features such as acoustic duration might be clues about processing ease and construction probability for the learner. These indicators could be compared with those found in native speech, in an attempt to highlight the specificities of learner speech processing.

Finally, it is worth considering the speech that learners get exposed to. Examining the spoken form of language input can help understand the acquisition process, by explaining why certain constructions may be easier to learn in some contexts. Thus, it has been said that words following the filled pause *er* are easier to remember (Corley, MacGregor, and Donaldson 2007). Phonological similarity, in the form of alliteration patterns, is also claimed to be relevant for language learning (cf. Gries 2011: 504). Phonetic and perceptual salience seems to be useful too, since it has been shown that constructions that are salient in learners' language input (for example by being stressed or more clearly articulated) tend to be acquired earlier (Collins et al. 2009). Such features may therefore help predict the ease with which constructions will be acquired or memorized.

This section has sought to demonstrate that speech offers numerous clues that can help understand the processes underlying foreign language learning: not only can the study of learner speech and its features (e.g. use of pauses or discourse markers, acoustic duration) tell us something about how learners process constructions or how their constructicon develops, but, in addition, the features of the spoken language input that learners receive can help predict their acquisition of constructions. Another interesting field of application, related to foreign language learning, is pedagogy. In the next section, we will see how the study of speech can help improve the teaching of constructions.

4.2 Improving foreign language teaching

Generally speaking, we can say that foreign language learners get relatively little exposure to (authentic) speech in the target language. In a typical foreign language situation, the target language is learned via instruction, and spoken input is often limited to teacher talk and oral pedagogical materials (Gilquin and Paquot 2008: 52). Some years ago, comparisons of textbooks and authentic speech emphasized the lack of authenticity of dialogues in textbooks (cf. Gilmore 2004, Römer 2004).

Things have changed slightly since then, both in terms of the quality of textbooks and additional opportunities that foreign language learners may have to receive spoken or spoken-like language input, especially for English (e.g. through TV series). However, it is still the case that authentic speech does not usually represent the main component of the language input that foreign language learners receive. In addition, it was underlined in Section 3.1 that learners tend to be unaware of stylistic differences between constructions. It is therefore important that learners should get exposed more to spoken constructions and should be made aware of their distinctive features and contexts of use. Typically spoken phenomena should also be incorporated into the foreign language curriculum (see also Gilquin and De Cock 2011: 159), including, for example, discourse markers, which are essential to "oil [...] the wheels of verbal interaction" (Stubbe and Holmes 1995: 63), but which are often underused and/or misused by foreign language learners (see, e.g., Aijmer 2011 or Gilquin 2016).

Potentially relevant from a pedagogical point of view are the recent approaches of dialogic syntax (Du Bois 2014) and dialogic Construction Grammar (Brône and Zima 2014), which consider that constructions can span several turns, thus relying on the interactional nature of speech. If we combine these approaches with De Pietro, Matthey, and Py's (1989) concept of "séquences potentiellement acquisitionnelles" (*sequences of potential acquisition*; see Perdue 2000), which describes interactional sequences conducive to learning, we can propose a dialogic construction for corrective feedback. Such a construction is illustrated in (8), taken from the Spanish component of LINDSEI, where A represents the interviewer and B represents the learner.

(8) B: he's he's using . some .. I don't know how   Communicative breakdown
do you say this . these things you use to paint
A: a **brush**   Expert intervention
B: **brush** okay yes thank you   Incorporation of feedback
(A: mhm)
B: yes she he's using some **brushes** to to
paint the picture
(LINDSEI-SP)

The first turn corresponds to a communicative breakdown: the learner does not know how to say *brush* and uses a paraphrase to describe the object (*these things you use to paint*), while clearly signaling the problem (*I don't know how do you say this*). The second turn shows the expert intervention, where the interviewer provides the right word (*a brush*). The learner then incorporates the expert's feedback by repeating the word *brush* and acknowledging that she has understood (*okay yes*). In her next turn, she integrates the word into the sentence (*he's using some brushes to to paint the picture*). The same type of dialogic construction is found twice in example (9), taken from the French component of LINDSEI, where the learner uses her mother tongue (cf. words in italics) to get the expert to help her.

(9)   Construction 1
B: I think they have er this room for for the   Communicative breakdown
whole family with er just erm .. erm <starts
whispering> er *fauteuil* how do you say that
A: a **chair**   Expert intervention
B: a **chair** yes . some chairs for the the family   Incorporation of feedback
in er . in the: in the corner and just erm .. er ..

	CONSTRUCTION 2
B: *oh la la* how do you say that er	Communicative breakdown
A: a **bookcase** *une armoire* a cupboard	Expert intervention
B: yes a **bookcase**	Incorporation of feedback
(LINDSEI-FR)	

Interaction, including teacher-learner interaction, can facilitate foreign language learning (Verga and Kotz 2013). Dialogic constructions building on such interactions, for instance to provide corrective feedback, are regularly used by teachers and they should be encouraged in the classroom or in any other setting where learning can take place. While they have already been examined from other theoretical perspectives (e.g. Mackey, Oliver, and Leeman 2003), their formalization within Construction Grammar could be a first step toward their closer investigation by (applied) construction grammarians.

Taking pedagogical intervention one step further, the teacher can engage in instructional manipulation. As Collins et al. (2009: 348) point out, "one of the distinct advantages of the classroom is the possibility of facilitating acquisition by manipulating input and output opportunities for learners". One well-known type of manipulation is the repeated exposure of learners to the same construction, as recommended by Nation (2001) for vocabulary acquisition. Following up on Collins et al.'s (2009) study on phonetic and perceptual salience (see Section 4.1), we could also recommend teachers to increase the salience of opaque constructions, e.g. through stress, intonation, or articulation, in order to help students notice these constructions and remember them better. Filled pauses could be used with the same effect (cf. Corley, MacGregor, and Donaldson 2007, Section 4.1). Presenting learners with written transcripts of spoken texts might be another useful type of manipulation, not suggested by Collins et al. (2009) but building on their observation that "encounters with new features in spoken contexts are fleeting, offering listeners little opportunity to reflect on the linguistic properties of what they hear" (Collins et al. 2009: 350). A written transcript could make these fleeting encounters more lasting, thus giving learners time to consider constructions that are typical of spoken language.

Finally, the study of spoken data could change attitudes towards nonstandard language. As pointed out by Lintunen and Mäkilä (2014: 378), "higher expectations are set for accuracy in writing, whereas spoken language allows many inaccuracies in form". By examining spoken native data, teachers and/or researchers might become more tolerant toward certain aspects of learner language, including what Waara (2004) calls "learner constructions", that is, utterances that are "slightly off" and consist in "form-meaning reconstructions" (Waara 2004: 51). An example would be the [*DISCUSS about* NP] construction, illustrated in (10), which is taken from the Finnish component of the International Corpus of Learner English. While such a construction is normally considered an error that should be corrected in learner language, the fact that it can be found in spoken native data (cf. (11), taken from the Corpus of Contemporary American English) might make some teachers hesitant to reject it categorically among their learners.

(10) Although the jury members are not allowed to follow the course of the events in the media or to **discuss about** the trial with each other, there are no garantees about that they will not do that. (ICLE-FI)

(11) Well, you come next year and then we'll **discuss about** that (COCA-SPEECH)

Similarly, Götz (2013), in a study on the fluency of native and non-native English speech, has shown that, although on average native speakers of English use fewer filled pauses than learners of English, there is some overlap between the two groups, with some native speakers actually using more filled pauses, and thus being arguably more disfluent, than certain learners. This seems to be the case if we compare example (12), uttered by a German learner, and example (13), uttered by a native speaker. While the former only includes one filled pause (and a vowel lengthening on *the*), the latter includes as many as three filled pauses, which are combined with other disfluent features (unfilled pause [indicated by the dot], repeat, vowel lengthening). Again, such findings could make teachers more tolerant toward the imperfections of their learners' language production.[5]

(12) I chose the movie Goodbye Lenin which is a movie about the[i:] **erm** German reunification (LINDSEI-GE)

(13) the film is basically about . **erm** the life of William Wallis who was a: a leader **erm** he was **erm** a fairly simple person (LOCNEC)

In this section, we have seen that the study of speech in Applied Construction Grammar can bring pedagogical benefits. It can encourage teachers to focus more on spoken constructions and stylistic issues. The manipulation of learners' language input (repeated exposure to certain spoken constructions, empha-

---

[5] This is not to say that teachers should necessarily tolerate in their learners' production anything that can be found in native speech. Maintaining certain standards in the foreign language classroom is arguably desirable in many teaching contexts.

sis through articulation or intonation, etc.) or the use of dialogic constructions (e.g. for corrective feedback) can also enhance the comprehension and acquisition of constructions. As for the study of native speech, it can increase our tolerance toward non-standard features in learner language. Having considered the applied perspective, we now move on to the final dimension, that of the possible theoretical implications of a better recognition of speech in Applied Construction Grammar.

5 Theoretical perspective

Including more speech in Applied Construction Grammar can have an impact on the model of Construction Grammar itself. One change that the study of spoken data can bring about is a shift to the more usual aspects of language, which reflects Bergs (2008) question: "Can we take Construction Grammar beyond sneezing napkins off tables?" Goldberg (2003: 291) points out that "unusual constructions shed light on more general issues, and can illuminate what is required for a complete account of language". However, we should also take the other side of the coin into account and recognize, as Stubbs (2002: 221) does, that "[u]nique events certainly occur, but can be described only against the background of what is normal and expected".

The POS n-gram analysis of LINDSEI described in Section 3.2 brought to light constructions that are so simple that they may almost seem disappointing in comparison with the types of constructions that are typically highlighted in Construction Grammar. This does not appear to be limited to learner speech, as native speech (at least native students' speech) also seems to rely predominantly on rather basic constructions (Gilquin 2018). Yet, it is important to bear in mind that the more mundane aspects of language have an essential role to play and thus deserve to take center stage in linguistic analysis.

Taking speech into account will also allow for a welcome acknowledgment of the phonological aspects of constructions. Phonological properties are part and parcel of the symbolic structure of constructions, as appears from Figure 2, taken from Croft (2001: 18), as well as Croft and Cruse's (2004: 247) statement that "[c]onstructions, like the lexical items in the lexicon, are 'vertical' structures that combine syntactic, semantic and even phonological information (for the specific words in a construction, as well as any unique prosodic features that may be associated with a construction)". However, as pointed out by Boas (2013: 239), "[w]hile constructional research has focused primarily on the role of semantic, pragmatic, and syntactic factors in licensing constructions, very few studies address the influence of phonological factors". Boas (2013: 240) adds that "phonological information may sometimes also be relevant for the licensing of constructions, and as such need to be included in formal representations when necessary". This can only be done through the careful analysis of spoken corpora, or more precisely speech corpora, which give access to the acoustic signal in addition to the transcripts.

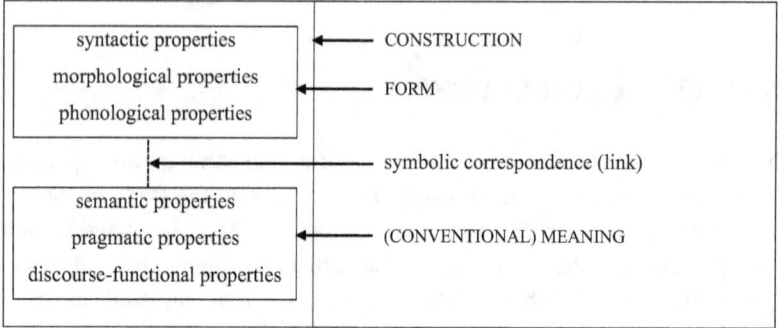

Figure 2: Representation of the symbolic structure of a construction (Croft 2001: 18).

Figure 2 also shows that stylistic features are part of the meaning pole of constructions, in the form of discourse-functional properties. Just like phonological properties, however, stylistic aspects, including differences between speech and writing, have often been neglected in Construction Grammar. Bergs and Diewald (2009a: 2) pointed out that "[s]o far, many studies in construction grammar have focused on (verb) semantic aspects. [. . .] most [studies] have treated pragmatics and *discourse* more or less in passing, so that there is still no systematic survey of this domain" (emphasis added). Their book (Bergs and Diewald 2009b) was a first attempt to consider these aspects more systematically in Construction Grammar. Recently, there has also been a growing "interest in genre-based or genre-sensitive constructions" (Nikiforidou and Fischer 2015: 139). More research on speech in Construction Grammar should further stimulate this interest in stylistic issues.

Research on speech can also help uncover new types of constructions. Phonological constructions were discussed in Section 3.2 and dialogic constructions in Section 4.2. Pragmatic markers have also been claimed to correspond to constructions, most notably by Fried and Östman (2005) and Fischer (2010). Filled pauses, which have been mentioned several times in what precedes, could be said to function as constructions too. In the literature, they have been described as *bona fide* words (Tottie 2015) – and since words are constructions, filled pauses must be constructions. Like constructions, they consist of a pairing of form (e.g. *er* or *erm*) and function (for example, keep the floor, request help to complete the utterance, invite the addressee to speak, or show politeness; see Clark and Fox Tree 2002 for a list of some of the functions of filled pauses). Unfilled pauses are more difficult to deal with. While they undoubtedly fulfill certain functions (cf. Esposito et al. 2007), some might object to silence being considered a linguistic form. And yet, if "silence speaks volumes", it must be a form of communication.[6]

At a more general level, the use of spoken data can help get closer to the ideal of psychological plausibility that characterizes (the more cognitive strand of) Construction Grammar (Boas 2013: 248). While experimentation is arguably the most suitable method to achieve this aim, among corpus data, speech may be said to be a better indicator of psycholinguistic processes, such as construction-forming or automaticity, than writing (see also Section 4.1). Speech can thus promote a more psychologically plausible form of (Applied) Construction Grammar.

This section has explored the idea that speech can contribute to (Applied) Construction Grammar as a theoretical model. Its study can help refine the model so that it explicitly accommodates the specificities of (learner) speech. It also draws our attention to properties of constructions that tend to be neglected, especially phonological and discourse-functional properties, and can lead to the discovery of new types of constructions. Finally, it can bring us closer to the ideal of psychological plausibility that (Cognitive) Construction Grammar strives for.

6 Conclusion

Lintunen and Mäkilä (2014: 377) rightly point out that "[t]here is an axiomatic difference between speech and writing, but together they form the essential parts of learners' L2 skills". Speech, therefore, deserves the attention of (applied) linguists and teaching practitioners just as much as writing. Adopting the perspective of Applied Construction Grammar, this paper has shown that research on speech can help provide better descriptions of spoken learner constructions, which may differ from written learner constructions or spoken native constructions, and can help approach the spoken learner constructicon. Spoken language research can also offer insights into the cognitive mechanisms underlying L2 acquisition, answering questions such as "how do learners build their constructicon?" or "how do they process constructions?" In addition, it can contribute to

---

[6] During the discussion time that followed my plenary talk at CALP-3, on which this paper is based, Thomas Herbst asked the interesting question of whether accent could be considered a construction. The jury is still out on whether this is the case or not.

the improvement of teaching practices by bringing stylistic issues to the forefront or by manipulating learners' language input. Finally, it can help refine the model of (Applied) Construction Grammar and widen its scope, by explicitly making room for typically spoken phenomena like interaction or disfluencies.

If research on speech can prove to be useful on all of these accounts, it is well worth devoting more time and energy to it in the developing field of Applied Construction Grammar. Of course, speech cannot be studied in isolation from writing. Research on written language therefore needs to be pursued in Construction Grammar, so that the distinctive features of speech can be easily highlighted. It is also important to take into account that speech and writing represent a continuum rather than a dichotomy, and that many of the new emerging genres, like tweets (cf. Paveau 2013) or TED talks (cf. Ludewig 2017), are mixed genres in terms of the mode they represent, combining features of speech and writing. This grey area between the spoken and written poles, as well as the evolution of modes, will have to enter the equation too, and should be on the research agenda of (applied) construction grammarians. Clearly, there's plenty to do, so let's get down to it!

References

Aijmer, Karin. 2011. *Well I'm not sure I think . . .* The use of *well* by non-native speakers. *International Journal of Corpus Linguistics* 16 (2). 231–254.

Algeo, John and Thomas Pyles. 2010. *The origins and development of the English language*. Sixth Edition. Boston, MA: Wadsworth.

Altenberg, Bengt & Marie Tapper. 1998. The use of adverbial connectors in advanced Swedish learners' written English. In Sylviane Granger (ed.), *Learner English on computer*, 80–93. London & New York: Addison Wesley Longman.

Bergs, Alexander. 2008. Can we take Construction Grammar beyond sneezing napkins off tables? In Klaus Stierstorfer (ed.), *Proceedings of the Anglistentag Münster 2007*, 269–276. Trier: WVT.

Bergs, Alexander & Gabriele Diewald. 2009a. Contexts and constructions. In Alexander Bergs & Gabriele Diewald (eds.), *Contexts and constructions*, 1–14. Amsterdam & Philadelphia: John Benjamins.

Bergs, Alexander & Gabriele Diewald (eds.). 2009b. *Contexts and constructions*. Amsterdam & Philadelphia: John Benjamins.

Boas, Hans C. 2013. Cognitive Construction Grammar. In Thomas Hoffmann & Graeme Trousdale (eds.), *The Oxford handbook of Construction Grammar*, 233–252. Oxford: Oxford University Press.

Brône, Geert & Elisabeth Zima. 2014. Towards a dialogic construction grammar: *Ad hoc* routines and resonance activation. *Cognitive Linguistics* 25 (3). 457–495.

Bybee, Joan. 1998. The emergent lexicon. *Chicago Linguistic Society* 34. 421–435.

Cappelle, Bert. 2006. Particle placement and the case for "allostructions". *Constructions* SV1-7/2006.

Cappelle, Bert & Natalia Grabar. 2016. Towards an n-grammar of English. In Sabine De Knop & Gaëtanelle Gilquin (eds.), *Applied Construction Grammar*, 271–302. Berlin: De Gruyter.
Clark, Herbert H. & Jean E. Fox Tree. 2002. Using *uh* and *um* in spontaneous speaking. *Cognition* 84 (1). 73–111.
Collins, Laura, Pavel Trofimovich, Joanna White, Walcir Cardoso & Marlise Horst. 2009. Some input on the easy/difficult grammar question: An empirical study. *The Modern Language Journal* 93 (3). 336–353.
Corley, Martin, Lucy J. MacGregor & David I. Donaldson. 2007. It's the way that you, er, say it: Hesitations in speech affect language comprehension. *Cognition* 105 (3). 658–668.
Croft, William. 2001. *Radical Construction Grammar. Syntactic theory in typological perspective*. Oxford: Oxford University Press.
Croft, William & D. Alan Cruse. 2004. *Cognitive linguistics*. Cambridge: Cambridge University Press.
Dahlmann, Irina & Svenja Adolphs. 2009. Spoken corpus analysis: Multimodal approaches to language description. In Paul Baker (ed.), *Contemporary corpus linguistics*, 125–139. London & New York: Continuum.
De Cock, Sylvie. 2004. Preferred sequences of words in NS and NNS speech. *Belgian Journal of English Language and Literatures (BELL), New Series* 2. 225–246.
De Knop, Sabine & Gaëtanelle Gilquin (eds.). 2016. *Applied Construction Grammar*. Berlin: De Gruyter.
de Pietro, Jean-François, Marinette Matthey & Bernard Py. 1989. Acquisition et contrat didactique: les séquences potentiellement acquisitionnelles de la conversation exolingue. In Dominique Weil & Huguette Fugier (eds.), *Actes du troisième colloque régional de linguistique, Strasbourg, 28–29 avril 1988*, 99–124. Université des Sciences Humaines/ Université Louis Pasteur.
Diessel, Holger & Michael Tomasello. 2001. The acquisition of finite complement clauses in English: A corpus-based analysis. *Cognitive Linguistics* 12 (2). 97–141.
Drummond, Rob. 2011. Glottal variation in /t/ in non-native English speech: Patterns of acquisition. *English World-Wide* 32 (3). 280–308.
Du Bois, John W. 2014. Towards a dialogic syntax. *Cognitive Linguistics* 25 (3). 359–410.
Ellis, Nick C. & Fernando Ferreira-Junior. 2009. Constructions and their acquisition. Islands and the distinctiveness of their occupancy. *Annual review of Cognitive Linguistics* 7. 187–220.
Eskildsen, Søren Wild. 2012. L2 negation constructions at work. *Language Learning* 62 (2). 335–372.
Eskildsen, Søren Wild. 2014. What's new? A usage-based classroom study of linguistic routines and creativity in L2 learning. *International Review of Applied Linguistics* 52 (1). 1–30.
Esposito, Anna, Vojtěch Stejskal, Zdeněk Smékal & Nikolaos Bourbakis. 2007. The significance of empty speech pauses: Cognitive and algorithmic issues. In Francesco Mele, Giuliana Ramella, Silvia Santillo & Francesco Ventriglia (eds.), *Advances in brain, vision, and artificial intelligence. Proceedings of the second international symposium, BVAI 2007, Naples, Italy, October 2007*, 542–554. Berlin & Heidelberg: Springer-Verlag.
Fillmore, Charles J., Paul Kay & Mary Catherine O'Connor. 1988. Regularity and idiomaticity in grammatical constructions: The case of *let alone*. *Language* 64 (3). 501–538.
Fischer, Kerstin. 2010. Beyond the sentence. Constructions, frames and spoken interaction. *Constructions and Frames* 2 (2). 185–207.
Fischer, Kerstin & Maria Alm. 2013. A radical construction grammar perspective on the modal particle-discourse particle distinction. In Liesbeth Degand, Bert Cornillie & Paola Pietrandrea (eds.), *Discourse markers and modal particles: Categorization and description*, 47–87. Amsterdam & Philadelphia: John Benjamins.

Francis, Elaine J. & Laura A. Michaelis. 2017. When relative clause extraposition is the right choice, it's easier. *Language and Cognition* 9 (2). 332–370.

Fried, Mirjam & Jan-Ola Östman. 2005. Construction Grammar and spoken language: The case of pragmatic particles. *Journal of Pragmatics* 37 (11). 1752–1778.

Gablasova, Dana & Vaclav Brezina. 2015. Does speaker role affect the choice of epistemic adverbials in L2 speech? Evidence from the Trinity Lancaster Corpus. In Jesús Romero-Trillo (ed.), *Yearbook of corpus linguistics and pragmatics 2015: Current approaches to discourse and translation studies*, 117–136. Dordrecht: Springer.

Gilmore, Alex. 2004. A comparison of textbook and authentic interactions. *ELT Journal* 58 (4). 363–374.

Gilquin, Gaëtanelle. 2015. The use of phrasal verbs by French-speaking EFL learners. A constructional and collostructional corpus-based approach. *Corpus Linguistics and Linguistic Theory* 11 (1). 51–88.

Gilquin, Gaëtanelle. 2016. Discourse markers in L2 English: From classroom to naturalistic input. In Olga Timofeeva, Anne-Christine Gardner, Alpo Honkapohja & Sarah Chevalier (eds.), *New approaches to English linguistics: Building bridges*, 213–249. Amsterdam & Philadelphia: John Benjamins.

Gilquin, Gaëtanelle. 2018. Exploring the spoken learner English constructicon: A corpus-driven approach. In Rosa Alonso Alonso (ed.), *Speaking in a second language*, 127–152. Amsterdam & Philadelphia: John Benjamins.

Gilquin, Gaëtanelle & Sylvie De Cock. 2011. Errors and disfluencies in spoken corpora: Setting the scene. *International Journal of Corpus Linguistics* 16 (2). 141–172.

Gilquin, Gaëtanelle, Sylvie De Cock & Sylviane Granger. 2010. *Louvain International Database of Spoken English Interlanguage. Handbook and CD-ROM*. Louvain-la-Neuve: Presses universitaires de Louvain.

Gilquin, Gaëtanelle & Sabine De Knop. 2016. Exploring L2 constructionist approaches. In Sabine De Knop & Gaëtanelle Gilquin (eds.), *Applied Construction Grammar*, 3–17. Berlin: De Gruyter.

Gilquin, Gaëtanelle & Sylviane Granger. 2015. Learner language. In Douglas Biber & Randi Reppen (eds.), *The Cambridge handbook of English corpus linguistics*, 418–435. Cambridge: Cambridge University Press.

Gilquin, Gaëtanelle & Magali Paquot. 2008. Too chatty: Learner academic writing and register variation. *English Text Construction* 1 (1). 41–61.

Ginzburg, Jonathan & Massimo Poesio. 2016. Grammar is a system that characterizes talk in interaction. *Frontiers in Psychology* 7. 1938. doi:10.3389/fpsyg.2016.01938.

Goldberg, Adele E. 2003. Constructions: A new theoretical approach to language. *Trends in Cognitive Sciences* 7 (5). 219–224.

Goldberg, Adele E. 2006. *Constructions at work. The nature of generalization in language.* Oxford: Oxford University Press.

Götz, Sandra. 2013. *Fluency in native and nonnative English speech*. Amsterdam & Philadelphia: John Benjamins.

Gries, Stefan Th. 2011. Phonological similarity in multi-word units. *Cognitive Linguistics* 22 (3). 491–510.

Gries, Stefan Th. 2013. Data in Construction Grammar. In Thomas Hoffmann & Graeme Trousdale (eds.), *The Oxford handbook of Construction Grammar*, 93–108. Oxford: Oxford University Press.

Hilpert, Martin. 2014. *Construction Grammar and its application to English*. Edinburgh: Edinburgh University Press.
Israel, Michael. 1996. The way constructions grow. In Adele E. Goldberg (ed.), *Conceptual structure, discourse and language*, 217–230. Stanford, CA: CSLI Publications.
Kay, Paul & Charles J. Fillmore. 1999. Grammatical constructions and linguistic generalizations: The *What's X doing Y?* construction. *Language* 75 (1). 1–33.
Kuperman, Victor & Joan Bresnan. 2012. The effects of construction probability on word durations during spontaneous incremental sentence production. *Journal of Memory and Language* 66 (4). 588–611.
Lambrecht, Knud. 1990. 'What, me worry?': Mad magazine sentences revisited. In Kira Hall, Jean-Pierre Koenig, Michael Meacham, Sondra Reinman & Laurel A. Sutton (eds.), *Proceedings of the sixteenth annual meeting of the Berkeley Linguistics Society*, 215–228. Berkeley: Berkeley Linguistics Society.
Linell, Per. 2005. *The written language bias in linguistics. Its nature, origins and transformations*. London & New York: Routledge.
Lintunen, Pekka & Mari Mäkilä. 2014. Measuring syntactic complexity in spoken and written learner language: Comparing the incomparable? *Research in Language* 12 (4). 377–399.
Ludewig, Julia. 2017. TED Talks as an emergent genre. *CLCWeb: Comparative Literature and Culture* 19 (1). http://docs.lib.purdue.edu/clcweb/vol19/iss1/2 (accessed 29 October 2018).
Lyngfelt, Benjamin, Lars Borin, Kyoko Ohara & Tiago Timponi Torrent (eds.). 2018. *Constructicography: Constructicon development across languages*. Amsterdam & Philadelphia: John Benjamins.
Mackey, Alison, Rhonda Oliver & Jennifer Leeman. 2003. Interactional input and the incorporation of feedback: An exploration of NS–NNS and NNS–NNS adult and child dyads. *Language Learning* 53 (1). 35–66.
Michaelis, Laura A. & Knud Lambrecht. 1996. Toward a construction-based theory of language function: The case of nominal extraposition. *Language* 72 (2). 215–247.
Nation, Paul. 2001. *Learning vocabulary in another language*. Cambridge: Cambridge University Press.
Nikiforidou, Kiki & Kerstin Fischer. 2015. On the interaction of constructions with register and genre. *Constructions and Frames* 7 (2). 137–147.
Paveau, Marie-Anne. 2013. Genre de discours et technologie discursive. Tweet, twittécriture et twittérature. *Pratiques* 157–158. 7–30.
Perdue, Clive. 2000. Untutored language acquisition. In Michael Byram (ed.), *Routledge encyclopedia of language teaching and learning*, 939–947. London & New York: Routledge.
Roehr-Brackin, Karen. 2014. Explicit knowledge and processes from a usage-based perspective: The developmental trajectory of an instructed L2 learner. *Language Learning* 64 (4). 771–808.
Römer, Ute. 2004. Comparing real and ideal language learner input: The use of an EFL textbook corpus in corpus linguistics and language teaching. In Guy Aston, Silvia Bernardini & Dominic Stewart (eds.), *Corpora and language learners*, 151–168. Amsterdam & Philadelphia: John Benjamins.
Sambre, Paul, Julien Perrez, Pascale Van Keirsbilck & Cornelia Wermuth. 2018. Constructing futurity: A contrastive approach to L1 and L2 Dutch and French. Paper presented at *Constructionist Approaches to Language Pedagogy 3 (CALP 3)*, 15–17 February 2018, Austin, TX.

Segalowitz, Norman & Jan Hulstijn. 2005. Automaticity in bilingualism and second language learning. In Judith F. Kroll & Annette M. B. De Groot (eds.), *Handbook of bilingualism. Psycholinguistic approaches*, 371–388. Oxford: Oxford University Press.

Shank, Christopher, Koen Plevoets & Julie Van Bogaert. 2016. A multifactorial analysis of *that*/zero alternation: The diachronic development of the zero complementizer with *think, guess* and *understand*. In Jiyoung Yoon & Stefan Th. Gries (eds.), *Corpus-based approaches to Construction Grammar*, 201–240. Amsterdam & Philadelphia: John Benjamins.

Smith, Adam. 2009. Light verbs in Australian, New Zealand and British English. In Pam Peters, Peter Collins & Adam Smith (eds.), *Comparative studies in Australian and New Zealand English: Grammar and beyond*, 139–154. Amsterdam & Philadelphia: John Benjamins.

Stubbe, Maria & Janet Holmes. 1995. *You know, eh* and other 'exasperating expressions': An analysis of social and stylistic variation in the use of pragmatic devices in a sample of New Zealand English. *Language & Communication* 15 (1). 63–88.

Stubbs, Michael. 2002. *Words and phrases. Corpus studies of lexical semantics*. Oxford: Blackwell.

Tizón-Couto, Beatriz. 2014. *Clausal complements in native and learner spoken English. A corpus-based study with LINDSEI and VICOLSE*. Bern: Peter Lang.

Tottie, Gunnel. 1991. Conversational style in British and American English: The case of backchannels. In Karin Aijmer & Bengt Altenberg (eds.), *English corpus linguistics: Studies in honour of Jan Svartvik*, 254–271. London & New York: Longman.

Tottie, Gunnel. 2015. *Uh* and *um* in British and American English: Are they words? Evidence from co-occurrence with pauses. In Rena Torres Cacoullos, Nathalie Dion & André Lapierre (eds.), *Linguistic variation: Confronting fact and theory*, 38–54. New York & London: Routledge.

Verga, Laura & Sonja A. Kotz. 2013. How relevant is social interaction in second language learning? *Frontiers in Human Neuroscience* 7. 550. doi:10.3389/fnhum.2013.00550.

Waara, Renee. 2004. Construal, convention, and constructions in L2 speech. In Michel Achard & Susanne Niemeier (eds.), *Cognitive linguistics, second language acquisition, and foreign language teaching*, 51–75. Berlin & New York: Mouton de Gruyter.

Wible, David. 2008. Multiword expressions and the digital turn. In Fanny Meunier & Sylviane Granger (eds.), *Phraseology in foreign language learning and teaching*, 163–181. Amsterdam & Philadelphia: John Benjamins.

Wood, David. 2010. *Formulaic language and second language speech fluency: Background, evidence and classroom applications*. London: Continuum.

Peter Uhrig, Susen Faulhaber, Ewa Dąbrowska, Thomas Herbst
L2-words that go together – more on collocation and learner language

> *Wortschatzlernen ist Kollokationslernen.*
>
> *Learning words is the learning of collocations.*
>
> Franz Josef Hausmann 1984

1 Collocation in learner language

What is there to be said about collocations? That you shall know a word by the company it keeps (Firth 1968 [1956]: 106–7)? That collocations present difficulties for foreign learners of a language because they are unpredictable (Hausmann 1985)? And that this is why the treatment of collocations in foreign learners' dictionaries (Cowie 1978, Hausmann 1984) and teaching materials (Herbst 2016) is so important? That collocations can be characterized in terms of frequency (Sinclair 1991, Evert 2004)? That some regard the unpredictability view and the frequency view of collocation as incompatible (Hausmann 2004, 2007), whereas others argue they are perfectly reconcilable with one another (see Section 6)? All this can be said, and, indeed, has been said in a vast body of research into the nature of collocation ever since interest in it was triggered in British linguistics in the first half of the twentieth century.[1]

What we are interested in are differences between speakers of English as a foreign language and native speakers of English and differences between individuals within these groups, as will be explained in more detail in Section 2.

In the light of the many different concepts of collocation, we should say that we see collocations as constructions which are characterized by a close affinity between two words which can be determined by frequency and/or unpredictability.[2] This is in line with Goldberg's (2019: 7) broadening of her original concept of constructions from purely non-compositional (Goldberg 1995) to one that also

---

[1] See Cowie (2009) and Barnbrook, Mason & Krishnamurthy (2013).
[2] For discussions of the various views on collocation see Handl (2008), Hausmann (2007), Herbst (1996, 2011); for lexicographic research see e.g. Herbst & Mittmann (2009), Herbst (2015), Siepmann (2005, 2008); for psycholinguistic and cognitive research Ellis, Frey & Jalkanen (2009), Gilquin (2007).

includes highly frequent combinations (Goldberg 2006), which now reads as follows:

> ... constructions are understood to be emergent clusters of lossy memory traces that are aligned within our high- (hyper!) dimensional conceptual space on the basis of shared form, function, and contextual dimensions.

In our view, collocations are to be located in the fuzzy green area of the lexicon-syntax continuum:

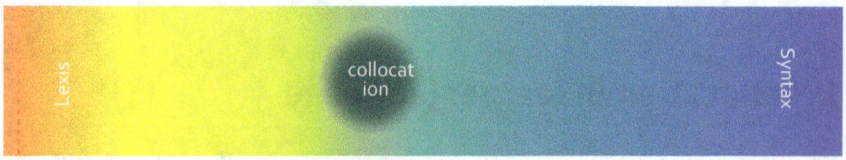

Figure 1: Collocations in the lexicogrammatical continuum.

What Figure 1 is supposed to illustrate is that we do not assume there to be a category of collocation constructions which could be separated by clear-cut boundaries from other types of construction. Rather, we take the term collocation to refer to a spotlight perspective which foregrounds a certain area of a continuum – probably in the neighborhood of word formation constructions and valency constructions. From a cognitive perspective this element of vagueness in the definition of collocation is certainly no disadvantage since one basic assumption of constructionist approaches is that the lexicogrammatical continuum consists of constructions of varying degrees of schematicity (Langacker 2008: 19). We will come back to this in Section 6.

2 Individual differences

As our research methods have become more and more sophisticated, so have the questions we are seeking to answer. The rise of corpus linguistics opened linguistics to quantification at an unprecedented scale (Sinclair 1991), so that, for instance, linguists were suddenly able to make statements about how often a noun such as *conscience* co-occurred with adjectives such as *good* and *clear*. Since this could be done with native speaker corpora and with learner corpora, statistical comparisons between learner language and language use by native speakers became possible.

This has produced interesting insights into the characteristics of learner language (Granger 2009, deCock 2000, Lorenz 1999) including findings about the so-called over- and underuse of certain forms by learners. At the same time, of course, one must not overlook that in many cases what is being compared is an average use of a particular construction in two or more corpora. Such studies are certainly of great value for the design of teaching materials. However, even in an ideal world of foreign language learning it would be rather awkward to argue that language teaching has been maximally successful if the percentage of several rivalling forms in a native speaker corpus is mirrored in a corpus of learner English, let alone in the output of an individual learner. If we find, for example, that *for example* occurs more than three times as often in the BNC than *for instance*, this does not mean, of course, that every speaker of British English uses *for instance* once for every three uses of *for example*. If this is more than obvious for native speakers, there is no reason at all to expect that sort of behavior from learners, however advanced.[3] Leaving aside all other factors determining the choice of a particular construction, one could call a foreign learner's performance native-like if it is within the range of that of individual native speakers, but not necessarily like the average of a native speaker corpus.

At present, it is still very difficult to get sufficiently large corpus material of one and the same person to make reliable claims as to how great individual differences between speakers are.[4] That such differences exist in the area of collocation has been shown in the *Words-that-go-together* test by Dąbrowska (2014), which comprises forty test items in which subjects had to indicate one out of five phrases that "sounds the most natural or familiar". The test contains 20 adjective-noun collocations as in (1) and 20 verb-noun collocations as in (2) and all targeted collocations have a t-score of at least 2, an MI score of at least 3 and a minimum frequency of 3 per 100 million (Dąbrowska 2014: 404–405).

(1) delicate tea
 feeble tea
 frail tea
 powerless tea
 weak tea

(2) deliver a speech
 hold a speech
 perform a speech
 present a speech
 utter a speech

---

3 Compare Paquot's (2009: 109) findings about the overuse of *for example* and *for instance* in learner language.
4 See also Dąbrowska (2012).

Dąbrowska's (2014: 406) test revealed huge differences (from 28% to 98%) between the 80 native speakers tested, who had been selected in such a way that their "distribution of qualifications roughly reflects that of the general UK population" (Dąbrowska 2014: 407).[5]

3 L2 words-that-go-together test

3.1 Test population

In order to be able to compare the performance of advanced foreign learners of English directly with that of native speakers, we replicated Dąbrowska's *words-that-go-together* test with 97 advanced foreign learners of English, all of whom were students of English at the Friedrich-Alexander-Universität Erlangen-Nürnberg in 2016. This means that our test population was more homogeneous than Dąbrowska's with respect to age and educational background. 82 (85.5%) were native speakers of German, with 5 people naming German and Turkish and one person German and Russian as their mother tongues. The 15 students who did not have German as their mother tongue named as their L1s: Russian (6), Italian (3), Ukrainian (3), Hungarian (2), and Armenian, Chinese, Dutch, Greek and Japanese (1 each).[6] Table 1 gives an overview of the participants in the test:

Table 1: Participants in the *L2-words-that-go-together* test.

Total number of questionnaires used:[7]						97		
Gender:	female:	77 (79.4%)	male:		19 (19.5%)	other:		1 (1.0%)
Age:	mean:		22.3	minimum:		18	maximum:	36
	median:		22	standard deviation:		3.3		
Semesters studied[8]:	mean:		4.6	minimum:		1	maximum:	13
	median:		2	standard deviation:		4.1		

---

5 For further details of the experiment see Dąbrowska (2014).
6 Multiple answers were possible.
7 All in all, 186 students took part in the experiment, which was administered in 5 first-year seminars and 5 third-/fourth year seminars in English linguistics. Participants were then given a questionnaire with questions about their language background, reading habits etc. 103 students returned these questionnaires (anonymously, of course); 6 of these were native speakers of English and thus excluded.
8 The questionnaire asked for the semesters in the current degree programme. To account for the BA degree, 7 semesters were added to the value for MA students.

In the remaining parts of Section 3, we will present those results of the *L2-words-that-go-together* test that are of interest in the context of foreign language teaching, leaving the comparison with the original *Words-that-go-together* test to Section 4.

3.2 L2WTGT and language instruction

The first areas where we looked for possible correlations with the *L2-words-that-go-together* tests concerned the duration of formal instruction that students had received as well as the grades they had achieved at school.

With respect to the duration of instruction or exposure to English, we used the age of participants and subtracted the age of the beginning of formal instruction in school (which was at age 8 for some and age 10 for others). If we take this rather rough calculation (which ignores any contact with English before the beginning of formal instruction at school) of duration as a basis, then it ranges from 8 years to 25 years, the mean being 13.5 years. On this basis, we can establish a significant positive correlation between the duration of learning the language and the performance in L2WTGT ($r = .341$, $p < 0.001$). However, the age of the participants is even more strongly correlated with the performance in L2WTGT ($r = .361$, $p < 0.001$),[9] suggesting that early onset English instruction in elementary school does not contribute to English proficiency later in life. This is in fact in line with the findings of Pfenninger and Singleton (2019).

If one compares the results of the tests carried out in the first-year seminars with those of more advanced students, we can observe a slight increase in the means value, which, however, only verges on the border of significance for the full dataset ($p = 0.0522$); see Table 2. With the outlier described in footnote 9 removed as in Table 2 (i.e. the top performer who was in his/her first semester at age 36 after several years abroad), the difference becomes significant ($t = -2.2$, $df = 88.3$, $p < 0.05$, $d = -0.45$).

---

9 Note that both correlation coefficients are overly optimistic due to one extreme outlier: The person with the highest L2WTGT score (32 points) was a first-semester student aged 36 years who had spent multiple years abroad in English-speaking environments. If we remove this person from the dataset, we obtain substantially lower values, which are however still significant ($r = .253$, $p < 0.05$ for years since instruction started; $r = .276$, $p < 0.01$ for age).

Table 2: Targeted answers in the *L2-words-that-go-together* test by first-year and more advanced students, one outlier removed.

	n	minimum	maximum	mean	median	standard deviation
total	96					
first-years	54	8	30	16.4	16	4.9
more advanced students	42	8	31	18.6	18	4.9

There is also a weak but significant positive correlation between the results of the L2WTGT test and the duration of study in semesters ($r = .214$, $p < 0.05$) as shown in Figure 2:

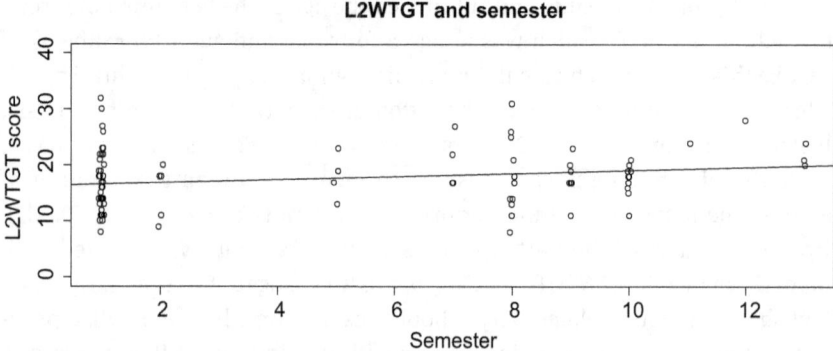

Figure 2: Targeted answers in the *L2-words-that-go-together* test by semester.

We were also interested in seeing whether there was any correlation between the marks students got in their school leaving certificates (*Abitur*) and the entrance exam that all BA- and *Lehramt*-students, who study to be teachers of English, have to take and L2WTGT.[10] Interestingly, we could not establish a significant correlation between the average mark of the *Abitur* and L2WTGT and only a slightly higher, but still not significant correlation between the marks for German and English in *Abitur* and from the two last years at school taken together and L2WTGT. As shown in Table 3, a significant correlation was only found for the FAU entrance exam and its components, with the FAU-Test (see footnote 10) as the most strongly correlated item.

---

[10] This entrance exam consists of a C-test, the Abitur-grade and an additional test testing for listening comprehension, prose composition, discourse completion, grammar and production skills ("FAU test").

Table 3: Correlation between L2WTGT and various pre-university qualifications; German grades, i.e. all correlations should be negative because in the L2WTGT test a higher score is better whereas in the German grading system a lower number is the better.

Total		97
	r	p
Average mark in Abitur	−0.019	0.86
English grade (Abitur & mean score of the last two years at *Gymnasium*)[11]	−0.082	0.47
German grade (Abitur & mean score of the last two years at *Gymnasium*)	−0.144	0.19
University entrance exam (50 % Average mark in Abitur + see below)	−0.326	0.01
C-test (10 % of University entrance exam)	−0.337	0.004
FAU-test (40 % of University entrance exam)	−0.473	0.00003

3.3 Input-related factors

In the light of the crucial role of input and motivation in foreign language learning (see Piske & Scholten-Young 2009, Madlener 2016), we included questions about why people study English, how much time they spend listening to English, or reading and writing English texts and also made use of an author recognition test that aims to measure print exposure.[12] There is a significant positive correlation between the author recognition test and L2WTGT, but no significant correlation between author recognition and time spent reading, writing or listening to English, as we can see in Table 4:

Table 4: Correlation between L2WTGT and the author recognition test with time spent reading, listening and writing.

	L2WGTW		Author recognition	
	r	p	r	p
total reading per week	0.158	0.123	0.101	0.325
total listening per week	**0.227**	**0.025**	0.036	0.728
total writing per week	−0.054	0.599	−0.063	0.543
author recognition	**0.406**	**0.000**		

---

11 If only one of the two grades was available, it was used nonetheless.
12 The questions asked were adapted from Acheson, Wells & MacDonald (2008). In the questionnaire, a scale was used with 11 different values (ranging from no time spent reading/writing/listening to a specified material to more than 7 hours per week). In our calculations we used the average, e.g. when the participant ticked "1/2 – 1 h", we calculated this with 45 minutes, i.e. 0.75 hours. For "> 7 h" we set the value in the calculations to 10 hours. The hours for the various types of materials were summed up and were used as the variable *total amount of reading*, *writing*, and *listening* respectively.

Since the amount of input learners receive in the foreign language can also be influenced by the amount of time they spend in an English-speaking country, we also collected information about that. 66 of the participants in the test spent vacations in an English-speaking country during the three years prior to the test, with the duration of stay varying between 5 and 326 days (mean 27 days). However, no significant correlation between vacation as such and L2WTGT could be found.

27 of the 97 participants spent time in an English-speaking country on an exchange programme or as an au pair etc. (between 24 days and almost 4 years; mean ca. 2.5 years). Here, a significant positive correlation between number of days spent abroad and L2WTGT can be established ($r = 0.355$, $p < 0.001$; $r = 0.223$, $p < 0.05$ with the outlier removed). If we combine time spent during holidays with time spent on exchange programs or working (altogether 69 people with a mean stay of some 3.5 months, plotted in Figure 3), the relationship is less solid and we lose significance without the outlier[13]:

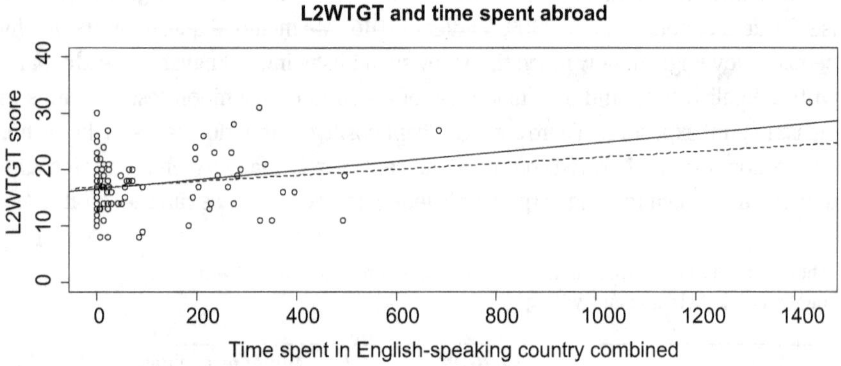

L2WTGT and time spent abroad

Figure 3: L2WTGT and time spent abroad: dashed regression line without outlier.

3.4 Overall exposure

In sections 3.2 and 3.3 we have discussed a range of factors ultimately related to exposure. In order to obtain a more robust and precise measurement of exposure, a composite score was calculated as follows:

---

[13] We also lose significance if we use the log of the time spent abroad, even though a histogram suggests that the data should be logged in order to come closer to a normal distribution.

1) During the years with English instruction at school we assume an average of 0.5 hours of exposure to English per day.
2) During the last two years of school (where most of the students attended intensive courses in English), we add half of their self-reported exposure (time spent reading and listening to English).
3) During their time at university we assume that their self-reported exposure (time spent reading and listening to English) was constant, i.e. for someone in their 5th semester, we add 2.5 years with the reported hours for 52 weeks.
4) During years spent abroad, we assume an average of 8 hours of exposure to English per day, following Dąbrowska, who works with "an eight-hour 'language day' – that is to say, that most people spend about eight hours a day engaged in some kind of linguistic activity (talking, reading, watching television, listening to the radio, browsing the Internet, etc.)" (Dąbrowska 2004: 19).

The resulting score leads to a higher correlation coefficient than the other measures of exposure ($r = 0.436$, $p < 0.001$). It is very stable in that its value does not change much when it is log-transformed (in fact, it increases slightly to $r = 0.446$) or when the outlier is removed.

3.5 Motivational factors

The questionnaire also contained a number of questions aiming at the motivation of the students for choosing English as a subject of study. They were given a variety of possible reasons (such as "want to become a teacher", "need English for my career", "love languages", "love an English-speaking country") and were asked to classify these on a Likert scale from 1 to 7. No significant correlations between any of these factors and L2WTGT could be established. Again, a composite score was created with those items deemed most relevant to motivation, but no significant correlation with L2WTGT was found.

3.6 Dictionary use

As far as dictionary use is concerned, we found a rather interesting significant correlation: the more often students use bilingual dictionaries for production purposes (to find collocations and constructions), the worse they performed in the L2WTGT test ($r = 0.28$, $p < 0.01$). No such correlation could be established for monolingual dictionaries.

4 Learner language

4.1 Learners and native speakers

If we compare the results of the L2WTGT test with those of the original test, we get the following picture:

Table 5: Overall results of L2WTGT test and the original WTGT test (Dąbrowska 2014).

	L2WGTW (learners)		WTGT (native speakers)	
N	97		80	
Minimum achievement	8	20%	11	28%
Maximum achievement	32	80%	39	98%
Mean	17.5		29.5	
Median	17		20	
Standard deviation	5.2		6.2	
Easiest item	raise prices 84.5% (native speakers: 93.8%)		blank expression 97.5% (learners: 32%)	
Most difficult item	hazard a guess 9.3% (native speakers: 70%)		striking example 29% (learners: 51.5%)	

As is to be expected, on the whole native speakers outperform learners. The difference is significant and shows a large effect size.

What is interesting, though, is that the differences between native speaker assessments and learner assessments is not spread evenly over the test items. In the original test, the items had been arranged according to increasing difficulty on the basis of a pilot study with 67 undergraduates (Dąbrowska 2014: 404). In the actual study, Dąbrowska then found a strong negative and highly significant correlation between rank of the item and the percentage of correct choice among native speakers ($r=0.81$, $p=0.000$), i.e. the earlier test items were more likely to be correct than the later items. For the learners taking part in L2WTGT, only a weak negative significant correlation was found ($r=-0.32$, $p=0.041$). The rank correlation between the results of the native speakers and the learners is relatively low (rho=0.35, tau=0.24). Tables 6 and 7 below show the items with the smallest and the biggest differences between learners and native speakers; it seems reasonable to assume that these differences are indicative of the different types of linguistic input (also with regard to text types) the participants in the various groups have experienced.

Table 6: Items where learners came close to native speaker performance or outperformed them (in bold).

	L2WGTW (learners)	WTGT (native speakers)	difference (percentage points)
striking example	**51.5%**	**28.8%**	**+ 22.7**
serious problem	**80.4%**	**73.8%**	**+ 6.6**
gain popularity	79.4%	81.3%	– 1.9
memorable phrase	41.2%	47.5%	– 6.3
raise prices	84.5%	93.8%	– 9.3
restore faith	50.5%	61.3%	– 10.8
witness an incident	70.1%	81.3%	– 11.2
close similarity	51.5%	65.0%	– 13.5
odd remark	52.6%	66.3%	– 13,7

Table 7: Items showing the greatest differences between learners and native speakers.

	L2WGTW (learners)	WTGT (native speakers)	difference (percentage points)
hazard a guess	9.3%	87.5%	– 78.2
blank expression	32.0%	97.5%	– 65.5
divert attention	12.4%	77.5%	– 65,1
lodge a complaint	10.3%	70.0%	– 59.7
dim view	14.4%	71.3%	– 56,9
bitter dispute	16.5%	70.0%	– 53.5
attractive proposition	24.7%	75.0%	– 50.3
issue a statement	18.6%	68.8%	– 50.2
boost production	33.0%	78.8%	– 45.8

4.2 Learners' alternative choices

It is interesting to see that in some cases there are clear favorites in the learners' choices, whereas in others the answers were more evenly distributed. Table 8 contains the cases in which 66% or more learners chose the same items:

Table 8: Items with a 66%+ favorite in learner reactions (targeted WTGT answers in bold) and some distractor results.

arouse suspicions	74%	revive suspicions	10%
		incite supicions	8%
harsh dispute	69%	**bitter dispute**	16%
fair share	74%	reasonable share	13%
gain popularity	78%	attract popularity	10%
raise prices	84%	lift prices	10%
serious problem	81%	significant problem	11%
witness an incident	71%	observe an incident	15%
		notice an incident	8%

The second group of test items still displays a clear favorite in the learners' responses, but the preference is below the two thirds mark. Table 9 gives a few examples.

Table 9: Selected test items with a clear favorite in learner responses (below 66%) (targeted WTGT answers in bold).

attract publicity	59%	make publicity	16%
		attain publicity	12%
		win publicity	8%
absolute silence	58%	pure silence	27%
		sheer silence	14%
odd remark	51%	peculiar remark	20%
		weird remark	17%
raise standards	46%	advance standards	18%
		elevate standards	16%
		lift standards	14%

Finally, there were a large number of test items where the learners taking part in the test did not show a clear preference, some of which are exemplified in Table 10:

Table 10: Items with no clear favorite in learner responses (targeted WTGT answers in bold).

write a complaint	49%	place a complaint	25%
		formulate a complaint	11%
		lodge a complaint	10%
risk a guess	47%	dare a guess	35%
		hazard a guess	9%

Table 10 (continued)

extend production	46%	**boost production**	34%
		double production	12%
blank expression	35%	plain expression	31%
		terrible expression	24%

It is obvious that what one has to bear in mind when assessing these results is – and this applies equally to L2WTGT and the original WTGT – that what has been classified as a "targeted" response is related to corpus data as well as to the question "sounds most natural". There is no implication that distractor collocations (such as *plain expression* or *terrible expression*) would necessarily lead to unidiomatic or unacceptable language use, whichever way we would wish to define it.

5 The role of input and foreign language teaching

5.1 Three important factors

The fact that we find positive correlations between the results in the WTGT test and the number of years they have been learning English, the point in time of their studies at university as well as time spent abroad can be taken as an indication of the fact that, as is to be expected, input plays a crucial role in acquiring a good collocational competence in the foreign language. This is supported by the correlation with the author recognition test, because one would assume people who perform well in this test to read a lot even if we could not establish any correlation between self-assessed reading time per week and test results.[14] It turns out that a score that takes into account exposure during formal instruction at school, institutionalized and individual exposure during the degree programme and increased exposure during time spent abroad is the second-best predictor of all factors we have investigated in this study. Even though one could claim that time spent in an English speaking country or reading English literature can also be taken as indicators of motivational factors, which in turn might result in positive learning effects, we found no relation between motivation as we tried to measure it in the questionnaire and performance.

How extended stays abroad actually affect collocational competence is not completely understood. Nesselhauf (2005: 236), in a study of verb-object colloca-

---

[14] See however the discussion of the exposition score in section 3.4.

tions also finds a correlation, but comes to the conclusion that the result of being exposed to English in a country where it is the L1 is not so much that learners would use collocations they had not used previously, but rather that they make less use of non-established combinations – in other words, the gain could be seen in pre-emption. This ties in very nicely with the results of Herbst's (1996) sentence completion task, in which learners used a larger variety of verbs to complete stimuli such as *I entirely ___* or *They badly ___*, and a collocation judgment task carried out by Granger (1998: 152–154), where learners also "marked a greater number of types of combinations than the native speakers."

5.2 Learners must be made aware of collocation and collocations

Obviously, these insights lead to the question of (whether and) how collocations can be taught? In a usage-based or, to use a term employed by Tyler and Ortega (2018), usage-inspired approach to foreign language teaching, two points seem to be of prime importance:
– that students should be made aware of the central role of phraseological units (including collocations) in producing and understanding language, i.e. the phenomenon of collocation, and
– that students should be taught the most important collocations of the words that they (are supposed to) learn.

And, of course, this is precisely what happens – to a higher or lesser degree – in many language courses all over the world. Looking at textbooks of English that are being used in Bavaria, for example, one finds occasional examples such as the following:[15]

to **take a risk**	...	ein Risiko eingehen
risk ...		Risiko
		(*Green Line New Bayern* 3: 99)
lonely ...	I'm often alone, but I don't always feel *lonely*.	einsam
		(*Green Line New Bayern* 4: 124)

---

15 For a suggestion for a slightly more systematic and a more communicative structure of the vocabulary parts of textbooks see Herbst (2018).

A certain potential for further improvement could be seen in an increase of the number of collocations (and other phraseological units as well as valency patterns) in the vocabulary parts of these textbooks. This could be modelled on the collocation boxes commonly used in monolingual dictionaries (such as the following one taken from LDOCE-online):

COLLOCATIONS – Meaning 1: to perform an action or activity DO + NOUN

do a job/task

> On Saturdays I usually do a few jobs around the house.

do some/any/ no etc work

> She was feeling too tired to do any work.

do the shopping/cleaning/ironing/cooking etc

> Who does the cooking in your family?

do the housework (=jobs in your home such as cleaning, washing clothes etc)

> I've been doing the housework all day.

do the dishes (also **do the washing-up** British English) (=wash the plates after a meal)

> Will anyone help me do the washing-up?

do the laundry (also **do the washing** British English) (=wash dirty clothes)

> Ellie was doing the washing.

do your homework

> My parents don't let me go out unless I've done my homework.

do a calculation/sum (=use numbers to find out a figure, price etc)

> I did a quick calculation on a piece of paper.

do business (=buy and sell goods, or provide services)

> The company does a lot of business in China.

do something/nothing/anything

> He lay on the sofa and did nothing all day.

Realistically, one has to say, however, that the demands made on textbooks and other teaching materials are enormous, and that the coverage of collocations and set phrases in some of them, at least, has reached a standard that leaves little room for improvement. This may vary from country to country, and this is why we can do no more than to underscore the importance of giving prominence to the phenomenon of collocation in textbooks and teaching materials.

When it comes to classroom teaching, one can think of various ways of making students aware of the phraseological nature of language. One possible approach consists in making students mark all expressions in a text that they would have phrased differently, and then to discuss the differences and keep record of all useful phrases of the original (see Götz 2011: 150). In classrooms with access to the Internet, large corpora like the British National Corpus or the Corpus of Contemporary American English can be used to demonstrate the nature of collocation. If students can see – or be made to find out – that the second most-frequent word (after *is*) occurring before *questionable* is *highly*, or that *popularity* tends to occur with forms such as *growing, gaining, increasing* and *enjoyed*, this may leave a more lasting impression on them than just being told. Obviously, this cannot be done in all classrooms, in all countries and only for languages for which sufficiently large corpora are freely available, but no doubt corpus work opens up a number of highly interesting options for foreign language teaching (Bernardini 2004, Klotz 2005, Granath 2009, Johansson 2009).

5.3 Dictionaries

Using corpora in the classroom and teaching language learners at least some basic skills as to what they can find out from a corpus and when and how to do it may seem particularly important in the light of the obvious limitations of dictionaries in this respect. Although, undeniably, remarkable progress has been made in the treatment of collocations in English learners' dictionaries since the 1970s, when the publication of *Longman Dictionary of Contemporary English* shattered the up to then unchallenged status of the *Oxford Advanced Learner's Dictionary* as the only dictionary of this type, they are nowhere near perfect. Take a look at the coverage of the collocations that are from the WTGT test in the online versions of three learners' dictionaries given in Table 11:

Table 11: Coverage of the collocations of the WTGW in the order in which they were presented in the online versions of the *Oxford Advanced Learner's Dictionary* (OALD), the *Macmillan English Dictionary* (MED) and the *Longman Dictionary of Contemporary English* (LDOCE). b: bold type; ex: example; phrase: separate phrase; coll box: collocations box; corpus ex: example in the corpus examples section; 0: no coverage.

	OALD		MED		LDOCE	
	collocate	base	collocate	base	collocate	base
blatant lie	ex	0	0	b-coll	ex	b-coll
blank expression	ex	0	phrase	0	ex	b-ex
attract publicity	0	0	0	coll-box	0	coll-box
fair share	0	0	0	ex	sep. entry	sep. entry
arouse suspicions	ex	ex	0	b-phrase	sep. entry	coll box

Table 11 (continued)

	OALD		MED		LDOCE	
raise prices	phrase	0	ex	coll-box	ex	coll box
hazard a guess	b-ex	b-ex	ex	0	b-ex	coll box
bend rules	idiom	idiom	sep. entry	sep. entry	cross ref	coll box
issue a statement	ex	bex	coll box	b-phrase	ex	coll box
raise standards	ex	0	ex	b-phrase	ex	coll box
boost production	0	0	0	0	corpus ex.	0
join the ranks	ex	b-ex	ex	b-phrase	0	b-ex
bitter dispute	ex	0	ex	0	b-phrase	coll box
absolute silence	phrase	b-ex	0	0	0	coll box
full confession	0	ex	0	ex	corpus ex	coll box
gain popularity	0	gain in p: bex	coll box	gain in p. b-phrase	gain in p. b-ex	gain in p. b-phrase & coll box
regular employment	0	0	0	0	0	coll box
witness an incident	ex	0	ex	0	0	0
achieve one's objectives	0	b-phrase	0	coll box	0	coll box
general direction	0	0	sep. entry	ex	b-ex	coll box
divert attention	ex	0	ex	b-phrase	b-phrase	b-phrase
serious problem	b-phrase	b-phrase	0	0	def & coll box	coll box
urgent matters	0	matter of urgency (b-ex)	0	0	0	coll box
close similarity	0	0	0	0	0	coll box
hear rumours	0	0	b-phrase	ex	ex	coll box
memorable phrase	0	ex	0	0	0	coll box
divert suspicion	0	0	0	0	b-ex	coll box
restore faith	ex	b-ex	0	b-phrase	ex	coll box
thorough search	0	ex	b-phrase	coll box	corpus ex	coll box
precise details	ex	0	ex	0	0	coll box
inflict punishment	0	b-phrase	coll box	0	0	coll box
attractive proposition	b-phrase	b-ex	ex	ex	b-phrase	coll box
dim view	idiom take a dim view	idiom take a dim view	0	0	sep. entry	b-phrase

Table 11 (continued)

	OALD		MED		LDOCE	
outspoken critic	0	ex	ex	0	ex	b-phrase
odd remark	0	0	0	0	0	0
striking example	0	0	ex	coll box	corpus ex	corpus ex
lodge a complaint	ex	b-phrase	ex	ex	sep. entry	coll box
obvious conclusion	0	0	coll box	coll box	0	coll box
overall responsibility	bex	ex	0	ex	0	coll box
refuse an application	ex	ex	0	0	corpus ex	coll box

It is relatively obvious that dictionaries couldn't possibly cover the whole collocation range of a lemma. Furthermore, the sample presented above only contains information that is freely available online and excludes all information that would have to be paid for. Nevertheless, the picture is very encouraging: OALD and MEDAL cover 29 out of the 40 collocations in one form or another; LDOCE comes out best – not only because it misses only two collocations altogether, but because it provides the information where it is needed, for productive purposes at least, namely under the base (Hausmann 2007: 218).

What this means for the teaching of collocation is perfectly obvious: once learners have understood the nature and the importance of collocation for producing idiomatic English, they must also be taught which tools there are and how to use them. Even the admirable collocation boxes in LDOCE require a certain type of reference skill, i.e. (a) not to be satisfied with the first three lines of a dictionary entry, and (b) knowing that there is more to be found. Training students in how to use a dictionary is just as much of a necessity with electronic dictionaries as with paper dictionaries, the main point being that you will only search for a particular type of information if you know you may expect to find it (Herbst, Heath & Kucharek 1989).

6 Collocation in speakers' constructicons

6.1 Individual variation

The WTGT test was developed by Dąbrowska (2014) to elicit differences between native speakers, but using it for advanced learners produced a similarly wide range of targeted hits, as shown in Table 5. There quite clearly is a considerable amount of variation both between L1-speakers and between L2-speakers. While this may be more surprising in the case of the native speakers, it is perfectly clear that individual variation is an extremely relevant factor in assessing the linguistic knowledge both in the L1 and the L2. Since the L2-learners taking part in this experiment were all students of English, we can even expect them to be less focused on a particular subject area in their competence than, say, students who take a course in English as part of business studies or law degree course and as such be more similar to native speakers. Nevertheless, it is obvious that the linguistic experience of students of English will vary considerably – just think of the situations and topic areas a person studying at university and a person being an au-pair in an English-speaking country for several months will have experienced.

6.2 Collocations or constructions or collocations as constructions?

Finally, a note about the nature of collocation. As pointed out in the introduction, Hausmann (1984, 2007) insists on the combinatorial unpredictability aspect as a criterion for defining collocations. From the point of view of foreign language teaching and foreign language lexicography, this is absolutely correct, of course. Nevertheless, one must also take into account that collocation is by no means the only area of language where such unpredictability can be observed. For instance, if someone understands how the German words *Zaun*, the Dutch word *tuin* and English *town* are etymologically related, would they, on the basis of knowing the meaning of one of these words, be able to predict what the other two mean? Certainly not, although it is easy to see how the different meanings – 'fence', 'garden', 'town' – could have developed from the same root.

It is equally plausible to see how *do*, *machen* and *faire* combine with the words for homework (*Hausaufgaben machen, faire ses devoirs, do one's homework*), but, of course, this is unpredictable for the learner. By the way, collocations are equally unpredictable to the learners if they happen to coincide with those of their L1 (Klotz & Herbst 2016: 110–120), just as a perfectly "harmless" combination such as that of the adjective *sandy* with the noun *beach* is not predictable – because hypothetically a translation of *Sandstrand* as *sandbeach*, which also exists, but seems to be restricted to technical language, is just as feasible (Herbst 2011).

We do not intend to question the usefulness of seeing collocation as an established, but unpredictable combination of two words in the language (Hausmann 1984) for the foreign language context in which it was developed at all, quite the contrary. However, doesn't such a view of collocation presuppose a pretty structuralist view of creating sentence meaning by putting words together while calling it into question at the same time? Cognitively, it seems far more appropriate to subsume collocation under what Langacker (2008: 19) describes as "an enormous inventory of units larger than words, representing usual ways of conveying certain notions".

If we shift our attention from the issue of combining words to that of expressing meaning, we will find a wide array of differences between languages in the ways in which the same meaning is expressed. Very often, one meaning is expressed by a simple lexeme (*bus – Bus*), a compound (*lighthouse – Leuchtturm*) or a collocation (*bad conscience – schlechtes Gewissen*) in two languages, but we also get cases where there is no such simple correspondence, with *sandy beaches – Sandstrand* or *The tide is coming in/going out – Es ist Flut/Ebbe* being cases in point (see Herbst 2011). All these expressions can rightly be called constructions in the Goldbergian (2019) sense, and the fact that linguists use terms such as word, compound, collocation, or phrasal verb for some of them at best serves the purpose of establishing a number of prototypes on a continuum. As a consequence, much of what we said about collocations applies equally to compounds or other multi-word units. Whether we (as linguists) call *the tide is coming in* a collocation, an idiomatic expression or an idiom is not particularly important as long as we describe its character as a partially schematic construction (*the tide is/was coming in/going out*) appropriately. What is important is that we understand that words in themselves are pretty useless, unless we see them as constructions within a network of constructions and at the same time as parts of larger constructions.

References

Acheson, Daniel J., Justine B. Wells & Maryellen C. MacDonald. 2008. New and updated tests of print exposure and reading abilities in college students. *Behavior Research Methods* 40(1), 278–289.
Barnbrook, Geoff, Oliver Mason & Ramesh Krishnamurthy. 2013. *Collocation. Applications and Implications*. Basingstoke: Palgrave Macmillan.
Bernardini, Silvia. 2004. Corpora in the classroom. An overview and some reflections on future developments. In John Sinclair (ed.), *How to use corpora in language teaching*, 15–36. Amsterdam & Philadelphia: Benjamins.
Bybee, Joan. 2010. *Language, usage and cognition*. Cambridge: Cambridge University Press.
Cowie, Anthony P. 1972. The place of illustrative material and collocations in the design of a learner's dictionary. In Peter Strevens (ed.), *In Honour of A.S. Hornby*, 127–139.
Cowie, Anthony P. 2009. The earliest foreign learners' dictionaries. In Anthony P. Cowie (ed.), *The Oxford History of English Lexicography*, 385–411. Oxford: Oxford University Press.
Dąbrowska, Ewa. 2012. Different speakers, different grammars: Individual differences in native language attainment. *Linguistic Approaches to Bilingualism* 2(3). 219–253.

Dąbrowska, Ewa. 2014. Words that go together: Measuring individual differences in native speakers' knowledge of collocations. *The Mental Lexicon* 9(3). 401–418.

De Cock, Sylvie. 2000. Repetitive phrasal chunkiness and advanced EFL speech and writing. In Christian Mair & Marianne Hundt (eds.), *Corpus Linguistics and Linguistic Theory*, 51–68. Amsterdam & Atlanta: Rodopi.

Ellis, Nick C., Eric Frey & Isaac Jalkanen. 2009. The psycholinguistic reality of collocation and semantic prosody (1). Lexical access. In Ute Römer & Rainer Schulze (eds.), *Exploring the Lexis-Grammar Interface*, 89–114. Amsterdam & Philadelphia.

Evert, Stefan. 2005. *The Statistics of Word Cooccurrences. Word pairs and collocations.* Ph.D. thesis, Institut für maschinelle Sprachverarbeitung, Universität Stuttgart. http://elib.uni-stuttgart.de/opus/volltexte/2005/2371/.

Firth, John Rupert. 1968 [1956]. Descriptive linguistics and the study of English, 96–113. In Frank Palmer (ed.) *Selected Papers of J. R. 1952–59*, 168–205. London: Longman.

Gilquin, Gaëtanelle. 2007. To err is not all: What corpus and elicitation can reveal about the use of collocations by learners. *Zeitschrift für Anglistik und Amerikanistik* 55(3). 273–291.

Götz, Dieter. 2011. Chunks and the effective learner – a few remarks concerning foreign language teaching and lexicography. In Thomas Herbst, Susen Faulhaber & Peter Uhrig (eds.), *The Phraseological View of Language. A Tribute to John Sinclair*, 147–158. Berlin & Boston: De Gruyter Mouton.

Goldberg, Adele E. 1995. *Constructions. A Construction Grammar approach to argument structure.* Chicago: Chicago University Press.

Goldberg, Adele E. 2006. *Constructions at work. The nature of generalization in language.* Oxford & New York: Oxford University Press.

Goldberg, Adele. 2019. *Explain me this. Creativity, competition, and the partial productivity of constructions.* Princeton, New Jersey: Princeton University Press.

Granath, Solveig. 2009. Who benfits from learning how to use corpora? In Karin Aijmer (ed.) *Corpora and Language Teaching*, 47–65. Amsterdam & Philadeelphia: Benjamins.

Granger, Sylviane. 1998. Prefabricated patterns in advanced EFL writing: collocations and formulae. In Anthony P. Cowie (ed.) *Phraseology. Theory, Analysis, and Applications*, 145–160. Oxford: Clarendon Press.

Granger, Sylviane. 2009. The contribution of learner corpora to second language acquisition and foreign language teaching: A critical evaluation. In Karin Aijmer (ed.) *Corpora and Language Teaching*, 13–32. Amsterdam & Philadelphia: Benjamins.

Groom, Nicholas. 2009. Effects of second-language immersion on second-language collocational development. In Andy Barfield & Henrik Gylstad (eds.), *Researching collocation in another language: multiple interpretations*, 21–33. New York: Palgrave Macmillan.

Handl, Susanne. 2008. Essential. collocations for learners of English: The role of collocational direction and weight. In Fanny Meunier & Sylviane Granger (eds.), *Phraseology in Foreign Language Learning and Teaching*, 43–66. Amsterdam & Philadelphia: Benjamins.

Hausmann, Franz Josef. 1984. Wortschatzlernen ist Kollokationslernen. Zum Lehren und Lernen französischer Wortverbindungen. *Praxis des neusprachlichen Unterrichts* 31. 285–406.

Hausmann, Franz Josef. 1985. Kollokationen im deutschen Wörterbuch. Ein Beitrag zur Theorie des lexikographischen Beispiels. In Henning Bergenholtz & Joachim Mugdan (eds.), *Lexikographie und Grammatik*, 118–129. Tübingen: Niemeyer.

Hausmann, Franz Josef. 2004. Was sind eigentlich Kollokationen? In Kathrin Steyer (ed.), *Wortverbdingen – mehr oder weniger fest*, 309–334. Berlin & New York: de Gruyter.

Hausmann, Franz Josef. 2007. Die Kollokationen im Rahmen der Phraseologie – systematische und historische Darstellung. *Zeitschrift für Anglistik und Amerikanistik* 55(3). 217–234.
Herbst, Thomas. 1996. What are collocations: *sandy beaches* or *false teeth* English Studies 77. 379–393.
Herbst, Thomas. 2011. Choosing *sandy beaches* – collocations, probabemes and the idiom principle. In Thomas Herbst, Susen Faulhaber & Peter Uhrig (eds.), *The Phraseological View of Language. A Tribute to John Sinclair*, 27–57. Berlin & Boston: De Gruyter Mouton.
Herbst, Thomas. 2015. Why construction grammar catches the worm and corpus data can drive you crazy: accounting for idiomatic and non-idiomatic idiomaticity. *Journal of Social Sciences*
Herbst, Thomas. 2016. Foreign language learning is construction learning – what else? Moving towards pedagogical construction grammar. In Sabine de Knop and Gaëtanelle Gilquin (eds.), *Applied Construction Grammar*, 21–51. Berlin & Boston: de Gruyter.
Herbst, Thomas. 2018. Über Kognition zur Konstruktion – Zielorientiertes Lernen fremdsprachlicher Konstruktionen von links nach rechts. In Jürgen Erfurt & Sabine de Knop (eds.), *Konstruktionsgrammatik und Mehrsprachigkeit*. Osnabrücker Beiträge zur Sprachtheorie 94, 149–172. Duisburg: Universitätsverlag Rhein-Ruhr OHG.
Herbst, Thomas, David Heath & Richard Kucharek. 1989. *Dictionary Techniques. Praktische Wörterbucharbeit mit dem DCE. Lehrerhandreichungen*. München: Langenscheidt-Longman.
Herbst, Thomas & Brigitta Mittmann. 2008. Collocation in English dictionaries at the beginning of the twenty-first century. *Lexicographica*. 103–119.
Johansson, Stig. 2009. Some thoughts on corpora and second-language acquisition. In Karin Aijmer (ed.) *Corpora and Language Teaching*, 33–44. Amsterdam & Philadeelphia: Benjamins.
Klotz, Michael. 2005. Translation und Technik. zum Einsatz EDV-basierter Ressourcen im Übersetzungsunterricht Englisch-Deutsch. In Thomas Herbst (ed.), *Linguistische Dimensionen des Fremdsprachenunterrichts*, 71–80. Würzburg: Königshausen & Neumann.
Klotz, Michael & Thomas Herbst. 2016. *English Dictionaries: a linguistic introduction*. Berlin: Schmidt.
Langacker, Ronald W. 2008. *Cognitive grammar. A basic introduction*. Oxford & New York.
Lorenz, Gunter. 1999. *Adjective intensification – learners versus native speakers: A corpus study of argumentative writing*. Amsterdam: Rodopi.
Madlener, Karin. 2016. Input optimization. Effects of type and token frequency manipulations in instructed second language learning. In Heike Behrens & Stefan Pfänder (eds.), *Frequency Effects in Language. What counts in language processing, acquisition and change*, 133–173. Berlin & New York: De Gruyter Mouton.
Nesselhauf, Nadja. 2005. *Collocations in a learner corpus*. Amsterdam & Philadelphia: Benjamins.
Paquot, Magali. 2008. Exemplification in learner writing: A cross-linguistic perspective. In Sylviane Granger & Fanny Meunier (eds.), *Phraseology: An interdisciplinary perspective*, 101–119. Amsterdam & Philadelphia: John Benjamins.
Piske, Thorsten & Martha Young-Scholten (eds.). 2009. *Input Matters in SLA*. Bristol: Multilingual Matters.
Siepmann, Dirk. 2005. Collocation, colligation and encoding dictionaries. Part II: Lexicographical aspects. *Lexicographica* 18. 409–444.

Siepmann, Dirk. 2008. Phraseology in learners' dictionaries: What, where and how? In Fanny Meunier & Sylviane Granger (eds.), *Phraseology in Foreign Language Learning and Teaching*, 185–202. Amsterdam & Philadelphia: Benjamins.
Sinclair, John. 1991. *Corpus, concordance, collocation*. Oxford: Oxford University Press.
Sinclair, John. 2008. The phrase, the whole phrase, and nothing but the phrase. In Sylviane Granger & Fanny Meunier (eds.), *Phraseology: An interdisciplinary perspective*, 407–410. Amsterdam & Philadelphia: John Benjamins.
Tyler, Andrea. E. & Lourdes Ortega. 2018. Usage-inspired L2-instruction: An emergentist, researched pedagogy. In Andrea E. Tyler, Lourdes Ortega, Mariko Uno & Hae In Park (eds.), *Usage-inspired L2 instruction. Researched Pedagogy*, 3–26. Amsterdam & Philadelphia: Benjamins.

Textbooks

Green Line New Bayern 3. 2005. Stephanie Ashford, Rosemary Heller-Jones, Marion Horner, Raimund A. Mader. Stuttgart: Klett.
Green Line New Bayern 4. 2006. Stephanie Ashford, Rosemary Heller-Jones, Marion Horner, Peter Lampater. Stuttgart: Klett.

Dictionary

Longman Dictionary of Contemporary English. https://www.ldoceonline.com [accessed 4th/5th March 2019]
Macmillan Dictionary. https://www.macmillandictionary.com [accessed 4th/5th March 2019]
Oxford Advanced Learner's Dictionary. https://www.oxfordlearnersdictionaries.com [accessed 4th/5th March 2019]

III **Learning and teaching constructions**

Sabine De Knop, Fabio Mollica
Construction-based teaching of German verbless directives to Italian-speaking learners

1 Introduction

At an intermediate or advanced level, language teaching should focus on various differentiated structures which represent authentic ways of expression in the foreign language. One of the grammatical topics that should be dealt with is the way in which speakers can express directive speech acts, i.e. speech acts aiming at causing a specific reaction with the addressee (Finkbeiner 2015: 18). These include giving commands, instructions or advice. Languages have several possibilities to do so. The most common way in German is the use of verbal imperative forms like *Gib mir bitte einen Saft* (lit. 'Give me please a juice')[1] or infinitives, e.g. *Alle einsteigen bitte!* (lit. 'All get in please!'). Declarative sentences like *Du gibst mir sofort den Schlüssel!* (lit. 'You give me immediately the key!') or sentences with modal verbs + infinitive are also possible, e.g. *Du sollst mir jetzt den Schlüssel geben!* (lit. 'You should give me the key now!').[2] Alternatively, passive sentences can also express directive speech acts, e.g. *Hier wird jetzt aber gearbeitet!* (lit. 'Here is now but worked!').

But speakers also have the possibility to use compact forms with adverbs (Germ. *Hierher!*, lit. 'here to (me)' or Italian *Avanti!,* lit. 'Come in!') or so-called

---

[1] Because these examples are quoted directly in the text, we simply give a literal translation. The numbered examples further down are first translated word by word according to the Leipzig glossing rules (https://www.eva.mpg.de/lingua/pdf/Glossing-Rules.pdf) and then followed by a more authentic English translation.

[2] There is of course a register difference between these expression forms. Thus, the use of infinitives is often used in public situations, at the train station for instance. Because of their conciseness, infinitives can sometimes appear to be a rough, not very polite way of expression. By contrast, the use of sentences with imperative forms is rather neutral and can be polite. We cannot go into register issues in this paper but refer to Genzmer (1995: 133) and to Weigand (2015: 216) for the variation among utterances according to the communicative purpose.

Notes: We thank the anonymous reviewers for their very constructive comments on an earlier version of the paper. The article is the result of close collaboration between the two authors; however, the two authors have dealt more specifically with different parts: Sabine De Knop is responsible for Sections 3.1, 3.2, 4 and 5 and Fabio Mollica for Sections 1, 2 and 3.

https://doi.org/10.1515/9783110746723-005

"verbless directives" (Jacobs 2008), i.e. verb-free structures which express directive speech acts. Our paper deals with such verbless directives in detail. The first extensive contribution dealing with them is Jacobs' (2008) study, which examines the potential of a constructionist approach for the exploration of such structures. Jacobs uses the German term "verblose Direktiva" to designate a range of instantiations which all express a motion event as in the following examples.

(1) *Her mit dem Geld!*
to me with the money
'(Give) To me the money!'

(2) *Ab ins Bett!*
off into the bed
'Off to bed!'

(3) *Hinein ins Vergnügen!*
into into the pleasure
'Let us enjoy!'

These examples have an illocutionary force and belong to the directive illocutionary speech acts in Searle's taxonomy (1979). They are quite common in German and in some Slavic languages (Wilder 2008). In Romance languages they are possible, but – as we show in this chapter – not so common.[3] As is well-known from studies on lexicalization patterns, German as a satellite-framed language (Talmy 2000) expresses motion along a trajectory frequently with satellites, i.e. prepositions and particles (De Knop 2019). Accordingly, verbless directives consisting only of satellites are good candidates to express such motion events.

Because of their illocutionary force, verbless directives mainly appear in oral discourse or in written fictional texts which simulate oral speech. The instances for this study have been extracted from the corpora of the Sketch Engine.[4] They can be considered to be representative of the actual use of this construction, as they have their origin in oral interaction in internet forums and simulated oral speech in direct discourse of belletristic literature. These instances thus repro-

---

3 Here we exclude adverbs like it. *fuori* 'outside', *avanti* 'go/off', *via* 'out', fr. *en avant* 'go/off', as they do not correspond to the structure of verbless directives.
4 It is important to realize that in the small corpora of oral data found in the database of spoken German (Datenbank Gesprochenes Deutsch (DGD) of the Institut für Deutsche Sprache (IDS) in Mannheim) hardly any instantiations of verbless directives could be found. That is why we opted for the corpora of the Sketch Engine, more specifically for the German deTenTen 13 corpus.

duce spoken discourse, although they are realized in written form (for conceptually oral speech see Koch and Oesterreicher (1985) and Feilke and Hennig (2016)). All instances were checked by native speakers to confirm their actual use in present German. Because of their conciseness, verbless directives are favored by speakers and writers to trigger the realization of some intentions. If we compare the following two examples in a mother-child context, we realize that example (4) is more compelling and – depending on the situation – is less friendly, but more energetic or determined than (5):[5]

(4) *Kairi kam mit Kari an. "So und nun <u>ab ins   Bett</u>".*
    So and now off into the bed
    'Kairi arrived with Kari. "So and now off to bed".'
                                            (Sketch Engine, deTenTen13)

(5) *Nun, <u>geh doch bitte ins Bett</u>, wir können morgen noch darüber reden.*
    Now, go after all please into the bed
    'Now, please go to bed, we can talk about it tomorrow.'

With example (4) a quick reaction without any contradiction is expected. Because of their impact several verbless directives can be found in one and the same sentence, as illustrated by (6) and further by (7):

(6) *Gutes Wetter draußen? Dann <u>rein in die Turnschuhe</u> und <u>ab in den Wald</u>.*
    Then into in the sport shoes and off in the wood
    'Good weather outside? Then into the sport shoes and off to the wood.'
                                            (Sketch Engine, deTenTen13)

Our analysis of the corpus data has also shown that verbless directives are frequently found in advertising, e.g. in tourism, because they are concise and should motivate possible addressees to buy the advertised product or to call on somebody's services:

(7) *<u>Raus aus der Stadt</u> und <u>hinein ins Vergnügen</u>.*
    Out of the town and into in the pleasure
    'Out of town and enjoy the pleasure.'   (Sketch Engine, deTenTen13)

---

5 This corresponds to the "Principle of Non-Synonymy of Grammatical Forms": two syntactic alternations of structures are semantically and/or pragmatically different (Goldberg 1995: 67). One of the reviewers commented that this principle was first proposed by Bolinger (1968).

(8) *Bei TMG Hotels, Flüge, Mietwagen einzeln oder zusammen als Pauschalreise buchen und dann <u>ab in den Urlaub</u>.*
                                 off into the holiday
'With TMG book hotels, flights, rented cars individually or together as package holiday and off on vacation.'   (Sketch Engine, deTenTen13)

Verbless directives have been described in various ways, depending on the syntactic theory. For projectionist models they constitute a great challenge (compare Jacobs 2008) as they do not contain any verb as head of the sentence, which predetermines its complements (see Welke 2011: 172). Domínguez Vázquez (2011) and Domínguez Vázquez et al. (2017) consider them to be elliptical with the omission of some arguments.[6] By contrast, Wilder (2008) holds the view that *mit*-directives are in fact imperative sentences with a non-explicit semantically empty verb *go*. Fortmann (2018) also argues that verbless directives result from syntactic structures with an empty verbal category as head of the structure.

Welke (2009) postulates structures consisting of a *pivot* as head with situational predicates (*raus* 'out', *nieder* 'down', *ab* 'off' and so on). He argues that verbless directives originate in sentences with a verb through analogy (valency inheritance or constructional change), e.g. *Auf zur Klassenfahrt* (lit. 'off to the school trip') vs. *Sie brachen auf zur Klassenfahrt* (lit. 'They started off to the school trip'). This may be true, but in actual German verbless directives are autonomous constructions with their own characteristics. Still, Eroms (2012: 42) claims that these constructions depend on the motion adverb which presents similar valency properties as a verb. This can be observed with the verb particle *ab* in constructions like *ab ins Bett* (lit. 'off to bed') or *ab in den Müll mit den Klamotten* (lit. 'off into the dustbin with these clothes') where *ab* expresses the inchoative Aktionsart of the verb.[7]

Like Jacobs (2008), who compares the projectionist approach with the constructionist model, it is our view that a constructionist description offers a more adequate model to describe the idiosyncrasies of these structures. More specifically, Goldberg's usage-based, non-formalistic description of language (1995, 2006 and 2013) grounded in the cognitive tradition allows us to define verbless direc-

---

6 Even if some constructions containing a verb are possible, e.g. *Sie steht da, ganz klein und fett, und schreit mich an: Geh ab ins Bett!* (lit. 'She stands there, small and fat, and shouts at me: Go off to bed!') (Sketch Engine, deTenTen13), other constructions with *mit*-directives are not acceptable in standard German if a verb is added: **Gib (geh, trag, bring, . . .) her mit dem Geld!*; **Bring (. . .) weg mit dem Krempel!*; **Mach (. . .) nieder mit den Studiengebühren!*; **Schmeiß (. . .) in den Müll mit den Klamotten!*; **Schick (. . . .) zur Hölle mit dieser Regierung!* (Examples from Müller (2011: 6); acceptability judgment like in the original; see also the discussion in Fortmann 2018).
7 *Ab* is in fact a particle, but because it can be in first position we consider it to behave like an adverb.

tives as entrenched and conventionalized form-meaning pairings, i.e. autonomous constructions[8] with their own semantic, syntactic and pragmatic properties.

Goldberg's entrenchment principle (2006) plays a major role in the definition of constructions for the idiosyncratic expression of a specific speech act in a particular language. It is this principle which makes it possible to generalize and to advocate schematic constructions which facilitate the learning of structures. Starting with the analysis of the data Section 2 presents a fine-grained description of the relevant properties in Goldberg's (1995, 2006, 2013) framework and a definition of several classes of instances where the same syntactic structure has different semantics.

A description of verbless directives is further interesting from a contrastive perspective, which the paper adopts in Section 3. It presents a smaller parallel collection of examples from two Belgian-French comic strips and their German and Italian translations (Hergé 1947, 1998, 1999; Jacobs 1980, 1991, 1993). The section focuses on typological differences between the Germanic language German and the Romance languages French and Italian. But having described the differences between German verbless directives and their counterparts in Romance languages is no guarantee that learners will be able to use such constructions.

For a more efficient learning of these constructions we developed a methodology inspired by studies on structural priming (among others Gries (2005), Hartsuiker et al. (2004), Loebell and Bock (2003) and Scheepers and Corley (2000)), which focuses on the learning of syntactic structures. The methodology was tested with Italian master students of German as a foreign language at the University of Milano. This study is presented in Section 4. Finally, Section 5 discusses some limitations of this method and perspectives for further research.

2 German verbless directives as constructions

Verbless directives are constructions in Goldberg's (2006) sense, i.e. form-meaning pairings which are productive and frequent in German and cognitively well-entrenched.[9] As already pointed out above, such constructions mainly express commands, instructions, recommendations and requests, which are supposed to motivate a quick reaction (compare Wilder 2008; Jacobs 2008: 15; De Knop 2021):

---

8 By contrast, Müller (2011) studies verbless directives in the framework of Generative Grammar and does not define them as constructions. For him they are composed of smaller units and their assembling can be explained by rules.
9 We are not dealing with the issue of compositionality of single instantiations (compare De Knop 2019).

(9) *Also auf die Plätze fertig los und <u>rein ins Vergnügen</u>.*
　　　　　　　　　　　　　　　　　into in the pleasure
　　'Ready, steady, go and enjoy'　　　　　　　　(Sketch Engine, deTenTen13)

(10) *Dir brennt noch etwas anderes auf der Seele. <u>Raus mit der Sprache</u>.*
　　　　　　　　　　　　　　　　　　　　　　　Out with the language
　　'Something else is bothering you. So now, tell us about it!'
　　　　　　　　　　　　　　　　　　　　　　　(Sketch Engine, deTenTen13)

(11) *Seine Empfehlung war: „<u>Ab ins Bett!</u>"*
　　　　　　　　　　　　　　Off into the bed
　　'His recommendation was: "Off to bed!"'.　　(Sketch Engine, deTenTen13)

For Jacobs (2008: 15) verbless directives express an underlying directional-resultative predication: "An entity should – literally or in a figurative sense – be moved along a path towards its endpoint and stay there" [our translation from German]. The motion path towards a goal is mainly expressed with a satellite – which is often a local preposition[10] – in German. If it is a two-way preposition it is combined with the accusative case for the expression of an incipient motion which is "not yet established" (Willems 2011; Willems et al. 2018). By contrast, the dative would designate an "established" location or goal. Such constructions are characterized by the "goal-over-source principle" (compare Stefanowitsch and Rohde (2004), Ungerer and Schmidt (1996), Verspoor, Dirven and Radden (1999)), because one can abstract away from the expression of the source of the motion event, but not of the goal. Jacobs (2008) distinguishes three construction types with verbless directives:

Type 1: [(directional) Adverb Prepositional Phrase$_{directional}$] (*Raus aus der Wohnung!*)
Type 2: [directional Adverb *mit*-Prepositional Phrase] (*Her mit dem Geld!*)
Type 3: [Prepositional Phrase$_{directional}$ *mit*-Prepositional Phrase] (*In den Müll mit diesem Hemd!*)

In the following sections we deal with each construction type in detail, and we will describe some further constructions to show that they all belong to a common semantic network.

---

10 Recently a discussion has started about the nature of satellites. Whereas Talmy (2000) also included prepositions in the class of satellites, Ibarretxe (2017), Filipovic and Ibarretxe-Antunano (2015) suggested to discard prepositions. Because prepositions combined with morpho-syntactic cases in German contribute to the expression of a motion path towards a goal we will consider them to be satellites as well.

2.1 Type 1: [(directional) Adverb Prepositional Phrase$_{directional}$]

Prototypical instantiations of this abstract construction contain an adverb in the first position, which is often a directional adverb (like *ab, vorwärts, zurück*) expressing motion. In some less prototypical examples the adverb can be a manner verb which does not express a direction, e.g. *schnell* ('quick') or *los* ('off') or it can simply be missing, as in *in den Hof!* (lit. 'into the yard!'), *ins Wasser!* (lit. 'into the water!'), or *ins Bett!* (lit. 'into the bed!'). Such instantiations are strongly context-dependent and only possible in specific usage. As these structures with a manner adverb or without any adverb express a directive meaning as well, we will also include them in our description of this category of examples (see Section 3):[11]

(12) *Jetzt muss nur noch der Wind wehen, dann kann es losgehen! Ab in die Luft!*
Off in the air
'Now we just need the wind to blow, then we can start! Off in the air!'
(Sketch Engine, deTenTen13)

(13) *Also ab unter die Dusche und los ins Nachtleben von Chicago!*
Off under the shower and off into the night life of Chicago
'So off under the shower and off to Chicago's night life!'
(Sketch Engine, deTenTen13)

The endpoint or goal is always expressed in this construction type, it can be more or less concrete or abstract, as can be seen in the following examples:

(14) *Dann zurück ins Bett. Mir ist verdammt kalt.*
Then back into the bed
'Then back to bed. I am damn cold.'

(15) *Zu Hause alles wohl gefunden? Na – dann kommen Sie! . . . Vorwärts ins Vergnügen!*
Forwards into the pleasure
'Found everything at home? Well – then come!. . . Go and enjoy yourself!'

---

[11] In some cases, a comma or an exclamation mark is used between the adverb and the prepositional phrase, e.g. *Los, ins Bett!* (lit. 'Go, into the bed!') or *Ab! Ins Bett!* (lit. 'Off! Into the bed!'). This is especially the case with adverbs like *los* ('go') or *vorwärts* ('forwards').

The path of motion is expressed with a local or motion preposition, e.g. *in*, *auf* and so on. This construction can be represented as follows:

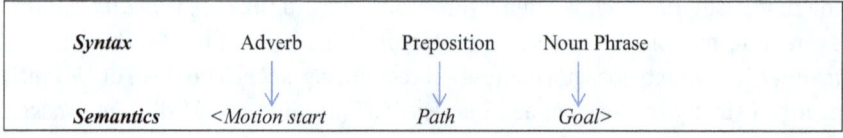

Figure 1: Abstract Type 1-construction of German verbless directives.

In the prototypical use the speaker wants the addressee to move into the direction which s/he requests. The addressee is "not only the causer of the motion, but at the same time the entity which has to be moved" (Jacobs 2008: 16 [our translation from German]):

(16)　*Morgen Jungs. Frühstückt schön und dann <u>ab zur[12] Schule</u>.*
　　　　　　　　　　　　　　　　　　　　　　　　then off to the school
　　'Morning boys. Have nice breakfast and then off to school.'
　　　　　　　　　　　　　　　　　　　　　(Sketch Engine, deTenTen13)

In the German deTenTen13-corpus of the Sketch Engine we can also find examples in which the moving entity is not the addressee but the speaker him-/herself. In these cases too, the construction keeps its directive character.

(17)　*Zurück ging es dann wieder bei strahlendem Sonnenschein entlang des Seeufers. Noch schnell was in der Jugendherberge gegessen und <u>auf zum nächsten Ziel</u>: Luzern. Auch hier haben wir uns erst mal verfahren. [. . .] Abends dann noch was in der Stadt essen, E-Mails abrufen und <u>ab ins Bett</u>.*
　　　　　　　　　　　　　　　　　　　　　　　　　off to the next goal
　　　　　　　　　　　　　　　　　　　　　off into the bed
　　'(Having) Quickly eaten something in the youth hostel and off to the next goal: Luzern. Here too we got lost.
　　[. . .] In the evening then eat something in town, download e-mails and off to bed.'　　　　　　　　　　　(Sketch Engine, deTenTen13)

---

12 The German preposition *zu* always requires the dative case because it expresses a telic motion focusing on the endpoint (see Section 3.1).

(18) *Deshalb sage ich jetzt einfach mal: <u>ab in die Ferien</u>, ich will meine Ruhe haben.*
　　　　　　　　　　　　　off into the vacation
　'Therefore I simply say: Off in the vacation, I want to be left in peace.'
　　　　　　　　　　　　　　　　　　　　　(Sketch Engine, deTenTen13).

In other less prototypical examples no directive speech act in the form of a command or invitation to do something is expressed, but the directional meaning is still present:

(19) *Für ihn heißt es bald: <u>Ab in die Ferien</u>.*
　　　　　　　　　　　　Off into the vacation
　'For him this means soon: Off in the vacation' (Sketch Engine, deTenTen13)

The schematic constructions can generate whole lists of instantiations:

(20)　a.　*Ab ins Bett!*
　　　　　　off into the bed
　　　　　　'Off to bed!'
　　　b.　*Ab durch die Hecke!*
　　　　　　off through the hedge
　　　　　　'Off through the hedge!'
　　　c.　*Ab hinter das Haus!*
　　　　　　off behind the house
　　　　　　'Off behind the house!'

(21)　a.　*Vorwärts ins Haus!*
　　　　　　forwards into the house
　　　　　　'Forwards into the house!'
　　　b.　*Vorwärts in die Zukunft!*
　　　　　　forwards into the future
　　　　　　'Forwards into the future!'
　　　c.　*Vorwärts auf den Berg!*
　　　　　　forwards onto the mountain
　　　　　　'Forwards upon the mountain!'

If a directional adverb is composed of a particle together with a local preposition, then the same preposition is frequently reduplicated in the prepositional phrase. In such cases the path is already announced with the directional adverb:

(22) *Rauf aufs Rad und rein in die Pedale!*
Upon onto the bike and into in the pedals
'On the bike and on the pedals!' (Sketch Engine, deTenTen13)

But the preposition in the directional adverb and the local preposition introducing the nominal phrase can differ:

(23) *Raus ins Freie und das ohne Kompromisse!*
Outside in the free
'Go outside and this without any compromise!' (Sketch Engine, deTenTen13)

2.2 Type 2: [Directional Adverb *mit*-Prepositional Phrase]

As opposed to Type 1 constructions, which have an abstract non-fixed structure, Type 2 includes a lexically fixed element, instantiated with the preposition *mit* ('with') and free slots:

(24) *Nieder mit der Diktatur!*
down with the dictatorship
'Down with the dictatorship!' (Sketch Engine, deTenTen13)

(25) *Her mit den Jeansjacken und Ballerinas!*
to us with the jeans jackets and the ballerinas
'Here with the jeans jackets and the ballerinas!' (Sketch Engine, deTenTen13)

(26) *Weg mit den Winterferien – dafür regulär zwei Wochen Urlaub an Ostern.*
away with the winter vacation
'Away with the winter holiday – instead two regular weeks of holiday.'
(Sketch Engine, deTenTen13)

Following Dobrovol'skij (2011) we call these structures "phraseme-constructions".[13] He defines them as structures "which have a lexical meaning as a whole, whereby

---

[13] We adopt Dobrovol'skij's terminology as it ideally reflects the continuum between lexically fixed phrasemes (phraseology) and constructions in free use (syntax).

some positions in their syntactic structure are lexically filled, while others are slots, which have to be filled [. . .]" (Dobrovol'skij 2011: 114; our translation from German). In traditional German phraseology research such constructions are called "Phraseoschablonen" (Fleischer 1997; 'phraseo-patterns') and they are assigned a special status (compare for instance Fleischer's (1997) and Burger's (2010 and 2015) descriptions). Phraseme-constructions are linguistic units at the borderline between phraseology and syntax (compare Fleischer 1997: 130–131). They have received relatively little attention, not only in research on syntax more generally, but also in phraseology. That is why Construction Grammar, which advocates a grammar-lexicon continuum, offers a more adequate model for their description.

Type 2 also includes a directional adverb and a prepositional phrase in its structure, but the preposition is always *mit* ('with'). Semantically, it also expresses motion, but as against Type 1 it is not directional motion with an endpoint, but motion which profiles a theme argument (Jacobs 2008: 15). In the first position one can find directional adverbs like *weg* ('away'), *nieder* ('down'), *her* ('towards me/us') which express the path and not the motion start as in Type 1, these adverbs are deictic (Jacobs 2008: 15). Constructions of Type 2 can be represented schematically as follows:

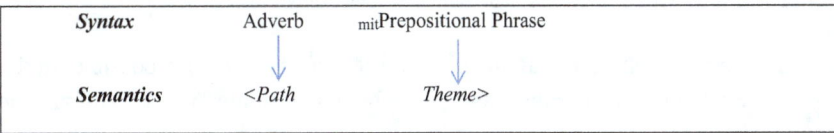

Figure 2: Abstract Type 2-construction of German verbless directives.

2.3 Type 3: [Prepositional Phrase_directional *mit*-Prepositional Phrase]

This construction type has similarities with the two other types of verbless directives. As in Type 1, the (directive) prepositional phrase expresses the goal of motion, whereas the preposition designates the path. But in contrast to Type 1, constructions of Type 3 do not start with a directional adverb. As in Type 2 the prepositional phrase introduced by *mit* cannot be substituted as it profiles the theme-argument (Jacobs 2008: 16). Here, too, the constructions are phraseme-constructions and they frequently instantiate swearing:

(27) *Zum Teufel mit den Wolfsgeschichten!*
       to the devil with the wolf stories
       'To hell with the wolf stories!'   (Sketch Engine, deTenTen13)

(28) *Zur Hölle mit dem Fernsehen, ich bin jetzt ein Kinostar.*
       to the hell with the television
       'To hell with the television, now I am a cinema star.'
                                                       (Sketch Engine, deTenTen13)

(29) *In den Müll mit solchen E-Mails.*
       in the trash with such e-mails
       'Away in the trash with such e-mails.'   (Sketch Engine, deTenTen13)

Type 3 constructions can be schematically represented as follows:

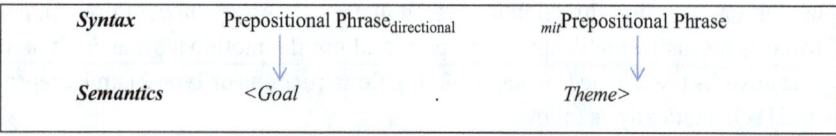

Figure 3: Abstract Type 3-construction of German verbless directives.

It is interesting to observe that mixed construction types are also possible. In the German Sketch Engine corpus, examples which instantiate Type 1 could also be found with a further prepositional phrase introduced by *mit* (see example 30). Example (31) as an instantiation of Type 3 constructions also has an additional adverb specifying the start of motion in first position:

(30) *Ab in die Küche mit Dir!!!*
       off into the kitchen with you
       'Off to the kitchen with you!!!'   (Sketch Engine, deTenTen13)

(31) *Ab in die Tonne mit dem Gesetz!*
       off into the trash can with the law
       'Off in the trash can with the law.'   (Sketch Engine, deTenTen13)

Still, such complex structures in which different construction types are combined are not so frequent in the corpus. This has to do with the function of verbless directives and the speaker's intentions: s/he chooses a short and striking way of expression with the hope to see her/his goal immediately attained. That is why we postulate – as opposed to Jacobs (2008) – a single macro-construction[14] (the highest and most schematic level), i.e. [(directional) Adverb Prepositional Phrase$_{directional}$ *mit*-Prepositional Phrase], which can be represented as follows:

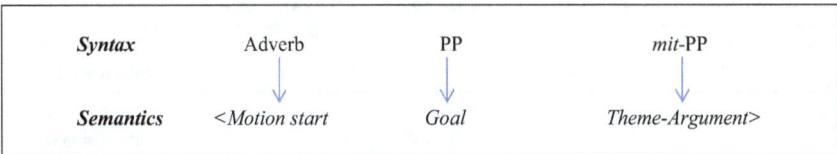

Figure 4: Abstract macro-construction [(directional) Adv PP$_{directional}$ *mit*-PP].

At the lower level (meso-constructions) the three construction types can then be distinguished. The similarities between the meso-constructions can be explained by Wittgenstein's (2001) concept of family resemblance. Meso-constructions are related structures which have common formal and functional properties and which differ very slightly from each other. The family resemblance concept has to be understood as an intransitive relation (compare Engelberg et al. (2011)), i.e. it implies that each family member is related to other (but not all) members of the same family and that not all family members have to share the same properties (Proost (2014 and 2017), Proost and Winkler (2015)).

Accordingly, Type 1 does not usually contain a prepositional phrase introduced by *mit*, but on the basis of Type 2 and 3 this prepositional phrase can appear with Type 1-constructions if the speaker wants to directly address the recipient of the message (*Ab ins Bett mit dir!*, lit. 'Off to bed with you!'). By contrast, in Type 2 and 3 the prepositional phrase introduced by *mit* expresses the theme-argument, it cannot be omitted (e.g. *Her mit dem Geld!*, lit. 'to me with the money!'/*Zur Hölle mit dem Geld!*, lit. 'to hell with the money!'). While a directional adverb fills the first syntactic slot of Type 1 and 2, in Type 3 a directional prepositional phrase is found. All three types share the directive semantics.

Table 1 contains some examples illustrating the three types of meso-constructions:

---

14 Following Traugott (2008: 236) we distinguish between different construction levels: "macro-constructions: meaning-form pairings that are defined by structure and function [. . .], meso-constructions: sets of similarly behaving specific constructions, micro-constructions: individual construction types, constructs: the empirically attested tokens [. . .]".

Table 1: Different construction types at the level of meso-constructions.

construction-type	Motion start	Path	Goal	Theme-argument
Type 1	*ab* ('off')	*zum* ('to the')	*nächsten Ziel* ('following goal')	
Type 3	–	*In den* ('in the')	*Müll* ('trash')	*mit den Klamotten* ('with the clothes')
Type 2	–	*runter* ('Down')	–	*mit den Steuern* ('with the taxes')

2.4 Network of verb-free constructions

Beyond the three construction types described by Jacobs (2008), German also has further structures without any verb but with the form [Nominal Phrase – directional Adverb], like *Hände hoch* ('hands up!'), *Finger weg* ('fingers away'), *Waffe runter* ('weapon down'). They are elliptical structures and correspond to verb-constructions (*Hände hoch halten/Finger weg nehmen/Waffe runter nehmen*, lit. 'to hold hands off/to take fingers away/to take weapon down'). These verb-free structures, however, are lexicalized in German and accordingly are entrenched constructions. Because of their reduced form, they are mostly used when the speaker expects an immediate reaction from the addressee. Such constructions can alternate with Type 2 constructions or with constructions with a verb but with hardly any meaning difference:

(32) "<u>Waffe runter auf den Boden! Waffe runter</u>", schreit Gößling.
      weapon down on the floor! Weapon down
      '"Weapon down on the floor! Weapon down", shouts Gößling.'
                                          (Sketch Engine, deTenTen13)

(33) *Eine Bewegung und ich leg ihn um.* <u>*Runter mit der Waffe*</u>.
                                     Down with the weapon
      'One movement and I knock him down. Down with the weapon.'
                                          (Sketch Engine, deTenTen13)

(34) *[. . .] er stoppte, als Miles seine Waffe lud.* "<u>*Leg die Waffe runter*</u>!"
                                                      Lay the weapon down
      '[. . .] he stopped when Miles loaded his weapon. "Put the weapon down!"'
                                                       (Sketch Engine, deTenTen13)

(35) *Hände hoch Mister Obama – Hände hoch für Waffenkontrolle.*
　　　　　　　　　　　　　　　　　　　Hands up for weapon control
　　　'Hands up Mister Obama – Hands up for the weapon control.'
　　　　　　　　　　　　　　　　　　　　　　　　(Sketch Engine, deTenTen13)

(36) *Hoch mit den Händen, lasst uns sehen, dass ihr gute Laune habt.*
　　　High with the hands
　　　'Hands up, let us see, that you are in good mood.' (Sketch Engine, deTenTen13)

(37) *Geht auch wenn alle am Boden liegen und die Hände hoch halten!*
　　　　　　　　　　　　　　　　　　　　　　　　the hands high hold
　　　'Works too when all on the floor lie and hold the hands up!'
　　　　　　　　　　　　　　　　　　　　　　　　(Sketch Engine, deTenTen13)

In the network of verbless directives the above quoted macro-construction [(directional) Adverb Prepositional Phrase$_{directional}$ *mit*-Prepositional Phrase] takes a central position as the prototypical verbless directive. By contrast, the construction [Nominal Phrase – directional Adverb] (*Hände hoch!* lit. 'Hands high') is the peripheral representative as it can be instantiated with or without a verb. Further peripheral representatives are directional adverbs which appear alone, e.g. *aufwärts* 'upwards', *abwärts* 'downwards', *hinauf* 'upwards', *runter* 'downwards', *rein/herein*[15] 'inside', *raus/hinaus* 'outside', and *nach rechts/links* 'to the right/left'.

Prepositional phrases [PP$_{directional}$] (*zum Flughafen!* lit. 'to the airport!'), which can be used alone belong to the same category of examples. Such short phrases have the function of adverbial complements. Although both constructions can be considered to be elliptical structures (E.g. *Fahren wir dahin/zum Flughafen!* lit.'(Let us) drive thereto/to the airport!' vs. *dahin/zum Flughafen!* lit. 'Thereto/to the airport!'), they are also part of the network of verbless directives. Both directional adverbs and prepositional phrases with directional semantics are realized in a reduced form to express directive speech acts (see Section 3.1). This is possible because they are also entrenched. The prototype and the peripheral constructions are related to each other by the links [+ directive semantics] and [- verb]. The following figure represents the network.

---

[15] *Hin* and *her* are particles which express the speaker's point of view or perspective: *hin* expresses a movement away from the speaker and *her* towards the speaker. As we see in the examples, they can be combined with prepositions which add another orientational aspect. They can also appear as reduced form *r* before the preposition, e.g. *rein, raus*.

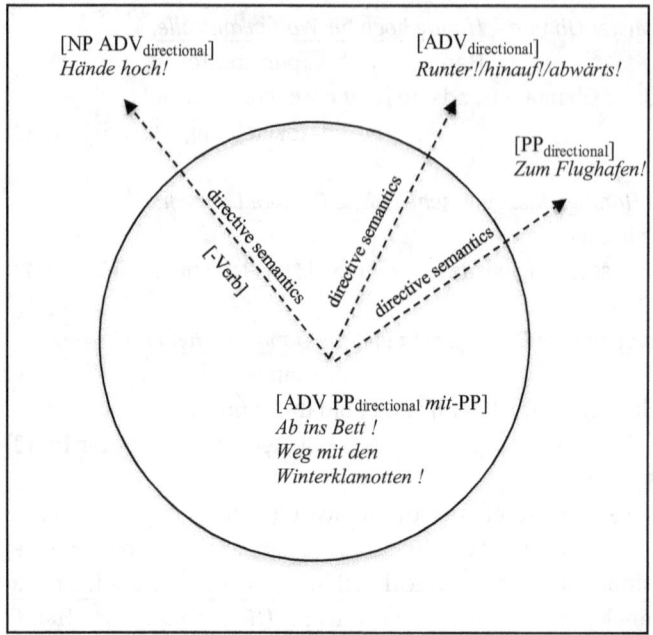

Figure 5: Network of verbless directives.

3 A contrastive (German-Italian) description of verbless directives

This section focuses on the question of how verbless directives are realized in Italian as opposed to German. This issue is far from trivial – especially if we take into account typological differences between Romance and Germanic languages. The differences depend on the linguistic realization of the path of motion. In German – like in other Germanic and some Slavic languages – the path of motion is often expressed with satellites, in Romance languages it is mainly realized with a full verb (Talmy 2000). This insight allows to explain why in German a sentence like *Wollen wir rübergehen/hinübergehen?* (lit. 'Do we want to go over?') with *rüber* or *hinüber* as separable satellites is preferred over a semantically similar sentence with a full verb *Wollen wir die Straße überqueren?*[16] (lit. 'Do we want to cross the

---

[16] The particle *über* is not separable in the verb *überqueren* and accordingly it does not function as a satellite.

street?'). The same sentence in Italian, for instance, would have the full verb *attraversare* ('to cross'), e.g. *Vogliamo attraversare (la strada)?/attraversiamo?*

As a general tendency we claim that satellites are not favored in Romance languages (Narasimhan et al. 2012: 3). The various constructionist approaches have different views on how constructions have to be described and operationalized in a cross-linguistic perspective. In Croft's Radical Construction Grammar (2001) constructions as well as syntactic categories are considered to be language-specific. Consequently, it is impossible to postulate some constructions as tertium comparationis for a cross-linguistic analysis. By contrast, Boas (2010) argues in favor of a construction-based cross-linguistic exploration (for an overview see Boas and Ziem (2018)). It can be expected that constructions within the same typological family present more similarities and as a result that their comparison is easier.

On that account, the comparison of constructions between German and Romance languages can be more difficult as there is no 1:1 correspondence between the constructions in the two languages. That is why this study starts from the directive illocutionary speech act and explores how this speech act is realized respectively in German and Italian with the aim of identifying which constructions can be interpreted as functional cross-linguistic constructional equivalents in some specific pragmatic contexts. Thus, the analysis does not focus on all possible verbless directives in Italian in detail. Still, we can quote the following most common verbless directive structures in Italian:

- [NP ADV$_{directional}$], e.g. *Mani in alto!* 'Hands up';
- [Adverb Prepositional Phrase$_{directional}$], e.g. *Presto all'aeroporto!* 'Quickly to the airport!',
- or reversely as [Prepositional Phrase$_{directional}$ Adverb], e.g. *All'aeroporto, presto!* 'To the airport, quickly!'

A precise description of Italian verbless directives with a focus on similarities and differences with other languages still constitutes an issue for further research.

3.1 A contrastive study on constructional preferences

In order to compare constructions from the point of view of their function across different languages, we present the results of a small-scale contrastive survey with examples from comics in German and Italian. We selected this type of literature because the language used is compact and it reflects oral language, espe-

cially direct speech.[17] That is why we expected to find many examples of verbless directives in this compact style. Here is the list of German comics we consulted:
– Hergé (1998), *Tim und Struppi – Die Krabbe mit den goldenen Scheren*.
– Jacobs, Edgar P. (1980), *Die Abenteuer von Blake und Mortimer. Die Diamanten-Affäre*

with the Italian counterparts,
– Hergé (1999), *Le avventure di Tintin. Il granchio d'oro*.
– Jacobs, Edgar P. (1993), *Blake e Mortimer. Il caso del Collier*.

Both the German and Italian versions of the same comics are translations of the original Belgian French version (comics have their origin in Belgium). This means that we compare two translations of the same original text. The examples were collected manually by going through the German version and looking for the Italian equivalents in the Italian version. We proceeded this way because we expected more verbless directives in German than in Italian. As a countercheck we also went through the French original version and looked for verbless directives as well which we recorded to find the equivalent translations in the German and Italian versions.

Our comparison of the German and Italian texts reveals some interesting tendencies.[18] In the German versions of Hergé's (1998) comics we found 13 examples of verbless directives and in Jacobs' (1980) comics 17 examples, mainly instantiated as Type 1, i.e. constructions consisting of an introductory adverb and a prepositional phrase in which the preposition expresses the path of motion. Six examples contain the modal adverb *schnell* ('quick') with a following prepositional phrase which has a directive semantics. A prompt reaction is expected from the addressee.[19]

(38) Germ. *Schnell! Hinter die Düne!. . . und absitzen!* (Hergé 1998: 38)
         quickly behind the dune
         'Quickly! Behind the dune! . . . and wait!'

---

17 For the characteristics of the language of comics, see among others Frahm (2010), Grünewald (2000), and Lenk and Suomela-Härm (eds.) (2016).
18 In the framework of this article, we cannot deal with translation strategies. For issues dealing with "positive and negative politeness" we can refer to Antoniou (2014), and for cultural differences between translated texts in the perspective of Cognitive Linguistics to Rojo & Ibarretxe-Antuñanu (eds.) (2013).
19 Sometimes this modal adverb and the prepositional phrase are separated by a comma or an exclamation mark.

(39) Germ. *Schnell, ins Auto!* (Jacobs 1980: 19)
 Quickly into the car
 'Quickly, in the car!'

(40) Germ. *Zum Hafen, Struppi!. . . Schnell zum Hafen. . .!* (Hergé 1998: 11)
 To the harbor Milou quickly to the harbor
 'To the harbor, Milou!. . . Quickly to the harbor. . .!'

The corresponding Italian equivalents for (38)-(40) also contain verbless directives, instantiated as [Adverb Prepositional Phrase$_{directional}$] (examples 38' and 39'), or, reversely as [Prepositional Phrase$_{directional}$ Adverb] (40'):

(38') It. *Presto: dietro le dune! e a terra!* (Hergé 1999: 36)

(39') It. *Presto in macchina!* (Jacobs 1993: 47)

(40') It. *Al porto, Milù. . . al porto presto!* (Hergé 1999: 9)

But although the Italian equivalents are – just like in German – verbless directives, a major difference between the two languages can be observed. In German, directionality is expressed in a more differentiated way than in Romance languages. On the one hand, this is possible because German has different prepositions which allow for a distinction between static processes vs. dynamic motion towards a goal. E.g., the preposition *bei* ('at/with') in *Er wohnt bei seinem Vater* (lit. 'He lives at his father') expresses a state, whereas the preposition *zu* ('to/towards') in *Er geht zu seinem Vater* (lit. 'He goes to his father') is used for a dynamic motion towards someone (= the father).[20]

In contrast, Italian has just one preposition, namely *a* for both conceptualizations, as illustrated by example (40'). The disambiguation takes place based on additional context, i.e. *presto!* (40'). On the other hand, the German morphosyntactic case-marking sustains expressions for different facets of motion events with the distinction between accusative and dative cases. This is particularly relevant for so-called "two-way prepositions" (Smith 1995), which can be used either with the accusative case for the expression of an incipient dynamic motion along a path and towards a goal or the dative case for locations or more static processes where no telic motion is implied (see also Section 2 and Willems (2011) or Willems

---

[20] For studies about German prepositions, see also Di Meola (2000), Breindl (1989), and Grießhaber (2007).

et al. (2018)). This explains, e.g., why the nominal phrases in (38) and (39) have an accusative case.

Verbless structures in the German example in (41) have varying equivalents in Italian, namely an imperative form in the second person plural in the first part and also a verbless directive in the second part (41').[21] This shows that verbless structures can alternate with structures with a verb in one and the same language:

(41) Germ. *An die Knarren, und jeder an seinen Platz.* (Jacobs 1980: 58)
 to the guns and everybody at his place
 'To the guns, and everybody at his place.'

(41') It. *Prendete le armi e ciascuno al suo posto!* (Jacobs 1993: 58)
 take the weapons and everybody at his place
 'Take the weapons and everybody at his place'.

The contrastive analysis of the examples reveals that the Italian versions mainly contain constructions with verbs, often in the imperative form – which does not surprise, because it is one of the possibilities to express directive speech acts. Most imperative forms in the Italian equivalents are in the first person plural, as illustrated by the following examples,

(42) Germ. *Fertig!. . . Schnell in Deckung* (Hergé 1998: 19)
 ready quickly in cover
 'Ready! . . . Quickly under shelter'

(42') It. *Ecco fatto, mettiamioci al riparo!* (Hergé 1999: 17)
 this done, let us put ourselves under shelter
 'This is done, let us go under shelter!'

(43) Germ. *Schnell!. . . Wieder nach oben. . .!* (Hergé 1998: 20)
 quickly again to upwards
 'Quickly!. . . Let us go up again. . .!'

(43') It. *presto! Risaliamo!* (Hergé 1999: 18)
 quickly we go up
 'Quickly! Let us go upwards!'

---

[21] The use of the verbal form in the Italian equivalent can also be a pure translation coincidence, a verbless structure like *Alle armi e ciascuno al suo posto!* could have been acceptable as well.

The imperative form in the first person plural in (42′) and (43′) is directed to an addressee, but it implies that the speaker him-/herself feels involved in the action.

The preference for short, compact verbless structures in German is also obvious with the long list of German examples which do not contain prototypical verbless directives in the narrow sense, as they consist only of a directional adverb. As explained above, these structures can be considered as peripheral representatives of the network of verbless directives, as they are often the reduced realizations of directive speech acts. They are interesting, because they illustrate the typological difference between German and Romance structures for the expression of motion events:

(44) Germ. *Oh! Eine Leiter!... Hinab!* (Jacobs 1980: 28)
              oh a ladder downwards
              'Oh! A ladder!... Downwards!'

(44') It.   *Oh! Una scaletta! Scendiamo!* (Jacobs 1993: 28)
              oh a ladder we go down
              'Oh! A ladder!... Let us go down!...'

(45) Germ. *Weiter!...* (Jacobs 1980: 47)
              farther
              'Go on!'

(45') It.   *Proseguiamo!* (Jacobs 1993: 47)
              we go on
              'Let us go on!'.

As we can see, the Italian equivalents are again structures with imperative forms in the first person plural. This is also the case with the following example, but the semantics of the equivalents differs from the meaning of motion events:

(46) Germ. *Schnell, hinterher!* (Jacobs 1980: 23)
              quickly behind
              'Quickly, after him/her/them!'

(46') It.   *Presto, andiamo a vedere!* (Jacobs 1993: 23)
              Quickly, we go to see
              'Quickly, let us go and see!...'

While the German instantiation expresses the idea of running after someone, the Italian equivalent has to do with looking at what is happening. Another option for expressing directive speech acts is in terms of a complex verbal form with a modal verb with an infinitive, as illustrated by the Italian version (47′):

(47)   Germ.   *Zuerst zum Sicherungskasten...* (Jacobs 1980: 9)
                first to the fuse box
                'First to the fuse box...'

(47′) It.   *Dobbiamo trovare il quadro elettrico!* (Jacobs 1993: 9)
                we must find the board electrical
                'We must find the electrical board!'

The Italian equivalent of (47′) does not express any motion like in German, but more the necessity to 'find' the fuse box. The modal verb form *dobbiamo* ('we must') expresses the absolute necessity to find the electrical board. It is interesting to realize that the translators of the comic strips under study sometimes become creative instead of sticking to the French original structure *D'abord: Trouver le tableau!...* (Jacobs 1991: 9) ('First: Find the board!...'). Instead they often adapt the translation according to the idiosyncrasies of the target language.

In our collection of German examples we found only one single instance of Type 2 constructions which is also realized with a verbless structure [Adverb Prepositional Phrase$_{directional}$] in the Italian equivalent:

(48)   Germ.   *Raus mit dir, du lausiger Bettler!* (Hergé 1998: 53)
                outside with you, you lousy beggar
                'Out of here, you lousy beggar!'

(48′) It.   *Fuori di qui, schifoso mendicante!* (Hergé 1999: 51)
                out of here lousy beggar
                'Out of here, lousy beggar!'

The small amount of Type 2 instances does not surprise, as this construction type is a very idiosyncratic and well-entrenched construction in German which does not have similar counterparts in Romance languages. This observation also applies to Type 3 constructions for which we did not find any instantiation in the comics.

The contrastive analysis of the examples collected in the translated versions of both comics has brought some evidence in favor of the hypothesis that German uses verbless directives more frequently, whereas Italian favors structures with verbal forms – mostly in the imperative.[22] But the different structures (with or without verb) realize the same pragmatic function of directive speech acts. Accordingly, the German and Italian equivalents can be considered to be parallel constructions for the same lexical and pragmatic meaning. This observation sustains Croft's (2001) insight that constructions are language-specific and that they are often realized with various syntactic structures in different languages.

3.2 Learning issues related to verbless directives

As explained in the introduction of this paper, to learn a foreign language at an intermediate or more advanced level means to acquire various structures and different ways of expression. Accordingly, this implies that learners should be able to use verbless directives as alternatives to constructions with verbal forms like imperative forms, infinitives or modal verbs. But in view of the typological differences described in the above sections, learners of German whose mother tongue belongs to Romance languages cannot be expected to use verbless directives preferentially when it comes to express directive speech acts.[23] In order to confirm this expectation we started an empirical contrastive study with 50 Italian master students of German at the University of Milano[24] (proficiency level B2-C1 in the Common European Framework of Reference for Languages (CEFR)) and with 15 master students of German language and letters with a specialization in German as a foreign language at the University of Regensburg[25] with the aim to see if the Italian-speaking learners used fewer verbless constructions than the German students. Both test groups received the same test consisting of sets of 3 to 4 pictures extracted from the following comics:

Hergé (1967a), *Tim und Struppi, Tim in Tibet*. Hamburg: Carlsen Verlag.
Hergé (1967b), *Tim und Struppi, König Ottokars Zepter*. Hamburg: Carlsen Verlag.
Hergé (1970), *Tim und Struppi, Kohle an Bord*. Hamburg: Carlsen Verlag.

---

[22] As discussed above, this has to do with the missing morpho-syntactic cases and different prepositions in Romance languages.
[23] Some studies in foreign language learning demonstrate that even constructions with imperative verbal forms are produced much later in the process of learning a foreign language. This can be explained by the sociological and psychological background in relation with expressions of politeness (Berretta 1995: 334). Compare among others Terrasi-Haufe (2004) for German and Berretta (1995) for Italian.
[24] We thank the master students of the Department of "Languages and Cultures for International Communication and Cooperation" at the University of Milano, who took part in the tests.
[25] We thank Dr. Svenja Brünger who conducted the tests with the German students.

Only picture sets representing motion events with possible directive speech acts were selected. In some of the bubbles accompanying the pictures, the text was deleted and each empty bubble received a number from 1 to 8. These were bubbles where we could expect a verbless directive. The students were asked to write sentences for the empty bubbles (1 to 8) on an extra sheet of paper. They did not receive any instructions, just the comment: "Please write sentences for the empty bubbles; think of the concise style of comics". Table 2 presents one example of a picture set with examples of sentences written by the Italian students.

Table 2: Test 1: Example of a picture set and sentences by the Italian students.

Example of the picture sets	Examples of sentences written by the students for picture 3
The picture set number 3 in our survey was taken from Hergé (1967b: 15). The first picture represents Tintin on the phone who hears a call for help. In the second picture you see Tintin putting on his coat and rushing outside. The third picture shows Tintin and Snowy rushing on the street. In the second picture, the words in the bubble were replaced by number 3.	laufen wir! Komm doch schnell! Ich muss mich beeilen, Raus! Schnell sie ist in Gefahr! 'Ich komme gleich, Ihnen zu helfen!

As can be seen from the examples in Table 2, the students mainly used constructions with verbs, verbless directives are hardly realized. Table 3 summarizes the results for the 8 sentences written by the 50 Italian-speaking students:

Table 3: Results of the sentence writing test for empty bubbles by Italian learners.

	Hits	Frequency	Examples of sentences written by the students
Verbless directive	5	1,3%	Raus mit dir! die Treppe runter; Schnell zum Flughafen! Los, runter in den Keller
Verbless directive without adverb	1	0,3%	Zu den Waffen!
Incorrect verbless directive	1	0,3%	Schnell! an der Polizeistation
Only adverb	8	0,2%	Vorwärts; Schnell; Raus!; Los!
Construction with imperative	158	39,6%	Renn nicht weg!gehen wir! Folge diesem Auto; Komm mit mir! Laufen wir schnell!
Construction with infinitive	0	0,0%	

Table 3 (continued)

	Hits	Frequency	Examples of sentences written by the students
Construction with modal verb + infinitive	74	18,5%	Ich muss weggehen; Wir müssen uns verstecken! Ich muss zum Kommissariat laufen; Wir müssen schnell sein! Schnell, wir müssen ihn schnappen!
Construction without verb (ellipses)	13	3,3%	Hinter mir; Ruhe; da lang;
Other constructions	138	34,6%	Vorsicht, es ist glatt Hast du keine Angst? Ich nehme den Dieb! Er ist dort, ich bin mir sicher; Wir haben keine Zeit zu verlieren!
No answer	1	0,3%	
TOTAL	399	100,0%	

As Table 3 shows, there is a clear tendency with the Italian learners to use imperatives (39,6%) or a modal verb with an infinitive (18,5%) to express directive speech acts. Infinitives are not used at all. Verbless directives are hardly used (1,3%) – in spite of the hint given to the students about the conciseness of the comic language. One verbless directive was used with a mistake (0,3%), e.g. *Schnell an der Polizeistation* ('Quickly to the police station') in which the dative case is incorrect. Others had no introductory adverb (0,3%), e.g. *Zu den Waffen* ('to the weapons'); 2,0% of the sentences written by the students were simple adverbs like *Vorwärts!* ('Forwards!'). As we have seen, these, too, can be considered to be peripheral representatives of the class 'verbless directives'.

To get a baseline that allows us to compare the results from learners with those of native speakers, the test was also performed with the German students. Table 4 summarizes the results by native German speakers and lists some of the sentences produced by them.

Table 4: Results of the sentence writing test for empty bubbles by German natives.

	Number of examples	Frequency	Examples by German students
Verbless directive	14	11,7%	Rein da! Schnell in den Wagen! Raus hier! Schnell ins Auto! Los, hier entlang!
Verbless directive without adverb	0	0,0%	/

Table 4 (continued)

	Number of examples	Frequency	Examples by German students
Incorrect verbless directive	0	0,0%	/
Only adverb	8	6,7%	Los Struppi! Halt stopp! Los, weg hier!
Construction with imperative	37	30,8%	Na warte! Beeil dich! He, warte doch auf mich! Sei vorsichtig! Versteckt euch!
Construction with infinitive	1	0,8%	Halt! Stehen bleiben!
Construction with modal verb + infinitive	12	10,0%	Wir müssen ihm helfen! Wir müssen ihn verfolgen.
Other constructions without verb	20	16,7	Stopp, Sie da! Ich doch nicht! Immer das Gleiche mit ihm...
Other constructions	28	23,3%	Also, ich werde mir Zeit lassen. Hoffentlich ist es nicht entwischt! Wo hast du den her? Das sieht doch ganz einfach aus!
No answer	0	0,0%	/
TOTAL	120	100,0%	

A direct comparison of the results by the Italian learners and by the German native speakers (see Table 5 hereunder) leads to insightful observations.

Table 5: Results by Italian learners and German natives in comparison.

	Native speakers		Learners	
	Number of examples	Frequency	Number of examples	Frequency
Verbless directive	14	11,7%	5	1,3%
Verbless directive without adverb	0	0,0%	1	0,3%
Incorrect verbless directive	0	0,0%	1	0,3%
Only adverb	8	6,7%	8	0,2%
Construction with imperative	37	30,8%	158	39,6%
Construction with infinitive	1	0,8%	0	0,0%
Construction with modal verb + infinitive	12	10,0%	74	18,5%
Construction without verb (ellipses)	20	16,7%	0	0,0%
Other constructions	28	23,3%	151	37,9%
No answer	0	0,0%	1	0,3%
TOTAL	120	100,0%	399	100,0%

The most striking difference in Table 5 can be observed with the verbless directives: 11,7% of the sentences produced by native speakers are verbless directives – compared with 1,3% produced by the learners of German. Our hypothesis is thus confirmed that verbless directives belong to the natural and authentic ways of expression by German natives in the context of comics. It can further be concluded that the mere use of an adverb for the expression of directive motion events is also favored among speakers of German (6,7% of the sentences by native speakers as opposed to only 0,2% by learners). Constructions with imperative verbal forms are a favorite way of expression in both groups which does not surprise as such structures correspond to the most common way of expressing directives (see introduction). Native speakers produced 30,8% of sentences in the imperative, learners with 39,6% even more. Alternative constructions with a modal verb + an infinitive are also common with native speakers (10%) and with learners (18,5%).

A comparison of the results by native speakers and those by learners also confirms our hypothesis that native speakers express themselves with a greater variation of constructions. Native speakers also produced many constructions without a verb (16,7%), which do not correspond to verbless directives. There were no such sentences by learners. The use of elliptical structures presupposes a good proficiency of the foreign language as they constitute a deviation from the norm. Consequently, our hypothesis that learners whose mother tongue is a Romance language will use verbless directives less frequently is confirmed. Because in some contexts it can be pragmatically more adequate to use verbless directives than in the context of other structures it is recommended to teach these structures more explicitly to our students. The following section describes some possibilities for teaching verbless directives more effectively.

4 Learning and teaching strategies

This section deals with the question of how learners can get used to foreign structures – in this specific case verbless directives – and how they can be instructed to use them in an appropriate context. In the scientific literature on psycholinguistics a method based on the principles of syntactic or structural priming has recently turned out to yield positive results (see among others Hartsuiker et al. 2004; Loebell and Bock 2003; Scheepers and Corley 2000). The basic assumption of this methodology is that "speakers tend to repeat the structure just encountered" (Gries 2005: 365). This means that by first reading or hearing a sentence with a specific structure, learners will probably re-use or echo this same structure in the sentences they produce immediately thereafter. The priming methodology is based on the repetition of structures (Loebell and Bock 2003) and on memory processes (Bernolet and Hartsuiker 2018). Similar structures are filled with various lexical material, in this sense syntactic priming meets entrenchment and frequency assumptions of Construction Grammar. More specifically, and

> [. . .] contrary to syntactic acquisition in L1, L2 acquisition in late learners begins with the learning of lexical representations without firm connections to abstract syntactic information. These item-specific lexical representations become more abstract with increasing proficiency, with abstraction taking place across words within the L2, and eventually also between languages. [. . .] [A]cross the learning trajectory, L2 representations become more and more integrated with existing L1 representations. (Bernolet and Hartsuiker 2018: 211)

Studies in syntactic priming have focused on different languages and experiments have been conducted according to various paradigms. To name just a few which are relevant for our analysis, Scheepers and Corley (2000) study priming effects in the order of arguments in German ditransitives in different configurations, i.e. the dative object before the accusative object, or the contrary order, namely the accusative object before the dative object, as well as monotransitives.

They show that the order of the arguments in the target language very much depends on the order in the prime. German-speaking participants were asked to complete sentence fragments, i.e. add a missing argument, either in the accusative or in the dative. By contrast, Loebell and Bock (2003) studied the alternation between prepositional vs. double-object datives and transitives, seeking some evidence for syntactic priming between German and English in a picture description task. Such an experimental design has the advantage of not influencing the learner by presenting pictures for the target, which have nothing to do with the semantics of the prime. It thereby allows one to focus on the syntactic structure. That is why we adopted a similar methodology in our experiments. This methodology turned out to be successful in Loebell and Bock's (2003) experiments in that it found priming effects between alternative forms of English datives and their German equivalents.

In contrast, priming effects could not be observed for the active vs. passive alternations. While they also use picture description tasks for their experiments, Hartsuiker et al. (2004) further deal with learning issues which can be fostered by priming processes. They focus on the language pairs Spanish and English and the linguistic phenomenon active vs. passive sentences with or without objects. Their experiment involves descriptions of English target pictures by Spanish speakers. They come to the conclusion that English passives are used more frequently when following a Spanish passive sentence.

Inspired by these experiments based on structural priming, we designed an empirical study (Test 2) with the aim to test whether this methodology can also foster the learning and use of verbless directives. The participants were the same group of 50 Italian master students of German as in the pretest (see Section 3.2). The test took place three weeks after Test 1, but this time in the class-room, completely unexpectedly. The teacher first handed out 2 pages with the following information:

Table 6: Instructional document for the students before Test 2.

- First read the examples:
  Schnell in den Keller!
  Ins Boot bitte!
  Ab ins Bett!
  Runter vom Sofa!
  Rauf auf den Berg!
  Weg mit dem Müll!
  Los, ins Wasser!
- Look at the pictures of comic strips and compare the structures
  (here were reproduced 6 contrasting picture sets German-Italian)

This second part of the document contained 6 sets of contrastive Italian-German pictures (which we cannot reproduce here because of a lack of space and copyright issues), representing the same scene. In the German version a verbless directive was used, e.g. *Hier hinein ... !* (Hergé 1998: 56) (lit. 'Here within ... '). By contrast, the same picture found in the Italian version contained an Italian verb-framed structure, e.g. *Entriamo qui! Ci sono addosso!* (Hergé 1999: 54) (lit. 'Let us enter here! They are on us!'). The students did not receive any instruction from the teacher, but should look at the two pages by themselves. After about 10 minutes the teacher asked the students to return the documents. The students then received the same test they had done as a pretest (see Test 1 in Section 3.2). Again, they had to write sentences for the 8 empty bubbles of Test 1. The results of Test 2 as posttest are summarized in Table 7.

Table 7: Results of the sentence writing test for empty bubbles by Italian learners (Test 2).

	Hits	Frequency
Verbless directive	123	30,8%
Verbless directive without adverb	66	16,5%
Incorrect verbless directive	47	11,8%
Only adverb	3	0,8%
Construction with imperative	129	32,3%

Table 7 (continued)

	Hits	Frequency
Construction with infinitive	5	1,3%
Construction with modal verb + infinitive	0	0,0%
Construction without verb (ellipses)	0	0,0%
Other constructions	2	0,5%
No answer	24	6,0%
TOTAL	399	100,0%

The results show a strong improvement in the use of verbless directives (30,8%). If we add to this figure the incorrect verbless directives (11,8%, e.g. *Los nach Hafen,* 'Off to harbor')[26] and the verbless directives without introductory adverb (16,5%, e.g. *Auf den Berg,* 'on the mountain') we get an overall result of 59,1% of verbless directives with satellites in Test 2, this corresponds to more than half of the sentences written by the students. The overall use of verbless directives including the incorrect ones and the ones with a missing introductory adverb in Test 1 was only 1,9%. But a comparison of the results from Test 1 as pretest and Test 2 as posttest bring some more interesting observations (see Table 8).

Table 8: Comparison of the results of Test 1 and Test 2 by Italian learners.

	Frequency Test 1 (Pretest)	Frequency Test 2 (Posttest)
Verbless directive	1,3%	30,8%
Verbless directive without adverb	0,3%	16,5%
Incorrect verbless directive	0,3%	11,8%
Only adverb	2,0%	0,8%
Construction with imperative	39,6%	32,3%
Construction with infinitive	0,0%	1,3%
Construction with modal verb + infinitive	18,5%	0,0%
Construction without verb (ellipses)	3,3%	0,0%
Other constructions	34,6%	0,5%
No answer	0,3%	6,0%
TOTAL	100,0%	100,0%

---

26 The mistakes were mostly morpho-syntactic in nature, i.e. the correct selection of the preposition or the case, e.g. *Los, nach dem Hafen/zu die Polizei* ('Go, to the harbour/to the police); *ab hinter dem Haus!* ('Off behind the house'). Only three students produced sentences with syntactic mistakes, e.g. *schnell ab!, Los auf!* and so on.

Imperative forms are used quite frequently both in the pretest (39,6%) and the posttest (32,3%). Constructions with a modal verb with an infinitive completely disappeared in the posttest, whereas they appeared in 18,5 % of the sentences in the pretest. A similar trend can be observed regarding the use of declarative or interrogative sentences. Also, consider the use of other constructions, which were used in 34,6 % of cases in the pretest and only 0,5% in constructions of the posttest (e.g., *Sollten wir hinter dem Haus gehen?* 'Should we go behind the house?', incorrect dative case; *Los, gehts* 'Go, goes it' incorrect forms). Interestingly, the number of cases where no answer was given at all increased from 0,3% in the pretest to 6,0 % in the posttest. This can perhaps be explained by the fact that some learners did not really recognize from the instructional document they received before the posttest the grammatical topic and the new structures. Perhaps they were quite confused when having to write down sentences.

The progress between all verbless directives in the pretest (1,9%) and posttest (59,1%) is so significant that it does not even have to be statistically validated. But, in spite of the good results we have to express some reservations about the methodology based on structural priming: First, experiments based on structural priming are mostly conducted in laboratories (see for instance the studies by Loebell and Bock 2003 or Hartsuiker et al. 2004), which was not the case with our students who were in a classroom setting. Second, in a strict sense, structural priming experiments are performed with students receiving (hearing or reading) one single sentence with a specific structure at a time, then seeing a picture depicting another scene which requires a different type of vocabulary.

Our experiment was performed differently: (1) Together with the instructional document our students first received a whole list of examples with the same structure for motion events. (2) They further received instructions saying that they had to pay attention to the structural contrasts between the pictures in their mother tongue and the corresponding ones in the foreign language. In this sense, they were actively influenced to metalinguistically reflect on the structures. (3) Third – and this is probably the main limitation of our empirical study – the posttest was performed immediately after the students had been confronted with the list of structures and the pictures illustrating the contrasts in both languages.

At this stage we cannot be sure that they actively integrated the knowledge of verbless directives and will remember them – and even more will use them on a regular basis in a few months' time. Therefore, a long-term posttest is needed to get more conclusive results. Of course, exercises allowing to practice the new structures – more specifically structures which are not so present in their native language, e.g. verbless directives – are a necessity. It is hard to imagine that learners fully understand and internalize verbless directives in their morpho-syntactic and pragmatic complexity simply on the basis of structural priming and are later able to use them actively.

5 Conclusions

In this chapter we proposed a network of verbless directives in which the prototypical construction [Adverb Prepositional Phrase$_{directional}$ *mit*-Prepositional Phrase] holds a central position. Verbless directives are concise structures which express directive speech acts and they can be used as an alternative to imperative constructions. In the literature, they have been analyzed by different theoretical approaches, in most cases they are considered to be elliptical structures. By contrast, the constructionist approach allows us to analyze them as autonomous constructions with a form that is paired with a specific function and meaning.

Even if verbless directives appear to be a rather marginal phenomenon in German, they should be mastered by intermediate or advanced learners – at least in a passive way. Students should be able to understand them pragmatically, as verbless directives frequently appear in specific text sorts, e.g. in advertisements. To acquire such constructions can be more difficult if they are not common in the learners' native language. Goldberg's constructionist approach constitutes an ideal model for the study of verbless directives as it makes it possible to generalize and to advocate schematic constructions which facilitate the learning of structures. Moreover, the entrenchment principle allows to define the constructions for the expression of a specific speech act which are idiosyncratic in a specific language. Therefore, verbless directives should be introduced in language pedagogy and discussed in a simple way in the framework of this Construction Grammar model.

The methodology based on syntactic priming also proved to be useful. Our experiment with Italian-speaking learners of German demonstrated that syntactic priming can lead to some positive learning outcomes. At the same time it is important to keep in mind that these positive results should be validated in a follow-up long-term study as German verbless directives are a complex linguistic phenomenon. They are complex morpho-syntactic constructions and to use them properly, learners need a very good knowledge of German grammar. They must know which adverb and/or preposition should be used in the schematic construction. They must also further understand the differences between morpho-syntactic cases in German and they have to be able to select the proper case after two-way prepositions.

Consequently, mastering the use of verbless directives is more than about mnemonic processes. Thus, we consider the priming methodology to offer a good start in the right direction, but we have to keep in mind that more explanations and exercises are needed – as one knows from the mastering of other phenomena in foreign language learning – so that learners will be able to use these structures in the correct grammatical and pragmatic context. In short: Structural priming is important, but as the proverb says "Skill comes with practice!"

References

Antoniou, Maria. 2014. Politesse et traduction: le cas du couple grec modern et français. *Language for international Communication: Linking interdisciplinary Perspectives*. University of Latvia. Faculty of Humanities, Department of English Studies and Centre for Applied Linguistics. 234–261.

Bernolet, Sarah & Robert J. Hartsuiker. 2018. Syntactic representations in late learners of a second language. A learning trajectory. In David Miller, Fatih Bayram, Jason Rothman & Ludovica Serratrice (eds.), *Bilingual Cognition and Language: The state of the science across its subfields*, 205–224. Amsterdam: John Benjamins.

Berretta, Monica. 1995. Imperativi in italiano: il ruolo della marcatezza pragmatica e morfologica nell'apprendimento di L2. In Anna Giacalone Ramat & Grayia Crocco Galèas (eds.), *From Pragmatics to Syntax. Modality in Second Language Acquisition*, 333–348. Tübingen: Gunter Narr.

Boas, Hans C. 2010. Comparing constructions across languages. In Hans C. Boas (ed.), *Contrastive Studies in Construction Grammar*, 1–20. Amsterdam/Philadelphia: John Benjamins.

Boas, Hans C. & Alexander Ziem. 2018. Constructing a constructicon for German. Empirical, theoretical, and methodological issues. In Benjamin Lyngfelt, Lars Borin, Kyoko Ohara, Tiago Timponi Torrent (eds.), *Constructicography Constructicon development across languages*, 183–228. Amsterdam: John Benjamins.

Bolinger, Dwight. 1968. Entailment and the meaning of structures. *Glossa* 2 (2). 119–127.

Breindl, Eva. 1989. *Präpositionalobjekte und Präpositionalobjektsätze im Deutschen*.Tübingen: Niemeyer.

Burger, Harald. 2010. *Phraseologie. Eine Einführung am Beispiel des Deutschen*. 4. Auflage. Berlin: Erich Schmidt.

Burger, Harald. 2015. *Phraseologie. Eine Einführung am Beispiel des Deutschen*. 5. Auflage. Berlin: Erich Schmidt.

Croft, William. 2001. *Radical Construction Grammar: Syntactic Theory in Typological Perspective*. Oxford: Oxford University Press.

De Knop, Sabine. 2019. Verblose Direktiva im Deutschen und Französischen. Eine kontrastive und konstruktionistische Untersuchung. In Barbara Lübke & Elsa Liste Lamas (eds.), *Raumrelationen im Deutschen: Kontrast, Erwerb und Übersetzung*, 47–67. Tübingen: Stauffenburg Verlag.

De Knop, Sabine. 2021. Von der Konstruktionsbeschreibung zum Konstruktionslernen illustriert am Beispiel der verblosen Direktiva. In Christoph Bürgel, Paul Gévaudan & Dirk Siepmann (Hrsg.), *Sprachwissenschaft und Fremdsprachendidaktik: Konstruktionen und Konstruktionslernen*, 241–261. Tübingen: Stauffenburg Verlag.

De Knop, Sabine & Fabio Mollica. 2018. Verblose Direktiva als Konstruktionen: ein kontrastiver Vergleich zwischen Deutsch, Französisch und Italienisch. In Jürgen Erfurt & Sabine De Knop (eds.), *Konstruktionsgrammatik und Mehrsprachigkeit*, 127–148. Universität Duisburg-Essen: Universitätsverlag Rhein-Ruhr OHG.

Di Meola, Claudio. 2000. *Die Grammatikalisierung deutscher Präpositionen*. Tübingen: Stauffenburg.

Dobrovol'skij, Dmitrij. 2011. Phraseologie und Konstruktionsgrammatik. In Alexander Lasch & Alexander Ziem (eds.), *Konstruktionsgrammatik III. Aktuelle Fragen und Lösungsansätze*, 110–130. Tübingen: Stauffenburg.

Domínguez Vázquez, María José. 2011. Verblose Direktiva?, Subjektlose Sätze? Zur Weglassbarkeit, Fakultativität und Ellipse am Beispiel der Regieanweisungen in Dürrenmatts "Die Physiker". In María José Domínguez Vázquez, Emilio González Miranda, Meliss Meike & Víctor Millet et al. (eds.), *A palabra no texto. Homenaxe a Carlos Buján*, 199–218. Santiago de Compostela: Universidade de Santiago de Compostela.

Domínguez Vázquez, María José, Ulrich Engel & Gemma Paredes Suárez. 2017. *Neue Wege zur Verbvalenz. Band 1: Theoretische und methodologische Grundlagen*. Frankfurt a. M.: Peter Lang.

Engelberg, Stefan, Svenja König, Kristel Proost & Edeltraud Winkler. 2011. Argumentstrukturmuster als Konstruktionen? Identität – Verwandtschaft – Idiosynkrasien. In Stefan Engelberg, Anke Holler & Kristel Proost (eds.), *Sprachliches Wissen zwischen Lexikon und Grammatik*, 71–112. Berlin: de Gruyter.

Eroms, Hans-Werner. 2012. Die Grenzen der Valenzen. In Klaus Fischer & Fabio Mollica (eds.), *Valenz, Konstruktion und Deutsch als Fremdsprache,* 25–46. Frankfurt a. M.: Peter Lang.

Feilke, Helmuth & Mathilde Hennig (eds.). 2016. *Zur Karriere von 'Nähe und Distanz': Rezeption und Diskussion des Koch-Oesterreicher-Modells*. Berlin: de Gruyter.

Filipovic, Luna & Iraide Ibarretxe-Antunano. 2015. Motion. In Eva Dabrowska & Dagmar Divjak (eds.), *Mouton handbook of cognitive linguistics*, 526–545. Berlin: Mouton de Gruyter.

Finkbeiner, Rita. 2015. *Einführung in die Pragmatik*. Darmstadt: Wissenschaftliche Buchgesellschaft.

Fleischer, Wolfgang. 1997. *Phraseologie der deutschen Gegenwartssprache*. Tübingen: Max Niemeyer.

Fortmann, Christian 2018. Vermeintlich verblose *Direktiva* – stumme Prädikatsbildung in Wurzelstrukturen. In Eric Fuß & Angelika Wöllstein (eds.), *Grammatiktheorie und Grammatikographie*, 63–92. Tübingen: Narr.

Frahm, Ole. 2010. *Sprache des Comics*. Hamburg: Philo Fine Arts.

Genzmer, Herbert. 1995. *Sprache in Bewegung. Eine deutsche Grammatik*. Frankfurt am Main: Suhrkamp.

Goldberg, Adele E. 1995. *Constructions. A Construction Grammar Approach to Argument Structure*. Chicago: University of Chicago Press.

Goldberg, Adele E. 2006. *Constructions at Work: The Nature of Generalization in Language*. Oxford: Oxford University Press.

Goldberg, Adele E. 2013. Constructionist Approaches. In Thomas Hoffmann & Graeme Trousdale (eds.), *The Oxford Handbook of Construction Grammar*, 15–31. Oxford: Oxford University Press.

Gries, Stefan Th. 2005. Syntactic priming: A corpus-based approach. *Journal of Psycholinguistic Research* 34 (4). 365–399.

Grießhaber, Wilhelm. 2007. Präposition. In Hoffmann Ludger (ed.), *Handbuch der deutschen Wortarten*, 629–656. Berlin: de Gruyter.

Grünewald, Dietrich. 2000. *Comics*. Tübingen: Niemeyer.

Hartsuiker, Robert J., Martin J. Pickering & Eline Veltkamp. 2004. Is syntax separate or shared between languages? Cross-linguistic syntactic priming in Spanish-English bilinguals. *Psychological Science* 15 (6). 409–414.

Ibarretxe-Antunano, Iraide. 2017. Introduction. Motion and semantic typology: A hot old topic with exciting caveats. In Iraide Ibarretxe-Antunano (eds.), *Motion and Space across Languages*, 13–36. Amsterdam: John Benjamins.

Jacobs, Joachim. 2008. Wozu Konstruktionen? *Linguistische Berichte* 213. 3–44.

Koch, Peter & Wulf Oesterreicher. 1985. Sprache der Nähe – Sprache der Distanz. Mündlichkeit und Schriftlichkeit im Spannungsfeld von Sprachtheorie und Sprachgeschichte. In *Romanistisches Jahrbuch* 36. 15–43.

Lenk, Hartmut E. H. & Elina Suomela-Härmä (eds.). 2016. *Sprache im Comic / Il linguaggio dei fumetti / La lengua de los comics*. Helsinki: Société Néophilologique.

Loebell, Helga & Kathryn Bock. 2003. Structural priming across languages. *Linguistics* 41 (5). 791–824.

Müller, Gereon. 2011. Regeln oder Konstruktionen. Von verblosen Direktiven zur sequentiellen Nominalreduplikation. In Stefan Engelberg, Anke Holler & Kristel Proost (eds.), *Sprachliches Wissen zwischen Lexikon und Grammatik Berlin*, 211–249. Berlin: de Gruyter.

Narasimhan, Bhuvana, Anetta Kopecka, Melissa Bowerman, Marianne Gullberg & Asifa Majid. 2012. Putting and taking events: A crosslinguistic perspective. In Anetta Kopecka, Bhuvana Narasimhan (eds.), *Events of putting and taking: A crosslinguistic perspective*, 1–18. Amsterdam: John Benjamins.

Proost, Kristel. 2014. Ditransitive transfer constructions and their prepositional variants in German and Romanian: An empirical survey. In Ruxandra Cosma, Stefan Engelberg, Susan Schlotthauer, Speranta L. Stanescu & Gisela Zifonun. (eds.), *Komplexe Argumentstrukturen. Kontrastive Untersuchungen zum Deutschen, Rumänischen und Englischen*, 19–84. Berlin: de Gruyter.

Proost, Kristel. 2017. The role of verbs and verb classes in identifying German search-construction. In Francisco José Ruiz de Mendoza Ibáñez, Alba Luzondo Oyón & Paula Pérez Sobrino (eds.), *Constructing Families of Constructions Analytical perspectives and theoretical challenges*, 17–51. Amsterdam: Benjamins.

Proost, Kristel & Edeltraud Winkler. 2015. *Familienähnlichkeiten deutscher Argumentstrukturmuster*. In OPAL – Online publizierte Arbeiten zur Linguistik 1 https://ids-pub.bsz-bw.de/frontdoor/index/index/docId/3628 (accessed 30 October)

Rojo, Ana & Iraide, Ibarretxe-Antuñanum (eds.). 2013. *Cognitive Linguistics and Translations. Advances in Some theoretical Models and Applications*. Berlin: de Gruyter.

Scheepers, Christoph & Martin Corley. 2000. Syntactic priming in German sentence production. In Lila R. Gleitman & Aravind K. Joshi (eds.), *Proceedings of the 22nd Annual Meeting of the Cognitive Science Society*, 435–440. Mahwah, NJ.: Psychology Press.

Searle, John R. 1979. *Expression and Meaning. Studies in the Theory of Speech Acts*. Cambridge, Mass.: Cambridge University Press.
Smith, Michael B. 1995. Semantic motivation vs. arbitrariness in grammar: Toward a more general account of the DAT/ACC contrast with two-way prepositions. In Irmengard Rauch & Gerald F. Carr (eds.), *Insights in Germanic Linguistics: Methodology and Transition*, 293–323. Berlin: Mouton de Gruyter.
Stefanowitsch, Anatol & Ada Rohde. 2004. The goal bias in the encoding of motion events. In Günter Radden & Klaus-Uwe Panther (eds.), *Studies in Linguistic Motivation*, 249–267. Berlin: Walter de Gruyter.
Talmy, Leonard. 2000. *Toward a Cognitive Semantics*. Cambridge, MA: MIT Press.
Terrasi-Haufe, Elisabetta. 2004. *Der Schulerwerb von Deutsch als Fremdsprache: Eine empirische Untersuchung am Beispiel der italienischsprachigen Schweiz*. Tübingen: Max Niemeyer.
Traugott, Elizabeth Closs. 2008. Grammaticalization, constructions and the incremental development of language: suggestions for the development of degree modifiers in English. In Regine Eckhardt, Gerhard Jäger & Tonjes Veenstra (eds.), *Variation, selection, development: probing the evolutionary model of language* change, 219–250. Berlin: De Gruyter.
Ungerer, Friedrich & Hans-Jörg Schmidt. 1996. *An Introduction to Cognitive Linguistics*. London: Longman.
Verspoor, Marjolijn, René Dirven & Günter Radden. 1999. Putting concepts together: Syntax. In René Dirven & Marjolijn Verspoor (eds.), *Cognitive Exploration of Language and Linguistics*, 87–115. Amsterdam: Benjamins.
Weigand, Edda. 2015. The Dialogic Principle Revisited: Speech Acts and Mental States. *Interdisciplinary Studies in Pragmatics, Culture and Society*, 209–232. https://link.springer.com/chapter/10.1007/978-3-319-12616-6_7
Welke, Klaus. 2009. Konstruktionsvererbung, Valenzvererbung und die Reichweite von Konstruktionen. *Zeitschrift für germanistische Linguistik* 37. 514–543.
Welke, Klaus. 2011. *Valenzgrammatik des Deutschen*. Berlin: de Gruyter.
Wilder, Christopher. 2008. The PP-*with*-DP construction. In Jacek Witkos & Gisbert Fanselow (eds.), *Elements of Slavic and Germanic Grammars: A Comparative View. Papers on Topical Issues in Syntax and Morphosyntax*, 235–253. Frankfurt a. M.: Peter Lang.
Willems, Klaas. 2011. The semantics of variable case marking (accusative/dative) after two-way prepositions in German locative constructions. Towards a constructionist approach. *Indogermanische Forschungen* 116. 324–366.
Willems, Klaas, Jonah Rys & Ludovic De Cuypere. 2018. Case alternation in argument structure constructions with prepositional phrases. *A case study in corpus-based constructional analysis*, 85–130. In Hans Boas & Alexander Ziem (eds.), *Constructional Approaches to Argument Structure in German*. Berlin: Mouton de Gruyter.
Wittgenstein, Ludwig (2001): *Philosophische Untersuchungen. Kritisch-genetische Edition*. Frankfurt am Main: Suhrkamp.

References for the data

Hergé. 1947/1982. *Les aventures de Tintin – Le Crabe aux pinces d'or*. Tournai: Casterman.
Hergé. 1967a. *Tim und Struppi – Tim in Tibet*. Hamburg: Carlsen Verlag.
Hergé. 1967b/1995. *Tim und Struppi – König Ottokars Zepter*. Hamburg: Carlsen Verlag.
Hergé. 1970/1994. *Tim und Struppi – Kohle an Bord*. Hamburg: Carlsen Verlag.
Hergé. 1998. *Tim und Struppi – Die Krabbe mit den goldenen Scheren*. Hamburg: Carlsen Verlag.
Hergé. 1999. *Le avventure di Tintin. Il granchio d'oro*. Roma Lizaed.
Jacobs, Edgar P. 1980. *Die Abenteuer von Blake und Mortimer. Die Diamanten-Affäre*. Hamburg: Carlsen Verlag.
Jacobs, Edgar P. 1991. *Les aventures de Blake et Mortimer – L'affaire du collier*. Bruxelles: Editions Blake et Mortimer.
Jacobs, Edgar P. 1993. *Blake e Mortimer. Il caso del collier*. Milano: Colori.
Sketch Engine: https://www.sketchengine.co.uk/

Tore Nesset, Laura A. Janda
Securing strategic input for L2 learners: Constructions with Russian motion verbs

1 Strategic input for L2 learners and linguistic profiling

Since L2 learners are sensitive to the frequency of the constructions they encounter (see e.g. Ellis and Wulff 2015 and Ellis et al. 2016: 47), it follows that L2 instructors should pay particular attention to the input they provide learners with. Without a doubt, it is strategic to expose L2 learners to frequently used language patterns, so that they can acquire the most important patterns in the language they are studying. But how can we identify what is the most strategic input? Traditionally, this task has been left to the intuition of L2 instructors and writers of textbooks, and as a result textbooks are often populated with invented sentences that probably "have not occurred in any natural speech situation before (and [. . .] probably never will)" (Römer 2004: 153). The purpose of the present study is to propose a more scientific basis for the identification of strategic input for L2 learners. On the basis of a case study of Russian motion verbs, we suggest a methodology combining two core concepts of constructional and usage-based approaches: constructional profiles and grammatical profiles. In the remainder of section 1, we will present linguistic profiling, before we give a short overview of Russian verbs of motion in section 2 and their basic constructions in section 3. After a brief discussion of morphological constructions in section 4, we turn to syntactic constructions in sections 5 and 6. In sections 7 and 8 we combine constructional and grammatical profiles, before the contribution of the article is summarized in section 9.

By "linguistic profile" we mean the statistical distribution of features related to a linguistic unit. Linguistic profiling, discussed at length by Kuznetsova (2015), represents a suite of methods for using corpus data to explore form-meaning relationships in language by means of relative frequencies. Linguistic profiles were pioneered by Divjak and Gries (2006), whose "behavioral profiles" summarized the statistical distribution of a large number of properties of linguistic units. In the present study, we will be concerned with two kinds of linguistic profiles: constructional profiles and grammatical profiles.

Tore Nesset, Laura A. Janda, UiT The Arctic University of Norway

A constructional profile (Janda and Solovyev 2009) is the relative frequency distribution of the syntactic or morphological constructions a linguistic unit occurs in. In their study of nouns denoting happiness and sadness in Russian they showed that while these words tend to occur in the same set of constructions, the frequency distribution of each word across those constructions is unique, and thus constructional profiles make it possible to tease apart differences between near synonyms.

A grammatical profile is the relative frequency distribution of the inflected forms of a lexeme (Janda and Lyashevskaya 2011: 719). Thus, the grammatical profile of a verb is the proportion of corpus attestations for present tense, past tense, etc. In their large-scale study of imperfective and perfective verbs in Russian, Janda and Lyashevskaya (2011) show that verb pairs based on prefixation and suffixation have similar grammatical profiles, while the profiles of imperfective verbs are clearly distinct from those of perfective verbs. At the same time, Janda and Lyashevskaya (2011) show that the grammatical profiles they investigate make it possible to identify "outlier verbs" that show strong affinities to certain grammatical forms, a fact they argue is of importance for L2 instruction.

In the present study, we will combine the use of constructional and grammatical profiles in order to identify strategic input for L2 learners. However, before we explore linguistic profiling, we will introduce the Russian verbs of motion, since constructions with these verbs are the empirical basis for the claims we make in the present article.

2 Russian motion verbs – a major obstacle for L2 learners

Constructions with Russian verbs of motion are challenging for L2 learners of Russian – Gor et al. (2010: 361) aptly describe the motion verbs as a "notoriously thorny topic". There are at least three main reasons for this: they come in pairs, they are involved in morphological constructions with aspectual prefixes, and there is no generic motion verb in Russian.

The first challenge is illustrated in (1) and (2), which show that Russian has two verbs meaning 'walk':[1]

---

[1] All numbered examples are from the Russian National Corpus (parallel subcorpus). The Russian National Corpus is freely available at www.ruscorpora.ru. Notice that we cite the Russian example first, regardless of whether the text in question is a translation from English to Russian or the other way around. The Russian examples are given in transliterated orthography. For the

(1) *Abbat byl čelovekom blagočestivym i šel^{uni} domoj spat' srazu že posle večernej messy.* (Brown 2003)
'The abbu was a deeply pious man who **went** home to bed immediately after mass.'

(2) **Xodil^{non}** *v zonu, vernulsja živoj i s den'gami.* (A. and B. Strugatsky 1971)
'I **went** into the Zone and came back alive and with money.'

In (1), the Russian text has the past tense form *šel* of *idti* 'walk', because we are dealing with movement in one direction towards a goal, whereas in (2) the past tense form of *xodit'* 'walk' is used, since the example describes a round trip (into the zone and back again). Verbs like *idti* in (1) are referred to as "unidirectional", whereas the label "non-directional" is used for verbs like *xodit'* in (2).[2] In addition to roundtrips as in (2), non-directional verbs are used in constructions describing multidirectional movement "round about" as in (3), where a woman is walking around in a room, and the ability to carry out the relevant type of motion as in (4), which is about a girl who is able to walk again after a serious illness.

(3) *Potom **xodit^{non}** po komnate, vidno, čto sderživaet slezy.* (Nabokov 1925–26)
'Then she **walks** around the room: it is evident that she is holding back tears.'

(4) *Slava bogu, ona teper' uže **xodit^{non}**.* (Dostoevsky 1878)
'Thank God, she can **walk** now!'

Russian has thirteen pairs of unidirectional and non-directional motion verbs distinguishing various manners of motion, but for the purposes of this article we will limit ourselves to discussing the pairs in Table 1, which are all highly relevant for L2 learners.[3] While the fact that Russian motion verbs come in pairs makes life hard for L2 learners, the situation is further exacerbated by a second challenge – the fact that the motion verbs interact with the notoriously complex Russian aspectual system. Both unidirectional and non-directional verbs are imperfec-

---

convenience of the reader, the relevant verbs or verb phrases are boldfaced, and unidirectional verbs are provided with the superscript "uni", while the tag "non" is used for non-directional verbs.

[2] Notice that the terminology shows some variation. Alternatives to "non-directional" are "multidirectional" or "indeterminate", while "determinate" is frequently used instead of "unidirectional". See Nesset (2000: 106–107) for discussion and references.

[3] For discussion of other motion verbs, see Nesset (2000: 106) and references therein.

tive and combine with aspectual prefixes in non-trivial ways. Thus, by adding the prefix *v-* 'into' to the unidirectional *idti* 'walk' we get the perfective verb *vojti* 'walk into', while the addition of *v-* to the non-directional verb *xodit'* yields the imperfective verb *vxodit'* 'walk into'. The details of this system are debated in the scholarly literature on Russian verbs of motion (see e.g. Nesset 2008), but for present purposes it is sufficient to notice that Russian has more than fifteen aspectual prefixes that create a large number of prefixed motion verbs of both aspects – which represent a major challenge for L2 learners. We present an overview of relevant prefixes in section 4 below.

Table 1: Pairs of unidirectional and non-directional motion verbs.

Unidirectional verb	Non-directional verb	English gloss
idti	*xodit'*	'walk'
exat'	*ezdit'*	'ride in a vehicle'
letet'	*letat'*	'fly'
plyt'	*plavat'*	'swim, sail'
vesti	*vodit'*	'lead'
vezti	*vozit'*	'transport'
nesti	*nosit'*	'carry'

A third challenge, in addition to the pairedness of motion verbs and their use with aspectual prefixes, is the fact that Russian lacks a generic motion verb. While English *go* can be used about motion on foot and by means of a vehicle, in Russian the verbs *idti/xodit'* 'walk' describe motion on foot, whereas *exat'/ezdit'* 'ride in a vehicle' are used when a vehicle is involved. Thus, in (1) the Russian translator of *The Da Vinci Code* had a choice between *idti* and *exat'*, and went for the former on the basis of the context – presumably the clergyman in question lives close enough to the church to make walking the most likely option for going home from mass. Although Russian lacks a generic motion verb, *idti/xodit'* can be generalized to motion that does not take place on foot (Rakhilina 2004, Nesset 2010). We will return to such uses in section 5 below. At this point, it is sufficient to notice that such generalized uses do not necessarily have any close parallels in English and other languages. A well-known example that L2 learners struggle with is the "weather construction" with *idti* 'walk' plus a noun. Thus, English *it rains* corresponds to *idet^{uni} dožd'* '(lit.) walks rain' in Russian.

Since, as we have shown, Russian motion verbs represent a complex system which does not have any direct parallel in English and other non-Slavic European languages, they are a major obstacle for L2 learners. How to provide strategic input to L2 learners is therefore a particularly pertinent question with regard to motion verbs. We address this question in the remainder of the article, exploring a number of morphological and syntactic constructions with Russian motion verbs.

3 Distribution of lexical items and the unidirectional/non-directional contrast

Our quest for strategic input starts with a simple question: Which lexical items are most important? As mentioned in section 1, we submit that frequency plays a key role here, i.e. that it is strategic to focus on verbs of high frequency, since such verbs will prove highly useful for L2 learners. In order to investigate the frequency distribution of the Russian motion verbs in Table 1, we turned to the Russian National Corpus (main corpus), a corpus of approximately 283 million words (August 2018). We carried out searches in the manually disambiguated subcorpus, which contains about six million words (August 2018). Since the Russian National Corpus is a balanced corpus that includes a variety of genres, it is likely that the data in Table 2 adequately reflect the overall situation in the language. Further studies of the frequency distribution in specific genres (e.g. oral speech) would be of interest, but for present purposes we limit ourselves to discussion of the data in Table 2.

Table 2: Frequency distribution of Russian motion verbs (Russian National Corpus, disambiguated part, searches performed in August 2017 and August 2018).

	Unidirectional	Non-directional	Total
Idti^{uni}/xodit^{non} 'walk'	6,763	2,292	9,055
exat'^{uni}/ezdit'^{non} 'ride in a vehicle'	1,500	712	2,212
letet'^{uni}/letat'^{non} 'fly'	602	226	828
plyt'^{uni}/plavat'^{non} 'swim, sail'	300	260	560
Vesti^{uni}/vodit'^{non} 'lead'	1,608	214	1,822
Vezti^{uni}/vozit'^{uni} 'transport'	327	173	500
Nesti^{uni}/nosit'^{uni} 'carry'	675	812	1,487
Total	11,775	4,689	16,464

Let us first consider each pair of motion verbs as a unit and explore the distribution of the seven relevant manners of motion: walk, ride in a vehicle, fly, swim/sail, lead, transport and carry. The distribution is visualized in Figure 1, which gives percentages based on Table 2. One observation can be made: the distribution is very skewed, and the verb pair with the meaning 'walk' is by far the most frequent. While 'walk' accounts for 55% of the examples, the other manners of motion range from 3% to 14%. In view of this, it seems strategic to pay particular attention to 'walk' in L2 instruction.

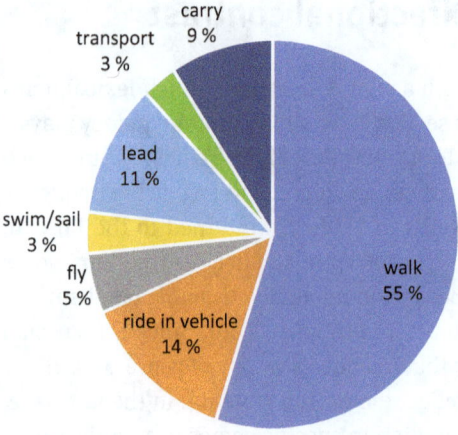

Figure 1: Distribution of manners of motion in percent (based on Table 1).

The data in Table 2 also make it possible to consider the distribution of unidirectional and non-directional verbs. Which type is most frequent and most relevant for strategic input for L2 learners? Figure 2 presents the distribution in percent based on the data in Table 2. As shown, unidirectional verbs cover almost three quarters of all examples with verbs of motion. This strongly suggests that L2 learners should pay particular attention to unidirectional verbs, and that it may be advantageous to start with unidirectional verbs and then proceed to non-directional verbs in L2 instruction. However, it is worth mentioning that there is one exception to the general trend. As shown in Table 2, for 'carry' the non-directional verb *nosit'* is more frequent than its unidirectional partner *nesti*. This suggests that in order to construct strategic input for L2 learners, it is important to take the properties of individual verbs into consideration. We will return to 'carry' in section 8.

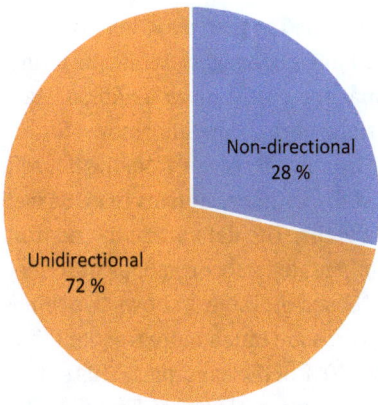

Figure 2: Distribution of unidirectional and non-directional motion verbs in percent (based on Table 1).

4 Morphological constructions: Prefixes

So far, we have only considered simplex (i.e. unprefixed) motion verbs. However, as mentioned in section 2, Russian verbs of motion combine with a number of aspectual prefixes. The prefixed verbs can be considered morphological constructions in the sense of Booij (2010). What would be strategic input for the morphological constructions with prefixes? In order to find out, we considered the frequencies of eight important prefixes:

(5) a. *v-* 'into'
 b. *vy-* 'out of'
 c. *pri-* 'to'
 d. *u-* 'away from'
 e. *pod-* 'up to'
 f. *ot-* 'away from'
 g. *pere-* 'across'
 h. *pro-* 'through'

The glosses give only rough approximations of the meanings, but are precise enough to show that the prefixes encode paths that the motion events in question follow. Since the path is marked by a prefix, while the manner of motion is described by the verb stem, Russian is a satellite-framed language in the typology of Talmy (2000: 222). Notice that the prefixes in (5a-f) constitute three pairs of antonyms: 'into' –

'out of', 'to' – 'away from', and 'up to' and 'away from'. The prefixes *u-* in (5d) and *ot-* in (5f) are given the same gloss, but are not used interchangeably. While the former describes movement out of a three-dimensional space (e.g. *uexat' iz Rossii* 'leave Russia'), the latter is used in situations where someone or something moves further away from a point in space (*ot''exat' ot doma* 'drive (further) away from the house').

Table 3 gives the frequencies of prefixed verbs with the prefixes in (5) as well as frequencies for the corresponding simplex verbs. The data are gathered from the Russian National Corpus (manually disambiguated subcorpus), as described in section 3. Figure 3, which gives percentages based on Table 3, shows two things clearly. First of all, it is evident that prefixed verbs are much more frequent than simplex verbs, since prefixed verbs account for 70% of the examples. This entails that it is strategic to provide input with prefixed verbs to L2 learners. Traditionally, students are first exposed to simplex verbs, and only when they have mastered the simplex verbs, they go on to study prefixed motion verbs (e.g. Muravyova 1995 and Mahota 1996). Frequency data of the type we present in Table 3 and Figure 3 may be taken as inspiration to rethink this traditional set-up. Would it be advantageous to start with prefixed verbs, and then proceed to simplex verbs instead? We leave this question open for future consideration, but note that constructional profiles of the kind reported in this article have potentially far-reaching implications for L2 instruction.

A second observation that can be made on the basis of Table 3 and Figure 3 is that not all prefixes are equally important. The two pairs of antonyms in (5a-d) account for almost 50% of the examples, while the remaining four prefixes in (5e-h) represent less than 25% of the examples. Clearly, therefore, it is strategic to focus on constructions with the four prefixes in (5a-d) in the input for L2 learners of Russian verbs of motion.

Table 3: Distribution of simplex and prefixed motion verbs (Russian National Corpus, disambiguated part, corpus searches carried out in August 2017. The forms given in parentheses for ezdit' and plavat' indicate that these verbs have different stems in prefixed verbs.

	Simplex	v- 'into'	vy- 'out of'	pri- 'to'	u- 'away from'	pod- 'up to'	ot- 'away from'	pere- 'across'	pro- 'through'
xodit^{mon} 'walk'	2,292	925	1,523	1,451	1,277	767	181	335	1,209
ldti^{uni} 'walk'	6,763	1,562	3,135	3,652	2,061	1,507	390	516	2,346
ezdit^{mon} (-ezžat') 'ride in a vehicle'	712	38	114	635	340	65	35	67	108
exat^{uni} 'ride in a vehicle'	1,500	73	203	1,739	898	112	38	177	140

Table 3 (continued)

	Simplex	v- 'into'	vy- 'out of'	pri- 'to'	u- 'away from'	pod- 'up to'	ot- 'away from'	pere- 'across'	pro- 'through'
letat[non] 'fly'	226	27	68	29	56	9	26	18	52
letet[uni] 'fly'	602	56	160	144	117	19	41	24	85
nosit[non] 'carry'	812	124	188	379	92	68	82	128	21
nesti[uni] 'carry'	675	285	275	932	140	121	205	217	51
vodit[non] 'lead'	214	133	142	497	77	81	85	180	793
vesti[uni] 'lead'	1,608	333	308	1,173	110	187	281	367	1,072
vozit[non] 'transport'	173	14	42	92	49	17	25	14	1
vezti[uni] 'transport'	327	12	98	556	175	36	115	45	8
plavat[non] (-plyvat') 'swim, sail'	260	3	28	6	27	10	7	7	30
plyt'[uni] 'swim, sail'	300	2	43	12	25	20	11	11	32
Total	16,464	3,587	6,327	11,297	5,444	3,019	1,522	2,106	5,948

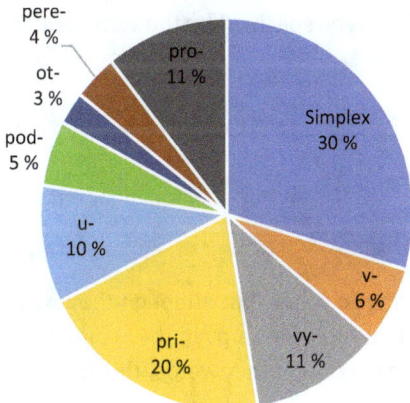

Figure 3: Distribution of simplex and prefixed motion verbs in percent (based on the bottom line in Table 3).

5 Constructional profiles: Specific, generalized and metaphorical uses

We now turn from morphological to syntactic constructions. Although in the previous section we argued that prefixed verbs deserve more attention, simplex verbs are nevertheless important. It makes sense to distinguish between three broad classes of constructions where simplex motion verbs involve what we refer to as "specific", "generalized" and "metaphorical" motion. We show that motion verbs have very different distributions across these three classes of constructions and argue that the differences help us pinpoint strategic input for L2 learners.

"Specific" constructions are found in examples where the verb describes physical motion with the manner of motion specified in the lexical meaning of the verb in question. By way of example, consider the following sentence from *Harry Potter*:

(6) Okazalos', on ne vral, on dejstvitel'no umel **letat**^{mon}. (J. K. Rowling 1997)
'He hadn't been lying, he could **fly**.'

Here it is clear that we are dealing with physical movement through space, and that the movement is of the kind specified by the lexical meaning – flying.

"Generalized" motion covers constructions with physical movement in space, but where the movement is not of the type specified by the verb's lexical meaning:

(7) Nad zamkom rejal flag, po zalivu **šli**^{uni} korabli ili stojali na jakore. (R. L. Stevenson 1886)
'There was a flag upon the castle, and ships **moving** or lying anchored in the firth.'

The ships in this example are clearly moving in space, but although the lexical meaning of *idti* 'walk' specifies movement on foot, the ships in the example are not moving on foot, since ships do not have feet. In other words, this is a construction of the generalized motion type.

"Metaphorical" motion is a type of constructions where the motion in question is not literal:

(8) U nas **idut**^{uni} peregovory s ee mužem o razvode. (L. Tolstoy 1878)
'We are **carrying on** negotiations with her husband about a divorce.'

In this example, there is no physical motion, but *idti* 'walk' is used metaphorically to indicate the progress of the negotiations.

In order to investigate the distribution of the specific, generalized and metaphorical constructions, we created a database of 100 corpus examples for each motion verb listed in Table 3. We used the Russian National Corpus (main corpus), and restricted the searches to examples from 1950 or later, since we are interested in the situation in modern Russian. Based on the searches we created a random sample of 100 examples for each verb. Each sample contained only one example per author. The samples were conflated to one large dataset, which was then annotated manually. The distribution is given in Table 4 and visualized in Figure 4.

Table 4: Constructional profiles for specific, generalized and metaphorical constructions with motion verbs.

	Specific	Generalized	Metaphorical	Total
vezti ^{uni} 'transport'	66	0	34	100
vozit' ^{mon} 'transport'	96	4	0	100
vesti ^{uni} 'lead'	11	0	89	100
vodit' ^{mon} 'lead'	46	37	17	100
exat' ^{uni} 'ride in a vehicle'	99	0	1	100
ezdit' ^{mon} 'ride in a vehicle'	100	0	0	100
Idti ^{uni} 'walk'	29	13	58	100
xodit' ^{mon} 'walk'	89	6	5	100
letet' ^{uni} 'fly'	71	13	16	100
letat' ^{mon} 'fly'	97	0	3	100
nesti ^{uni} 'carry'	34	7	59	100
nosit' ^{mon} 'carry'	9	50	41	100
plyt' ^{uni} 'swim, sail'	55	9	36	100
plavat' ^{mon} 'swim, sail'	81	3	16	100
Total Unidirectional	365	42	293	700
Total Non-directional	518	100	82	700
GrandTotal	883	142	375	1400

Three observations can be made on the basis of Table 4 and Figure 4. First, it is clear that motion verbs have quite different constructional profiles – all motion verbs are not born equal. Second, if we compare the pairs of verbs with the same lexical meanings (located next to each other in the figure), we see considerable differences. While some pairs (e.g. *exat'-ezdit'* 'ride in a vehicle') predominantly involve specific constructions, other pairs such as *nesti-nosit'* 'carry' tend to occur in generalized and metaphorical constructions. Third, the members of some pairs display quite different constructional profiles. A case in point is *idti-xodit'* 'walk', where the former is largely generalized and metaphorical, while the latter is dominated by constructions of the specific type.

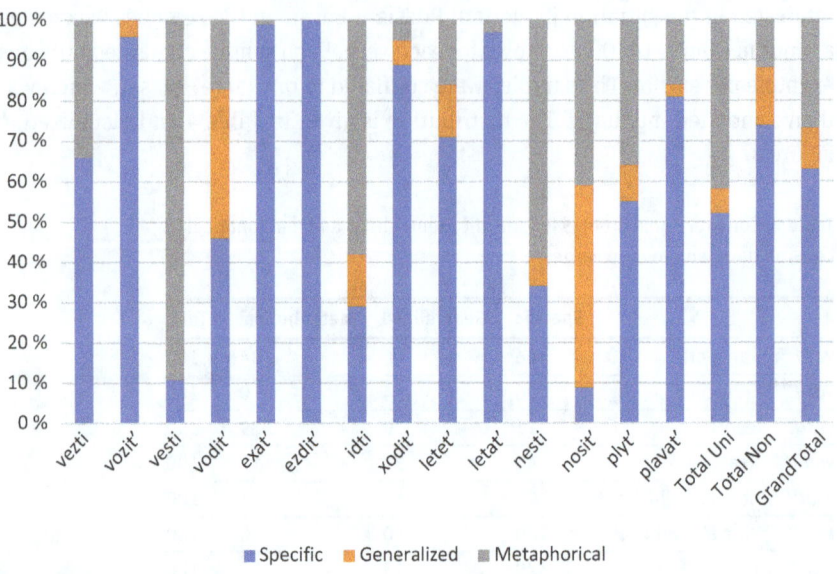

Figure 4: Constructional profiles for specific, generalized and metaphorical constructions with motion verbs.

What are the implications of the constructional profiles for L2 instruction? If we want to create strategic input for L2 learners, it seems clear that the differences shown in Figure 4 cannot be ignored. In particular, it appears important to introduce generalized and metaphorical constructions at an early stage, especially for those verbs where such constructions are prevalent.

6 Constructional profiles: Directionality

We now zoom in on the specific constructions. In section 2, we pointed out that non-directional verbs are used in three different types of constructions involving multidirectional motion, round trips, and the capacity to carry out a particular kind of motion. In what follows, we present constructional profiles for these three classes of constructions, and show that they have important implications for strategic input for L2 learners.

The constructional profiles were extracted from the database described in the previous section. The results are summarized in Table 5 and visualized in Figure 5. Notice that we ignore *nosit'* 'carry' in this section, since, as shown in the previous section, this verb is largely used in generalized and metaphorical constructions. We return to *nosit'* in section 8 below. With regard to round trip constructions, we have included both single round trips and multiple round trips.

Table 5: Constructional profiles for non-directional verbs: non-directional, round trip and capacity constructions.

	Multidirectional	Round Trip	Capacity	Total
vozit'^{non} 'transport'	48	48	0	96
vodit'^{non} 'lead'	16	30	0	46
ezdit'^{non} 'ride in a vehicle'	38	62	0	100
xodit'^{non} 'walk'	38	48	3	89
letat'^{non} 'fly'	47	17	33	97
plavat'^{non} 'swim/sail'	31	3	19	53
Total	218	208	55	481

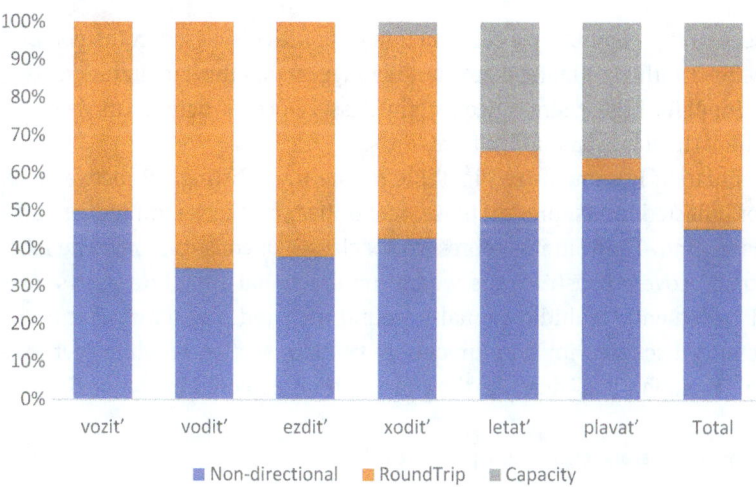

Figure 5: Constructional profiles for non-directional verbs: multidirectional, round trip and capacity constructions.

Table 5 and Figure 5 indicate a relatively even distribution for non-directional constructions; non-directional motion is well attested for all the verbs under scrutiny, and they vary between 35% (*vodit'* 'lead') and 58% (*plavat'* 'swim/sail'). With regard to strategic input, it would not make much difference which verbs were used to introduce this type of construction to L2 learners.

The distribution of round trips and capacity, on the other hand, display differences. Capacity is only attested for three verbs (*xodit'* 'walk', *letat'* 'fly', and *plavat'* 'swim/sail'), and only for two of them (*letat'* and *plavat'*) does capacity cover more than 30% of the examples. This is not surprising, since both flying and swimming are skills one has to learn. In L2 instruction, it seems strategic to introduce capacity constructions through *letat'* and *plavat'*, where this class of constructions is frequent.

As shown in Figure 5, capacity and round trips are in nearly complementary distribution; the verbs where capacity is frequent have few or no examples with round trips, and vice versa. Hence, we argue strategic input for round trip constructions should focus on *vozit'* 'transport', *vodit'* 'lead', *ezdit'* 'ride in a vehicle', and *xodit'* 'walk', which are verbs that occur frequently in this type of construction.

7 Constructional and grammatical profiles combined

In this section, we combine the constructional profiles discussed in the two previous sections with grammatical profiles. We suggest that this facilitates creating strategic input for L2 learners, since certain classes of constructions are used frequently in particular grammatical forms.

The situation is summarized in Table 6. The rows distinguish between six groups of inflected forms: present tense, imperative, past tense, infinitive, participle and gerund. The columns represent six classes of constructions. The label "Directional" covers constructions where unidirectional verbs are used about physical movement. "Multidirectional", "round trip" and "capacity" refer to the constructions discussed for non-directional verbs in section 6, while "generalized" and "metaphorical" describe the constructions explored in section 5.

Table 6: Constructional and grammatical profiles combined.

	Directional	Multi-directional	Round trip	Capacity	Generalized	Metaphorical	Total
Present	114	66	49	7	68	163	467
Imperative	16	1	4	0	3	3	27

Table 6 (continued)

	Directional	Multi-directional	Round trip	Capacity	Generalized	Metaphorical	Total
Past	118	74	104	7	48	114	465
Infinitive	75	68	47	25	34	35	284
Participle	29	14	6	16	20	57	142
Gerund	6	1	1	0	4	3	15
Total	358	224	211	55	177	375	1400

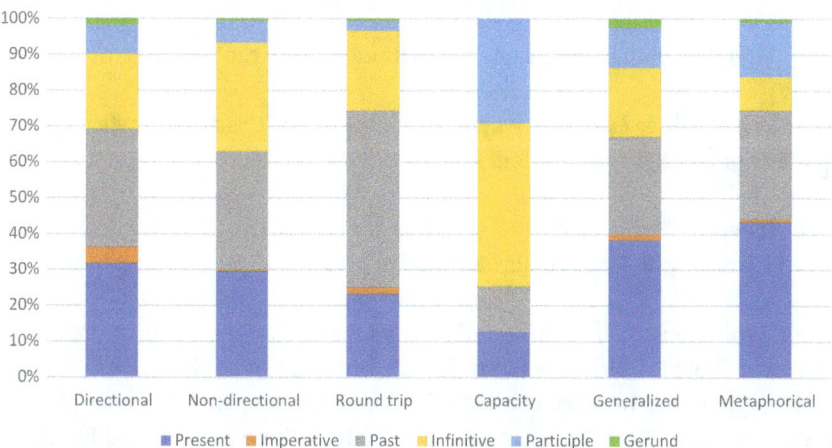

Figure 6: Constructional and grammatical profiles combined.

Table 6 and Figure 6 show that there are correlations between grammatical and constructional profiles. In particular, two observations can be made. First, we see that capacity constructions are very frequently used with the infinitive. Second, round trip constructions show a strong affinity to the past tense. With regard to the input to L2 learners, we argue that it would be strategic to focus on the infinitive for capacity constructions and the past tense for round trip constructions.

8 Case study: *nosit'* 'carry'

In this section, we report on a small case study concerning the non-directional verb *nosit'* 'carry', which as demonstrated in section 5, strongly prefers generalized and metaphorical constructions. We show that three generalized/metaphorical constructions are particularly important. First, we have examples where *nosit'* combines with the noun *xarakter* 'character':

(9) *Vsja scena* **nosila**[non] ***xarakter*** *privyčnoj intimnosti.* (F. Scott Fitzgerald 1925)
 'There **was an** unmistakable **air of** natural intimacy about the picture.'

Second, we have examples of the following type, where *nosit'* takes a word for 'name' as its grammatical object:

(10) *Krome togo, každyj iz nix* **nosit**[non] ***imja****, kotoroe ja terpet' ne mogu.* (Fowles 1963)
 'And they both **have** the one man's **name** I really can't stand.

Third, we consider examples where the object of *nosit'* is a noun referring to a garment or another clothing item such as glasses:

(11) *On* **nosil**[non] ***očki****, i volosy u nego byli sil'no rastrepany.* (J. K. Rowling 1997)
 'He **wore glasses**, and his hair was very untidy.'

The distribution of the "character", "name" and "garment" constructions is shown in Table 7, which is organized in the same way as Table 6 in the previous section. However, we have conflated the categories imperative, participle and gerund to "other" in Table 7, since in our database these grammatical forms are not attested frequently for *nosit'*.

Table 7: Constructional and grammatical profiles for nosit' 'carry'.

	Character	Name	Garment
Present	12	7	17
Past	9	2	15
Infinitive	2	1	13
Other	1	2	3
Total	24	12	48

Although we are dealing with a small dataset, it seems clear that the three constructions have somewhat different grammatical profiles. In particular, the infinitive is only frequent for the garment construction. With regard to input for L2 learners, it seems strategic to include the infinitive for the garment construction,

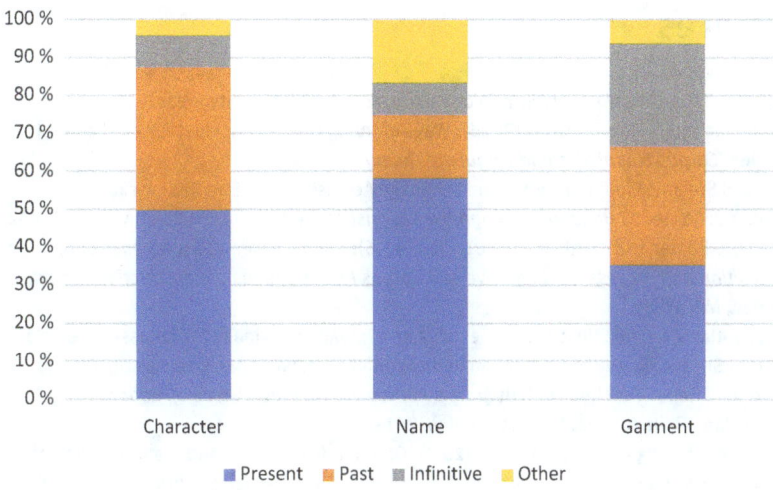

Figure 7: Constructional and grammatical profiles for nosit' 'carry'.

but not for the character and name constructions. More generally, the case study with *nosit'* shows that it is necessary to consider each verb individually, since both grammatical and constructional profiles for each verb may involve idiosyncrasies that have consequences for the creation of strategic input for L2 learners.

9 Concluding remarks

In conclusion, we would like to make two remarks. First, on a general level we have explored the question of how to create strategic input for L2 learners. How to provide learners with input that reflects frequent patterns and therefore facilitates their learning? We have proposed a general methodology involving the combination of constructional and grammatical profiles. This methodology, we have argued, enables us to pinpoint patterns that are of particular relevance for L2 learners.

Our second concluding remark concerns verbs of motion in Russian. Since these verbs represent a major obstacle for L2 learners of Russian, providing L2 learners with strategic input is particularly important. We have shown that creating constructional profiles for the syntactic environments of each verb and combining these profiles with grammatical profiles that show which grammatical forms appear in each construction has the potential to transform the way we teach Russian.

References

Booij, Geert (2010): *Construction morphology*. Oxford: Oxford University Press.
Divjak, Dagmar and Stefan Th. Gries (2006): Ways of trying in Russian: clustering behavioral profiles. *Corpus Linguistics and Linguistic Theory* 2: 23–60.
Ellis, Nick and Stefanie Wulff (2015): Second Language Acquisition. In: Ewa Dabrowska and Dagmar Divjak (eds.) *Handbook of Cognitive Linguistics*. Berlin: Mouton de Gruyter, 409–432.
Ellis, Nick, Ute Römer and Matthew B. O'Donnell (2016): *Usage-based Approaches to Language Acquisition and Processing: Cognitive and Corpus Investigations of Construction Grammar*. Malden, MA: Wiley.
Gor, Kira, Svetlana V. Cook, Vera Malyushenkova and Tatyana Vdovina (2010): Russian verbs of motion: Second language acquisition and cognitive linguistics perspectives. In Victoria Hasko and Renee Perelmutter (eds.): *New Approaches to Slavic Verbs of Motion*. Amsterdam/Philadelphia: John Benjamins, 361–381.
Janda, Laura A. and Olga N. Lyashevskaya (2011): Grammatical profiles and the interaction of the lexicon with aspect, tense and mood in Russian. *Cognitive Linguistics* 22.4: 719–763.
Janda, Laura A. and Valery D. Solovyev (2009): What Constructional Profiles Reveal About Synonymy: A Case Study of Russian Words for SADNESS and HAPPINESS. *Cognitive Linguistics* 20.2: 367–393.
Kuznetsova, Julia (2015): *Linguistic profiles: going from form to meaning via statistics*. Berlin: De Gruyter Mouton.
Mahota, William (1996): *Russian motion verbs for intermediate students*. New Haven and London: Yale University Press.
Muravyova, Larisa S. (1995): *Verbs of motion in Russian*. Moscow: Russkij jazyk.
Nesset, Tore (2000): Iconicity and prototypes: A new perspective on Russian verbs of motion. *Scando-Slavica* 46: 105–119.
Nesset, Tore (2008): PATH and MANNER: An Image-Schematic Approach to Russian Verbs of Motion. *Scando-Slavica* 54: 135–197.
Nesset, Tore (2010): Metaphorical walking: Russian *idti* as a generalized motion verb In Victoria Hasko and Renee Perelmutter (eds.): *New Approaches to Slavic Verbs of Motion*. Amsterdam/Philadelphia: John Benjamins, 343–360.
Rakhilina, Ekaterina V. (2004): There and back: the case of Russian 'go'. *Glossos* 5: 1–34.
Römer, Ute (2004): Comparing real and ideal language learner input: The use of an EFL textbook corpus in corpus linguistics and language teaching. In: Guy Aston, Silvia Bernardini and Dominic Stewart (eds.): *Corpora and Language Learners*. Amsterdam: John Benjamins, 151–168.
Talmy, Leonard (2000): *Toward a Cognitive Semantics*. Volume 2. Cambridge, Massachusetts and London, England: The MIT Press.

Amanda L. Patten, Florent Perek
Pedagogic applications of the English Constructicon

1 Introduction

This paper outlines a proposal for a new constructicon of English before examining its potential as a pedagogic resource. Constructicon research is an emerging field of linguistics (see Lyngfelt et al. 2018a) which relates to a practical application of the central theoretical tenet of Construction Grammar: that language is not a system of rules that govern how we combine words to make sentences, but is a network of symbolic units (form-meaning pairings) of varying size and complexity (see e.g. Fillmore, Kay, and O'Connor 1988). The linguistic network of the mind has been referred to as a constructicon (e.g. Jurafsky 1991: 18) or construct-i-con (e.g. Goldberg 2003: 219). As descriptive resources, constructicons are structured repositories of the lexicogrammatical constructions of a particular language, typically in electronic form. The development of such resources involves the application of lexicographic practices to construction grammar theories (a method labelled *constructicography* by Lyngfelt et al. 2018a). Constructicons may be, by design, of varying sizes and scope, and current constructicon projects are in various stages of development. Nevertheless, a large-scale constructicon – one which aims for substantial coverage of a particular language – is ultimately a model of that language (Janda et al. 2018: 170).

In this paper, we describe what we think is an exciting opportunity, as well as a genuine need, for a more comprehensive constructicon of the English language that combines the existing resources of FrameNet and the COBUILD Grammar Patterns. We show how such a resource would be of benefit to the field of English language learning and teaching, and would complement a pedagogic model of construction grammar. In Section 2, we provide a short overview of the evidence in support of constructional theories of language learning, before explaining some of the principles that lie behind a constructional approach to language teaching. We then summarise the existing literature on the pedagogic applications of constructicon resources, before presenting our plans for a new English Constructicon in Section 3. In Section 4, we explore the additional value

Notes: We would like to thank two anonymous reviewers for their valuable comments on an earlier version of this article. We are grateful to Adrienne Hughes for sharing her reflections on teaching English grammar.

https://doi.org/10.1515/9783110746723-007

of such a resource for language pedagogy, illustrating and enriching this discussion through a case study that compares a test case for the proposed constructicon with existing pedagogic works designed to support teachers and learners in English grammar. Our focus here is on verb complementation, specifically the patterns **V -ing** and **V to-inf** (see Francis, Hunston, and Manning 1996: 80–96).[1] We conclude, in Section 5, that constructicon research has much to offer for language learners and language teachers, and that the development of user-friendly constructicons is essential for the successful implementation of construction grammar models of language teaching.

2 The role of construction grammar in language learning and teaching

2.1 Language learning as construction learning

Over the last twenty years, constructional theories of language have become increasingly popular in the field of linguistics, accompanied by growing empirical evidence that much of language is learned and stored as constructions; that is, as pairings of form and meaning. Experimental research in both first and second language acquisition suggests that language knowledge emerges out of multiple experiences with recurring patterns (see Ellis, Römer, and O'Donnell 2016). This supports the usage-based model of acquisition on which every aspect of the speaker's linguistic knowledge is learned from the language input; the speaker inductively generalises over instances to form mental schemas (a process referred to as 'pattern-finding' by Tomasello (2003, 2009: 70)) which are represented as constructions in the language system.

The empirical evidence that language is stored in the mind as constructions comprises numerous studies, including sentence-sorting experiments (see Bencini and Goldberg 2000; Liang 2002; Gries and Wulff 2005, 2009; Valenzuela Manzanares and Rojo López 2008). In these studies, participants are asked to group sentences into categories. This means making a choice of either construction-based sorting (for example, both *Chris threw Linda the pencil* and *Beth got Liz an invitation* are instances of the ditransitive construction) or categorising sentences according to the verbs contained within them (as in the pairing of *Chris*

---

[1] In line with formatting conventions in the field, we use bold font for the names of patterns listed in the COBUILD Grammar Patterns (see Hunston and Francis 2000).

threw Linda the pencil with *Pat threw the keys onto the roof*) (Gries and Wulff 2005: 200). The results of these studies show that constructions have a 'psychological reality' for both native and non-native speakers of English, and that among the non-native speakers, it is the more proficient learners who demonstrate a greater use of construction-based sorting (see Liang 2002, cited in Goldberg 2006: 116–117). We can assume from this that knowledge of constructions is crucial for language learning and that the entrenchment of mental schemas is important for obtaining greater language proficiency.

2.2 Construction Grammar and language teaching

This psycholinguistic research suggests that a constructional approach to language teaching could benefit learners of English, and there is an emerging body of literature on this topic (see Wee 2007; Holme 2010a, 2010b; and the contributions in De Knop and Gilquin 2016). Many of these authors argue that as a theory of language, Construction Grammar is particularly well suited, not only to language learners, but also to today's language teaching classroom. As Herbst (2016: 33) notes, there is little formalism in much of the literature on Construction Grammar, and so the theory is relatively amenable to applications outside of the academic community (see also Boas 2013: 249). Furthermore, Construction Grammar is consistent with many of the most recent developments in language pedagogy, including corpus-based (or corpus-aided) approaches to language learning and the concomitant focus on collocation and phraseology. Construction Grammar incorporates both collocation and phraseology into the concept 'construction', and as a usage-based theory, it is committed to the study of authentic language use.

Consequently, Construction Grammar should also work well alongside the *communicative approach* to language teaching, which involves the study of texts written (or spoken) for authentic communicative purposes. The communicative approach emphasises interaction, as learners practise performing different communicative intentions that are meaningful to them. Wee (2007: 21) highlights concerns among teachers that the communicative approach as it stands does not provide enough explicit grammar instruction: "ideas take precedence" over grammatical accuracy, "leading to poor language use." Wee suggests that since Construction Grammar emphasises the symbolic nature of language as comprising pairings of form and meaning, its application in language teaching would enable due attention to grammatical form "without sacrificing the focus on communicative function" (2007: 23).

In a similar discussion, Littlemore (2009) notes that Construction Grammar would help to balance out the heavy focus on vocabulary and fixed phrases in the *lexical approach* to language teaching. Construction Grammar recognises a continuum between the lexicon and the grammar, with fixed lexical expressions treated as (partially) motivated instances of more regular grammatical patterns. Littlemore claims that this would be of benefit to the language learner, with construction grammar offering "a sort of middle ground between the categorical yet inadequate traditional 'grammar rules' approach and the more accurate yet potentially overwhelming 'lexical' approach" (p.169) (see also De Knop and Mollica 2016).

The Construction Grammar approach to language teaching centres around the following key recommendations:

(1) *Enrich the input*

In order to help learners to acquire mental representations that generalise over instances, they should be exposed to authentic and varying instantiations of the construction (as containing different lexical items), which should be presented repeatedly in differing contexts.

Gilquin (2016) shows that English as a Second Language (ESL) students, who have comparatively more exposure to natural input than English as a Foreign Language (EFL) students, have a more native-like knowledge of constructions, and that they generalise at a more abstract level. EFL students, who receive limited input and more explicit instruction, tend to generalise at a more concrete level. However, she concludes that neither group of students seemed to have received sufficient exposure to recognise the full productivity of the construction considered.

Holme (2012) recommends a strategy of *input engineering*, in which the teacher very consciously provides students with exposure and then re-exposure to varying instances of the construction, for example, via texts that "recycle new tokens of previously taught constructions" (Holme 2010a: 127). This should be accompanied by explicit instruction, to ensure that students *notice* the "different instantiations and related shifts in meaning" (Holme 2010a, 127). Holme's (2010b) classroom-based study suggests that combining sufficient exposure of constructions with explicit teaching results in greater accuracy than exposure alone.

However, the constructional view of language learning, as a usage-based model, also recognises what may be the limits of classroom-based exposure and instruction. As Holme (2010b: 373) comments, "we need to recognise that progress in a language is equivalent to building an inventory of its constructions, and there is almost no point at which that process can be declared complete. Constructions can be entrenched through naturalistic processes of usage, but correct usage is itself promoted by conscious processes of exploration."

(2) *Teach according to the constructional network*

The constructional approach also makes recommendations for the organisation of learning, with language material being presented in a way that reflects the constructional network. Ideally, students should begin with prototypical associations between word and construction, before expanding out into extended, coerced instances or fixed phrases (see Langacker 2008: 83). For example, the lexical content of the verb *give* (as transference of possession) corresponds with the constructional meaning of the ditransitive, while other verbs occurring in this construction (*knit*, for example) do not: *give me a sweater, knit me a sweater* (see Goldberg 1995: 35); Holme (2010b: 363) concludes, "[t]eachers who want to exemplify a construction's meaning should therefore look for lexis whose decontextualized meaning is congruent with it".

There is considerable evidence that light verbs (which are often prototypical verbs) can act as *pathbreakers* in constructional learning, serving as "prototype[s] with which other verbs may be associated" (Goldberg, Casenhiser, and Sethuraman 2004: 304, see also Ellis and Ferreira-Junior 2009), and that this makes for a more efficient learning experience (Sung and Yang 2016). However, as Holme (2010a: 123) observes, finding pathbreaker verbs "is not always straightforward". As an alternative, he suggests grouping the verbs into subcategories of meaning, with teachers presenting the construction "as a productive group of connected category meanings" (2010a: 125). Holme (2010a: 125) claims that this approach will encourage learners to treat the construction "as a fully productive or 'empty' pattern rather than as one built around a handful of specific verbs". Holme (2010a: 123) recognises that "previous lexical work can help" teachers to organise constructions into meaning groups, making explicit reference to the Collins COBUILD research.

The constructional network should also influence the larger syllabus of grammar instruction, with constructions taught in relation to similar constructions. Ruiz de Mendoza Ibáñez and Agustín Llach's (2016) study suggests that it is easier to learn constructions that share conceptual and formal structure, and that this strategy is especially helpful in cases where one of the constructions does not have a clear equivalent in the learners' first language (the L1). Sung and Yang's (2016) study suggests that learning only one construction helps in the translation of another, and that these effects are strongest when the constructions are related by a direct link in the constructional network. The authors conclude that organising foreign language teaching in accordance with the constructional network is one way of compensating for limited exposure to natural language input, as it "maximizes learning gains" (Sung and Yang 2016: 109).

(3) *Teach lexis and grammar together*

As noted above, Construction Grammar recognises a continuum between the lexicon and the grammar. Teaching along this continuum means exploring the relationship between words and constructions, rather than separating out knowledge of vocabulary from knowledge of grammar (as in the 'dictionary and grammar book' model (Taylor 2010, 2012)). Holme (2010a: 130) suggests teaching new vocabulary alongside grammar instruction: "[w]ords and their meanings should be looked at inside the constructions where they are found to occur"; likewise, "[t]eaching new lexis can be interpreted as an opportunity for looking at the constructions that typify its use". Holme (2010a: 128) observes that grammar exercises typically involve 'fill the gap' sentences (cloze procedures) in which students are asked to enter either the correct grammatical form of a given word or the appropriate closed class word (such as a preposition); he suggests that these 'fill the gap' exercises could also be used to ask students "to provide appropriate lexical items", making for "a more creative and compositional use of the cloze procedure".

Teaching along the continuum also means that elements at the lexical end of the scale, such as fixed phrases (e.g. *over the years; in the first place*), are discussed not only as formulaic expressions or 'chunks', but are integrated into the constructional network in a way that reveals their regularity and (potential) productivity. As Littlemore (2009: 174) notes, this presents formulaic phrases as being partially motivated rather than purely arbitrary.

(4) *Emphasise meaning at every opportunity*

Construction Grammar emphasises the symbolic nature of language as comprising form and meaning pairs. Its application in language teaching means not only a return to focusing on grammatical form, but also proper attention to the meaning of grammatical structures. Through a constructional approach, students should understand the constraints that meaning imposes on the behaviour of constructions (i.e. which lexical items they can combine with), and how the various meanings of a particular construction are related to one another. On this view, it is not enough to describe the rules or tendencies of grammar; "we need to explain to the learner why the foreign language should be as it is" and "promote the learner's insight into the foreign language system" (Taylor 2008: 57). In this way, the constructional approach – building on work in applied cognitive linguistics – emphasises *motivation* in the language system, whether this resides internally to the construction (in the mapping between form and meaning) or in the relation between a construction and the larger language network (as noted in point (3) above with regards to formulaic phrases).

2.3 Constructicons and language pedagogy

The above section outlined the key principles behind a Construction Grammar approach to language teaching. However, the successful implementation of this approach is dependent upon the provision of appropriate resources. As Loenheim et al. (2016: 344) comment, "One can hardly expect teaching materials to display a constructionist perspective unless their authors have had access to corresponding descriptive resources". Ideally, this means a resource that pays equal attention to both lexis and grammar, and that attends systematically to both form and meaning. As Herbst (2016: 45) notes, we need a resource that combines "information that traditionally was found in a dictionary and information that was traditionally found in a grammar book".

Fortunately, in the case of English, there is an abundance of existing resources that provide useful lexicogrammatical representations of the language. The pioneering lexicographic analysis of English corpus data conducted as part of the COBUILD project (founded by John Sinclair) confirmed that natural language is made up of recurrent patterns in which lexical and grammatical information is intertwined (see Hunston and Francis 2000, ch.1). This research led to a transformation in the lexicographical practices of dictionary production; learner dictionaries of English now routinely incorporate language patterns (information about the syntactic environment of lexical items) into their word entries (see Hunston 2004). Lexical reference works aimed at linguistic researchers, such as the FrameNet database (Ruppenhofer et al. 2016) and the Valency Dictionary of English (Herbst et al. 2004), focus explicitly on the combinatorial properties of lexical items. From the opposite perspective, grammatical reference works, such as the COBUILD Grammar Patterns series (Francis, Hunston, and Manning 1996, 1998) and the Erlangen Valency PatternBank (Herbst and Uhrig 2009) provide lists of the lexical items attested as occurring in syntactic patterns centred around verbs, nouns and adjectives.

However, each of these resources has a particular focus of attention. For example, in the case of FrameNet, the combinatorial properties of a lexical unit (or word sense) are described in terms of the theory of Frame Semantics (Fillmore 1985). In contrast, the COBUILD Grammar Patterns series provides a much more thorough description of linguistic form, with a less systematic approach to meaning (see Hunston and Francis 2000: 86). In Section 3, we outline plans for an English Constructicon that combines information from these two existing resources into a more comprehensive and multifunctional lexicogrammatical resource that better captures the relationship between words and constructions and between form and meaning. By integrating this information into a constructional network (i.e. a constructicon), we add a description of the relationship *between* constructions.

As Herbst (2016: 45) comments, the diversity of a truly lexicogrammatical resource is better suited to an electronic, rather than print-based medium, and indeed much of the discourse around the topic of constructicons and pedagogy relates to the usability of the web interface providing access to the constructicon and the accessibility of the resource to non-linguists. Suggestions for a pedagogic constructicon include:

- A user-friendly interface, which is easily searchable "for both lexical and grammatical information" (Herbst 2016: 45), and which presents information in ways familiar to language teachers and learners. For example, listing constructions alphabetically may not be the most transparent method of organisation, contra Loenheim et al. (2016: 346).
- Constructional entries that contain as little complex linguistic terminology as possible. Herbst (2016: 44) notes that in language teaching, terminology should be "restricted to a useful minimum", and should be employed consistently. We follow the approach taken in the COBUILD Grammar Patterns, outlined in Hunston and Francis (2000: ch.6), of describing grammatical structure using a 'flat' notation that is easy for non-expert users to interpret.
- An option for users to select a simplified version of constructional entries, following the approach taken in the Swedish Constructicon (see Lyngfelt et al. 2018b). Following the previous point, some specialist terminology could be included in the "full" version of the constructional entries, but the simplified version should avoid this as much as possible, and this should be the one shown to the public by default.
- The provision of a pedagogic tool, giving examples of teaching materials developed using the resource. Such a tool is under development as part of the Swedish Constructicon project (see Loenheim et al. 2016: 349).

There is, as yet, less discussion in the emerging constructicography literature on how constructicons can be employed in language teaching and learning. Loenheim et al. (2016: 343) speculate "that access to patterns and constructions becomes more and more important *at higher proficiency levels*, with an increasing focus on *idiomatic language use*" (emphasis added). We agree that this kind of information would indeed be useful to advanced learners.

However, there is no real reason why constructicon resources could not be implemented in the teaching of learners across all levels of proficiency. Ultimately, this is dependent upon the scope and the design of the constructicon. For example, the FrameNet Constructicon project (Fillmore, Lee-Goldman, and Rhodes 2012) was designed as a complement to the FrameNet database, capturing aspects of grammatical behaviour not covered by the FrameNet lexical entries. Its focus is therefore on the more idiosyncratic constructions of English (Lee-Goldman and Petruck 2018). In the next section, we outline a proposal for a much more comprehensive English Constructicon, which differs in key ways from existing constructicon projects. We go on, in Section 4, to show how this proposed constructicon would be of value to language teachers and learners in ways that are consistent with a constructional approach to language pedagogy.

3 A new English Constructicon

At present, there are existing or planned constructicons for a number of different languages, including the Brazilian Portuguese Constructicon (Torrent et al. 2014), the Swedish Constructicon (Lyngfelt et al. 2012), the Japanese Constructicon (Ohara 2013), the German Constructicon (Boas and Ziem 2018), and the Russian Constructicon (Janda et al. 2018). The FrameNet Constructicon (Fillmore, Lee-Goldman, and Rhodes 2012), which actually pioneered the field of constructicography, is a constructicon of English. However, as noted above, this constructicon was designed as a complement to the FrameNet database.

FrameNet aims to describe the meaning of English words in terms of semantic frames, defined as "coherent schematization[s] of experience or knowledge" (Fillmore 1985: 223) that capture common aspects of conceptual content shared between lexical items. For each lexical unit, which is a pairing of a frame and a word form, the database also includes valency information derived from annotated corpus examples. While these annotations capture the "regular" behaviour of words, or 'core' grammar (as it is traditionally referred to in generative approaches), the FrameNet Constructicon, also called the 'Beyond the Core' project, is meant to capture grammatical information that cannot be adequately represented in the valency information of FrameNet. Therefore, the constructions it describes tend to be idiosyncratic ones with irregular grammatical properties or some other distinctive feature, rather than common and fully regular structures. Examples include "be_recip" (e.g. *Sue is good friends with Bob*, cf. Lee-Goldman and Petruck 2018) and "non-canonical" syntax (e.g. ellipsis constructions such as gapping, *I had a salad and Mary a burger*), but not more general constructions, such as the ditransitive (e.g. *You gave me a book*) or other argument structure constructions.

The FrameNet Constructicon was instrumental in laying the foundations of constructicography research, but it seems that it was never intended as a comprehensive inventory of the constructions of English. This is in keeping with the tendency of Construction Grammar studies to focus on separate constructions or families of constructions, with such hallmark examples as the caused-motion construction or the *way*-construction persistently cited as evidence for the approach. In contrast, comparatively little progress has been made to expand the empirical coverage of Construction Grammar; as Lyngfelt (2018: 1) notes, the internal structure of the language network "is still largely unchartered territory". Regrettably, this leaves the Construction Grammar approach open to criticism for having limited reach (see e.g. Michaelis 2012), as it remains an open question whether the machinery that works well for small pockets of the language network is really sufficient to capture the network as a whole, as put forward by Fillmore, Kay, and O'Connor's (1988) seminal work (*inter alia*). More relevant to the context of the present study, comprehensive constructicons are likely to enable Construction Grammar to better present itself as a serious alternative to other grammatical frameworks in various areas of applied linguistics. In particular, if language teaching professionals are to implement construction grammar as a pedagogic tool, or as a framework for designing course materials, it is essential for them to have at their disposal substantial descriptions of what constructions there are to teach.

Against this backdrop, building a more comprehensive constructicon of English that would complement the FrameNet Constructicon is a highly desirable enterprise. Similarly to the approach of the Swedish Constructicon (Lyngfelt et al. 2018b), we propose that a particularly effective and efficient way to achieve this goal would be to combine existing resources. Our proposed constructicon consists in combining the COBUILD Grammar Patterns (Francis, Hunston, and Manning 1996, 1998) on the one hand, and FrameNet (Ruppenhofer et al. 2016) on the other.

The COBUILD Grammar Patterns series was an offshoot of the COBUILD project. While information about the syntactic environment of lexical items was incorporated into the lexical entries of the COBUILD English Dictionary (Sinclair et al. 1995), the COBUILD Grammar Patterns series approaches things from the opposite perspective, cataloguing instead the environments, or the "patterns", of those lexical items, focusing on verbs (in Volume 1: Francis, Hunston, and Manning 1996) and nouns and adjectives (in Volume 2: Francis, Hunston, and Manning 1998). In most cases, it lists all of the lexical items attested in each pattern, totalling thousands of lexical entries. **V n *of* n** is an example of a verb pattern, corresponding to a verb followed by a direct object noun phrase and a prepositional phrase headed by *of*, e.g. *They convicted him of theft* (Francis, Hunston, and Manning 1996: 399).

The approach to language description utilised in the COBUILD Grammar Patterns, outlined in Hunston and Francis' (2000) *Pattern Grammar*, conforms to many of the same principles as Construction Grammar (Hunston and Su 2019), despite it having been developed independently. At least at first glance, patterns seem very similar to constructions, as also noted by Hunston and Su (2019), since they are conceptualised as single coherent grammatical units posited somewhat independently of the words they combine with, and consist of fixed parts and open slots. However, while each pattern's entry includes lexical sense information, and the lexical items are sorted into intuitive "meaning groups" (e.g. the second sense of the verb *suspect* in the COBUILD English dictionary is a member of 'the acquit and convict group' in the **V n *of* n** pattern (Francis, Hunston, and Manning 1996: 400)), patterns are not semantically motivated; contrary to constructions, patterns are not explicitly paired with meaning or semantic role descriptors. We suggest that FrameNet can be used to provide the semantic component that is missing in patterns, and that, paired with FrameNet, the COBUILD patterns can provide the basis for a more comprehensive English Constructicon, focusing in particular on the grammar of verbs, nouns, and adjectives.

Our approach, described in detail in Perek and Patten (2019), consists in matching every lexical item in each of the COBUILD pattern entries to the corresponding frame in FrameNet, which ultimately allows us to describe the general meaning(s) conveyed by the pattern, turning it into one or more constructions. In this approach, a construction is seen as a pairing of a pattern with a FrameNet frame or some other kind of general frame-semantic information. The matching procedure can to some extent be done automatically by means of a computer program, using the XML distribution of FrameNet and a machine-readable version of an updated and revised COBUILD Grammar Patterns, kindly provided to us by HarperCollins Publishers. The automatic procedure matches the lexical entries of patterns to frames by searching for that pattern in the valency annotations of the relevant lexical unit in FrameNet. However, this procedure leaves many gaps due to missing information in FrameNet; these gaps have to be filled manually by finding the appropriate frame (see Perek and Patten 2019 for details).

Once this process has been carried out, we obtain a complete picture of the semantic coverage of each pattern, allowing us to identify constructions by grouping frames according to frame-to-frame relations (especially inheritance relations showing that one frame is a more specific instance of another) and other kinds of similarities between frames. Various levels of generality can be identified, allowing us to relate constructions in a hierarchy. Though less common, "horizontal" relations between constructions are also allowed, for instance to indicate paraphrase relations (cf. Goldberg 1995, Cappelle 2006, Perek 2012, 2015).

By way of example, the **V that** pattern (e.g. *I said that I would do it*, see Francis, Hunston, and Manning 1996: 97) occurs with verbs evoking such frames as `Statement`[2] (*say, claim*), `Request` (*ask, order*) and `Commitment` (*promise, vow*), among others, which allows us to posit constructions corresponding to these frames (cf. Perek and Patten 2019). These frames and many others inherit from the `Communication` frame, allowing us to posit a higher-level 'Communication **V that** construction'. Conversely, the 'Statement **V that** construction' generalises over a number of possible lower-level constructions that correspond to frames inheriting from `Statement`, such as `Affirm_or_deny` (*confirm, deny*) or `Complaining` (*complain, moan*). As is likely the case for many patterns, the **V that** pattern does not correspond to one single high-level construction; besides the 'Communication **V that** construction', **V that** constructions include other generalisations over semantic groups of lexical units, such as `Mental_activity` and `Perception`, themselves further divided into a hierarchy of more specific constructions (see Perek and Patten 2019 for details).

According to Hunston and Su (2019), there are about 200 patterns listed in Francis, Hunston, and Manning (1996, 1998). Considering that most of these patterns are likely to correspond to more than one, possibly many constructions, a constructicon resulting from the combination of this resource with FrameNet would be unmatched in terms of size. Another difference between our constructicon and many of the existing similar resources is that, due to its design, its constructional entries will already come replete with exhaustive lists of the lexical items that can occur in the corresponding constructions – information that is inherited from the COBUILD Grammar Patterns resource. This will allow users to search the constructicon from the lexical end, find constructions according to the words that occur in them, and obtain information about the range of constructions that each word can be used in. Following the practice of the COBUILD Grammar Patterns, we intend for our Lexical Index to contain relative frequency information, as this may guide the user's selection of words and would be particularly helpful in pedagogic contexts.[3]

---

[2] In line with formatting conventions in the field, we use Courier font for frame names, and SMALL CAPS for names of frame elements.

[3] Our constructicon will therefore contain valuable information about the relative frequency of lexical items *across constructions*, and about the *type frequency* of constructions, i.e. the number of word-construction combinations e.g. *claim* that. However, in its initial conception, it will not provide the *token frequency* of each constructional type i.e. the frequency with which a given lexical item appears within a particular construction. To include this information would require further corpus analysis, guided by the constructions identified in the English Constructicon.

4 The pedagogic applications of a more comprehensive English Constructicon

As we saw in Section 3, our proposed constructicon differs in its starting point from other existing constructicon projects. It centres primarily on general or semi-fixed constructions whose substantive components are function words (like prepositions and particles) rather than contentful lexical items. In this way, our constructicon sits at a higher level of generality than those that focus on more idiosyncratic constructions. As a result, it includes grammatical structures that are familiar (or at least appropriate) to learners at elementary and intermediate levels of proficiency – as well as to more advanced learners. As Holme (2010a: 127) comments, in focusing on such structures "L2 curricula may be implicitly construction based". It follows that our constructicon can take a more central role in the English language classroom. Information from the constructicon could be integrated into existing grammar instruction, while the resource would offer opportunities for students to engage in 'discovery learning', either by accessing the resource directly as a homework task or via material selected by the teacher.

The constructicon's unique coverage also means that it could be used to design a new syllabus of grammar instruction that better suits a constructional approach to language learning. As we saw in Section 2.2, there is evidence to suggest that highlighting the relationships between constructions in a way that reflects the organisation of the constructional inheritance hierarchy can be beneficial to learners. Of course, this does not mean that learners should work through the constructional network incrementally, stepping from one construction to the next. Grammar instruction requires the learning and re-learning of constructions at different levels of proficiency, "conceptualis[ing] the new through the known" (Holme 2010b: 362). The constructicon would provide an opportunity for learners to build upon their knowledge of fundamental grammatical structures, both revising and supplementing their classroom learning.

In this section, we illustrate the potential pedagogic value of our proposed constructicon through a case study of verb complementation, specifically the patterns **V -ing** and **V to-inf**. Understanding the relationship between these two constructions forms a fundamental grammar point of English language learning: one that is taught, typically, at *every* level of proficiency. Its teaching centres on three main observations:

- There are verbs that occur in the gerundive pattern (**V -ing**), such as: *avoid, enjoy, finish*
- There are verbs that occur in the infinitive pattern **(V to-inf)**, such as: *hope, manage, offer*

- There are verbs that occur in both patterns (**V -ing** and **V to-inf**), such as: *like, remember, try*

In course books and reference works, it is normal for these three observations to structure the learning experience, such that each one is presented within a separate unit or group of units. The third observation deserves special mention because the occurrence of the same verb in the two patterns sometimes results in a difference of meaning. For example, the verb *remember* with the -ing form in (1) "looks back at the past", while with the to-infinitive in (2) it "looks forward in time – at things that one still has or still had to do at the moment of remembering" (Swan 2016: §105).

1) I still remember buying my first bicycle.
2) You must remember to fetch Mr Lewis from the station tomorrow.
(examples from Swan 2016: §105)

The two interpretations are presented to learners as information they must memorise about this particular lexical item. Verbs that undergo a change of meaning may be listed together in a table; but for the most part, they are discussed separately. As the *New Total English Intermediate Teacher Book* (Moreton 2011: §5.2) advises, "Check that [students] realise that there is no rule for verb patterns and that they must try to remember the patterns".

In what follows, we consider the usefulness of our proposed constructicon for teaching and learning this fundamental grammar point. Throughout the discussion, we make comparisons with existing teaching resources and course books. In particular, we draw from two highly respected reference works designed to support teachers in the area of English grammar instruction: Swan's (2016) *Practical English Usage*, which relies mainly on expert grammatical knowledge, and Carter and McCarthy's (2006) *Cambridge Grammar of English*, which is informed by corpus research. We also examine materials from two very popular course books: Pearson's *New Total English* series, which takes a communicative approach to learning, and McCarthy's (2012) *English Grammar in Use*, which is intended either as a "reference and practice book" for self-study or as a source of additional grammar activities for the classroom.

(1) *Enriching the input*

As we saw in Section 3, one distinctive aspect of our proposed constructicon is that, in most cases, it offers a comprehensive list of the lexical items that are attested as occurring in each construction (in a large corpus of English). We aim also for each pairing of word and construction to be illustrated by an authentic corpus example. Consequently, the constructicon resource will provide access to varied instantiations of an individual construction, and so would help to enrich the limited input of English language learners in a way that encourages them to recognise the full productivity of the construction. This is a great advantage over other pedagogic grammar resources. Drawing from the COBUILD Grammar Patterns (Francis, Hunston, and Manning 1996, 1998), our constructicon offers 155 lexical units occurring in the pattern **V -ing** and 204 lexical units occurring in the pattern **V to-inf**. In contrast, if we take McCarthy's (2012) *English Grammar in Use* as an illustration of students' classroom exposure, this amounts to 18 words that are followed by -ing, 20 words that are followed by to-inf, and 15 words that occur in both patterns.

Of course, teachers must be selective in the examples they choose to illustrate a new construction – classroom time constraints and learner vocabulary level dictate this. However, the way that the selection is presented to students can sometimes lead to misunderstanding. For example, McCarthy (2012: §53) chooses to present *stop* as a verb followed by -ing. While there is nothing amiss about discussing the use of this verb in this pattern, the subsequent presentation of yet another group of verbs noted for their ability to occur both with -ing and to-inf would seem to indicate that use of *stop* in the **V to-inf** construction is unacceptable. The accompanying exercise makes this suggestion more evident. Provided with the example in (3), students are asked to "Put the verb into the correct form, -ing or to ... ", with the correct answer given as *asking* (p.348). While the -ing verb form is certainly the better match for this imperative sentence, the pairing of the verb *stop* with the to-infinitive *to ask me questions* is acceptable English, as in the utterance *people often stop to ask me questions*.

3) Please stop _____ me questions!   (ask)

Rather than being an isolated example, this represents a pervasive, if unintended, consequence of approaches that overemphasise the degree of contrast between the two patterns, in order to simplify instruction. For example, the *New Total English Starter Student's Book* (Bygrave 2012: §6.3) presents '*like* + -*ing*' and '*want* + infinitive' as alternatives exemplified by pairings such as *like watching TV* and *want to watch TV*. The accompanying exercise asks students to complete sentences such as (4) with either *like* or *want* and a verb "in the correct form". While the preceding discussion encourages the answer *like playing* as the correct match, *like to play* would also be perfectly acceptable English in this context.

4) Do you _____ football? There's a sports centre near here.

Likewise, at elementary (Foley and Hall 2011: §9.3) and pre-intermediate (Crace 2011: §1.1) levels, students are informed that "we use a verb in the -ing form or a noun" after *like, love, hate, prefer* and *can't stand*, which implicitly precludes the use of these verbs with the to-infinitive.

The contrastive approach is made more explicit in the *New Total English Intermediate Student's Book* (Roberts 2011: §5.2). Here, students are provided with a list of verbs and are asked to put them "under the correct headings". The Reference page provides the information in (5).

5) Verbs following by -ing: verbs of feeling, e.g. *can't stand, like, love, enjoy, don't mind, hate, adore*
   Verbs followed by the infinitive: verbs about future plans, e.g. *agree, promise, want, choose, decide, hope, expect, plan, would like, refuse, prefer*

It seems that the purpose of this exercise is to help learners associate the two structures with different communicative functions (expressing feelings vs. making future plans) and with two corresponding lists of verbs. However, this presentation severely underplays the degree of overlap between **V -ing** and **V to-inf**, since *can't stand, like, love, hate, prefer, want* and *plan on* are actually found in both constructions (Francis, Hunston, and Manning 1996: 92, 84–85). The treatment of *prefer* is especially problematic, since this verb is associated with **V -ing** at starter, elementary and pre-intermediate levels (see above). In this exercise, the category "Verbs followed by -ing or infinitive" is restricted to verbs that undergo a discernible "change of meaning", in this case *try, stop* and *remember*.

In relying on reference grammars that are also selective in their presentation, teachers' access to the varying instantiations of a construction may also be somewhat limited, leading to a lack of appreciation of the full productivity of the construction. Swan (2016: §100, §97, §105) provides a list of 37 verbs "normally followed by -ing forms", 47 "verbs that can be followed by infinitives" (which includes to-infinitives, bare infinitives and noun phrase + infinitive e.g. *I want her to be happy*), and 24 verbs that can occur either with -ing forms or some type of infinitive.

Carter and McCarthy's (2006: 514–517) corpus analysis provides a similar selection of the 43 "most common verbs only followed by -ing", the 50 "most common verbs which may be followed by an infinitive clause", and 11 verbs "that can be followed either by -ing or a to-infinitive". Grouping the verbs into these three categories can give the wrong impression that verbs listed as occurring with only one of the patterns are unacceptable in the other. For both Swan (2016: §97) and Carter and McCarthy (2006: 516–517), the list of verbs followed by infinitives includes *like, love, hate, try, want* – all of which can occur in both patterns.

Indeed, Carter and McCarthy (2006: 514) give a clear indication that the list of verbs followed by -ing should be interpreted as exclusive, labelling them as "*only* followed by -ing" (emphasis added) "as opposed to the infinitive". Despite this, the verbs *dread* and *can't stand* are listed here, both of which are attested with **V to-inf** in other corpus studies (Francis, Hunston, and Manning 1996: 92).

Relying exclusively on resources that offer selective presentations of constructions, and that emphasise contrast between constructions, can cause confusion for learners and their teachers. It is common to see them ask for clarification on internet grammar forums: after coming across the sentence in (6), a teacher writes "Besides, I was always taught and have been teaching others that we usually use V–ING form after stand when it means dislike sth, or has a similar meaning as bear" (wordreference.com).

6) She can't stand to hear them arguing

This speaks to the need for teachers and materials designers to consult resources that provide a more comprehensive coverage of the productivity of linguistic patterns, so that even if the learner is presented with selective information, they are not imparted with *rules of correct usage* that are at odds with authentic language data. A more comprehensive English Constructicon would prevent learners from making misassumptions based on the selective presentation of constructional tokens.

Swan (2016: §100) acknowledges the problem; he notes, "Unfortunately, there is no easy way to decide which structures are possible after a particular verb. It is best to check in a good dictionary". The constructicon provides this easy solution, without requiring that users already know in which lexical items they are interested. However, following the COBUILD Grammar Patterns, our constructicon does "not state explicitly what cannot be said" or what words can *only* occur with what pattern; instead, it allows teachers and learners to compare for themselves the distribution of words with each construction (Hunston and Francis 2000: 263). On this approach, the absence of corpus evidence is, as far as is possible, not misrepresented as negative evidence.

(2) *Teaching according to the constructional network*

In our constructicon, constructional types (lexically specific constructions, e.g. *enjoy -ing*) are organised into subconstructions of the **V -ing** construction, which are effectively meaning groups. These subconstructions are based upon the semantic frame information evoked by the lexical item (when it occurs within a particular construction) and by the frame-to-frame relations posited in the FrameNet database. They are also informed by the intuitive meaning groups distinguished in the COBUILD Grammar Patterns, which more closely correspond to lexical sense information. The subconstructions can be used to identify an appropriate construction grammar syllabus that works well alongside a communicative approach to language teaching. This represents an advantage over teaching resources that simply list the lexical items occurring in each pattern in alphabetical order – as is the case for both Swan (2016) and Carter and McCarthy (2006). Teachers and material designers can use the constructicon to identify constructional types (lexical items occurring in the construction) that would work well together in the teaching of a particular communicative function.

To some extent, this already happens in resources that take a communicative approach to language teaching. For example, the *New Total English Elementary Student's Book* (Bygrave 2012: §9.3) encourages students to "Talk about personal preferences" using *like*, *love*, *hate* and *prefer*, while a larger range of verbs is introduced at pre-intermediate level (Crace 2011: §1.1) to "Discuss likes and dislikes", such as *keen on*, *mind*, and *can't stand*. However, in other cases, the highlighted communicative function has little to do with the semantic content of the selected verbs, and is reflected instead in the examples chosen for illustration. For example, students are introduced to the use of *stop*, *remember*, and *try* in the **V -ing** and **V to-inf** patterns using examples containing deontic modals (e.g. *you must remember to phone the dentist*). While the verbs *stop*, *remember*, and *try* do not represent a coherent meaning group, the common theme is that the examples allow students to both "Discuss illnesses and give advice" (Crace 2011: §7.3). Although we recognise the merits of teaching according to highly practical topics, a purely phrase-book approach could limit students' ability to apply the linguistic patterns to other language situations. In contrast, our constructicon promotes linguistically motivated communicative functions that have a wider applicability.

Consulting a comprehensive constructicon would certainly improve the accuracy of the information presented as part of a communicative approach (see Wee 2007, discussed in §2.2 above). As we saw above, in point (1), the *New Total English* series draws too sharp a distinction between **V -ing**, associated with "verbs of feeling" such as *like*, and **V to-inf**, associated with "verbs about future plans" such as *want* (see Roberts 2011: §5.2 and Bygrave 2012: §6.3). As Swan (2016: §95) observes, the often-taught generalisation that "infinitives are used when the reference is forward in time" is "a bad rule", as "there are too many exceptions".

Nevertheless, the constructicon can help students and teachers to identify useful and observable generalisations, without nurturing the misconception that they translate into "rules". For example, the constructicon shows that more verbs that evoke semantic frames related to emotion (Experiencer_focused_emotion and `Emotions_of_mental_activity`) are attested as occurring with the **V -ing** pattern, while verbs that evoke the frames of `Choosing`, `Commitment`, `Desiring`, and `Deciding` are almost exclusively associated with the pattern **V to-inf**. A comparison of the distribution of these verbs (or rather, a selection of verbs appropriate to the learner's level of vocabulary) could help learners to uncover a useful generalisation. The Venn diagram in Figure 1, accompanied by authentic examples, would provide such a point of comparison.

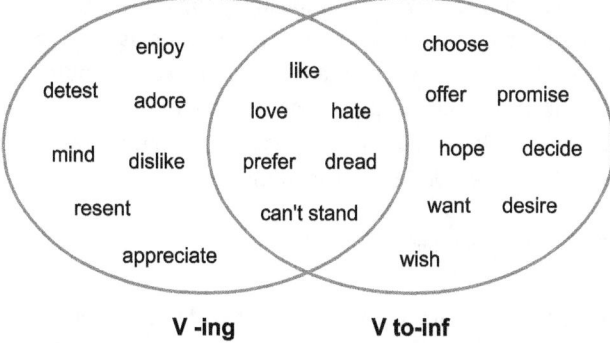

Figure 1: A Venn diagram showing the intersection of verbs of emotion and verbs of choosing in the patterns **V -ing** and **V to-inf**.

In discussing the distribution of semantically related verbs, the three "categories" of verbs (those that occur with **V -ing**, those that occur with **V to-inf** and those that occur in both patterns) are better integrated. For example, the distribution of verbs across Figure 1 provides a good opportunity to contextualise the meaning difference that can sometimes arise when the verb *like* occurs in each of the two patterns. While in the **V -ing** pattern of (7a) the meaning of *like* is similar to *enjoy*, in (7b) *like* with the to-infinitive indicates the subject's choice or habit – it does not necessarily involve a positive emotion towards the activity.

7) a) I like cleaning the kitchen (= I enjoy it)
    b) It's not my favourite job, but I like to clean the kitchen as often as possible
       (= I think it is a good thing to do but I don't necessarily enjoy it)
                                                            (from McCarthy 2012: §58)

The meaning of *like* in (7b), and the selection of verbs occurring in the second circle of Figure 1, accord with the observation that the **V to-inf** pattern is associated with indicating the subject's volition in performing an action or habitual choice. In the linguistics literature, this association is provided with a historical explanation: since it is related to the directional preposition *to*, the to-infinitive indicates a pathway towards a goal that may or may not be actualised (see De Smet 2004). As was noted above, it is common for reference grammars to present verbs that occur in only one pattern and verbs that occur in both patterns in separate units.

For example, Swan (2016: §105), discusses the subtle meaning difference in using *like, love, hate* and *prefer* in each pattern, and he notes that the verb *enjoy* can occur only in the pattern **V -ing** (§100); however, these are presented as completely isolated and decontextualised facts. An approach that organises instances into meaning groups, rather than into purely structural categories, is better able to capture generalisations that may have different consequences for different verbs. The constructicon encourages learners and teachers to identify differences in the productivity and use of patterns that have overlapping functions, without presenting them with a system of (potentially misleading) rules.

(3) *Teaching lexis and grammar together*

As we have already noted, our proposed constructicon provides comprehensive lexical information as part of our constructional entries. Consequently, the English Constructicon would be a useful resource to support the teaching of new lexis alongside grammar instruction. In consulting the list of lexical items attested as occurring in their chosen construction, teachers can select some more challenging vocabulary to be incorporated into traditional grammar exercises. As Holme (2010b: 362) suggests, learners can then be asked to experiment with the lexical substitution of a constructional token and discuss any changes in meaning. While most 'fill the gap' exercises focus on the learner's grasp of grammatical features, a task like (8) would encourage learners to use the two constructions productively to make new instances. More advanced learners could access the constructicon themselves to identify new vocabulary that would be appropriate in a particular lexical slot, in a particular communicative context.

8) remember   forget   manage   fail   recall   miss   neglect   contrive   recollect

   Choose a verb from the list above to complete the following sentences.
   Susan _____ listening to her grandfather's stories
   Alex _____ to get us tickets to the play
   Derek won't _____ visiting his aunt in Paris
   The salesman _____ to tell me about the faulty brakes
   Amy _____ hearing a loud bang at 3am

The constructicon can also be used either as a direct source of corpus examples, or as an aid to conducting a separate corpus search by selecting level-appropriate vocabulary items associated with the relevant grammatical structures: It is of course much easier to locate syntactic structures in a corpus if lexical information can be specified as part of the search. Gilquin (2016: 145) recognises that "inductive learning tends to be time-consuming and time is of the essence in the classroom". She suggests presenting students with a list of authentic, but carefully selected, corpus examples as a useful and relatively quick way of making them aware of the productivity of a construction. The constructicon therefore assists teachers in designing materials that encourage "grammatical consciousness-raising", even if the focus is on identifying new vocabulary (Hunston and Francis 2000: 262). As Hunston (2002: 176) notes, such exercises encourage learners to recognise the importance of patterns and to "notice patterns wherever they are met, not only when the teacher draws attention to them".

Indeed, it is clear that a much greater understanding of the concept of construction (or "pattern") as a structure comprised of fixed parts and open slots is required. The exercise in Figure 2 is taken from the *New Total English Advanced Student's Book* (Wilson 2012: §7.2). In this activity, students are asked to fill the gap "with two words", using the information in the "Active grammar" box for inspiration.

Confusingly, these two words might fill slots for the main verb and gerundive (as in example 9: *she **stopped writing** letters to me last year*); the to-infinitive without the preceding main verb (as in example 8: *I remembered **to take** traveller's cheques this time*); a phrasal verb (as in example 10: *she **went on** to become a famous lawyer*); or even for a gerundive and the article of the following noun phrase (shown in example 1: *I don't remember **taking this** photo*). This exercise is a very challenging one, and this is a consequence of its design, rather than the level of language proficiency required. Indeed, it is difficult even for a native speaker to complete.

In many cases, it is unclear which construction the sentence is a token of or which grammatical slots should be filled. The exercise does not help learners to identify the grammatical components of a particular construction, and could indeed be detrimental. It therefore makes a good argument for why a constructional approach is needed in language teaching. Asking students to complete a structured "substitution table" by incorporating new vocabulary into predefined slots, or helping them to abstract a grammatical pattern over authentic corpus examples (see Holme 2010a : 129, see also Hunston 2002: 178) would represent a more appropriate advanced-level exercise.

The constructicon is therefore useful as a way of enabling students to observe unfamiliar vocabulary in familiar constructions and in encouraging them to be

10 Complete each sentence (1–12) with two words. Use patterns from the Active grammar box.

1. I don't remember _____ photo, but it has turned out really well, one of my best!
2. After six hours of driving, we _____ have a break by the roadside.
3. We _____ visit the cathedral, but it was closed that day.
4. Even after I told her to be quiet, she went _____ loudly.
5. She regrets _____ so early this morning. Now she's really tired.
6. Getting fit means _____ smoking and drinking completely. You'll also have to go to the gym.
7. I didn't mean _____ the window. I lost control of the ball!
8. I remembered _____ traveller's cheques this time. Last time, I forgot and I lost all my money.
9. She used to send letters regularly, but she _____ to me last year. We're not in touch any more.
10. After leaving Oxford with a law degree, she _____ to become a famous lawyer.
11. We regret _____ you that you have not been accepted by the college.
12. If you have problems sleeping, you should _____ hot milk before you go to bed.

Active grammar

Some verbs can be followed by both the infinitive or the -ing form. Sometimes the meaning changes.

mean

1. Which underlined verb phrase means 'intended'? Which means 'involved'?

   Going to the Danakil Depression *means walking into hell on Earth*.
   David *meant to write* a book after his trips.

remember

2. Which underlined verb phrase describes 'a responsibility or something that you need to do'? Which describes 'a memory of the past'?

   He *remembers experiencing* a feeling of emptiness when he arrived.
   They tell you ... to *remember to drink* even when you're not thirsty.

regret

3. Which underlined verb phrase means 'a feeling of sadness about something in the past'? Which is used in a formal apology?

   I *regret to inform* you that your application for a visa has been turned down.
   I didn't *regret going* to the Danakil Depression.

stop

4. Which underlined verb phrase means 'paused in order to do something'? Which means 'completely finished something'?

   We *stopped to visit* a ghost town.
   David *stopped looking* for vegetation and wildlife once he realised nothing survived in the Danakil Depression.

try

5. Which underlined verb phrase describes an experiment to see what will happen (as a solution to a problem)? Which describes an effort to do something difficult?

   They had *tried to build* a railway.
   He *tried drinking* more water but he still felt absolutely terrible.

go on

6. Which underlined verb phrase means 'continued an action'? Which means 'did something after finishing something else'?

   They waved and *went on riding*.
   David Hewson *went on to write* a book.

Figure 2: A grammar activity on the theme *Going to Extremes* (Wilson 2012: §7.2).

more creative in producing new instances of a construction. In addition, the constructicon provides learners with semantic frame information, which is claimed to be useful for vocabulary acquisition (see Boas and Dux 2013; Boas, Dux, and Ziem 2016; Lorenz et al. 2020). As noted in Section 3, our constructicon incorporates information from FrameNet – a database that describes the English lexicon in terms of the theory of Frame Semantics. That information about semantic frames should be useful for vocabulary acquisition is based on the notion that "a word's meaning can be understood only with reference to a structured background of experience, beliefs, or practices, constituting a kind of conceptual prerequisite for understanding the meaning" (Fillmore and Atkins 1992: 76–77). A word may evoke different frames in different contexts, including grammatical contexts, and so cannot be separated from knowledge of constructions.

An understanding of frames helps to contextualise word sense information. For example, the verb *mean* has a different sense in the **V -ing** construction than in the **V to-inf** construction. We can paraphrase (9) as 'involve/necessitate' and the verb in (10) as 'intend'. In the constructicon, these verbs are shown to evoke different frames. In the **V -ing** construction, we interpret *mean* as evoking the `Have_as_requirement` frame, involving a REQUIREMENT (*studying hard*) and a DEPENDENT (*it*, referring to *pass the exam*). In contrast, *mean* in the **V to-inf** construction evokes the `Purpose` frame, in which "An Agent wants to achieve a Goal, or an object".[4] As an advantage over dictionary sense information, the constructicon offers other words that evoke the same frame and can occur in the same construction. For example, the verbs *involve, necessitate* and *require* also evoke the frame `Have_as_requirement` when occurring in the **V -ing** pattern; they are not attested with **V to-inf**.

9) If you want to pass the exam, it will mean studying hard

10) I don't think she means to get married for the moment   (from Swan 2016: §105)

Boas and Dux (2013) show that online lexical resources containing information about semantic frames can support the acquisition of new vocabulary in grammatical constructions. Their study focuses on the German Frame-semantic Online Lexicon (G-FOL), which is designed for English-speaking learners of German. Since there is often insufficient time in the foreign language classroom to "teach the detailed aspects of word meaning and grammar that are necessary for proper usage", Boas, Dux, and Ziem (2016: 322) suggest that this frame-based online resource "enable[s] language learners to learn the meaning and usage of new words outside of the classroom".

(4) *Emphasising meaning at every opportunity*

The constructicon also provides an opportunity for learners to make generalisations about meaning that go beyond the relationship between a lexical item

---

[4] All frame definitions provided in this and subsequent sections are taken from the online version of The FrameNet database (http://framenet.icsi.berkeley.edu).

and a semantic frame. For example, the verb *try* is analysed as evoking the same `Attempt` frame (in which "An Agent attempts to achieve a Goal") when it appears in both the **V -ing** and **V to-inf** patterns. Nevertheless, we can observe a subtle difference in meaning between the examples in (11) and (12). When occurring in the **V -ing** pattern, *try* means to do something as an experiment, "to see what will happen"; when occurring in **V to-inf**, it means "making an effort to do something difficult" (Swan 2016: §105).

11) I tried sending her flowers, but she still wouldn't speak

12) I tried to change the wheel, but my hands were too cold
(from Swan 2016: §105)

Learners are required to remember this distinction as a fact about the verb *try* when occurring in these patterns. No explanation is provided for why such meaning differences occur. However, the constructicon provides an explanation as to why this subtle difference in meaning should exist. The **V to-inf** pattern occurs with a number of verbs that evoke the `Work` frame in which "An Agent expands effort towards achieving a Goal" or verbs that involve some `Hostile_Encounter` "to reach a specific Purpose". These are listed in (13).

13) Battle, endeavour, fight, grapple, labour, scrabble, strain, strive, struggle, work

These two frames, and the verbs that evoke them, are not associated with the **V -ing** pattern. However, **V -ing** does occur with two verbs that evoke the `Daring` frame, in which "An Agent performs some Action which is considered imprudent", that are not found with **V to-inf**: *chance* and *risk*. The distribution of different kinds of verbs occurring in the two constructions therefore accounts for the subtle shades of meaning of *try*, as involving either effort (with **V to-inf**) or experimentation (with **V -ing**). Consequently, we can say that this meaning difference is motivated by the different *families of verbs* that occur in the verbal slot of each construction.

This represents an 'added value' of our constructicon, beyond the simple sum of the FrameNet database and the COBUILD grammar patterns, in that it clarifies the meaning shared between the lexical items of a construction and how this then contributes to the identification of constructional meaning – in this case, influencing how we interpret a particular lexical item *in context*. While the meaning groups of the COBUILD grammar patterns go some way towards this, it is worth noting that in this reference work the verb *try* is assigned to 'the try group' in both verb patterns. There is therefore a clear benefit to using FrameNet as the semantic component to pair with the COBUILD patterns, in that it adds considerable semantic detail. Likewise, since frames are defined independently of constructions, the subtle consequences of constructional meaning are not apparent in FrameNet.

There have been various studies to suggest that finding a motivation or explanation for linguistic phenomena can enhance language learning and memorisation (see Boers, De Rycker, and De Knop 2010; De Knop and Mollica 2016). According to Deconinck, Boers, and Eyckmans (2010), it does not matter whether the motivation for a form-meaning correspondence is "scientific or universally shared; as long as it is there for a particular learner, it can have mnemonic potential". The constructicon can therefore be used as a device for teachers and their learners to identify (potentially subjective) generalisations which can be of use to them.

In addition to finding motivation within semantic frame information or from the distribution of the lexical items that occur in a particular construction, the constructional network of the constructicon would also offer a greater "insight into the foreign language system" (Taylor 2008: 57). We can illustrate this with an examination of how aspectual verbs behave in the **V -ing** and **V to-inf** constructions.

From Swan's (2016: §100, §105) *Practical English Usage*, we learn that some aspectual verbs occur only in the pattern **V -ing** and not **V to-inf**, namely *finish* and *give up*, and that others exhibit a change of meaning when occurring in the two patterns, for example *stop*. When followed by -ing, *stop* means 'stop what one is doing', shown in (14). However, *stop* can also appear with to-inf, meaning 'pause in order to do something', as in (15). Swan (2016: §105) informs us that such examples contain "an infinitive of purpose".

14) I stopped running

15) I stopped to rest   (from Swan 2016: §105)

This distinction is captured by the semantic frames of Activity_stop, in which "An agent ceases an Activity without completing it", and the Halt frame, involving a "Theme ceasing Motion". In the **V to-inf** construction, the THEME *stops* for a PURPOSE: that is, the valency pattern is NP_Theme and VPto_Purpose.

When we examine the network of frames evoked by the verbs in each construction, shown in Figures 3 and 4, we can see that there are eight verbs attested with **V -ing** that evoke either the Activity_stop frame or the Activity_finish frame (the number of verbs that evoke each frame are given in parentheses). These verbs are listed in (16). In contrast, in the **V to-inf** construction, only one verb – *cease* – evokes the `Activity_stop` frame (to be discussed below). Besides *stop* and *cease*, the other verbs listed in (16) are not attested with this pattern.

16) discontinue, finish, quit, give over, give up, leave off, cease, stop

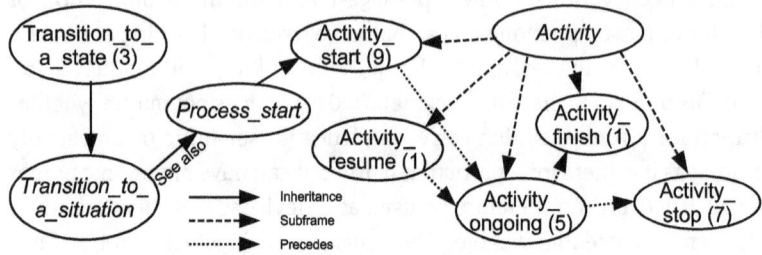

Figure 3: The network of aspectual frames in the **V -ing** construction.[5]

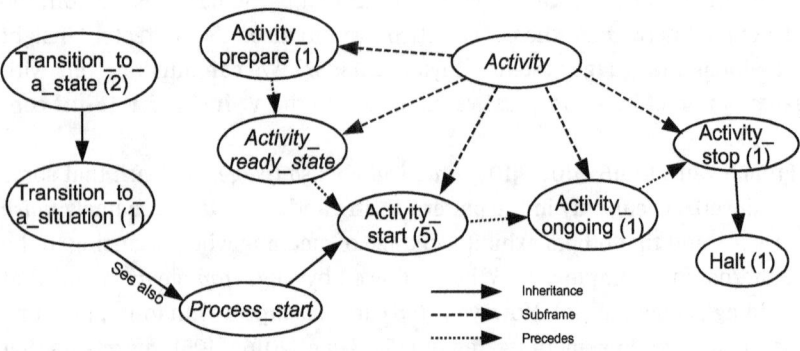

Figure 4: The network of aspectual frames in the **V to-inf** construction.

In sum, the network of frames reveals that while instances of the **V -ing** pattern evoking the `Activity_stop` frame are *motivated*, in that they are supported by a number of different lexical units in the network (shown in Figure 3), they are not productive in the **V to-inf** construction. Thus, while Swan (2016: §100, §105) presents the restriction of the verbs *finish* and *give up* to the **V -ing** pattern in a

---

5 The 'See also' relation is technically not a frame-to-frame relation in FrameNet, and is used only to encourage the human user to examine frames that "are similar and should be carefully differentiated, compared and contrasted" alongside one another (Ruppenhofer et al. 2016: 85). In this regard, 'See also' relations often indicate semantic associations between frames that are worth considering, and therefore are relevant in the discussion of frame-to-frame relations, even though the exact nature of the relation is underspecified.

different unit of instruction from the change in meaning of *stop*, we can see that the two facts are motivated by the same network of relations.

We can identify a similar motivation for the change in meaning of the phrasal verb *go on*. In (17), occurring in the **V -ing** construction, *go on* means 'continue'. However, in (18), its use in the pattern **V to-inf** suggests "a change of activity" (Swan 2016: §105).

17) She went on talking about her illness until we all went to sleep

18) She stopped talking about that and went on to describe her other problems
(from Swan 2016: §105)

Again, the distinction can be captured by a difference in the semantic frames evoked in each instance. The former use can be assigned to the Activity_ongoing frame, while the latter is better described in relation to the Activity_start frame.[6] As shown in Figures 3 and 4, there are five verbs attested with **V -ing** that evoke the Activity_ongoing frame, listed in (19). Only one of these verbs – *continue* – evokes this frame when occurring in the **V to-inf** construction (to be discussed further below).

19) keep, carry on, keep on, go on, continue

Assuming a usage-based model of language, on which the likelihood of generalisations being made is dependent on type frequency, we can conclude that the Activity_ongoing frame is much better supported in the **V -ing** construction, which in turn provides a motivation for the interpretation of *go on* in (17).

The constructicon also contextualises subtler differences in meaning involving aspectual verbs. While McCarthy (2012: §56) tells learners that *begin, start* and *continue* "can be followed by **-ing** or **to** . . . with no difference in meaning", Swan (2016: §105) observes that for *begin* and *start* the to-infinitive is "preferred with *understand, realise* and *know*", shown in (20).

---

6 Since *go on* in the **V to-inf** construction also entails that there was an activity preceding the new activity, this meaning could be better captured by a more specific frame inheriting from Activity_start, of which *proceed* might also qualify as a member. The Activity_start frame really captures only the to-infinitive part of the sentence in (18). We have the opposite situation with the verb *stop* which is assigned the Halt frame in FrameNet. As shown in Figure 4, Halt inherits from the Activity_stop frame, but the PURPOSE meaning of the to-infinitive (which is a non-core frame element of Halt) is not captured in the frame-to-frame relations.

20) I slowly began to understand how she felt (~~NOT...began understanding...~~)
He started to realise that if you wanted to eat you had to work (~~NOT...started realising...~~) (Swan 2016: §105)

Begin and *start* evoke the `Activity_start` frame when occurring in both constructions; however, their usage can be explained as a product of constructional meaning. The network of frames in Figures 3 and 4 shows that the subframes of the `Activity` frame (which refer to the sequential components of a more complex Activity) are better motivated in the **V -ing** construction, being evoked by 23 lexical units, in contrast to 8 lexical units in the **V to-inf** construction. We can see that together, the frames `Transition_to_a_state` and `Transition_to_a_situation` are evoked by 3 lexical units in each of the two constructions. In the **V -ing** construction, these lexical units are all phrasal verbs, shown in (21); here, the combination of the verb meaning with the particle *up* indicates attainment of an endstate. However, the verbs that evoke these frames in the **V to-inf** construction, listed in (22), do not always indicate attainment of an endstate outside of this construction (e.g. *grow*) and evoke different frames when occurring with -ing: *come* is assigned to the `Arriving` frame when occurring in the **V -ing** pattern (shown in (23));[7] *get* is assigned to the `Activity_start` frame (shown in (24)).

21) Verbs of transition with -ing: *end up, finish up, wind up*

22) Verbs of transition with to-inf: *come, get, grow*

23) They came stalking in here yesterday and demanded to see me
(Francis, Hunston, and Manning 1996: 81)

24) We need to get thinking, talking and acting on this before it is too late
("get 12" collinsdictionary.com)

When occurring in the **V to-inf** construction, *grow*, *come* and *get* acquire the transitional meaning of the frame `Transition_to_a_state`, in which "An Entity ends up in a Final_category, Final_situation, or Final_quality which it was not in before", shown in (25–27).

---

[7] The assignment of *come* to the `Arriving` frame is drawn from FrameNet. However, it does not capture the element of surprise (mirativity) or heightened emotional involvement in sentences such as (23).

25) Over the years she grew to hate him.
(Transition_to_a_state framenet.icsi.berkeley.edu)

26) She said it so many times that she came to believe it.
("come 7" collinsdictionary.com)

27) He treated us okay but I never got to like him.
(Francis, Hunston, and Manning 1996: 88)

These verbs of transition take states or non-agentive achievements as their complements, which includes *understand, realise* and *know*. The association of *begin* and *start* with such complements therefore suits the constructional profile of the **V to-inf** pattern.

That **V to-inf** may have a constructional meaning that better suits frames involving a transition to new states and situations also accounts for the exceptional behaviour of *cease* and *continue*, noted above. As shown in Figure 4, the frames Activity_stop and Activity_ongoing are not well motivated in the **V to-inf** construction – *cease* and *continue* are the only verbs evoking these frames. However, their use in the **V to-inf** construction can be explained once we observe that they predominantly take states and nonagentive processes as complements, shown in (28). This contrasts with their prototypical occurrence with dynamic, sequential and iterative activities in the **V -ing** construction, shown in (29) (see Kaleta 2012).

28) ceased to be, ceased to exist, continue to have, continue to grow

29) cease trading, cease fighting, continue working, continue talking
(from Kaleta 2012)

While the occurrence of *cease* and *continue* with states and nonagentive processes in the **V to-inf** construction is one of degree and gradience,[8] this usage would be better represented by the frames Transition_to_a_state and State_continue

---

[8] This is also influenced by stylistic factors. The **V to-inf** construction is preferred if the verb is in the progressive form, shown in (i). This avoids a sequence of -ing forms, shown in (ii), which Ross (1972) discusses as the "doubl-ing constraint". Stylistic factors therefore account for some instances of *cease* and *continue* taking dynamic complements, which more clearly evoke the Activity_stop and Activity_ongoing frames.

(i) I'm beginning to learn karate
(ii) ?I'm beginning learning karate (examples from Swan 2016: §105).

respectively. This reflects the prototypical use of these verbs in the **V to-inf** construction, and captures the influence of constructional meaning on these lexical fillers. Kaleta (2012) relates both of the scenarios – transition from one state of affairs to another and the continuation through time of a stable situation – with an association between the **V to-inf** construction and the historical derivation of *to* as a preposition denoting a path from A to B.

We can capture this constructional meaning as we derive subconstructions of **V -ing** and **V to-inf** from the network of frames depicted in Figures 3 and 4. Since the `Activity` frames are evoked by 23 lexical units attested in the **V -ing** pattern, there is evidence for positing an overarching 'Activity **V -ing** construction' as the prototype of aspectual **V -ing** instances, depicted in the constructional network of Figure 5. However, there is little evidence for positing this overarching construction for the **V to-inf** pattern (see Figure 4). Instead, we might argue for two lower-level constructions: the '`Activity_start` **V to-inf** construction' and the 'Transition_to_a_state **V to-inf** construction', with the constructional types not fully captured by these constructions represented as lexically specific entries: '*cease* **V to-inf** construction', '*continue* **V to-inf** construction', '*stop* **V to-inf** construction', and '*prepare* **V to-inf** construction'. As we have seen in our discussion of the behaviour of *begin* and *start* above, the `Activity_start` and `Transition_to_a_state` frames are closely related. Likewise, we have seen that lexical units that correspond to the end of an activity (evoking the frames `Activity_stop` and `Halt`) can also be interpreted as involving transition to a new situation (*cease to exist*) or the start of a new activity (*stop to talk*). Nevertheless, as Figure 5 demonstrates, generalisation across constructional types is more available for the aspectual **V -ing** constructions.

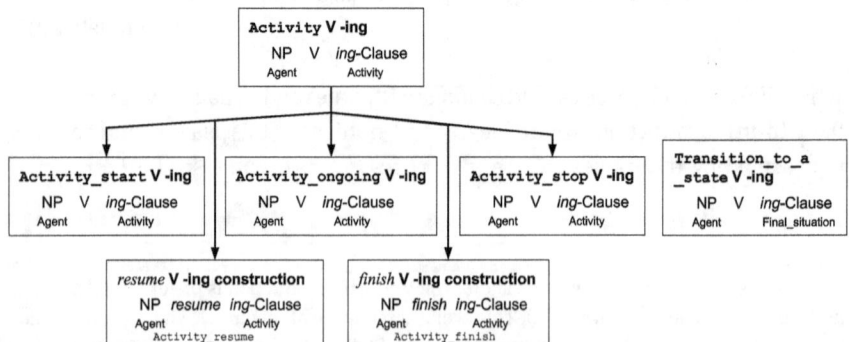

Figure 5: The network of aspectual **V -ing** constructions.

Of course, we recognise that drawing such subtle observations from these constructional networks is not a simple task either for a learner or teacher.[9] Our lower-level constructional entries will include descriptions that encourage users to notice how differences in the subconstructions of **V -ing** and **V to-inf** reflect and reveal semantic differences between the two constructions. We intend for our proposed constructicon to also describe the influence of constructional meaning in the constructional entry for the relevant type (that is, the combination of a particular word and a construction). This is especially important in cases where the changes to meaning and use are subtle, and are not so straightforwardly captured by semantic frame information alone. As Taylor (2008: 58) comments, "The challenge of applying cognitive linguistic insights to a pedagogical grammar lies precisely in searching for descriptively adequate, intuitively acceptable, and easily accessible formulations of these meanings". The advantage of the English Constructicon is that teachers and learners can explore the full range of meanings and lexical items associated with a particular construction, and examine the relationships between subconstructions. In this way, learners are not only told of a motivation for a particular linguistic phenomenon; they can be shown it, and can explore other related consequences of it. As Holme (2010a: 130) suggests, we may particularly help advanced "students by encouraging them to consider whether forms that they think of as 'basic' in fact possess more complicated category meanings that need to be separated out and then subsequently related one to another through some common conceptualisation".

5 Conclusion

As Loenheim et al. (2016: 344) comment, "One can hardly expect teaching materials to display a constructionist perspective unless their authors have had access to corresponding descriptive resources". Ultimately then, the systematic application of construction grammar research to language teaching cannot proceed without the development of constructicons for the languages that are taught (see also Littlemore 2009: 173).

In this paper, we have outlined a proposal for a new English Constructicon that is built upon the merging of two existing corpus-based lexicographic

---

9 We recognise, too, that our choice to label constructions in accordance with the frames of FrameNet would not be transparent in pedagogic contexts. Our intention is to consult teachers and learners in our use of labelling and terminology, and to incorporate more descriptive formulations into the simplified version of the English Constructicon (see §2.3).

resources: the COBUILD Grammar Patterns (Francis, Hunston, and Manning 1996, 1998) and the FrameNet database (Ruppenhofer et al. 2016). Frame information provides the semantic component for constructions based on grammar patterns. Largely due to the expansive coverage of the COBUILD Grammar Patterns, the culmination of our project would result in a far more comprehensive English constructicon than is currently available. In addition, this would be a truly lexicogrammatical resource. Unlike other constructicon projects (see Lyngfelt et al. 2018b), a comprehensive (corpus-based) list of the lexical items contained within each construction is provided.

As a resource, the English Constructicon compares favourably to reference grammars and course books designed to support teachers and learners in English grammar. We have demonstrated this with a case study of the patterns **V -ing** and **V to-inf**. The existing reference works typically offer a selective and alphabetical presentation of the range of lexical items that occur in each pattern, and discuss items that occur in both patterns within separate units of instruction. We have shown that this approach under-represents the degree of overlap present in natural language data, resulting in misunderstanding. In contrast, our proposed constructicon organises constructional types (the combination of word and construction) into meaning groups based upon semantic frame information. Its comprehensiveness will make it a valuable resource for enriching the limited input of learners, encouraging the acquisition of new vocabulary as part of grammar instruction, and refining mental representations based on insufficient data or misleading information. This makes the resource especially useful for advanced learners "whose teachers often sense that there is no more grammar to teach but that what has been taught has not been satisfactorily learnt" (Holme 2010a: 130). Given the often-noted limits on class time for attending to detailed points of vocabulary and grammar, this is an important benefit. This concern is echoed by language teaching practitioners themselves, as shown by this personal account:

> . . .if I allowed the students to do all of the grammar questions in class it would take up way too much of my lesson. [. . .] The concepts are not easy so it deserves teacher time and good explanations but equally students also seem to need quite some time to understand and absorb grammar so it's important not to devote too much class time to teaching it, especially when a topic is first introduced (English language teacher, personal email communication)

The organisation of the constructicon, which is based on semantic frame relations, makes it a suitable resource for incorporation into a communicative approach to language teaching. While we do not debate that Pearson's *New Total English* is an excellent series, we have seen that claims questioning the accuracy of some of the grammatical information in communicative approaches, as implemented in this work, are well founded. The English Constructicon benefits from the inherent pedagogic value of both COBUILD Grammar Patterns (in listing all lexical items that occur within a single structure) and the FrameNet database (in providing semantic frame information) and has the added bonus of incorporating this information into constructional entries organised within a constructional network. Together, this information provides opportunities for discovering useful motivations for linguistic phenomena, helping learners to identify and understand the productivity and use of a construction, and to build networks of constructions.

References

Bencini, Giulia M. L. & Adele E. Goldberg. 2000. The contribution of argument structure constructions to sentence meaning. *Journal of memory and language* 43(4). 640–651.

Boas, Hans C. 2013. Cognitive construction grammar. In Thomas Hoffmann & Graeme Trousdale (eds.), *The Oxford handbook of construction grammar*, 233–254. Oxford: Oxford University Press.

Boas, Hans C. & Ryan Dux. 2013. Semantic frames for foreign language education: Towards a German frame-based dictionary. *Veredas* 17 (1)[Special issue on Frame semantics and its technological applications]. 82–100.

Boas, Hans C., Ryan Dux, & Alexander Ziem. 2016. Frames and constructions in a German-English online learner's dictionary. In Sabine De Knop, & Gaëtanelle Gilquin (eds.), *Applied construction grammar*, 303–326. Berlin & New York: Mouton de Gruyter.

Boas, Hans C. & Alexander Ziem. 2018. Constructing a constructicon for German: Empirical, theoretical, and methodological issues. In Benjamin Lyngfelt, Lars Borin, Kyoko Ohara & Tiago T. Torrent (eds.), *Constructicography: Constructicon development across languages*, 183–228. Amsterdam: John Benjamins.

Boers, Frank, Antoon De Rycker & Sabine De Knop. 2010. Fostering language teaching efficiency through cognitive linguistics: Introduction. In Sabine De Knop, Frank Boers & Antoon De Rycker (eds.), *Fostering language teaching efficiency through cognitive linguistics*, 1–26. Berlin & New York: Mouton de Gruyter.

Bygrave, Jonathan. 2012. *New total English starter student's book*, 2nd edn. London: Pearson Longman.

Cappelle, Bert. 2006. Particle placement and the case for "allostructions." *Constructions* Special Volume 1. 1–28.

Carter, Ronald & Michael McCarthy. 2006. *Cambridge grammar of English: A comprehensive guide*. Cambridge: Cambridge University Press.

collinsdictionary.com. Available at https://www.collinsdictionary.com/ (accessed 28 September 2018)

Crace, Araminta. 2011. *New total English pre-intermediate student's book*, 2nd edn. London: Pearson Longman.

Deconinck, Julie, Frank Boers & June Eyckmans. 2010. Helping learners engage with L2 words. The form–meaning fit. *AILA Review* 23. [Special issue on Applied cognitive linguistics in second language learning and teaching]. 95–114.

De Knop, Sabine & Gaëtanelle Gilquin (eds.). 2016. *Applied construction grammar*. Berlin & New York: Mouton De Gruyter

De Knop, Sabine & Fabio Mollica. 2016. A construction-based analysis of German ditransitive phraseologisms for language pedagogy. In Sabine de Knop & Gaëtanelle Gilquin (eds.), *Applied construction grammar*, 53–88. Berlin & New York: Mouton De Gruyter.

De Smet, Hendrik. 2004. Semantics and variation in complement constructions: Gerunds and infinitives following the verb like. *Belgian Journal of English Language and Literature* 2. 247–260.

Ellis, Nick & Fernando Ferreira-Junior. 2009. Construction learning as a function of frequency, frequency distribution, and function. *The modern language journal* 93(3). 370–385.

Ellis, Nick C., Ute Römer & Matthew Brook O'Donnell. 2016. *Usage-based approaches to language acquisition and processing: Cognitive and corpus investigations of construction grammar*. Malden MA, Oxford & Chichester: Wiley-Blackwell.

Fillmore, Charles. J. 1985. Frames and the semantics of understanding. *Quaderni di Semantica*, VI(2), 222–254.

Fillmore, Charles. J. & Atkins, Beryl. T. S. 1992. Towards a frame-based lexicon: The semantics of RISK and its neighbors. In Adirenne Lehrer & Eva Kittay (eds.), *Frames, fields and contrasts: New essays in semantic and lexical organization*, 75–102. Hillsdale: Erlbaum.

Fillmore, Charles J., Paul Kay & Mary C. O'Connor. 1988. Regularity and idiomaticity in grammatical constructions: The case of 'let alone'. *Language* 64(3). 501–538.

Fillmore, Charles. J., Russell R. Lee-Goldman & Russell Rhodes. 2012. The FrameNet Constructicon. In Hans C. Boas & Ivan A. Sag (eds.), *Sign-Based Construction Grammar*, 283–322. Stanford: CSLI.

Foley, Mark & Diane Hall. 2011. *New total English elementary student's book*, 2nd edn. London: Pearson Longman.

framenet.icsi.berkeley.edu. Available at https://framenet.icsi.berkeley.edu/fndrupal/ (accessed 28 September 2018)

Francis, Gill, Susan Hunston & Elizabeth Manning. 1996. *Collins COBUILD grammar patterns 1: Verbs*. London: HarperCollins.

Francis, Gill, Susan Hunston & Elizabeth Manning. 1998. *Collins COBUILD grammar patterns 2: Nouns and Adjectives*. London: HarperCollins.

Gilquin Gaëtanelle. 2016. Input-dependent L2 acquisition: Causative constructions in English as a foreign and second language. In Sabine De Knop & Gaëtanelle Gilquin (eds.) *Applied construction grammar*, 115–148. Berlin & New York: Mouton De Gruyter.

Goldberg, Adele E. 1995. *Constructions: A Construction Grammar Approach to Argument Structure*. Chicago: Chicago University Press.

Goldberg, Adele E. 2003. Constructions: A new theoretical approach to language. *Trends in cognitive sciences* 7(5). 219–224.

Goldberg, Adele E. 2006. *Constructions at work: The nature of generalization in language*. Oxford: Oxford University Press.

Goldberg, Adele E., Devin M. Casenhiser & Nitya Sethuraman. 2004. Learning argument structure generalizations. *Cognitive Linguistics* 15(3). 289–316.

Gries, Stefan Th. & Stefanie Wulff. 2005. Do foreign language learners also have constructions? Evidence from priming, sorting, and corpora. *Annual review of cognitive linguistics* 3. 182–200.

Gries, Stefan Th. & Stefanie Wulff. 2009. Psycholinguistic and corpus-linguistic evidence for L2 constructions. *Annual review of cognitive linguistics* 7. 163–186.

Herbst, Thomas. 2016. Foreign language learning is construction learning – what else? Moving towards pedagogical construction grammar. In Sabine De Knop & Gaëtanelle Gilquin (eds.) *Applied construction grammar*, 21–52. Berlin & New York: Mouton De Gruyter.

Herbst, Thomas, David Heath, Ian F. Roe & Dieter Götz. 2004. *A valency dictionary of English: A corpus-based analysis of the complementation patterns of English verbs, nouns, and adjectives*. Berlin & New York: Mouton De Gruyter.

Herbst, Thomas & Peter Uhrig. 2009. *The Erlangen valency patternbank*. Available at http://www.patternbank.uni-erlangen.de/cgi-bin/patternbank.cgi (accessed 28 September 2018)

Holme, Randal. 2010a. Construction grammars: Towards a pedagogical model. *AILA Review* 23. 115–133.

Holme, Randal. 2010b. A construction grammar for the classroom. *IRAL* 48. 355–377.

Holme, Randal. 2012. Cognitive linguistics and the second language classroom. *TESOL Quarterly* 46(1). 6–29

Hunston, Susan. 2002. Pattern grammar, language teaching, and linguistic variation: applications of a corpus-driven grammar. In Randi Reppen, Douglas Biber & Susan Fitzmaurice (eds.), *Using corpora to explore linguistic variation*, 167–186. Amsterdam: John Benjamins.

Hunston, Susan. 2004. The corpus, grammar patterns, and lexicography. *Lexicographica* 20: 99–112.

Hunston, Susan & Gill Francis. 2000. *Pattern grammar: A corpus-driven approach to the lexical grammar of English*. Amsterdam: John Benjamins.

Hunston, Susan & Hang Su. 2019. Patterns, constructions, and local grammar: A case study of 'evaluation'. *Applied Linguistics* 40(4). 567–593.

Janda, Laura A., Olga Lyashevskaya, Tore Nesset, Ekaterina V. Rakhilina & Francis M. Tyers. 2018. A constructicon for Russian: Filling in the gaps. In Benjamin Lyngfelt, Lars Borin, Kyoko Ohara & Tiago T. Torrent (eds.), *Constructicography: Constructicon development across languages*, 165–182. Amsterdam: John Benjamins.

Jurafsky, Daniel. 1991. An On-line Computational Model of Human Sentence Interpretation: A Theory of the Representation and Use of Linguistic Knowledge. Doctoral dissertation. University of California, Berkeley.

Kaleta, Agnieszka. 2012. The English gerund vs. the to infinitive: The case of aspectual constructions. *Selected Papers from UK-CLA Meetings* 1: 323–341 http://uk-cla.org.uk/proceedings (accessed 28 September 2018)

Langacker, Ronald W. 2008. Cognitive grammar and language instruction. In Peter Robinson & Nick Ellis (eds.), *Handbook of cognitive linguistics and second language acquisition*, 66–88. New York: Routledge.

Lee-Goldman, Russell & Miriam R. L. Petruck. 2018. The FrameNet Constructicon in action. In Benjamin Lyngfelt, Lars Borin, Kyoko Ohara & Tiago T. Torrent (eds.), *Constructicography: Constructicon development across languages*, 19–40. Amsterdam: John Benjamins.

Liang, Junying. 2002. *Sentence comprehension by Chinese learners of English: Verb-centered or construction-based*. Guangdong: Guangdong University of Foreign Studies MA thesis.

Littlemore, Jeannette. 2009. *Applying cognitive linguistics to second language learning and teaching*. New York: Palgrave Macmillan.

Loenheim, Lisa, Benjamin Lyngfelt, Joel Olofsson, Julia Prentice & Sofia Tingsell. 2016. Constructicography meets (second) language education: On constructions in teaching aids and the usefulness of a Swedish constructicon. In Sabine de Knop & Gaëtanelle Gilquin (eds.), *Applied construction grammar*, 327–356. Berlin & New York: Mouton De Gruyter.

Lorenz, Alexander, Cori Crane, John Benjamins & Hans C. Boas. 2020. L2 German Learners' Perceptions and Use of an Online Semantic Frame-Based Dictionary. *Die Unterrichtspraxis/Teaching German* 53(2). 191–209.

Lyngfelt, Benjamin. 2018. Introduction: Constructions and constructicography. In Benjamin Lyngfelt, Lars Borin, Kyoko Ohara & Tiago T. Torrent (eds.), *Constructicography: Constructicon development across languages*, 1–18. Amsterdam: John Benjamins.

Lyngfelt, Benjamin, Lars Borin, Markus Forsberg, Julia Prentice, Rudolf Rydstedt, Emma Sköldberg, E., & Sofia Tingsell. 2012. Adding a Constructicon to the Swedish resource network of Språkbanken. *Proceedings of KONVENS 2012 (LexSem 2012 workshop), Vienna.* 452–461.

Lyngfelt, Benjamin, Lars Borin, Kyoko Ohara, & Tiago T. Torrent (eds.). 2018a. *Constructicography: Constructicon development across languages*. Amsterdam: John Benjamins.

Lyngfelt, Benjamin, Linnéa Bäckström, Lars Borin, Anna Ehrlemark & Rudolf Rydstedt. 2018b. Constructicography at work: Theory meets practice in the Swedish constructicon. In Benjamin Lyngfelt, Lars Borin, Kyoko Ohara & Tiago T. Torrent (eds.), *Constructicography: Constructicon development across languages*, 41–106. Amsterdam: John Benjamins.

Michaelis, Laura. 2012. Making the case for construction grammar. In Hans C. Boas & Ivan A. Sag (eds.), *Sign-Based Construction Grammar*, 31–69. Stanford: CSLI.

McCarthy, Michael. 2012. *English grammar in use: Self-study reference and practice book for intermediate learners of English*. Cambridge: Cambridge University Press.

Moreton, Will. 2011. *New total English intermediate teacher's book*, 2nd edn. London: Pearson Longman.

Ohara, Kyoko. 2013. Toward constructicon building for Japanese in Japanese FrameNet. *Veredas* 17(1). 11–27.

Perek, Florent. 2012. Alternation-based generalizations are stored in the mental grammar: Evidence from a sorting task experiment. *Cognitive Linguistics* 23(3). 601–635.

Perek, Florent. 2015. *Argument structure in usage-based construction grammar: Experimental and corpus-based perspectives*. Amsterdam: John Benjamins.

Perek, Florent & Amanda L. Patten. 2019. Towards an English Constructicon using patterns and frames. *International Journal of Corpus Linguistics* 24 (3).[Special issue on Constructions in Applied Linguistics]. 354–384.

Roberts, Rachael. 2011. *New total English intermediate student's book*, 2nd edn. London: Pearson Longman.

Ross, John R. 1972. Doubl-ing. *Linguistic Inquiry* 3. 61–86.

Ruiz de Mendoza Ibáñez, Francisco José & María del Pilar Agustín Llach. 2016. Cognitive pedagogical grammar and meaning construction in L2. In Sabine de Knop & Gaëtanelle Gilquin (eds.) *Applied construction grammar*, 151–184. Berlin & New York: Mouton De Gruyter.

Ruppenhofer, Josef, Michael Ellsworth, Miriam R. L. Petruck, Christopher R. Johnson, Collin F. Baker & Jan Scheffczyk. 2016. *FrameNet II: extended theory and practice*. Berkeley: ICSI. Retrieved from https://framenet2.icsi.berkeley.edu/docs/r1.7/book.pdf

Sinclair John McH., Gwyneth Fox, Stephen Bullon & Elizabeth Manning (eds.). 1995. *Collins COBUILD English Dictionary*, 2nd edn. London: HarperCollins.

Sung, Minchang & Hyun-Kwon Yang. 2016. Effects of construction-centered instruction on Korean students' learning of English transitive resultative constructions. In Sabine de

Knop & Gaëtanelle Gilquin (eds.) *Applied construction grammar*, 89–114. Berlin & New York: Mouton De Gruyter.
Swan, Michael. 2016. *Practical English usage*, 4th edn. Oxford: Oxford University Press.
Taylor, John R. 2008. Some pedagogical implications of cognitive linguistics. In Sabine De Knop & Teun De Rycker (eds.), *Cognitive approaches to pedagogical grammar: A volume in honour of René Dirven*, 37–66. Berlin: Mouton de Gruyter.
Taylor, John R. 2010 Language in the mind. In Sabine De Knop, Frank Boers & Teun De Ryker (eds.), *Fostering Language Teaching Efficiency through Cognitive Linguistics*, 29–58. Berlin: Mouton de Gruyter.
Taylor, John R. 2012. *The Mental Corpus: How language is represented in the mind*. Oxford: Oxford University Press.
Tomasello, Michael. 2003. *Constructing a Language: A usage-based theory of language acquisition*. Cambridge, MA: Harvard University Press.
Tomasello, Michael. 2009. The usage-based theory of language acquisition. In Edith L. Bavin (ed.), *The Cambridge handbook of child language*, 69–87. Cambridge: Cambridge University Press.
Torrent, Tiago. T., Ludmilla M. Lage, Thais F. Sampaio, Tatiane S. Tavares & Ely E. S. Matos. 2014. Revisiting border conflicts between FrameNet and construction grammar: Annotation policies for the Brazilian Portuguese constructicon. *Constructions and Frames* 6(1). 34–51.
Valenzuela Manzanares, Javier & Ana María Rojo López. 2008. What can language learners tell us about constructions? In Sabine De Knop & Teun De Rycker (eds.), *Cognitive approaches to pedagogical grammar: A volume in honour of René Dirven*, 197–230. Berlin: Mouton de Gruyter.
Wee, Lionel. 2007. Construction grammar and English language teaching. *Indonesian Journal of English Language Teaching* 3(1). 20–32.
Wilson JJ. 2012. *New total English advanced student's book*, 2nd edn. London: Pearson Longman.
wordreference.com. Retrieved from https://forum.wordreference.com/threads/cant-stand-to-do-vs-cant-stand-doing.1753862/ (accessed 28 September 2018)

Karin Madlener-Charpentier
Learned attention beyond typological bootstrapping: Constructional repertoires and constructional complexity in the spatial language domain

1 Introduction

Spatial language is a cognitively as well as linguistically challenging domain, where complex cognition is reflected by complex language. Spatial language covers linguistic constructions that are used to describe static and dynamic spatial relations, such as localizations (e.g., *The book is on the table*), spontaneous motion (e.g., *He jumped over the fence*), caused motion (e.g., *He drove her to the hospital*), and fictive/figurative motion (e.g., *A river runs through the valley*). Spatial metaphors, spatial language constructions, and their component parts are fundamental for the understanding of other domains such as mathematics (cf. Niederhaus, Pöhler & Prediger 2016, prepositions) or biology (cf. Maak 2018, motion constructions).

Spatial relations and spatial language are acquired early in first language (L1) development. For instance, German children use directional verb particles such as *rein* 'in', *raus* 'out', *rauf* 'up', and *runter* 'down' from age 1;10 on, both in isolation (Bryant 2012: 170–172) and with intransitive and transitive verbs of motion (e.g., *reingehen* 'go in', *reinstecken* 'stick in' [1;10]; *raufklettern* 'climb up', *draufsetzen* 'seat on top' [1;11], Bryant 2012: 177). In English, one-word productions such as *up*, *down*, *in*, and *out* have even been documented from age 1;6 on, combinations of particles/prepositions with figure or ground elements shortly afterwards (e.g., *bug on, on monkey-bars*, Tomasello 1987, cited in Bryant 2012: 157).

Cross-linguistic differences are well documented in the spatial language domain, regarding differences in *information focus* – which elements of the spatial event are typically selected for verbalization, which distinctions are obligatory – and *information locus* – which linguistic means are typically used for the verbalization of spatial relations. In some languages, particular aspects of information (e.g., manner of motion) may be more frequently expressed and thus more prominent or accessible than in other languages (Gentner & Bowerman 2009). The concept of *typological bootstrapping* (Slobin 2001: 441) refers to the related assumption that frequent lexicalization patterns and corresponding concepts will be acquired early and lead to the entrenchment of attentional routines geared toward these patterns over time, thus gradually shaping our ways of *Thinking for Speaking* (TfS; Slobin 1996).

https://doi.org/10.1515/9783110746723-008

Research in second language (L2) development inspired by TfS assumptions posits that cross-linguistic influence can be understood in terms of learned selective attention to the L1 lexicalization patterns (Ellis & Cadierno 2009). With respect to the verbalization of motion events, L1 lexicalization patterns and attentional routines may lead to deviant L2 information packaging, primarily with respect to the expression of manner and path (cf. Cadierno 2008). However, TfS-inspired research has only just begun to take into account more fine-grained aspects of this question (e.g., Harr & Hickmann 2016; Pavlenko & Volynsky 2015).

The present study thus combines a TfS-inspired approach focusing on aspects of information *packaging* with a usage-based approach focusing on information *density* (cf. Madlener, Skoruppa & Behrens 2017) to look at two languages – English and German – that are typologically closely related and share the relevant basic lexicalization patterns in order to go beyond established findings in terms of the TfS-inspired path-manner dichotomy. The main research question is thus: How do L2 constructional repertoires, constructional variability, and constructional complexity unfold in the spatial language domain for these two languages, and to what extent do we find evidence for and effects of learned attention beyond basic lexicalization patterns?

In the following, I will summarize and discuss selected aspects of the theoretical background and empirical findings concerning spatial language use and acquisition from the L1 (Section 2) and L2 perspectives (Section 3). Section 3 concludes with an overview of the research questions. The methodology and data of the study are presented in Section 4. Section 5 discusses selected findings regarding constructional repertoires, preferences, and complexity in the spatial language domain in English as compared to German and in first as compared to second language use. Implications, for instance, for construction-based second language teaching, are briefly outlined in Section 6.

2 Spatial language in L1 use and acquisition: Constructional repertoires, preferences, and selective attention

The term *spatial language* is used here as a cover term for utterance schemas used for the description of localizations, spontaneous and caused motion events,[1]

---

[1] Fictive/figurative motion is excluded here as most participants only produce very few of these constructions; see De Knop & Dirven (2008: 310–317) for discussion.

which are connected through largely overlapping conceptual slots. Following Talmy (1985, 2000), these slots correspond to (i) the basic concept of *motion/ localization*, typically expressed in the verb; (ii) the *figure* (i.e., the localized or moving entity); and (iii) the trajectory (*path*) or, more generally speaking, the spatial relation between this figure and some *ground* element(s) (e.g., the source or goal). Additional information regarding, for instance, aspects of *manner* (e.g., figure orientation, speed, or an instrument) or the *agent* of a caused motion event may also be expressed. Examples English and German utterance schemas are given in (1) to (3) below:

(1) Localization
(1a) *The book*   was   on   *the table.*
(1b) *Das Buch*   lag   auf   *dem Tisch.*
     'The book   was lying   on   the table'.
     FIGURE   LOCALIZATION (+MANNER)   PATH   GROUND

(2) Spontaneous motion
(2a) *He*   *jumped*   over   *the fence.*
(2b) *Er*   *hüpfte*   über   *den Zaun.*
     'He   jumped   over   the fence'.
     FIGURE   MOTION + MANNER   PATH   GROUND

(3) Caused motion
(3a) *He*   put   *the book*   on(to) *the table.*
(3b) *Er*   legte   *das Buch*   auf   *den Tisch.*
     'He   laid   the book   on(to) the table'.
     AGENT   MOTION (+MANNER)   FIGURE   PATH   GROUND

Examples (1) to (3) show that the basic lexicalization patterns of English and German largely overlap for all three event types, in terms of *information focus* – which aspects of the spatial scene or event are typically selected for verbalization – and *information locus* – at which slot and how the corresponding information is typically encoded – for spatial language: *Motion/location* and (more or less optionally) *manner* are typically expressed in the main verb, *path* (and *ground*) in satellites (e.g., particles, prepositional phrases[2]). However, *manner* is possibly more frequently expressed in German than in English (e.g., De Knop & Dirven

---

2 Cf. Beavers, Levin & Tham (2010) for a discussion of prepositional phrases as satellites.

2008 for English/German caused motion constructions; Pavlenko & Volynsky 2015 for manner optionality in English motion event descriptions).

Similarities become more evident if we compare the above English and German utterance schemas (1) to (3) to the preferred lexicalization patterns in other languages. For instance, examples (4) and (5) below illustrate the difference (in the motion domain) between so-called verb-framed (V-framed) and satellite-framed (S-framed) lexicalization patterns (Talmy 2000). In S-framed languages such as English, *path* information is encoded in a satellite, leaving the main verb free to encode *manner* (4). These languages have accordingly been claimed to be manner-salient, as manner information tends to be given in most verbalizations of motion events, tuning the speakers' attention to this kind of information (cf. Slobin 1996, 2006). By contrast, in V-framed languages such as French, *path* is typically encoded in the main verb (5). As *manner* information is encoded in an additional satellite (e.g., a gerund), increasing the complexity of the overall utterance, manner tends to be overtly encoded only in case this information is highly salient or unexpected (cf. Beavers et al. 2010); importantly, manner verbs are altogether excluded in boundary crossing events (cf. Özçalışcan 2015).

(4) Satellite-framed
    He   jumped   across   the road.
    FIGURE   MOTION+MANNER   PATH   GROUND

(5) Verb-framed
    Il   traversa   la route   (en sautant).
    'He   crossed   the road   (by jumping)'
    FIGURE   MOTION+PATH   GROUND   (MANNER)

Now, of course, S-framed languages also allow for V-framed expressions, for instance, you may well *enter a building* or *cross a road* in English, but it would be highly unexpected to say you *entered the building running* or you *crossed a road crawling*. Reversely, V-framed languages may show some aspects of more manner-salient, S-framed behavior (cf. Beavers et al. 2010) and some languages (e.g., Mandarin Chinese) may be best described as *equipollently-framed*.

Yet, even if Talmy's initial binary categorization has turned out to be overly simplifying (cf. also Berthele 2004a), it has still been shown that the corresponding language-specific lexicalization patterns are acquired early in L1 development. For instance, Ochsenbauer and Hickmann (2010) show that from three years of age on, German children already produce rather complex, information-dense utterances, corresponding to their S-framed L1's lexicalization patterns. They claim that "from the earliest age tested onward (three years), German speakers express MANNER and PATH in compact utterances, encoding MANNER in the finite verb and PATH mostly in verbal particles" (Ochsenbauer & Hickmann 2010: 234).

In terms of static localization events, languages prefer different frames of spatial reference – so-called relative, intrinsic, and absolute (cf. Levinson 2003) or geo-centric, ego-centric, and object-centric (cf. Shusterman & Li 2016) – and different cut-off points for differentiating, for instance, between containment, attachment, or support relations (cf. Bowerman & Choi 2001, 484–484). The latter also holds for the corresponding dynamic localization (or caused motion) events, where languages such as English and Korean display diverging categorical differentiations (Bowerman & Choi 2001: 481–484): Whereas in English, the main distinction is between containment (*in*) and support (*on*) relations, Korean prioritizes the distinction between *tight-fit* and *loose-fit* relations. For both languages, the relevant distinctions are acquired early, such that "from their first productive uses of spatial words [at 16 to 20 months of age], the [monolingual English or Korean speaking] children categorized spatial events language-specifically" (Bowerman & Choi 2001: 488) in terms of information focus as well as information locus. English-speaking children focus on containment and support relations, using verb particles such as *in* or *up* for both spontaneous and caused motion events, whereas Korean-speaking children use different verb sets to refer to spontaneous vs. caused motion, tight- and loose-fit relations (Bowerman & Choi 2001: 488–489). Harr and Hickmann (2016) obtain similar results for the verbalization of static and dynamic localizations in German and French, based on elicited productions from four- and six-year-old children and adults. Again, children display language-specific lexicalization preferences in terms of both information focus (which aspects of the event are chosen for verbalization) and information locus (how the meanings are expressed, basically, in the main verb or in a satellite).

These and related findings constitute strong evidence for the TfS hypothesis (Slobin 1996), a "lighter" version of (neo-Whorfian) linguistic relativity assumptions. TfS does not assume language to influence cognition in general (i.e., non-verbal cognition and memory),[3] but to influence the processes of selective attention and perspective taking when speech processing is prepared, that is, speakers' "pre-articulatory patterns of attention allocation" (Flecken, Carroll, Weimar & von Stutterheim 2015). Through processes of *typological bootstrapping* (Slobin 2001: 441), language-specific lexicalization patterns – i.e., preferred ways of saying, frequent utterance-level constructions, and frequent options of infor-

---

[3] Findings are actually inconclusive to date, cf. the discussion in Pavlenko & Volynsky 2015: 34.

mation packaging – direct and attune language users' selective attention to those specific aspects of events that are typically selected for verbalization (information focus) and to the linguistic means that are typically used to express these meanings (information locus) from early on. With increasing linguistic competence, these patterns are increasingly well entrenched and represent strong cognitive and linguistic routines for L1 speakers.

In addition to early target-like behavior in terms of information packaging, Harr and Hickmann (2016) also show some degree of gradual development in terms of constructional complexity (cf. also Bamberg 1994, Bryant 2012), as information density and specificity increase with age (2- vs. 4-year-olds). They point out the following: "In both languages [French and German], children express gradually more specific information and this developmental progression concerns the verb as well as other linguistic devices" (Harr & Hickmann 2016: 140–141). Madlener et al. (2017) show that, in German, gradual development in the spatial language domain continues well into middle childhood and that it does not only concern increases of local slot-filler complexity. Based on reanalyses of spontaneous speech from two- and four-year-olds as well as picture book retellings by three-, five- and nine-year-olds and adults (CHILDES Leo, Rigol, and Bamberg corpora), *local* complexity levels were found to gradually increase for preferred slot-filler types at the individual conceptual slots. For instance, older speakers produce significantly more lexical verbs with manner specification (Madlener et al. 2017: 775) and more complex path types such as prepositional phrases and multi-stage paths (Madlener et al. 2017: 776).

Importantly, however, (younger) children do not only produce fewer locally complex slot-fillers, but they use them differently from adults by avoiding combinations of several locally more complex slot-fillers within one *globally* highly complex, condensed utterance. In other words, (younger) children display significant "partial trade-off tendencies between pairs of slot-fillers such that, if one slot is filled by a relatively complex element, the other slot will likely be filled by a structurally and/or semantically light(er) element" (Madlener et al. 2017: 778). Even though language-specific, compact satellite-framed lexicalization patterns are available as early as age 2;6, the mastery of "increasingly complex structural means of expression within the constructional repertoire for each of the constructional slots and [the integration of] the various slot-fillers into complex, informative utterances" gradually extends over the preschool and early school years (Madlener et al. 2017: 793). This suggests that manner does *not* come "for free" in satellite-framed languages (as assumed by Slobin 2003: 162) and that it is still a long way from emergence to mastery (Berman 2016: 461).

3 Spatial language in L2 use and acquisition: Learned attention and the reconstruction of constructional repertoires

Over the last years, TfS-inspired approaches have also gained ground in L2 research, intersecting with usage-based reconceptualizations of cross-linguistic influence (CLI) as effects of learned selective attention (Ellis 2006). In this line of research, CLI is understood as the challenge of re-attuning selective attentional routines to the relevant L2 cues and categories and learning new ways of *thinking for speaking* while reconstructing L2 constructional repertoires (Ellis & Cadierno 2009). CLI in this sense is due to the strong, life-long entrenchment of selective attentional routines attuned to the cues and categories of one's L1 (Ellis 2006), which is necessary, as it makes L1 processing fluent, robust, and idiomatic.[4]

L1 learned attention comprises very abstract attentional routines at the level of information packaging, measurable, for example, as time-lines of selective attention (eye gaze) to the figure, to aspects of the ground, to boundary-crossing, and/or to endpoints of movement while language users prepare to verbally describe a spatial scene (Flecken et al. 2015). Influence of learned attention has been found at different levels of in L2 processing, for instance, pre-articulatory attention (e.g., Flecken et al. 2015), language processing (e.g., Sagarra & Ellis 2013), and gesture (Gullberg 2009); CLI may be bi-directional in bilinguals and L2 learners (e.g., Brown & Gullberg 2011; Daller, Treffers-Daller & Furman 2011).

L2 motion event descriptions have been explored, from a TfS perspective, following Slobin (1996, 2003, 2004, 2006). The basic distinction between V- and S-framed languages led to expectations of CLI, based on the respective L1 lexicalization patterns, in L2 acquisition and use, with a strong initial focus on the acquisition of S-framed L2s by users with a V-framed L1. The basic challenge in this case is that of learning to *condense* information more tightly into compact, complex spatial language utterances, impacting several levels of L2 processing.

First, the vocabulary level, as S-framed languages "allow for an economical expression of manner of motion in the main verb of a clause [and thus] make habitual use of manner verbs when encoding motion events, and have developed large lexicons with many fine-grained distinctions of manner, in comparison with smaller and less differentiated manner lexicons in V-languages" (Slobin 2003: 163). Second, the level of information packaging, as L2 users need to identify the

---

4 Beyond the role of formulaic sequences (cf. Pawley & Syder 1983)

target-like lexicalization patterns, involving the habitual expression of manner in the main verb and the expression of path and ground in satellites such as particles and prepositional phrases. Third, the level of path complexity, as S-framed languages "allow for detailed description of paths within a clause, because the syntax makes it possible to accumulate path satellites to a single verb" (Berman and Slobin 1994: 118–119), whereas each milestone along the path necessarily selects a new verb in V-framed languages. Fourth, the overall level of utterance complexity and information condensation, given that "S-framed languages [. . .] permit high levels of structural complexity and semantic specificity with respect to path/ground information as well as verb semantics" (Madlener et al. 2017: 760–761).

L2 users of S-framed language must thus identify the preferred lexicalization patterns of the target language from the available input, re-attune their selective attentional routines to the relevant L2 cues and categories (i.e., information focus, information locus), reorganize their constructional repertoires, and at the same time achieve considerable levels of information condensation and global utterance complexity. Empirical studies show that this is in fact a challenge (e.g., Bauer 2012; Schroeder 2009), even if long-term changes in speech and gesture are not excluded (cf. Stam 2015).

However, learning to express motion events in a V-framed language is not a trivial task either for L1 speakers of manner-salient S-framed languages, who basically face the challenge of learning to *reduce* information density within spatial language utterances (e.g., Cadierno 2004; Coscoñas 2018; Hendricks & Hickmann 2015). Treffers-Daller and Tidball (2016) show that, when retelling wordless cartoons, at least beginning English learners of L2 French tend to be overly informative in general, using relatively more (tokens of) manner verbs (Treffers-Daller & Tidball 2016: 169). They also use relatively more manner adverbials (such as *quickly* or *at full speed*) in combination with manner verbs (Treffers-Daller & Tidball 2016: 171) and, most importantly, even advanced learners still have to learn to respect the boundary crossing constraint in V-framed French. This is needed to avoid non-target-like utterances combining, in a typically condensed S-framed way, manner verbs of motion and boundary-crossing directional satellites (e.g., **c'est un homme qui court dans la banque* 'it is a man who runs into the bank' instead of *il entre dans la banque en courant* 'he enters into the bank running', Treffers-Daller & Tidball 2016: 174–175).

Recent research shows that even if the L1 and the L2 are typologically close, learned attentional routines may need restructuring. For instance, Hijazo-Gascón (2018) shows intra-typological differences in motion event descriptions by French as opposed to Italian users of L2 Spanish. The point here is that, although French, Italian, and Spanish are all V-framed (with *path* being typically expressed in main verbs such as *enter, exit,* or *cross*), path may also be expressed, in a small range of set expressions such as *andare via* 'go away' and *andare su* 'go up', in low-frequency "pseudo-satellites" in Italian (Hijazo-Gascón 2018: 243). Hijazo-Gascón (2018: 254) finds that, in elicited retellings, L1 French and L1 Italian speakers differ significantly from each other in terms of path/ground expression in their L2 Spanish (although neither group significantly differs from the Spanish L1 baseline) to the extent that Italian L1 speakers overtly express *path/ground* more often and more often in addition to path verbs (and to a similar extent as L1 German users of L2 Spanish). This is attributed to CLI due to diverging French and Italian L1 lexicalization patterns (Hijazo-Gascón 2018: 256).

The initial V-framed-vs-S-framed dichotomy (Talmy 2000) has in fact come to be understood as a cline along which languages may display higher or lower degrees of manner and/or path salience (Slobin 2004, 2006; cf. Hijazo-Gascón 2018: 242). Pavlenko and Volynsky (2015), for instance, critically discuss the categorization of English as a typical S-framed language, as the expression of manner in the main verb is actually *not* obligatory in spontaneous motion descriptions (as opposed to Russian, where manner verbs are used over 95% of the time), given wide-ranging, high-frequency generic verbs such as *go* or *get*.

In sum, although both English and German are S-framed languages in terms of their basic lexicalization patterns, manner salience in the spatial language domain may be assumed to be higher in German than in English. This is assumed to be due to the overall high degrees of manner salience observed in German (cf. De Knop & Gallez 2013), whereas manner salience has been questioned for English, with respect to static and dynamic localizations (e.g., De Knop & Dirven 2008; Gullberg 2009) and spontaneous motion (cf. Pavlenko & Volynsky 2015). The main research questions discussed in the reminder of this contribution are thus the following:

1. Do we find intra-typological differences in L1 encoding in the spatial language domain between English and German, that is, effects of learned attention in terms of information *density* (constructional complexity) rather than information *packaging*? And if yes, . . .
    1a. . . . do differences concern different spatial language constructions – e.g., localization and spontaneous motion – to a similar degree and in similar ways?
    1b. . . . do differences primarily concern manner salience (encoding of manner) and/or also the encoding of paths?
    1c. . . . do differences concern the *local* complexity level (constructional repertoires and/or preferences at individual slots within the spatial language constructions) and/or the *global* complexity level (combinatorial potential of slot filler types at the utterance/clause level)?

2. Do we find effects of learned attention in L2 encoding in the spatial language domain for typologically close languages such as English and German, that is, beyond the assumed basic lexicalization patterns? And if yes, ...
   2a. ... do differences concern different spatial language constructions – e.g., localization and spontaneous motion – to a similar degree and in similar ways?
   2b. ... do differences primarily concern the encoding of manner and/or of paths?
   2c. ... do differences concern the *local* and/or also the *global* complexity level?
   2d. ... do learned attention effects differ between L2 German and L2 English?

4 Data and methods

The study presented here is part of a larger project investigating constructional repertoires, constructional preferences, and constructional complexity in L2 German, English, and French. For the overall project, retellings of 20 cartoon sequences (Cavandoli 2003) and two wordless picture books (Haughton 2014; Mayer 1969) were elicited from a total of 36 participants. More specifically, they were elicted from 12 intermediate/advanced users of S-framed L2 German (six of which with English as their L1, 6 others with French as their L1), 12 intermediate/advanced users of S-framed L2 English (six of which with German as their L1, 6 others with French as their L1), and 12 intermediate/advanced users of V-framed L2 French (six of which with English as their L1, 6 others with German as their L1).

4.1 Methods & participants

The current discussion is based on data from 12 participants, that is, six native speakers of English (L2 German) and six native speakers of German (L2 English), who retold the cartoons and picture books in their respective L1 and L2. Data collection took place in a quiet office at two points in time within seven to 15 days for each participant.[5] Cartoon and picture book stimuli were presented on a

---

[5] For one participant, ID16 (L1 German), time between sessions was one year; one participant, ID 22 (L1 English) only showed up for one session, thus retelling each item either in L1 English or L2 German only.

computer screen and participants were asked to watch each stimulus twice before retelling the story and moving on to the next item.

Stimuli were pseudo-randomly ordered and counterbalanced across participants and points in time. All stimuli were presented for retelling in both the L1 and L2 for each participant, which allows for intra-individual comparison between L1 and L2 retellings. For reasons of familiarization with the tasks and procedures, at time 1, all participants first retold ten cartoon sequences and one picture book in their L1 before completing the L2 part (another 10 cartoon sequences and the second picture book). At time 2, all participants completed the L2 part (retelling in the L2 the stories previously retold in the L1) before the L1 part, in an attempt to balance potential CLI and carry-over effects.

All participants discussed here were undergraduate and graduate students and indicated that they grew up monolingually (either L1 German[6] or L1 English), although some participants indicated additional competences in foreign languages such as Italian, Spanish, French, or Swedish. The German native speakers had primarily learned English at school (for 6 to 9 years; mean: 8 years), four of them had also spent 9 to 12 months in an English-speaking country; their self-estimations in terms of English competences range from upper intermediate (3x B2) to advanced (2x C1, 1x C2). The English native speakers had learned German for four to 20 years (mean: 6 years). Three of them had also spent at least one year in a German-speaking country, two others were studying at a German-speaking university at the time of the data collection. Their (self-) estimated German competences also range from upper intermediate (4x B2) to advanced (2x C1), even if they are slightly lower than the German native speakers' estimated English competences.[7]

4.2 Data & coding

Participants' retellings were audio-recorded and transcribed. As all stimuli represented stories (e.g., a cartoon showing a man who is fishing and a pelican who steals his fish from the fishing rod, the man thus throws his fishing rod at the pelican, then falls into the water), participants generally produced several utter-

---

[6] Differences between standard and dialectal (Swiss) German are not taken into account here, but see Berthele (2004b) for discussion, e.g. of deverging path complexity; analyses for the current data set are ongoing.
[7] An anonymous reviewer suggests that L2 users with study-abroad experience might display better tuning to the target-language patterns; this seems a reasonable hypothesis, but it can unfortunately not be considered here, given the small number of participants.

ances per item. All utterances were transcribed, segmented into clauses, and coded for participant, language (L1 German, L1 English, L2 German, L2 English), task type (cartoon, picture book), item, and type (spatial language yes/no). All clauses containing spatial language (n=4582, Table 1) were then coded, amongst other things, for spatial event type (localization, motion, caused motion), syntactic structure/phrasal complexity at the relevant slots (figure, verb, path, ground, agent; see Table 2), and manner information beyond the verb slot (e.g., adverbs, gerunds).

Table 1: Corpus size per language group (in clauses).

	L1 German	L2 German	L1 English	L2 English
localization	194	159	219	229
spontaneous motion	831	540	811	837
caused motion	189	87	232	201

Essentially, syntactic coding follows the methodology outlined by Madlener et al. (2017), taking into account both semantic and structural complexity (cf. Table 2, with slot-filler complexity increasing bottom-up for each category). For instance, lexical verbs are semantically richer than copula verbs (Vcop) or modal verbs (Vmod), and lexical verbs with manner specifications (Vman, e.g., *jump, crawl* or *sit, stand*) are richer than those without (Vlex, e.g., *move, follow*). In terms of paths, deictic adverbs (Deic, e.g., *there*) are less informative/complex than other adverbs (Adv, e.g., *below, above*) or verb particles (Part, e.g., *up, down*), which in turn are less complex than prepositional phrases (e.g., *on the floor, into the water*), let alone complex multi-stage paths (e.g., *out of the window into the garden*). Virtual examples illustrating the categories listed in Table 2 below are given in (6) to (9):

(6)   *the man jumps onto the pedestal*
        NP   Vman P   NP

(7)   *he is sitting on the back of the little horse*
        Pro Vman   P   NPcompl

(8)   *and goes away quickly*
        e   Vlex Part   Manner

(9)   *they came back home from the forest*
        Pro   Vlex   Compl   NP

For parts of the statistical analyses (e.g., Section 5.1), numeric re-coding was used to reduce the number of factor levels for each category, with increasing numbers indicating increasing phrasal/local complexity per category (see column NUM* in Table 2), while all category levels are used for the more fine-grained pattern analyses (e.g., Section 5.2). Virtual examples of numeric recoding are given in (10) and (11) (repeated from (6) and (8) above):

(10) the man jumps onto the pedestal
     NP   Vman   P   NP
     2   3   3   2   == 10

(11) and goes away quickly
     e   Vlex Part Manner
     0   2   2   1   == 5

Table 2: Syntactic coding at the phrase level (complexity increasing bottom-up for each category; locally relatively complex elements are shaded light grey).

Slot	Code	Explanation	Example(s)	NUM*
figure/ agent	NPcompl	complex noun phrase	the man who shouts	3
	PP	prepositional phrase (in caused motion passives)	[he was pushed over] by the horse	2
	NP	noun phrase	the man	2
	N	proper name	Mike, La Linea	1
	Pro	pronoun	he	1
	e	ellipsis	–	0
verb	Vman	lexical verb with manner specification	run, jump, tiptoe	3
	Vlex	lexical verb	go, come, move	2
	Vmod	modal verb	want	1
	Vcop	copula verb	be, stay	1
	e	ellipsis	–	0
path	Complex	complex, multi-stage path		
		– with 2 or more prepositional phrases	– out of the jar through the window into the garden	6
		– with only 1 prepositional phrase	– back home from the forest	5
		– without any prepositional phrase	– up and down	4

Table 2 (continued)

Slot	Code	Explanation	Example(s)	NUM*
	ComplPleo	pleonastic path (mainly in German)	*oben drauf* 'onto on top'; *auf den Tisch drauf* 'onto the table on top'	4
	P(P)	preposition(al phrase)	*on, from, into X*	3
	Inf	infinitive	*[go] to see*	2
	NP	noun phrase	*[follow] the line*	2
	Part	particle	*up, down, away*	2
	Adv	adverb	*above, behind*	2
	Deic	deictic adverb	*there*	1
	e	ellipsis	–	0
ground	S	clause	*[back to] where he came from*	3
	NPcompl	complex noun phrase	*[on] the topmost branch of the tree*	3
	NP	noun phrase	*[on] the tree*	2
	N	proper name	*[behind] Mike*	1
	Pro	pronoun	*[on] it*	1
	Deic	deictic adverb	*[from] there*	1
	e	ellipsis	–	0

5 Results and discussion

The following sections explore intra-typological differences and effects of learned attention in L1 and L2 encoding in the spatial language domain in English and German. As English and German are typologically (and genetically) close, we expect potential effects to surface in terms of information *density* (constructional preferences and global complexity at the clause/utterance level) rather than information *packaging* (constructional repertoires, information locus, local constructional complexity). The focus is on localization and spontaneous motion events; as predictions for some spatial language constructions are inconsistent – for instance, with respect to manner salience in spontaneous motion event descriptions (cf. Slobin 2004 vs. Pavlenko & Volynsky 2015) – results are reported separately for localization and motion descriptions.

Section 5.1 provides a general overview of *global* complexity trends across language groups. It shows that globally speaking, clause complexity is lower in L1

English than in L1 German, and that L2 German speakers stick more closely to their L1 preferences than L2 English users. Section 5.2 takes a closer look at the actual patterns that are preferred in L1 and L2 encoding in English and German respectively, uncovering more detailed effects of learned attention in L2 English and L2 German. Sections 5.3 and 5.4 investigate English and German L1 and L2 preferences for manner and path/ground encoding more deeply. Section 6 summarizes the results and discusses selected implications for second language teaching. Overall, the results are in line with Pavlenko & Volynsky (2015), showing intra-typological differences in terms of learned attention in both L1 and L2 usage of English and German beyond the basic S-framed lexicalization pattern, namely at local as well as global levels of constructional complexity and with respect to manner as well as path/ground.

5.1 Global complexity at the clause level

This section provides a global overview of constructional complexity preferences across language groups. The analyses are based on numerically recoded phrasal complexity values (cf. Table 2, column NUM*); inter-group differences are evaluated based on non-parametric Kruskal-Wallis rank sum tests (KW) and pairwise Wilcoxon signed-rank tests (W) for dependent samples.[8] Results are reported separately for the *figure—verb—path* pattern and for the more inclusive *figure—verb—path—ground* pattern. The latter is more informative to the extent that it takes into account fine-grained combinatorial preferences at the path/ground slots, distinguishing between prepositional paths with pronoun ground elements (e.g., on *it*), with simple noun phrases (e.g., on *a tree*), and with complex noun phrases (e.g., on *the topmost branch of a huge tree*). Note that, with the exception of this distinction, differences in terms of global complexity do not reveal encoding differences at specific slots, for example, differences in manner salience; these are further explored in Sections 5.2 to 5.4.

5.1.1 Localization

For localization events – such as *The man is sitting on the floor* – usage preferences in terms of global constructional complexity significantly differ across the data set both for *figure—verb—path* combinations (KW=34.01, df=3, p<0.001) and for the more inclusive *figure—verb—path—ground* pattern (KW=30.06, df=3,

---

8 All statistical analyses were performed with the software R (R Core Team 2015).

p<0.001). Pairwise comparisons reveal significant differences between L1 German and L1 English (W=28058.5, p<0.001; W=27669.5, p<0.001 with *Ground*). Figure 1 indicates that global utterance complexity is significantly higher in German than in English, both for *figure—verb—path* (German: median=7 [range: 3–12]; English: median=5 [range: 3–9]) and for *figure—verb—path—ground* (German: median=9 [range: 3–15]; English: median=8 [range: 3–14]). Encoding preferences thus differ intra-typologically.

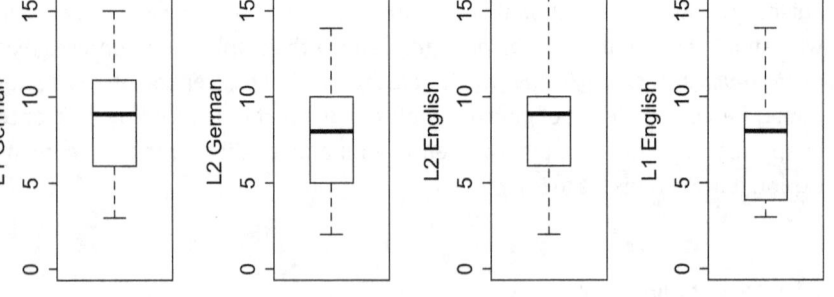

Figure 1: Global complexity: *Localization*.

As for L2 usage, L2 German is significantly different from the target L1 German (W=18430, p=0.001; W=18123.5, p=0.004 with *Ground*) and also from L1 English (W=15057, p=0.022; W=15146, p=0.03 with *Ground*). L2 English usage is significantly different from the target L1 English (W=20636.5, p=0.001; W=20410, p=0.001 with *Ground*) and different from L1 German (W=25541, p=0.007; W=24893.5, p=0.031 with *Ground*). For both language groups, L2 performance is thus significantly different from the speakers' respective L1 preferences and from the target language baseline, taking a middle ground between the speakers' L1 and the target language's constructional complexity profiles. In both cases, L2 users seem to have begun to restructure their preferences in terms of overall constructional complexity, without having definitely tuned in to the target language trends yet, thus displaying so-called hybrid behavior (cf. Treffers-Daller & Tidball 2016: 152). This finding is in line with TfS-inspired research showing that neither learning to increase constructional complexity (cf., Gullberg 2009) nor learning to reduce information density is a trivial task for L2 users (cf., Treffers-Daller & Tidball 2016). It is interesting to the extent that our data show that this is even the case with the basic lexicalization patterns being the same in the L1 and the L2.

5.1.2 Motion

Usage preferences in the domain of spontaneous motion events – such as *The man jumps onto the horse* or *They fall down from the cliff into a river* – significantly differ across the four language groups in terms of global constructional complexity, both for *figure–verb–path* (KW=33.45, df=3, p<0.001) and for *figure–verb–path–ground* patterns (KW=32.34, df=3, p<0.001). Again, L1 German preferences significantly differ from the L1 English trends for both schemas (W=374534, p<0.001; W=365214.5, p=0.003 with *Ground*), with L1 German speakers preferring globally more complex combinations in both cases (German: median=7 resp. 9; English: median=6 resp. 8; Figure 2). This finding is in line with intra-typological English-Russian contrasts as reported in Pavlenko and Volynsky (2015). Interestingly, however, differences in the current data set seem to be task-dependent. Whereas the two L1 baselines do actually not differ for the picture book retelling data (W=54171.5, p=0.508 n.s.; W=53451.5, p=0.725 n.s. with *Ground*), they significantly differ from each other for cartoon retellings (W=143264.5, p<0.001; W=138977, p<0.001 with *Ground*); the reason for this divergence is as of yet unclear and needs further investigation.

L2 users of German are faced with the challenge of increasing constructional complexity in L2 processing. Figure 2 illustrates that they cannot yet meet this challenge: For the *figure–verb–path* pattern, L2 German global constructional preferences do not diverge from the same speakers' L1 English usage (W=238881.5, p=0.085), but from the L1 German baseline (W=261558.5, p<0.001). Following Treffers-Daller & Tidball (2016: 151), this is evidence for L1 influence, possibly encouraged by general interlanguage trends towards less complex structures. Interestingly, for the more inclusive *figure–verb–path–ground* pattern, L2 German users' preferences differ both from the L1 German baseline (W=264465, p<0.001) and from the same speakers' L1 English preferences (W=239967, p=0.003). The resulting hybrid behavior (cf. Treffers-Daller & Tidball 2016: 152) is due to the fact that L2 German users' constructions (median=7) are actually globally less complex than both the L1 German baseline pattern (median=9) and the L1 English constructions (median=8). This suggests that the more complex the constructional pattern is in itself, the more L2 users (at least at intermediate competence levels) tend to avoid globally complex combinations of locally complex slot-fillers across increasing numbers of conceptual slots (here: *path* and *ground*).

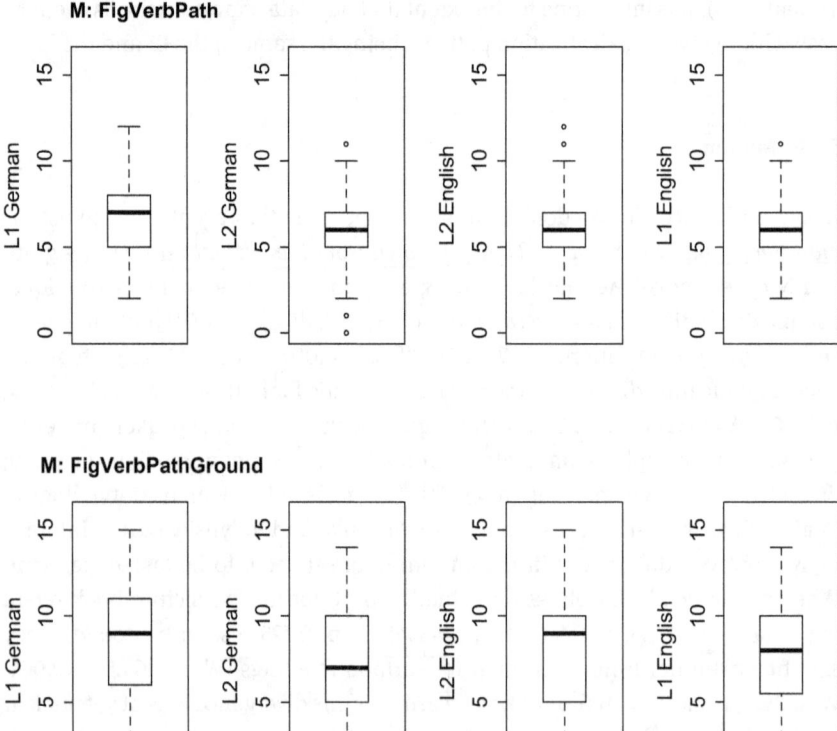

Figure 2: Global complexity: *Spontaneous motion* (zero values in L2 German reflect utterances consisting in an onomatopoetic expression only).

In contrast, English L2 users face the challenge to reduce global constructional complexity levels. Restructuring seems to be successful in the case of spontaneous motion event descriptions. L2 English use does not differ from the L1 English baseline (W=341645.5.5, p=0.814 n.s.; W=331274, p=0.397 n.s. with *Ground*), but differs from, that is, is globally less complex than the same speakers' L1 German baseline (W=388523, p<0.001; W=368529.5, p=0.034 with *Ground*). Thus, complexity reduction from the L1 to the L2 seems to be more easily available in the domain of spontaneous motion than information condensation, as in the case of L2 German (recall that additionally, L2 English users display a slightly higher overall competence level than the L2 German users, cf. Section 4.1); Sections 5.2. and 5.3 investigate to what extent this is due to restructuring at the verb slot, that is, to reduced manner salience.

5.1.3 Interim summary

So far, there are two main findings: First, global constructional complexity is significantly lower in L1 English than in L1 German for both spatial event types, although both are S-framed languages. This is in line with recent evidence of intra-typological divergences (Hijazo-Gascón 2018 for path expressions in V-framed languages; Pavlenko & Volynsky 2015 for manner salience in S-framed languages). As Section 5.2 will show, the difference is well reflected in the native speaker groups' preferred spatial language patterns.

Second, as a consequence, L2 users are faced with diverging challenges, independently of the close typological relationship between English and German. German learners of L2 English need to reduce global constructional complexity (similar to but to a lesser extent than L2 users of V-framed languages coming from an S-framed L1, cf. Cadierno 2004; Treffers-Daller & Tidball 2016), whereas English learners of L2 German need to increase and condense global constructional complexity (similar to but to a lesser extent than L2 users of S-framed languages with a V-framed L1, cf. Bauer 2012; De Knop & Gallez 2013). At this point, it is impossible to pin down encoding differences at specific slots, for example, diverging levels of manner salience, as sources of diverging global complexity preferences; Sections 5.2 to 5.4 will explore this issue in more detail.

Overall, information reduction seems to be more easily accessible, with L1 German users of L2 English largely displaying restructuration – such that their L2 preferences do not differ from the L1 target language baseline, but significantly differ from the L1 source language preferences (cf. Treffers-Daller & Tidball 2016: 151) – which is possibly supported by general interlanguage simplification trends. In contrast, information condensation seems to be harder to achieve, as L1 English users of L2 German display more transfer and hybrid behavior, significantly differing from the L1 target language preferences in both cases (Treffers-Daller & Tidball 2016: 152).

5.2 Preferred patterns in L1 and L2 German and English

Let us take a closer look at the preferred patterns for verbalizing localization and motion events. In order to identify the range of patterns used in total as well as the most frequent patterns for each language group, data frames were generated merging the categorical codes at the *figure, verb,* and *path* slots for each event type (cf. Table 2). The output – of the type *NP Vman PP* for utterances such as *the man jumps onto the pedestal* – was ordered by frequency of occurrence per language group, it thus reflects the range of patterns used per group as well as encoding preferences (by token frequency). Patterns at this level thus show *which* slots are typically filled ("e" indicating ellipsis, i.e., the absence of an overt slot-filler) and *how complex* the individual slot-fillers are in each combination.

Differences at the pattern level provide further insights regarding differences in information *focus* and information *locus* as well as the combinatorial potential of slot-filler types. The patterns thus provide an initial answer to the question of whether group differences in terms of global constructional complexity are due to general preferences for higher/lower levels of information compression (e.g., in L1 as compared to L2 use), or whether they are due to more specific local constructional preferences in terms of the selection of particular constructions or particular slot-filler types (e.g., verbs with/without manner specification, light/complex path descriptions) and their combinatoriability. The focus is on the L2 users here.

5.2.1 Localization

In the domain of localization, theoretically, English and German share the main lexicalization patterns. However, manner information (here: figure orientation as sitting, standing, lying etc.) is more frequently encoded in the main verb in L1 German (n=96/194; 49%) than in L2 German (n=53/159; 33%), L1 English (n=59/219; 27%), and L2 English (n=86/229; 38%); see Section 5.3.1 for more detail.

As for German, only two of the four most frequent L1 patterns are part of the preferred L2 patterns, namely (12) *Pro Vman PP* (n=22 in L1 German, n=12 in L2 German) and (13) *NP Vcop PP* (n=8 in L1 German, n=21 in L2 German; see Table 3), but in reversed orders of preference.

(12) *und sie liegen jetzt im Teich* 'an they are lying in the pond right now' (ID13, L1 German)

(13) *während das ist der Junge in einem Baum* 'at the same time, the boy is in a tree' (ID23, L2 German)

Overall, the preferred L2 patterns are "lighter" than the L1 German baseline patterns. For instance, the three most frequent L2 patterns take copula verbs – *NP Vcop PP* (n=21), *Pro Vcop PP* (n=19), *NP Vcop Deic* (n=14) – , whereas the two most frequent L1 patterns select lexical verbs with manner specifications (*NP Vman PP* [n=29], *Pro Vman PP* [n=22]). In L2 German, *manner* is expressed in the main verb only from the fourth frame (*Pro Vman PP*, n=11) on. In other words, L2 German users tend to background manner information in their preferred patterns. At the same time, L2 German patterns are more complex than the same speakers' L1 English choices, as *path (ground)* is expressed through a prepositional phrase in the two most frequent L2 frames (*NP Vcop PP* [n=21], *Pro Vcop PP* [n=19]). In contrast, L1 English selects deictic adverbs at the *path* slot in the most frequent frames (*NP Vcop Deic* [n=25], *Pro Vcop Deic* [n=21]), with prepositional phrases following in patterns three to seven (Table 3).

However, all of the four patterns that are preferred in L2 German are among the six most frequent L1 English frames. This suggests that even if L2 German usage preferences are significantly different from global complexity preferences in L1 English (cf. Section 5.1.4), they are still strongly influenced by L1 English constructional preferences. If we look beyond the most frequent patterns, differences between L1 and L2 German persist in terms of pattern preferences: The globally most complex pattern in L1 German is (14) *NPcompl Vman Compl* (n=2), with semantically/structurally complex slot-fillers across all conceptual slots, in contrast to the most complex L2 combination, (15) *NPcompl Vman PP* (n=5).

(14) *ein pink-orangener Vogel sitzt ganz gemuetlich auf einem Ast im Wald direkt vor ihnen* 'a pink-orange bird is sitting very comfortably on a branch in the forest, directly in front of them' (ID14, L1 German)

(15) *aber am andere Seite der Meeres steht der kleinste Elfe* 'but the smallest elf is standing at the other side of the sea' (ID__, L2 German)

As for L2 English, the more detailed pattern is different from the L2 German group, in spite of both groups looking similar in terms of global constructional complexity (Section 5.1.1). Overall, L2 English choices tend to be *more* complex than the L1 English baseline. Interestingly, L2 preferences both at the verb slot and at the path/ground slot are more complex than in the L1 English baseline, whereas only the former is typologically expected. Prepositional phrases are selected for the expression of *path (ground)* in the most frequent L2 patterns (*NP e PP* [n=26], *NP*

Vman PP [n=23; (16)], *NP Vcop PP* [n=18], *Pro Vman PP* [n=17], *e Vman PP* [n=16]), as opposed to deictic adverbs in the two most frequent English L1 frames (*NP Vcop Deic* [n=25; (17)], *Pro Vcop Deic* [n=21]).

(16) *and the LaLinea man is lying on . on the . on the floor* (ID11, L2 English)

(17) *our frog might be here* (ID24, L1 English)

Semantically rich verbs with manner specification are not selected in the four most frequent English L1 patterns (see Table 3), whereas manner verbs are present from the second most frequent L2 English pattern (16) onwards. This comparatively dense second most frequent L2 English pattern *NP Vman PP* (n=23) is actually not part of the most frequent L1 English patterns (n=3), but is the most frequent L1 German choice (n=29). This indicates that trends towards higher levels of constructional complexity in L2 English are at least partially influenced by L1 German schemas and routines. This is reflected by overall maximal complexity in L1 and L2 patterns: The globally most complex frame (18) *NPcompl Vman Compl* is only attested in L2 English (n=1), not in L1 English; *NPcompl Vman PP* is attested equally in L2 English (n=5) as in L1 English (n=3). In contrast, the globally "light" combination *Pro Vcop Deic* is clearly less frequent in L2 (n=13) than in L1 English (n=21). Even if L2 English users' preferences are thus significantly different from L1 German complexity trends (Section 5.1.1), they are still influenced by (globally comparatively complex) L1 routines.

(18) *a tiny cute cat is sitting next to him on his li . left side* (ID12, L2 English)

Table 3: Most frequent patterns (Figure—Verb—Loc) for *localization* per language group (globally complex patterns with three locally relatively complex components are shaded grey; patterns with two locally complex slot-fillers are shaded light grey).

L1 German		L2 German		L1 English		L2 English	
NP Vman PP	29	NP Vcop PP	21	NP Vcop Deic	25	NP e PP	26
Pro Vman PP	22	Pro Vcop PP	19	Pro Vcop Deic	21	NP Vman PP	23
Pro Vcop Adv	9	NP Vcop Deic	14	NP e PP	20	NP Vcop PP	18
NP Vcop PP	8	Pro Vman PP	11	NP Vcop PP	20	Pro Vman PP	17
				Pro Vman PP	18	e Vman PP	16
				Pro Vcop PP	17	NP Vlex e	15
				NPcompl Vcop PP	12	Pro Vcop PP	14
				NPcompl Vcop Deic	10	Pro Vcop Deic	13
				e Vman PP	10	NP Vcop Deic	10

5.2.2 Motion

In the spontaneous motion domain, restructuring seems to be easier for L2 German users, in spite of global complexity preferences indicating L1 influence (Section 5.1.2). Six out of the seven most frequent L2 German frames actually mirror frequent L1 German choices (Table 4): (19) *Pro Vman PP* (L2: n=51; L1: n=73), (20) *Pro Vman Part* (L2: n=47; L1: n=57), (21) *NP Vman Part* (L2: n=37; L1: n=51), (22) *Pro Vlex PP* (L2: n=28; L1: n=23), (23) *NP Vman PP* (L2: n=26; L1: n=53), and (24) *e Vman PP* (L2: n=23; L1: n=43), with manner verbs selected to a similar degree in the most frequent L1 and L2 German patterns (12/15 in L1 German, 6/7 in L2 German).

(19) *er hat über diese Dinge gejumpt* 'he jumped over these things' (ID25, L2 German)

(20) *und dann ist er runtergefallen* 'and then he fell down' (ID24, L2 German)

(21) *aber die Vogel hat nochmal weggeflogen* 'but the bird flew away once more' (ID23, L2 German)

(22) *so jetzt gehen sie mit dem Leiter auf den Baum, alle drei* 'so now they go up the tree with the ladder, all three of them' (ID21, L2 German)

(23) *und daher die vier Jaeger laufst durch den Wald* 'and thus the four hunters walk through the forest' (ID25, L2 German)

(24) *und springt auf der Schildkroete* 'and jumps on(to) the turtle' (ID21, L2 German)

This is less remarkable once we take into account that, at the same time, all of the seven most frequent L2 German frames are also among the 11 most frequent choices in L1 English, thus highly routinized in the learners' L1, too. Good overall approximation to the L1 German target preferences is thus facilitated by substantial overlap between frequent patterns in L1 German and L1 English. This may actually be due less to restructuring than to convergence or CLI, for instance, in the case of the *Pro Vlex PP* "intruder" in the L2 German top five, which is considerably less frequent in L1 German (n=23), but is highly frequent in L1 English (n=54). CLI might also impact upper limits of global complexity: Maximally complex *NPcompl Vman compl* is attested in both L1 (n=1; [25]) and L2 German (n=1; [26]), but complexity preferences diverge among the most frequent patterns.

Thus, the most complex pattern attested at least 20 times in L1 German – *NP Vman Compl* (n=30) – is globally denser than the most complex frequent frame in L2 German (*NP Vman PP*, n=26). Similarly, among patterns attested at least six times, maximal constructional complexity of *NPcompl Vman PP* in L1 German (n=8) is higher than L2 *NPcompl Vlex PP* (n=6), where increased complexity at the figure slot seems to trigger a complexity trade-off at the verb slot (although the pattern is attested 16 times in L1 English). Overall, two of the seven most frequent L1 German frames select locally relatively complex elements across all three slots (shaded grey in Table 4), and another three for two slots (shaded light grey in Table 4).

In contrast, only one of the seven most frequent L2 German pattern has locally relatively complex slot-fillers across all three slots, namely *NP Vman PP* (n=26), which is produced to a similar extent in L1 English (n=28). Another three L2 German frames have two relatively complex elements (*Pro Vman PP*, n=51; *NP Vman Part*, n=37; *e Vman PP*, n=24), all of which are again frequent in L1 English, too (80, 24, and 41 tokens respectively). In sum, seemingly good overlap between preferred patterns in L1 and L2 German in the motion domain is thus partially explained by corresponding L1 English routines, with L2 patterns showing partial L1 influence. For instance, in the cases of (23) *NP Vman PP* (underuse in L2 German) and (22) *Pro Vlex PP* (overuse in L2 German, but possibly in the course of restructuring, given the pattern is even more frequent in L1 English) as well as in terms of overall (lower) complexity preferences in general (see also Section 5.1.2); the latter may of course also be due to general interlanguage complexity reduction trends, which may also explain that none of the most frequent L2 German patterns contains a multi-stage path and that the globally rather "light" pattern *Pro Vman e* (without overt path) is more frequent in L2 German than both in L1 German and in L1 English.

As for the L2 English users, almost all of their most frequent patterns correspond to the most frequent L1 English choices (11/13, Table 4). However, these are frequent patterns in L1 German, too. There are subtle indicators of diverging choices – thus, CLI – , for instance, globally more complex *NP Vman PP* with three locally relatively complex slot-fillers is twice as frequent in L2 English (n=53) as in L1 English (n=25), but as frequent as in L1 German (n=53). Overall, L2 users of English seem to prefer manner verbs to a higher degree than L1 users of English. Eight of the top ten L2 English patterns select manner verbs, against only six in L1 English. Furthermore, the most frequent pattern with a complex path selects manner verbs in L2 English (*Pro Vman Compl*, n=26, cf. (25)) but non-manner verbs in L1 English (*Pro Vlex Compl*, n=28, cf. (26)). And, finally, the most complex combination *NPcompl Vman Compl* is only attested in L2 English (n=2) and in L1 German (n=2), whereas the most complex L1 English combinations are

NPcompl Vman ComplPleo (n=4) and *NPcompl Vlex Compl* (n=2). So even if only in subtle ways, the entrenched more complex L1 German pattern routines still seem to influence at least some aspects of global complexity preferences in L2 English.

(25) *he's always walking on his . on the white line in front of him to the left side* (ID12, L2 English)

(26) *but then it comes back up from out of the screen* (ID21, L1 English)

Table 4: Most frequent patterns (Figure—Verb—Path) for *motion* per language group (globally complex patterns with three locally relatively complex components are shaded grey; patterns with two locally complex slot-fillers are shaded light grey).

L1 German		L2 German		L1 English		L2 English	
Pro Vman PP	73	Pro Vman PP	50	Pro Vman PP	80	Pro Vman PP	99
Pro Vman Part	57	Pro Vman Part	47	Pro Vlex PP	54	e Vman PP	70
NP Vman PP	53	Pro Vman e	43	Pro Vman Part	49	NP Vman PP	53
NP Vman Part	51	NP Vman Part	37	e Vman PP	41	Pro Vlex PP	47
e Vman PP	43	Pro Vlex PP	28	e Vlex PP	38	Pro Vman Part	46
e Vman Part	43	NP Vman PP	25	Pro Vlex Part	29	e Vman e	32
NP Vman Compl	31	e Vman PP	23	NP Vman PP	28	e Vlex PP	32
Pro Vman Compl	28			Pro Vlex Compl	28	NP Vman Part	31
NP Vlex PP	28			Pro Vman e	27	Pro Vman Compl	26
NP Vman e	24			NP Vman Part	24	Pro Vman e	26
Pro Vlex PP	23			e Vman Part	23	NP Vman e	24
e Vman Compl	22			e Vman e	23	NP Vlex e	23
NP Vlex Part	21			Pro Vlex e	21	e Vman Part	21
e Vman e	21					Pro Vlex NP	20
e Vman ComplPleo	20						

5.2.3 Interim summary

The analyses of each language group's preferred patterns for the encoding of the localization and spontaneous motion events provide more detailed insight into the findings regarding L1 and L2 global constructional complexity trends (Section 5.1), but, importantly, also some qualifications. For instance, we find underlying L1 influence even in cases where global complexity trends indicated good L2 restructuring (e.g., motion in L2 English) or hybrid L2 behaviour (e.g., localizations in L2 German).

For localizations, both L2 German and L2 English display *hybrid* behavior in terms of global complexity preferences (Section 5.1.1). Yet, for L2 German, preferred patterns still strongly overlap with frequent L1 English patterns, whereas the overlap with L1 German is low. In particular, slot-fillers at the verb slot tend to be lighter in L2 German than in L1 German, following the L1 English preference for copula verbs. Path encoding in L2 German is more complex than in L1 English, suggesting that increasing complexity at the path slot might be more easily available than at the verb slot. For L2 English, both verbs and path elements are more complex than in L1 English, and very light combinations such as *Pro Vcop Deic* are underused.

For spontaneous motion, seemingly good overlap between the most frequent patterns in L2 and L1 German turns out to be not very significant, as the overlap between L2 German and L1 English preferences is also very high, including the highly frequent L1 English pattern (22) that goes against the strong L1 German preference for manner of motion to be overtly expressed at the verb slot. This explains why global complexity trends suggest transfer (resp. hybrid) behavior for L2 German (Section 5.1.2). Yet a closer look at the preferred patterns shows that there is substantial overlap between the most frequent patterns in L1 German and L1 English, such that L2 behavior may actually reflect surface convergence (in the sense of Treffers-Daller & Tidball 2016: 152) rather than hybrid behavior (ibid.). The degree of overlap between patterns preferred in L1 and L2 English is even larger, resulting in good restructuring in spite of selective L1 German influence, for instance, with respect to L2 English users' highly frequent *NP Vman PP* pattern.

As for maximal complexity, L1 German speakers produce highly complex patterns both in their L1 German and in their L2 English, frequently selecting maximally complex slot-fillers across all slots within one utterance/clause (e.g. *NPcompl Vman Compl*),[9] whereas L1 English speakers do so much less, whether in their L1 English or in their L2 German.

5.3 Expression of manner

Now, to what extent are differences in terms of preferred patterns (5.2) or preferred levels of global constructional complexity (5.1) actually due to diverging degrees

---

[9] With the notable exception of caused motion constructions, where such maximally dense patterning is absent in L2 English, suggesting that the higher level of (cognitive and linguistic) complexity of this structural pattern *per se* leads to some trade-off trend at the level of the (combination of) local slot-fillers.

of manner salience (or attention to manner information)? Recall that German and English dispose of the same range of (S-framed) constructional means to express manner information – for instance, with regard to posture, manner or instruments of movement – , namely primarily in the main verb, e.g., *to run, to sit*. However, verbs may also be more generic, as in *he moved on, he was in his car*. Manner information may also be expressed in additional satellites, e.g., *quickly, with his scooter, like a track-runner,* or *swimming*. Both languages have thus been assumed to be highly manner salient (Slobin 2004: 225), but recently, the actual degree of manner salience has been questioned for English for static and dynamic location events (cf., Gullberg 2009) as well as for spontaneous motion (cf. Pavlenko & Volynsky 2015).

5.3.1 Localization

Language groups differ from each other with respect to the expression of manner in the main verb in localization events (Table 5). In L1 German retellings, almost twice as many manner verbs are used compared to L1 English (mean: 56% vs. 32%). In L1 German, manner verbs such as *stehen* 'to stand' (n=50), *sitzen* 'to sit' (n=31), or *liegen* 'to lie' (n=5) are frequent choices in the verbalization of localization events as opposed to highly frequent copula *be* in L1 English (n=118). The L2 German mean is only slightly above the L1 English baseline (35%), indicating that L2 German users stick closely to their L1 routines (i.e., copula *sein* 'to be', n=69) when it comes to verb specificity. L2 English takes a middle ground between L1 German and L1 English (46%). However, manner verb proportions partly cover group differences, as choices also diverge when no manner verb is chosen. For instance, L1 English/L2 German users very clearly prefer copula verbs, whereas L1 German/L2 English speakers use copula verbs (n=65 resp. 91) as well as a small range of lexical verbs without manner specification such as *sich befinden* 'to find oneself' (n=11 resp. 9) to describe localizations. L2 English users thus not only use proportionally more manner verbs than L1 English users (46% vs. 32%), they also use relatively more lexical verbs than L1 English speakers (5% vs. 1%).

Additional manner information is sometimes also expressed in satellites in all groups. However, L2 users make less use of this additional option than L1 users. In L1 German, additional information primarily refers to emotional states of the figure (n=5) – e.g., a frog *happily* sitting in a jar (ID12) or a bird *calmly* sitting on a tree branch (ID11) – as well as figure orientation (n=2) – e.g., a man standing at the end of his walkway *with his arms crossed* (ID12). In each of these cases, manner information is expressed both in the main verb and in an additional satellite within the same utterance. In L1 English, additional manner information also refers to the figure's emotional state (n=3) – e.g., a family of frogs *happily sitting together* (ID24) – or body posture (n=4) – e.g., a man standing on a pedestal *like a statue* (ID21). In L2 German, there is only one occurrence of additional manner satellites, referring to the figure's emotional state – a man sitting *sadly* on the floor (ID21) – whereas in L2 English, all manner satellites refer to posture (n=6) – e.g., a man standing on top of a pedestal *like a statue* (ID13).

Table 5: Verb types produced across language groups (token counts) for *localization*.

	copula verbs	modal verbs	lexical verbs without manner information	lexical verbs with manner info	mean manner verbs
L1 German	65	0	11	96	0.56 (range 0.4 to 0.74)
L2 German	94	0	3	53	0.35 (range 0.24 to 0.5)
L1 English	121	0	2	59	0.32 (range 0.17 to 0.45)
L2 English	91	0	9	86	0.46 (range 0.38 to 0.51)

5.3.2 Motion

Manner verbs are also less frequent in L1 English than in L1 German for motion event descriptions (54%[10] vs. 69%); the upper limit of the L1 English range (0.63) actually corresponds to the lower limit in L1 German (0.61; Table 6). This does not exclude the occurrence of rare (e.g., *pole-vault, pounce, creep, hurdle, scurry, tumble*) and creative manner-verb coinages in L1 English, such as *and he just scooters up* (ID21), indicating attention to manner by L1 English users. However, for a similiar number of motion event descriptions (Table 1), L1 German users produce a substantially larger overall number of different verb lemmas (Vman: n=86; Vlex: n=34) than L1 English users (Vman: n=68; Vlex: n=20); the L1 English sample is heavily skewed towards the verb *go* (n=173; see below).

---

10 Interestingly, this is substantially less than the 65.2% of manner verb use reported in Pavlenko & Volynsky (2015: 42). This divergence might be due to task effects, as Pavlenko &Volynsky (2015) is based on picture book retellings only, whereas the current data regroup picture book retellings and animated cartoon retellings, cf. Section 5.1.2.

L2 English motion event descriptions take a middle ground between L1 English and L1 German in terms of manner verb selection (mean: 61%). The fact that L2 English users seem to be overinformative at the global constructional level (cf. 5.1.2) can thus at least partially be attributed to their verb choices (cf. also 5.2.2). Importantly, *go* is only the third most frequent L2 English choice (n=75), after *fall* (n=100) and *jump* (n=82), and closely followed by *walk* (n=61) and *run* (n=58).

L2 German users are close to the L1 German mean, suggesting good restructuring in terms of manner verb proportions (66% vs. 67%, with largely overlapping ranges). Their intention to express manner information is also evident in their nonce-borrowings – for instance *jump* (ID25, n=3), *paddle* (ID26), and *somersault machen* (ID26) – and their creative coinages *klatten/kletten* (ID22, n=3, approximating German *klettern* 'climb') and *schlaedden/schlidden* (ID25, n=2; ID26, approximating German *Schlitten fahren* 'to bobsled').[11]

However, there are 21 cases of inadequate uses of *gehen* 'go' in L2 German, mainly in contexts of driving (n=7), but also for falling (n=4), climbing (n=3), flying (n=3) as well as rolling, jumping, floating, and sinking events (n=1 each, Table 7). Such **gehen* errors – where *gehen* is used as a generic motion verb in the sense of *move*, whereas in German, *gehen* implies motion on foot, thus, walking – are actually expected for L2 German users with V-framed first languages, lacking selective attention to the preferred S-framed target pattern expressing manner of motion in the main verb. In line with assumptions of manner optionality in English (Pavlenko & Volynsky 2015: 35), *go* is actually more than twice as frequent (n=173) as the second most frequent motion verbs *come* and *fall* (n=79 each) in L1 English, whereas it is only marginally more frequent (n=90) than the second most frequent verb *fall* (n=86) in L1 German. **gehen* errors might thus indicate reduced attention to manner by the English-speaking users of L2 German, as argued in Pavlenko & Volynsky (2015: 45). Yet, as the L2 German speakers in the current data sample do display sensitivity to manner (see above), **gehen* errors in this population might just indicate local occurrences of lexical/semantic transfer from English – where one can in fact *go* down a hill on a bobsleigh or *go* up a tree with a ladder – not an overall divergence in learned selective attention (in the sense of conceptual transfer; cf. Hasko 2009, 2010; Pavlenko 2010; Pavlenko & Volynsky 2015 for similar **go* errors in American users of L2 Russian and early Russian-English bilinguals respectively).

---

11 Both nonce-borrowings and approximations were counted as manner verbs.

Table 6: Verb types produced across language groups (token counts) for *spontaneous motion*.

	copula verbs	modal verbs	lexical verbs without manner information	lexical verbs with manner info	% manner verbs
L1 German	4	9	256	550	0.67 (range 0.61 to 0.83)
L2 German	3	2	178	350	0.66 (range 0.55 to 0.91)
L1 English	0	0	372	432	0.54 (range 0.47 to 0.63)
L2 English	0	0	324	499	0.61 (range 0.36 to 0.79)

Table 7: *gehen errors (other errors, e.g., missing prepositions or case errors, are not signalled here).

ID	Scenario	L2 production	missing manner verb
21	a man bobsledding over hills	und der Mann *geht diese großen Hügeln 'and the man *goes these big hills'	(Schlitten) fahren
21	a man bobsledding over hills	er *geht oben und unten 'he *goes above and below'	(Schlitten) fahren
21	a man bobsledding over hills	und auf einmal *geht er unter unsere Sicht 'and suddenly he *goes below our sight'	(Schlitten) fahren
21	a man bobsledding over hills	und dann *geht er runter 'and then he *goes down'	(Schlitten) fahren
21	a bowling ball flying through the air	auf den ersten Mal *geht es im Luft 'the first time, it *goes into the air'	fliegen
21	a bowling ball falling/ breaking through the ground	und es *geht durch die Linie 'and it *goes through the line'	fallen, brechen
21	three characters climbing up a tree	um aufs Baum zu *gehen 'to *go up the tree'	klettern, steigen
21	three characters climbing up a tree	So jetzt *gehen sie mit dem Leiter auf den Baum 'so now, they *go up the hill with the ladder'	klettern, steigen
21	a wall breaking/falling down	und dann fangt der Mauer an *unterzugehen 'and then the man starts *going down'	fallen, brechen

Table 7 (continued)

ID	Scenario	L2 production	missing manner verb
21	a man driving up a hill in a car	er *geht über einen Hügel 'he *goes over a hill'	(Auto) fahren
21	fish jumping out of the water into the air and back	und wieder *reingehen 'and *go back in'	springen
22	a character falling into a lake	Einer der größte Elfen *geht unter der Wasser 'one of the biggest elves *goes under the water'	fallen
22	a man bobsledding over hills	und *geht über die Hügel, dann unter die Hügel 'and *goes over the hills, then under the hills'	(Schlitten) fahren
23	three characters floating across a lake on a tree trunk	sie *gehen in diesem / in diesem See 'they *go in this lake'	schwimmen, gleiten
23	a man falling/ breaking through the ground	und La Linea [...] ist durch der Boden *gegangen 'and La Linea [...] *went through the floor'	fallen, brechen
23	a bowling ball flying through the air	der erste Ball *geht oben / oben diese Ball 'the first ball *goes above / above this ball'	fliegen
23	a bowling ball flying through the air	und dann die nächste Ball hat sehr stark oben diese Ball *gegangen 'and then the next ball *went very strongly above this ball'	fliegen
23	a bowling ball falling/ breaking through the ground	und dann die letzte hat direkt vor diese Pins unten / [...] unter [...] den Boden *gegangen 'and then the last one *went directly in front of these pins below / [...] under [...] the floor'	fallen, brechen
25	three characters climbing up a tree	Die drei Jäger *gehen im Baum 'the three hunters *go in the tree'	klettern, steigen
26	a box rolling away	und die Kiste ist *weggegangen 'and the box *went away'	rollen
26	a man driving up a hill on a scooter	und *geht vorwärts auf ein Hüglein 'and *goes forwards onto a little hill'	(Roller) fahren

L1 German users also produce most additional manner satellites (n=101; vs. L2 German: n=41, L1 English: n=53, L2 English: n=52). Interestingly, the language groups also differ with regard to their preference for specific semantic categories.

In L1 German, 35 manner satellites refer to the emotional state of the moving figure – for instance, a man running away *vor Schreck/voller Angst* 'in fear' (ID12, 14) – and another 40 to manner of motion in the narrower sense – for instance, speed (n=11), body posture (n=15, e.g., *kopfüber* 'head over heels', ID11; *etwas gebückt* 'slightly bent over', ID12; *rücklings* 'backwards', ID15), and degrees of caution/power (n=9, e.g., *leise* 'quietly', ID11; *mit Kraft* 'forcefully', ID12). 16 manner satellites refer to the instrument of motion, including vehicles (n=9, e.g., *mit dem Roller* 'on the/his scooter', ID15; *mit einem Floß* 'with the/their raft', ID15) and other resources such as ladders for climbing up trees (n=3). Additionally, there are four present participle satellites, two of which describe simultaneous actions (*schreiend* 'screaming', ID12; *kläffend* 'barking', ID11), the other two manner of motion in (a typically V-framed) combination with the non-manner verbs *folgen* 'to follow' and *sich bewegen* 'to move' (*schwimmend* 'swimming', ID12, n=2).

Strikingly, in L2 German, there is only one reference to the figure's emotional state (i.e., a man walking *ganz sorglos* 'carelessly' [ID21]). Most frequently, L2 German manner satellites refer to instruments of motion (n=22, e.g., *mit diesem Auto* 'in this car', ID23; *mit diesem Pferd* 'on the horse', ID23; *mit seinem Hut als ein Schiff* 'in his hat (used) as a boat', ID25). Manner satellites also refer to speed of motion (n=8), degrees of caution/power (n=3) – or both, as in *sehr langsam und still* 'very slowly and quietly' (ID26) – and body posture (n=3, e.g., *mit Beine und Hände* 'on his legs and hands', ID26).

In L1 English, the figure's emotional state is also referred to (n=12), but reference to manner in the narrow sense is most frequent (n=35; e.g., speed, n=7; degrees of power/caution, n=7; body posture, e.g., *like a track runner*, n=2, ID23), including three references to instruments of motion (*on his little car*, ID21; *on their branch*, ID25; and *with their ladder*, ID23). Interestingly, there are also six present participles – *hopping* (ID24), *sailing* (ID26, n=2), *chasing* (ID26), *swimming* (ID24), and *swishing* (ID26) — specifying manner of motion (in typically V-framed patterns) in combination with deictic verbs (e.g., *came hopping up to them* [ID24], *comes swishing out of the tree* [ID26]).

No such participle constructions are found in L2 English, but L2 English manner satellites mirror L1 English categories well. They refer to the figure's emotion (n=12) less often than to manner in the narrow sense (n=31; e.g., speed, n=7; degree of caution/power, n=6; body posture, e.g., *head forward*, ID11; *like pole-jump*, ID13; or *one leg after the other*, ID11); however, they include relatively more mentions of vehicles (n=9).

5.3.3 Interim summary

Manner information is encoded relatively more frequently in the main verb in L1 German retellings than in L1 English for localization and spontaneous motion descriptions; this is in line with Pavlenko & Volynsky (2015). Overall, learned attention to manner thus seems to be higher in L1 German than L1 English, although both are S-framed.

In line with corresponding assumptions regarding L2 effects of learned attention to preferred L1 patterns, L2 German users produce fewer manner verbs and fewer manner satellites in localization constructions, where they overuse copula verbs. They display selective L1 influence in spontaneous motion constructions, in the form of *gehen errors, although they approximate the L1 German baseline in terms of overall manner verb selection well.

L2 English users seem to take a middle ground between the L1 English target baseline and L1 German with respect to the selection of manner verbs in both localization and motion event descriptions; in terms of manner satellites, they display good restructuring to the lower degree of manner salience in L1 English.

5.4 Expression of path/ground

As suggested above and by our findings regarding gradual development of constructional complexity (Madlener et al. 2017), expression of manner, as strongly focused upon by TfS-inspired approaches, may represent only one relevant aspect of constructional complexity for L2 users. Recall that in the case of L1 German, younger children produce fewer locally complex slot-filler types than older children and adults (e.g., fewer prepositional phrases and multi-stage paths) and development continues well into middle childhood (cf. Section 2). Importantly, however, children also use locally complex slot-fillers differently from adults, such that even nine-year-olds avoid combinations of several locally complex slot-fillers within one globally complex utterance. With respect to L2 users, cognitive or linguistic trade-off strategies similar to those of the less routinized L1 users may be expected, given that overall, higher cognitive loads can be assumed for L2 processing. This section thus takes a closer look at the number, make-up, and distribution of complex path types in L2 German/L2 English, as compared to the L1 German/English baselines.

5.4.1 Preferred path categories

Proportions of structurally complex path types across the language groups differ less than expected, which is probably due to the fact that for L2 users, the schemas are also strongly entrenched in the corresponding L1 and thus relatively easily accessible.

Let me point out two main observations here, though. First, L1 German displays the largest proportions of the most complex path types – complex multi-stage paths and pleonastic complex paths (Table 8): 17% for localizations (as compared to 7% for L2 German, 4% for L1 English, 7% for L2 English), 23% for spontaneous motion (as compared to 12% for L2 German, 17% for L1 English, 14% for L2 English). This suggests that it is not only the expression of manner that makes a difference in terms of global complexity trends in L1 German and L1 English (Section 5.1), but also relative path complexity, particularly for localizations (17% vs. 4% of complex paths). Second, L2 German users lag way behind the L1 German baseline for complex path proportions (localization: 7% vs. 17%; motion: 12% vs. 23%). All L1 English participants actually produce about twice as many complex paths in their L1 English as in their L2 German (up to five times more for ID24).

Table 8: Number of path types per group per event type (increasing complexity from bottom to top; more complex path types are shaded light grey; *Ger* stands for German, *Eng* for English).

	Localization				Motion			
	L1 Ger	L2 Ger	L1 Eng	L2 Eng	L1 Ger	L2 Ger	L1 Eng	L2 Eng
Complex	28	9	7	15	116	43	92	107
ComplPleo	5	2	2	1	74	22	42	8
PP	111	92	124	154	271	173	304	353
Inf, NP	0	0	0	0	37	21	55	59
Part, Adv	29	19	16	13	231	161	189	160
Deic	17	35	66	38	2	3	12	5
e	4	2	3	8	100	117	116	144

Once prepositional phrases are additionally taken into account, group differences tend to level out, with overall proportions of relatively complex path types – complex multi-stage paths, pleonastic complex paths, and prepositional phrases – ranging between 61% and 74% for localizations and between 44% and 56% for spontaneous motion. Yet, by trend, L2 German users produce fewer tokens of relatively complex path types than L1 German users (localization: 65% vs. 74%; motion: 44% vs. 55%), whereas the trend is reversed for L2 as compared to L1

English in the domain of localizations (74% vs. 61%). This finding is in line with the overall trends: L2 German users tend to produce less complex spatial descriptions (than German L1 users), L2 English users tend to produce overly complex spatial language constructions (as compared to L1 English). Path/ground elements must thus be taken into account in addition to the verbs (manner salience).

5.4.2 Complexity of path-ground combinations

The internal make-up of complex path types provides additional insight into preferred levels of path complexity and potential trade-off effects (cf. Madlener et al. 2017). In the following, we therefore look at the distribution of complex ground elements – complex noun phrases (NP) including modifiers (e.g., an adjective, a relative clause, a prepositional phrase, such as *the topmost branch of the tree*) – within relatively complex path types (i.e., multi-stage paths, pleonastic complex paths, and prepositional phrases).

For localizations, distributions of simple vs. complex NPs are quite even, with the exception of L2 English, with comparatively more complex NP ground elements both in prepositional phrases and in multi-stage paths than the other language groups (Table 9). This is in line with the overall trend of this group to produce highly complex spatial language descriptions and shows that this trend impacts different levels of analysis. Interestingly, however, the proportions of complex ground elements (as compared to simple NPs) within complex path types drop sharply for motion in L2 English (Table 10) and even more for caused motion.[12] This suggests that even for advanced L2 users, these constructions are *per se* more challenging, such that, in a kind of trade-off, complexity levels are locally reduced at the ground slot (within complex path types).[13]

---

[12] Zero occurrences of complex ground NPs with complex multistage or complex pleonastic paths; only 10 occurrences of NPcompl within simple prepositional phrases as compared to 60 simple NPs

[13] The same decrease is found for L2 German users, such that, actually, neither L2 group produces any combination of complex multi-stage paths with complex ground elements in caused motion constructions, whereas both L1 groups produce at least some (n=3 each).

Table 9: Complex path tokens combined with complex ground descriptions: *Localizations*.

L	L1 G		L2 G		L1 E		L2 E	
	NP	NPcompl	NP	NPcompl	NP	NPcompl	NP	NPcompl
Complex	18	5	7	2	5	2	9	6
ComplPleo	5	0	1	0	1	0	0	0
PP	75	28	71	21	85	24	86	41

Table 10: Complex path tokens combined with complex ground descriptions: *Motion events*.

M	L1 G		L2 G		L1 E		L2 E	
	NP	NPcompl	NP	NPcompl	NP	NPcompl	NP	NPcompl
Complex	72	25	32	5	51	25	67	25
ComplPleo	55	5	21	1	23	7	3	0
PP	207	41	135	23	213	54	220	85

Additionally, we can ask which types of path elements complex multi-stage paths are made up from. For all language groups, the large majority of complex paths consists either of one prepositional phrase plus one or more adverbs or particles (spontaneous motion, Table 12) or of two prepositional phrases (localization, Table 11), whereas very complex multi-stage paths (with 3+ prepositions) are rare.

Table 11: Make-up of multi-stage paths: *Localizations* (incl. errors).

L	L1 German	L2 German	L1 English	L2 English
2 or more adverb(s)/particle(s)/infinitves . . .	4	0	0	0
1 preposition + adverb(s)/ particle(s)	18	4	6	6
2 prepositions	5	7	2	10
2 prepositions + adverb(s)/ particle(s)	2	0	1	1
3+ prepositions	2	0	0	0
3+ prepositions + adverb(s)/ particle(s)	0	0	0	0
maximal complexity	3 prepositions	2 prepositions	2 prepositions + adverb	2 prepositions + adverb

For spontaneous motion, complex paths including two or more prepositions (and possibly also one or more adverbs or particles) are still frequent in all language groups (L1 German: n=46; L2 German: n=18; L1 English: n=20; L2 English: n=32), but least frequent in L1 English (15%; as compared to L1 German: 25%; L2 German: 30%; L2 English: 28%). As expected, L2 German users produce less complex multi-stages paths than all other groups for both localization and motion event descriptions (Tables 11, 12).

Table 12: Make-up of multi-stage paths: *Motion events* (incl. errors).

M	L1 German	L2 German	L1 English	L2 English
2 or more adverb(s)/ particle(s)/infinitves ...	20	12	17	14
1 preposition + adverb(s)/ particle(s)	121	31	96	69
2 prepositions	30	16	13	25
2 prepositions + adverb(s)/ particle(s)	13	2	5	3
3+ prepositions	1	0	2	3
3+ prepositions + adverb(s)/ particle(s)	2	0	0	1
maximal complexity	3 prepositions + 2 particles	2 prepositions + adverb + particle	4 prepositions	3 prepositions + 2 particles

5.4.3 Distribution of complex path categories

Let us finally look at the distribution of complex path types (multi-stage paths, pleonastic complex paths, prepositional phrases) as a function of complexity at the verb slot, that is, proportions of complex path types in combination with semantically less complex lexical verbs without manner information (-Vman) as compared to semantically richer manner verbs (+Vman, cf. Table 13). Do some language groups tend to combine semantically complex verbs with structurally complex paths, or do we rather see trade-off trends, such that, if one of the slots is filled with a locally complex slot-filler, the second one tends to be relatively "light" (cf. Madlener et al. 2017), resulting in globally less complex constructions? We focus on the domain of spontaneous motion here.

As expected, a general trend towards combinations of (structurally) more complex path types and (semantically) more complex manner verbs is found for

L2 English users – with non-complex path types (*other*) evenly distributed across lexical verbs with and without manner specification (111:114, Table 13), whereas (structurally) more complex paths are more frequently combined with (semantically) rich manner verbs than with generic lexical verbs (302:155). At the same time, however, we find a slight negative trade-off trend within the more complex path types in L2 English, such that prepositional phrases (i.e., the least complex of the complex path types) are two times as likely to be combined with manner verbs as compared to lexical verbs without manner specification (238:110). In contrast, the trend is reduced for multi-stage paths (61:40).

This effect is even stronger for both L1 English and L2 German. Prepositional phrases are more likely to be combined with semantically rich verbs by L1 English speakers in both their L1 English (179:124) and their L2 German (113:58), whereas the most complex multi-stage paths are only as likely to appear with manner verbs as with generic lexical verbs (21:21, L2 German) or even more likely to appear with semantically lighter verbs (50:39, L1 English). In L1 German, in contrast, prepositional phrases are about twice as often combined with manner verbs as with generic lexical verbs (185:85) and multi-stage paths even almost three times as often (81:31). It is impossible to say, at this point, whether this pattern arises from learned attention effects in L2 German (with the trade-off carried over from L1 English) and advanced restructuring in L2 English (overcoming L1 German learned attention trends), or whether both L2 groups display the trade-off due to more general interlanguage complexity reduction trend.

Table 13: Verb type – path/ground type combinations: *Motion events* (more complex path types are shaded light grey).

	L1 German		L2 German		L1 English		L2 English	
	-Vman	+Vman	-Vman	+Vman	-Vman	+Vman	-Vman	+Vman
Complex	31	83	21	21	50	39	40	61
ComplPleo	23	47	8	14	22	20	5	3
PP	85	185	58	113	124	179	110	238
Other	90	173	65	114	130	126	111	114

5.4.4 Interim summary

Our data strongly suggest that diverging constructional patterns and preferences for the expression of path (and ground) provide additional insights into global constructional complexity trends – with respect to information density rather than information packaging – between L1 English and L1 German spatial language encoding as well as between L1 and L2 encoding. L1 German users produce the highest numbers of complex path types (Section 5.4.1), and by trend also the most complex multistage paths (Section 5.4.2), indicating highly complex and condensed encoding of paths (and ground elements). Consequently, localization descriptions in L1 German are more complex than in L1 English, both in terms of manner expression (as L1 English users largely prefer copula verbs) and in terms of path/ground descriptions (as L1 German users produce more complex paths).

For spontaneous motion, L1 German users produce more complex multi-stage paths (46 items with two or more prepositions, against 20 in L1 English) and also tend to combine the most complex path types with semantically rich manner verbs, whereas L1 English users show a (partial) trade-off effect for path vs. verb complexity (Section 5.4.3). Path/ground descriptions are also revealing with regard to interlanguage restructuring in L2 German as compared to L2 English.

For instance, in addition to lower degrees of manner information (Section 5.3), L2 German users produce fewer complex multi-stage paths than L1 German users. The proportion of relatively complex path types is lower for L2 German than L1 German even if prepositional phrases are taken into account in addition to multi-stage and pleonastic complex paths. Finally, the internal complexity of complex multi-stage paths is by trend lower in L2 than L1 German. L2 German constructional choices thus display reduced constructional complexity in terms of manner, path (local complexity, Sections 5.3, 5.4), and their combinatorial potential (Sections 5.1, 5.2, 5.4.3).

As for L2 English users, who globally display higher global constructional complexity levels than the L1 English baseline (Section 5.1), a closer look at their local slot-filler repertoires and preferences reveals that this is actually not only a result of divergent choices (learned attention) in terms of manner (where L1 English seems to take a middle ground between L1 English and L1 German), but also of complex path/ground complexity (Sections 5.4.1, 5.4.2) and the combinatorial potential of paths with semantically rich verbs (Section 5.4.3).

6 Summary, discussion, and implications

Our data provide detailed insight into the use of complex spatial language constructions and constructional complexity in the spatial language domain in L1 and L2 English and German. This language pair is an interesting test case, as, typologically speaking, both languages display the same, S-framed basic lexicalization patterns at the utterance level and also share relevant subschemas (e.g., prepositional phrases) and semantic categories (e.g., semantics of spatial prepositions), which should allow for positive transfer in the L2 spatial language domain. However, English has been shown to be less manner-salient than other S-framed languages (e.g., Gullberg 2009, Pavlenko & Volynsky 2015), such that the actual information *focus* – that is, the degree to which manner is expressed (manner salience) – might differ between these closely related languages, while the information *locus* does not (i.e., if manner is expressed, it will be expressed in the main verb). To what extent do we thus find intra-typological differences in L1 encoding in the spatial language domain between English and German, that is, effects of learned attention beyond basic lexicalization patterns (research question 1), and also corresponding effects of learned attention in L2 acquisition and use (research question 2)?

With respect to research question 1, our data are clearly in line with prior research indicating that English is less manner-salient than German (pace Slobin 2004). Interestingly, German is more manner-salient – in the sense that manner information is more frequently encoded in the main verb (Slobin 2006) – across different spatial event types, for instance spontaneous motion events (as is Russian, cf. Pavlenko & Volynsky 2015) as well as localizations (as is Dutch, cf. Gullberg 2009). Importantly, however, our data show that manner salience is not the only cause for higher overall global complexity preferences at the clause/utterance level in German, but that path descriptions contribute to this effect.

This observation is again in line with Pavlenko & Volynsky (2015), who find that, in addition to divergent manner salience, the segmentation/representation of paths is less fine-grained in English than in Russian motion event descriptions. Therefore, further investigations of cross-linguistic differences in the spatial language domain will probably want to go (i) beyond the question of basic lexicalization patterns to include aspects of optionality and constructional complexity to arrive at a more fine-grained understanding of information focus and information packaging (inter- and intratypologically); (ii) beyond the local slot-filler complexity level to take into account convergent and divergent trends at the global, combinatorial complexity level; and (iii) beyond the TfS-inspired focus on (learned attention to) manner salience, to include more detailed investigations of other constructional elements, namely the constructional ranges and preferences for path/ground descriptions (and possibly also figure complexity, cf. Madlener et al. 2017).

As for research question 2 regarding CLI, in fact, we find fine-grained effects of learned attention in L2 encoding in the spatial language domain for typologically close languages such as English and German, beyond the assumed effects of L1-tuning for the basic S-framed lexicalization patterns. Again, these effects hold across local and global complexity levels for different spatial event types – but, according to the intra-typological differences in L1 encoding, they differ between L2 German users (with L1 English) and L2 English users (with L1 German). Whereas L2 German users need to *increase* constructional complexity in their L2 (even though to a lesser extent than learnes with a V-framed L1, cf. De Knop & Gallez 2013), L2 English users need to learn to *reduce* constructional complexity in their L2, with the latter challenge being more easily met, as it seems.

For both L2 groups, typological similarity most certainly reduces the challenge of L2 acquisition and use to a substantial extent, but some level of restructuring of constructional repertoires and preferences – that is, of reattuning selective attention to the preferred L2 patterns (Section 5.2) as well as levels of global (Section 5.1) and local constructional complexity (Sections 5.3–5.4) – is still needed. This suggests that what makes a difference for L2 processing is not only knowing which kind of information is typically selected for verbalization and at which conceptual slots this information is encoded (i.e., information packaging), but also with which levels of optionality (e.g., intratypological degrees of manner salience) and of local and global constructional complexity (i.e., information density).

Now, what are potential implications for second language teaching, given that for neither L2 group there is anything strictly speaking *wrong* in terms of constructional repertoires in the spatial language domain (except for the *gehen errors by L2 German users, cf. Section 5.3)? In other words, this is not a case where misleading L1 routines need obvious "unlearning" (Della Putta 2016), as cross-linguistic effects of learned attention – within typologically close languages – do not lead to incorrect language use in this case, but just to partially diverging choices at the local and global constructional complexity levels. Such complex and abstract discourse phenomena – for instance, L2 users of German producing slightly less information-dense utterances than L1 German speakers and L2 users of English producing slightly more information-dense utterances than L1 English users – will probably be rather inconspicuous in everyday language use and even in classroom activities focusing at the sentence level. It might still be necessary or at least desirable for advanced learners to grasp the detail of the respective target language preferences, if they want to be fully idiomatic at the discourse level, too.

As the phenomena targeted here are very subtle, abstract, and complex, positive evidence – as provided by (large numbers of) exemplars of the target languages' preferred patterns (cf. Section 5.2) as models, even with optimal frequency distributions (cf. Madlener 2015) – or indirect negative evidence – for instance, through recasting – will probably not trigger sufficient noticing for interlanguage restructuring to take place. For learners of L2 Russian, Pavlenko and Volynksy (2015: 46) suggest the use of dynamic visualizations in the form of video clips – and possibly animated cartoons as used for data collection in this study – as well as explicit consciousness raising activities, where students attend to and reflect upon which aspects of spatial language events are typically selected for verbalization, through which kind of linguistic means and with which degrees of optionality. This includes explicit comparison of L1 and L2 patterns and preferences (as well as L1 and L2 conceptualizations, cf. De Knop & Dirven 2008: 319) and discussions of potential misunderstandings due to inappropriate lexical and constructional choices or (lack of) precision. In line with Pavlenko and Volynsky (2015: 46), I would like to suggest that teaching L2 spatial language must go beyond vocabulary teaching and create meaningful contexts for (negotiating) form-meaning mappings in order to facilitate cognitive restructuring.[14] In the light of the current analyses, these meaningful contexts should highlight the target language's repertoire of form-meaning mappings and constructional preferences regarding both (i) information focus and optionality (i.e., local complexity, e.g., manner salience) and (ii) preferred patterns and information density trends (i.e., combinatorial potential and global, utterance-level complexity levels).

References

Bamberg, Michael (1994). Development of linguistic forms: German. In R. Berman & D. I. Slobin (Eds.), *Relating events in narrative: A crosslinguistic developmental study*, 189–238. Hillsdale: Lawrence Erlbaum.

Bauer, Lena (2012). Transfer von L1-Strukturen in Beschreibungen von Bewegungsereignissen bei japanischen DaF-Lernern. *Info DaF* 39 (1), 17–30.

Beavers, John, Beth Levin & Shiao W. Tham (2010). The typology of motion expressions revisited. *Journal of Linguistics*, 46, 331–377.

Berman, Ruth A. (2016). Language development and use beyond the sentence. In E. L. Bavin & L. Naigles (Eds.), *The Cambridge handbook of child language* (2nd edition), 458–480. Cambridge: Cambridge University Press.

Berman, Ruth A. & Dan I. Slobin. (1994). Overview of linguistic forms in the frog stories. In R. Berman & D. I. Slobin (Eds.), *Relating events in narrative: A crosslinguistic developmental study*, 109–126. Hillsdale: Lawrence Erlbaum.

Berthele, Raphael (2004a). The typology of motion and posture verbs: A variationist account. In: B. Kortmann (Ed.): *Dialectology meets Typology. Dialect Grammar from a Cross-Linguistic Perspective*, 93–126. Berlin/New York: Mouton de Gruyter.

---

14 Cf. also De Knop & Dirven (2008) for the outline of a conceptual approach to motion/location in German; Fischer (2018) for a range of activities based on pedagogical *Focus on Form* and *Concept-based Instruction*, targeting, for instance, overuses of generic verbs such as *kommen* 'come' and *gehen* 'go'.

Berthele, Raphael (2004b). Wenn viele Wege aus dem Fenster führen – Konzeptuelle Variation im Bereich von Bewegungsereignissen. *Linguistik Online*, 20 (3), 73–91.

Bowerman, Melissa & Soonja Choi. (2001). Shaping meanings for language: Universal and language-specific in the acquisition of spatial semantic categories. In M. Bowerman & S. C. Levinson (Eds.), *Language acquisition and conceptual development*, 475–511. Cambridge: Cambridge University Press.

Brown, Amanda & Marianne Gullberg (2011). Bidirectional crosslinguistic influence in event conceptualization? Expressions of path among Japanese learners of English. *Bilingualism: Language and Cognition*, 14, 79–94.

Bryant, Doreen (2012). *Lokalisierungsausdrücke im Erst- und Zweitspracherwerb. Typologische, ontogenetische und kognitionspsychologische Überlegungen zur Sprachförderung in DaZ*. Baltmannsweiler: Schneider Verlag Hohengehren.

Cadierno, Teresa (2004). Expressing motion events in a second language: A cognitive typological perspective. In M. Achard & S. Niemeier (Eds.), *Cognitive Linguistics, Second Language Acquisition, and Foreign Language Teaching*, 13–49. Berlin/New York: Mouton de Gruyter.

Cadierno, Teresa (2008). Learning to talk about motion in a foreign language. In P. Robinson & N. C. Ellis (Eds.), *Handbook of cognitive linguistics and second language acquisition*, 239–275. New York/London: Routledge.

Cavandoli, Osvaldo (2003). *La Linea*. Monitorpop Entertainment.

Coscoñas, Raquel (2018). *Zweitspracherwerb: Verbalisierung von Bewegungsereignissen als Herausforderung beim Erlernen des Spanischen*. Unpublished MA thesis, University of Basel.

Daller, Michael H., Jeanine Treffers-Daller & Reyhan Furman (2011). Transfer of conceptualization patterns in bilinguals: The construal of motion events in Turkish and German. *Bilingualism: Language and Cognition*, 14, 95–119.

De Knop. Sabine & René Dirven (2008). Motion and location events in German, French and English: A typological, contrastive and pedagogical approach. In S. De Knop & T. De Rycker (Eds.), *Cognitive Approaches to Pedagogical Grammar. A Volume in Honour of René Dirven*, 295–324. Berlin: Mouton de Gruyter.

De Knop, Sabine & Françoise Gallez (2013). Manner of motion: A privileged dimension of German expressions. In T. Li (Ed.), *Compendium of Cognitive Linguistics Research*, 25–42. Hauppage: Nova Science Publishers.

Della Putta, Paolo (2016). Do we also need to unlearn constructions? The case of constructional negative transfer from Spanish to Italian and its pedagogical implications. In S. De Knop & G. Gilquin (Eds.), *Applied Construction Grammar*, 237–267. Berlin/Boston: De Gruyter Mouton.

Ellis, Nick C. (2006). Selective attention and transfer phenomena in L2 acquisition: Contingency, cue competition, salience, interference, overshadowing, blocking, and perceptual learning. *Applied Linguistics*, 27, 164–194.

Ellis, Nick C. & Teresa Cadierno, (2009). Constructing a second language. Introduction to the special section. *Annual Review of Cognitive Linguistics*, 7, 111–139.

Fischer, Maria (2018). *Thinking Spanish for Speaking German. Sprachspezifische Perspektivierung von Bewegungsereignissen und ihre Vermittlung im DaF-Unterricht*. Unpublished MA thesis, Humboldt-Universität Berlin.

Flecken, Monique, Mary Carroll, Katja Weimar & Christiane von Stutterheim (2015). Driving Along the Road or Heading for the Village? Conceptual Differences Underlying Motion

Event Encoding in French, German, and French-German L2 Users. *The Modern Language Journal*, 99, Supplement, 100–122.

Gentner, Dedre & Melissa Bowerman (2009). Why some spatial semantic categories are harder to learn than others: The typological prevalence hypothesis. In J. Guo, E. V. M. Lieven, N. Budwig, S. E.-T. K. Nakamura & S. Özçalışcan (Eds.), *Crosslinguistic approaches to the psychology of language: Research in the tradition of Dan Isaac Slobin*, 465–480. New York: Taylor & Francis.

Gullberg, Marianne (2009). Reconstructing verb meaning in a second language. How English speakers of L2 Dutch talk and gesture about placement. *Annual Review of Cognitive Linguistics* 7, 221–244.

Harr, Anne-Katharina & Maya Hickmann (2016). Static and dynamic location in French and German child language. In P. Guijarro-Fuentes, K. Schmitz & N. Müller (Eds.), *The acquisition of French in multilingual contexts*, 118–144. Bristol et al.: Multilingual Matters.

Hasko, Victoria (2009). The locus of difficulties in the acquisition of Russian verbs of motion by highly proficient learners. *Slavic and Eastern European Journal*, 53, 360–385.

Hasko, Victoria (2010). Semantic composition of motion verbs in Russian and English: The case of intratypological variability. In V. Hasko & R. Perelmutter (Eds.), *New approaches to Slavic verbs of motion*, 197–224. Philadelphia/Amsterdam: John Benjamins.

Haugthon, Chris (2014). *Shh! We have a plan.* London: Walker.

Hendriks, Henriette & Maya Hickmann (2015). Finding one's path into another language: On the expression of boundary crossing by English learners of French. *Modern Language Journal*, 99, Supplement, 14–31.

Hijazo-Gascón, Alberto (2018). Acquisition of motion events in L2 Spanish by German, French and Italian speakers. *The Language Learning Journal*, 46 (3), 241–262.

Levinson, Stephen C. (2003). *Space in language and cognition: Explorations in cognitive diversity*. Cambridge: Cambridge University Press.

Maak, Diana (2018). *Sprachliche Merkmale des fachlichen Inputs im Fachunterricht Biologie. Eine konzeptorientierte Analyse der Enkodierung von Bewegung*. Berlin, Boston: De Gruyter.

Madlener, Karin, Katrin Skoruppa & Heike Behrens (2017). Gradual development of constructional complexity in German spatial language. *Cognitive Linguistics*, 28 (4), 757–798.

Mayer, Mercer (1969). *Frog, Where Are You?* New York: Dial.

Niederhaus, Constanze, Birte Pöhler & Susanne Prediger (2016). Relevante Sprachmittel für mathematische Textaufgaben – Korpuslinguistische Annäherung am Beispiel Prozentrechnung. In E. Tschirner, O. Bärenfänger & J. Möhring (Eds.), *Deutsch als fremde Bildungssprache: Das Spannungsfeld von Fachwissen, sprachlicher Kompetenz, Diagnostik und Didaktik*, 135–162. Tübingen: Stauffenburg.

Ochsenbauer, Anne-Katharina & Maya Hickmann. 2010. Children's verbalization of motion events in German. *Cognitive Linguistics*, 21 (2), 217–238.

Özçalışcan, Şeyda (2015). Ways of crossing a spatial boundary in typologically distinct languages. *Applied Psycholinguistics*, 36 (2), 485–508.

Pavlenko, Aneta (2010). Verbs of motion in L1 Russian of Russian–English bilinguals. *Bilingualism: Language and Cognition*, 13, 49–62.

Pavlenko, Aneta & Maria Volynsky (2015). Motion Encoding in Russian and English: Moving Beyond Talmy's Typology. *The Modern Language Journal*, 99, Supplement, 32–48.

Pawley, Andrew & Frances H. Syder (1983). Two puzzles for linguistic theory: Native-like selection and native-like fluency. In J. C. Richards & R. W. Schmidt (Eds.), *Language and Communication*, 191–226. London/New York: Longman.

R Core Team (2015). *R: A language and environment for statistical computing. Version 3.2.2*. R Foundation for Statistical Computing, Vienna/Austria. https://www.Rproject.org/.

Sagarra, Nuria & Nick C. Ellis (2013). From seeing adverbs to seeing verbal morphology. Language experience and adult acquisition of L2 tense. *Studies in Second Language Acquisition*, 35, 261–290.

Schroeder, Christoph (2009). *Gehen, laufen, torkeln*: Eine typologisch gegründete Hypothese für den Schriftspracherwerb in der Zweitsprache Deutsch mit Erstsprache Türkisch. In K. Schramm & C. Schroeder (Eds.), *Empirische Zugänge zu Sprachförderung und Spracherwerb in Deutsch als Zweitsprache*, 185–202. Münster/New York: Waxmann.

Shusterman, Anna & Peggy Li (2016). Frames of reference in spatial language acquisition. *Cognitive Psychology*, 88, 115–161.

Slobin, D. I. (1996). From "thought and language" to "thinking for speaking". In J. J. Gumperz & S. Levinson (Eds.), *Rethinking linguistic relativity*, 70–96. Cambridge: Cambridge University Press.

Slobin, Dan I. (2001). Form–function relations: How do children find out what they are? In M. Bowerman & S. Levinson (Eds.), *Language acquisition and conceptual development*, 406–449. Cambridge: Cambridge University Press.

Slobin, Dan I. (2003). Language and thought online: Cognitive consequences of linguistic relativity. In D. Gentner & S. Goldin-Meadow (Eds.), *Language in mind. Advances in the study of language and thought*, 157–191. Cambridge: MIT Press.

Slobin, Dan I. (2004). The many ways to search for a frog. Linguistic typology and the expression of motion events. In S. Strömqvist & L. Verhoeven (Eds.), *Relating Events in Narrative Volume 2: Typological and Contextual Perspectives*, 219–257. Mahwah: Lawrence Erlbaum.

Slobin, Dan I. (2006). What makes manner of motion salient? Explorations in linguistic typology, discourse, and cognition. In M. Hickman & S. Robert (Eds.), *Space in languages: Linguistic systems and cognitive categories*, 83–101. Amsterdam/Philadelphia: John Benjamins.

Stam, Gale (2015). Changes in Thinking for Speaking. A longitudinal case study. *The Modern Language Journal 99*, Supplement, 83–99.

Talmy, Leonard (1985). Lexicalization patterns. Semantic structure in lexical forms. In T. Shopen (Ed.), *Language typology and syntactic description: Grammatical categories and the lexicon*. Vol. 3, 57–149. Cambridge: Cambridge University Press.

Talmy, Leonard (2000). *Toward a cognitive semantics*. Cambridge: MIT Press.

Tomasello, Michael (1987). Learning to use prepositions: A case study. *Journal of Child Language*, 14 (1), 79–98.

Treffers-Daller, Jeanine & Françoise Tidball (2016). Can L2 learners learn new ways to conceptualize events? A new approach to restructuring in motion event construal. In P. Guijarro-Fuentes, K. Schmitz & N. Müller (Eds.), *The Acquisition of French in Multilingual Contexts*, 145–184. Bristol et al.: Multilingual Matters.

IV Frame-based teaching and learning

Maggie Gemmell Hudson
Teaching second year German using frames and constructions

1 Innovating and invigorating the second year German curriculum

This paper describes how to use a free open educational resource for German, the German Frame-Semantic Online Lexicon (G-FOL), to structure the curriculum of a second year German course at the university level. While the practical elements of this paper are most relevant to teachers of foreign languages, specifically German, the application of Frame Semantics and Construction Grammar to the foreign language classroom may also interest linguists and language students who find these theories useful in other kinds of research. The paper first examines strategies for overcoming the challenges faced by second language learners when acquiring vocabulary, then touches briefly on the recent shift toward open educational resources and their benefits for students. Then, I introduce the online resource G-FOL and outline some principles for creating a second year curriculum plan using the G-FOL. Finally, I discuss benefits of this approach, implications for the future, and the significance of this work within the broader field of foreign language pedagogy.

As linguistic research advances our understanding of language and its relation to cognition, so too should foreign language teaching methods and materials advance to reflect this new understanding. Current work in cognitive linguistics has provided two powerful descriptive and analytical tools for linguists that can be adapted for use in the classroom: *frames* and *constructions*.[1] The former is a way to define a generalized scenario that constitutes the real-world background knowledge evoked (or accessed) by a speaker when they use (or interpret) words and expressions whose meanings involve that kind of situation. Each frame can be broken down into the participants or actors in the scenario, known as *frame elements*, whose definitions and interrelations make up the meaning of the frame. For example, the word *schlafen* in German ('to sleep') would evoke the Sleep Frame, which includes only one frame element, the Sleeper, who enters (and will eventually leave) a state of unconsciousness.

---

[1] For a more complete view of how cognitive linguistics contributes to and informs foreign language pedagogy, see Holme (2012).

In this simple example, the frame is evoked by a verb with a straightforward meaning. Frames can also be evoked, however, by idioms or grammatical constructions. The second linguistic tool that this paper draws on is the *construction*. These are grammatical structures that impart meaning, much in the same way as words and expressions. Traditionally, grammatical structures have been separated from the lexicon (e.g. textbooks do not often include grammatical structures with vocabulary lists). Cognitive linguistics has shown, however, that this separation is superficial and unnecessary; there is no clear boundary between grammar and lexicon (see Langacker 1987, 2013 and Croft 2001, among others). Therefore, frame-based approaches set out that specific pairings of a form and a meaning evoke each frame.

Two kinds of form-meaning pairs can be identified: *lexical unit* refers to words, parts of words or expressions relative to their meaning in a particular frame (e.g. a word in one of its senses), and *construction* refers to a pairing of form with meaning/function (Goldberg 1995). The ditransitive construction in German is one such case: [X] verbs [Y] [Z], as in *Der Mann gibt dem Hund den Ball*. 'The man gives the dog the ball.' This is an arrangement of a verb and three nouns in different cases (nominative, accusative and dative) that evokes the meaning of transfer, where an item (the direct object, realized in accusative case) begins in the possession of one individual (the subject, in nominative case) and moves to another place (the indirect object, in dative case), which is typically the possession of a different individual, as in the example.

For learners, frames can provide a way to contextualize vocabulary and grammar, and to explore the differences and similarities between vocabulary items in and across languages with relation to a consistent frame of reference (pun intended!). Constructions provide a way of linking grammar to the meaning it conveys, so that learners clearly understand the part grammar plays in the language and why it is important for communication. A pedagogical approach based on frames and constructions assumes no strict division between grammar and the lexicon, underscoring the idea that language is made up of form-meaning pairings that can exist at various levels of complexity, far beyond a simple word like *Apfel* ('apple') and its referent – for example, the possessive "s" in English, the ditransitive construction, and so on. This places grammar and vocabulary on equal footing when it comes to communicating in the target language, which is the primary goal of second year language study at the university level. Furthermore, this justifies the inclusion of explicit grammar instruction as a necessary part of the language learner's experience when the learning objective is effective communication (Ellis 2002).

To implement a pedagogical approach to second year German that incorporates frames and constructions, teachers can take advantage of a free online resource known as the G-FOL (German Frame-Semantic Online Lexicon, coerll. utexas.edu/frames). This site describes a variety of frames well suited to teaching intermediate German, complete with definitions of their frame elements and lists of relevant lexical units that evoke each frame. Connected to every lexical unit, there are notes on usage and any relevant cross-cultural differences, example sentences, templates for how to use the lexical unit in a sentence (relative to frame elements), alternate forms (e.g. noun plurals, past tense verb forms), and grammar notes that explain relevant grammatical structures that are commonly used with that lexical unit.

All of this was designed with the learner in mind (Boas & Dux 2013, Boas et al. 2016). This means that infrequent or impractical vocabulary items are avoided in favor of a more concise list of lexical units for each frame. The frames should therefore not be seen as complete, but rather as sufficient for giving students the means to communicate about the topic described by the frame. Comparisons drawn between German and American culture can be found in the Details of each entry, and foster cross-cultural awareness and intercultural competence by explicitly conveying these differences (e.g. the broad use of English *friend* for close and not-so-close relationships, versus the use of German *Bekannte* 'acquaintance' to distinguish more distant relationships from closer friends designated as *Freunde* 'friends').

2 Challenges and strategies for learning L2 vocabulary and grammar

Before introducing a new approach to teaching and learning vocabulary in a foreign language, there must be room for improvement over existing methods; this paper seeks to improve the ways target language meanings are taught. Communicative, contextualized and proficiency-based instructional models dominate the foreign language teaching landscape in U.S. universities today, and given their popularity and success, this will likely continue. Research has shown that vocabulary is better retained when learning activities are contextualized rather than in list form (Redouane 2011), and the focus on communication and proficiency in communicative settings (e.g. ordering food in a restaurant, interacting with salespeople or the police) has produced speakers who can make their way in the world using the target language. The current approach appreciates these advances in language pedagogy and works within these methodological frameworks, using frames as a means for contextualizing learning, and adding explicit instruction regarding meaning of lexical units to achieve the goal of proficient communication on the topics covered in the frames.

Even in textbooks that make it a point to contextualize their lessons and emphasize the acquisition of communication skills, it has been difficult to transcend the basic "vocabulary list with glosses" format of presenting new vocabulary, and analysis of the vocabulary activities in current textbooks reveals an emphasis on this form-meaning connection (Neary-Sundquist 2015). In fact, Neary-Sundquist's analysis of five beginning-level German textbooks showed that the books provided virtually no way to discover information "concerning the underlying concept and referents that were associated with a word" (Neary-Sundquist 2015: 74–75). Language students and teachers alike easily view vocabulary learning as memorizing a word and matching it to its translation equivalent in the native tongue. This perspective is contrary to what teachers and students know about the difficulties of one-to-one translation, the importance of cultural context to interpreting the language, and the role of grammar as another way to convey meaning (Schmitt 333–334). In my own classes, I have seen students who rely on a simple gloss, and quickly realize this is impractical when they encounter homonyms or homophones. For example, when learning color words, a student objected to German *hell* ('light,' as in *light blue*), claiming that in Duolingo, he had learned the form *Licht* ('light,' as in *turn the light on*).

Ellis (2019: 52) notes that an imbalanced approach (either a broad focus on meaning or a broad focus on grammar) tends to accomplish its main goal, but may do so with reduced competence in the other area (i.e. grammatical competence with low fluency or communicative competence with low accuracy). Because this approach assumes no strict division between grammar and vocabulary, its goal is to strike a balance that fosters both communicative and grammatical competence (especially with regard to grammatical structures with greater expressive power). This means instructors should introduce any and all useful and relevant linguistic forms (whether lexical or grammatical in nature) that will help learners to become effective communicators regarding the topic at hand. This section presents research that highlights the importance of teaching meaning explicitly and providing opportunities for learners to induce meaning from language input, both in relation to vocabulary and to grammar. The focal points of this section are the difficulties encountered by teachers and learners with respect to vocabulary and grammar acquisition, and strategies for overcoming these difficulties.

2.1 Explicit instruction and how to allocate it

Researchers of foreign language pedagogy recognize that there is a need for rich vocabulary instruction, while also acknowledging that the average college level course is limited by time constraints and the level of cognitive demand required for learning a language (Ellis 1997, 2002, 2007; Nation 2001). Laufer and Nation (2012) characterize priority vocabulary items as those that are frequent (and therefore generally useful), and those that are useful to individual learners based on their own circumstances, regardless of frequency (2012: 164). Of those useful items, some have meanings very close to the translation equivalent in the L1, while others differ significantly in meaning, usage, or both. For practical purposes, a language curriculum should aim to follow the 80/20 rule[2] by focusing explicit instructional efforts on the smaller percentage of useful vocabulary that differ from the L1; this will give learners the broadest ability to communicate effectively.

This means that frequent or useful words that can be straightforwardly translated (such as German *spielen* 'to play' or *Tisch* 'table') should not receive as much attention, while words that have cross-linguistic differences in meaning or use should be explicitly taught and the differences explained (e.g. German *Freund/Freundin* 'male/female friend' or 'boyfriend/girlfriend,' depending on how it is used). Teaching cross-linguistic differences alerts learners to the mismatch between the conceptual structure they use in their L1 and that of the L2, which can be a major source of difficulty in vocabulary acquisition (Jiang 2020). Finally, to most effectively allocate explicit instruction, it should focus on input that provides repeated encounters with the vocabulary (Ellis 2009, Laufer and Nation 2012), encouraging learners to focus on the forms presented and engage with them in some way; not necessarily by producing them; attending to them or understanding them and acting on that knowledge also improves likelihood of acquisition (Kim 2011, Robinson et al. 2012, Shehadeh and Coombe 2012).

Ellis (1997) argues that semantic features of new vocabulary (i.e. word meaning) is learned consciously and explicitly. When learning words in context (e.g. viewing a picture with labels of new vocabulary items or guessing the meaning of a word in a text), the learner is actively engaged in determining what that word's semantic properties are and fitting it into their mental lexicon. Whenever new vocabulary is introduced, a learner must fit it into their version of the target language. This process can be fostered through explicit vocabulary instruction, whereby learners encounter clear explanations of semantic information. Foreign language learners must link their pre-existing conceptualizations of the world to new language forms, and are thus subject to interference from their

---

2 The 80/20 rule, related to the Pareto distribution, is the principle that in many contexts, 80% of the output is produced by 20% of the effort. This suggests that where you focus your efforts is of great importance; doing a few highly productive activities will make you more efficient at the greater task than overworking yourself or scattering your efforts to accomplish things that barely add to your productivity.

native language with regard to the ways in which the world is partitioned and expressed linguistically (Ellis 1997).

In the foreign language classroom, this means that explicit vocabulary instruction must include references to the native language in a way that distinguishes its conceptual structure from that of the target language (because learners might assume their current perspective constitutes the only way the world perceived). This explicit instruction helps learners identify which parts of their conceptual structure need to be augmented to fit the meanings of the new forms, and allows them to communicate effectively with those forms faster than would have been possible if no explanation had been given.

It is fair to say that all language instructors include explicit vocabulary instruction for some vocabulary that they know to be problematic for the learners they teach, but it is unreasonable and impractical to leave it completely up to instructors to determine which vocabulary items require explanation and which do not. Unfortunately, this is exactly what traditional foreign language textbooks do when they limit the presentation of vocabulary to lists with translations.[3] An ideal vocabulary resource would focus on the most relevant, common and useful vocabulary for a variety of topics, and explicitly state which items are used differently in the target language (and how).

Norris and Ortega (2000) showed that explicit grammar instruction is more effective than implicit grammar instruction, which is in line with its relation to vocabulary acquisition discussed above. Fujii (2005) describes how the increasing importance of communication in language pedagogy led to the realization that grammar should be taught explicitly, as it is an important part of discourse (research in discourse analysis contributed largely to this conclusion). Fujii argues for dealing with grammar beyond the sentence level (2005: 292–293), but that approach was designed for more advanced students who can produce longer discourse than learners in the second year of instruction.

Of course, learners' ability to use grammatical constructions to express themselves must be fostered and developed from the beginning, so simple, sentence level constructions that increase learners' communicative capabilities are a good place to start. As learners become more capable, they take on more difficult constructions. Different structures vary in ease of acquisition; factors such as how common the construction is, how familiar it is to learners from knowledge of their native grammar, and how complex it is (i.e. how many units comprise it), surely

---

3 It should be noted that modern textbooks use activities to incorporate more than simple glosses; see Neary-Sundquist (2015) for a detailed look at five German textbooks and how they convey information about vocabulary.

influence the degree of difficulty learners experience, just as Willis and Ohashi (2012) found with regard to vocabulary. Given that grammatical structures are form-meaning pairings in the same way as lexical units, we should expect no stark differences in how the two are acquired, challenges learners encounter, or strategies for aiding acquisition.

2.2 Inductive and deductive approaches

Herron and Tomasello (1992) clarify the difference between inductive and deductive approaches to grammar teaching. The former, espoused by contextualized, communicative approaches of the time, exposes learners to a new grammatical structure through authentic texts and encourages them to create and apply grammatical rules in order to use the structure to communicate. The latter approach begins by explicitly presenting the grammatical rules, then asks learners to practice using it by completing exercises designed for that purpose (1992: 708). With their Guided Induction approach, Herron and Tomasello (1992) take the best elements of both; learners are first exposed to language sequences that contain the targeted form, then given the opportunity to complete a model sentence (designed to guide them to discover the rule) based on what they have observed.

In their study, the authors found Guided Induction to be more effective than deduction (1992: 715). More current approaches draw on newly available corpora to magnify the input available to students in an approach known as data driven learning (Hidalgo, Quereda and Santana 2007, Smart 2014, Lin and Lee 2015). Smart's (2014) study compared an inductive, data driven approach to a deductive, corpus-informed approach and a traditional deductive approach (without using corpus data) and found that learners benefitted significantly from the inductive, data-driven method of teaching. Tsai (2019) provides evidence that the deductive approach is better suited to learning word meanings (and thus to earlier levels) while inductive is better suited to learning collocations (and thus more appropriate for more advanced learners).

2.3 Considerations for a curriculum

Research has shown that frequency is an important factor in how useful vocabulary is to a beginning learner (for details see Rankin 2020). Nation (2001) emphasizes the importance of learning high-frequency words (2001: 16), criticizing the lack of distinction between high and low frequency words in second language acquisition studies that suggest knowing a large number of words is key to learners' success. Nation rightly points out that learning a higher proportion of commonly used terms will allow a learner to use the language more effectively than learning a higher proportion of uncommon terms, and that amassing a large vocabulary is not a necessary goal in the short-term, but is more appropriate as a long-term learning objective (2001: 9). Nation (2013) proposes that learners should study highly frequent words early on, and then continue with less frequent words as they advance (2013: 57).

Crossley et al. (2013) found that the best indicator of whether beginning learners would use a particular word in discourse is word frequency for nouns, and versatility for verbs, i.e. that they can be used in diverse contexts (2013: 727). For example, a word like *gehen* 'to go' in German is learned early on and used frequently, whereas *fahren* 'to drive' and *reisen* 'to travel' are progressively less versatile and learners thus take longer to incorporate them into their discourse. This means that beginning language instruction (i.e. first year university level) is right to focus on frequent nouns and versatile verbs, and that intermediate level instruction (second year university level) should begin to expand students' lexical range by providing ways for them to practice using more specialized (for verbs) and specific (for nouns) vocabulary. This is not to say, however that basic forms should be left out altogether; on the contrary, Nation (2013) emphasizes the utility and effectiveness of fluency development activities, in which learners are encouraged to produce language about basic concepts quickly and in large quantity (54–55).

Based on an analysis of advanced learner discourse, Fujii (2005) recommends that a primary goal for teachers when designing learning tasks should be to "target grammatical items that we know are challenging to learners." (2005: 330). This is the essence of how grammar instruction fits into a communicative or proficiency based approach. Crossley et al. (2013) emphasize that frequency is the best predictor of language acquisition in studies that test constructions, just as with vocabulary acquisition (2013: 728). With grammar too, we encounter the familiar loop of commonality, familiarity, usefulness and versatility all playing into one another. Therefore, common and versatile grammatical constructions are both more important and easier for learners because they are encountered continuously. So again we see that when instructors select content for a language course, they can ensure that it is serving learners well by choosing the most productive, versatile and also commonly used structures possible in novice level classes, and increasing specificity and specialization as learners advance.

A good example of this is the genitive case in German. Of all the German cases, this one may just be the simplest (in its form) because it has fewer variations than the others, and its meaning is straightforward: it conveys possession like English 'of,' which is a commonly used concept. Is this a form that beginning learners should study? Well, no, and that's because there is another form, a single word, *von* ('of'), that has a straightforward equivalent in English and serves the same function. Because students can use this one word, *von*, to get around using a case that does not exist in their native language, and because this structure is not very versatile, there is no reason for first year (native English speaking) German students to attempt it. The genitive case is much better saved for the second year of instruction, when discourse is developing further and students are actually able to take advantage of some of the more complex concepts that can combine with this structure, such as genitive prepositions like *statt* ('instead of') or *trotz* ('in spite of'), which stretch beyond the basic nature of beginner discourse.

2.4 Achieving deep understanding through input, engagement and repetition

Schmitt (2008) describes different kinds of knowledge necessary for a deep understanding of vocabulary, and claims that different approaches to teaching vocabulary are appropriate at different levels; beginners may need to focus on the form-meaning pairing (explicit instruction), while more advanced learners may begin to associate collocations implicitly through extensive language input (2008: 334–335). Nation (2001) found that learners need to see and interact with vocabulary in a variety of contexts and ways to retain it well, and that a deeper understanding of its meaning is what allows learners to use vocabulary correctly in context. A study by Laufer and Rozovski-Roitblat (2015) showed that the kind of activity used to practice vocabulary is more important for acquisition than frequency. In their study, the best retention results were achieved after a reading task combined with a focused word activity, regardless of number of encounters (other tasks tested were reading only and reading with a dictionary). Input-based instruction need not be paired with language production to achieve these goals; Shintani (2012) showed that negotiation of meaning and a focus on linguistic form are possible with listen-and-do tasks. In fact, research has shown that simple input-based teaching can be more effective in terms of acquisition than poorly designed output-based tasks that nonetheless engage learners (Hamavandy and Golshan 2015).

Teaching grammatical forms in context is very important; it allows learners to engage with and interpret the new forms as they interpret the meaning, and during this process (especially with explicitly directed attention, e.g. focus on form tasks), they become more familiar with how they are applied (Omaggio Hadley 1993). Ellis (1997) argues that the formal elements of language (e.g. phonological structure, part of speech) are learned through analyzing sequences in discourse (consciously or not). In the earliest levels of instruction, students develop a feel for the structures of the target language in an unconscious way through exposure to the language and by learning chunks first (longer phrases such as *my name is . . .*). Structures that are similar to the native language pass into the student's conceptualization of the target language without much effort (which underscores the importance of language exposure for acquisition, particularly early on), while more complex structures require increasing amounts of attention, engagement, explanation and practice.

Just as noun frequency and verb versatility are good predictors for which vocabulary items are most readily produced by learners (Crossley et al. 2013), frequency of a linguistic item in learner input is a strong predictor of acquisition (Ellis 2002). These frequency effects are two sides of the same coin: production and comprehension. The more common a concept is in everyday life and language, the more likely one is to talk about it; the more often one hears a word, the more likely one is to remember it and start using it. Exposure to target language input is key to vocabulary acquisition, and indeed language acquisition in general (Crossley et al. 2013: 728). Nation (2001) found that learners could be exposed to vocabulary items up to 16 times before learning them, and that without continued exposure over a longer period, new vocabulary was forgotten within 24 hours of instruction. This demonstrates the need for practice and validates teachers' inclinations toward frequent review sessions. Willis and Ohashi (2012) showed that along with frequency, the degree of "cognateness" (i.e. similarity to words in the native language) and word length (in morphemes) were good predictors of how easily a word could be acquired. It's no surprise that foreign words are easier to learn when they're closer to those of your first language, or that longer words are more difficult. Thus while reviewing is necessary and effective, it is best done using activities where learners engage with the vocabulary explicitly and intentionally, rather than in list or overview form. Combining quality input with explicit engagement is a powerful way to help learners retain vocabulary.

Due to the variable nature of many constructions, it is important to afford learners repeated opportunities to engage with the concept and practice producing it in different contexts. After the first round of explicit instruction and practice, applying the construction in new contexts should get much easier. Bogaards (2001) showed that in the realm of vocabulary, multiword expressions made up of familiar words are more easily acquired than novel words (2001: 331–332), and that previous knowledge of a word form is significantly helpful for acquiring new senses of that form while the degree of relatedness to the first learned sense is not very helpful at all (2001: 335–336). If we extend these conclusions to grammatical constructions, it seems that solid knowledge of a construction in one context (e.g. reflexive verbs in the context of grooming in German, e.g. *Sie waschen sich die Hände*, 'They wash their hands') would be key to extending it to new contexts (e.g. reciprocal use of reflexive verbs, e.g. *Sie treffen sich um 10*, 'They meet each other at 10').

2.5 From theory to implementation

There are three main areas in which to implement the strategies discussed above: (1) instructional efforts (explicit instruction and guided induction), (2) course content and sequencing, and (3) strategies for fostering deep understanding of the language. Section 2.1 showed the benefits of explicit instruction for both vocabulary and grammar acquisition (Ellis 1997, Norris and Ortega 2000). Section 2.2 showed that guided induction is an effective way to incorporate authentic data (e.g. from a corpus) in order to let learners construct their own understanding of how the language functions while still receiving guidance from the instructor (Herron and Tomasello 1992, Smart 2014). Curricular considerations were discussed in Section 2.3, namely, how to determine which linguistic units and constructions to include and how to sequence them effectively. It is clear from the discussion that the most common (frequent) and versatile (for verbs, specifically) items should be included at the earliest levels of instruction, with a gradual expansion toward somewhat less frequent items as learners progress (Nation 2001, Laufer and Nation 2012, Crossley et al. 2013, Rankin 2020). To prevent the problem of L1 concepts structuring use of L2 forms, it is also helpful to explicitly teach items with cross-linguistic differences in meaning (Jiang 2020).

Decisions about sequencing course material should weigh the following considerations to maximize acquisition and communicative utility: (1) the closer a L2 form is to an equivalent in the L1, the easier it will be acquired (Willis and Ohashi 2012); (2) the more frequently a concept or linguistic form appears in everyday discourse, the more useful it will be to a learner (this includes topics of conversation, i.e. frames, as well as lexical units and constructions) (Nation 2001, Laufer and Nation 2012, Nation 2013, Crossley et al. 2013, Rankin 2020); (3) the more versatile a linguistic form is (i.e. the more contexts it can appear in and the more other forms it can combine with), the more it contributes to communicative competence, even if these contexts are introduced one at a time, because subsequent new applications will likely be easier to acquire (Crossley et al. 2013). As course material progresses from beginner to intermediate level, inductive grammar teaching becomes more effective as learners are able to acquire more kinds of knowledge about a form (more than what a gloss or definition can convey) (Tsai 2019). At more advanced levels, instruction should be aimed at concepts that instructors believe (or find) is challenging to learners, and corpus data may be used more to move beyond the sentence level toward a more discourse-based approach (Fujii 2005).

Section 2.4 reviewed the value of repetition (both in input and in production) and active engagement for acquisition, which is consistent with Schmitt's (2008) view that a deep understanding of linguistic forms is necessary for their proper use in communication. The most significant strategies are providing sufficient input (Ellis 2002, 2009, Laufer and Nation 2012), allowing learners to actively incorporate new forms into their previous knowledge using strategies appropriate to their level (Ellis 1997, Schmitt 2008) and perhaps most important of all, fostering genuine engagement and interaction with the material (Laufer and Rozovski-Roitblat 2015).

Building a curriculum for second year language instruction is an enormous task, especially when not relying on a commercially produced textbook. There are, however, ways to find appropriate teaching materials online. Section 3 describes open educational resources and why they are flooding into institutions of higher education.

3 The case for open educational resources (OER)

Open educational resources, those that are freely available online, are accessible to anyone with internet access, and reach a wider range of learners, beyond those who participate in traditional educational institutions. At the university level, open resources alleviate some of the financial burden shouldered by students who are paying ever-increasing tuition costs and seeing less value in paying hundreds of dollars for a language textbook, even if it does last them for a whole year of classes. Of course, there are downsides to open resources; they may be of poor quality, difficult to navigate, out of date or incomplete.

The U.S. Department of Education is encouraging educators to use openly sourced materials with their #GoOpen campaign (https://tech.ed.gov/open/), and modern technology is making it easy. The U.S. Department of Education also funds 16 National Foreign Language Resource Centers (http://nflrc.org/), of which one is completely devoted to OER for language teaching and learning: COERLL, the Center for Open Educational Resources & Language Learning, at The University of Texas at Austin (http://coerll.utexas.edu). The free availability of language materials has allowed universities across the nation to drop their textbooks – which can cost upwards of $300 for one year of study – in favor of using a laptop in class or getting a printed version of the free materials (well under $50). This paper is an effort to bring similar benefits to teachers and students of second year German, using one of the online resources hosted at COERLL.[4]

---

[4] The G-FOL project was developed in collaboration with the Center for Open Educational Resources and Language Learning (COERLL) at the University of Texas at Austin and supported by funds from Title VI grants P229A140005 and P229A180003 from the U.S. Department of Education.

4 Frames, constructions and related linguistic resources

The open educational resource G-FOL (German Frame-semantic Online Lexicon) aims to provide richer vocabulary resources for teaching and learning German and to align learning materials with current linguistic theory. It bridges the gap between frames and constructions as descriptive tools for linguists and as a tool for helping language learners grasp new linguistic forms and their functions. This section gives background information on the G-FOL.

Section 4.1 provides a brief overview of the theory of Frame Semantics (Fillmore 1982, 1985; Fillmore & Atkins 1992). Section 4.2 describes the corpus-driven online database known as FrameNet (Baker et al. 1998, Fillmore et al. 2003 Background, Fillmore & Baker 2010), which is based on Frame Semantics. Section 4.3 gives an overview of the G-FOL, together with contrastive examples from the Grooming frame in both G-FOL and FrameNet.

4.1 Frame Semantics

In Frame Semantics *frames* can be seen as "specific unified frameworks of knowledge, or coherent schematizations of experience" (Fillmore 1985: 223). The basic unit of linguistic meaning in Frame Semantics, paired with a form (such as a word or idiomatic expression), is called a *lexical unit* (LU). A word in one of its senses is the prototypical example of a lexical unit (see Petruck 1996 and Fillmore & Atkins 1992 for more details). Even grammatical structures are viewed as form-meaning pairs; these are typically referred to as *constructions*, following the complementary theory of Construction Grammar (Goldberg 1995, Boas & Sag 2012). Lexical units and constructions are studied with reference to frames, which allows syntactic realizations of semantic properties to be analyzed.

Frame elements, specific to each frame, represent the participants in the frame, so in (1) below,[5] they are defined with respect to the Motion frame (other frames would have different frame elements; even if two frames have a frame element with the same name, they are distinct). The Motion frame involves these participants (frame elements): something that is moving (Theme), the area in which it moves (Area), the direction it moves (Direction), the distance it moves (Distance), where it started (Source), the path it moves along (Path), and the location it moves to (Goal). In (1), for example, the Theme is encoded as the subject

---

5 This and all other examples are taken from the annotations in FrameNet II, available online.

of the target verb *roll* (which evokes the Motion frame), and the frame elements Path and Goal are also realized:

(1) Suddenly [_Theme_it] slipped from his hand and *ROLLED*^Target [_Path_down the bank] [_Goal_into the water].[6]

4.2 FrameNet

Berkeley's FrameNet Project (http://framenet.icsi.berkeley.edu; Baker et al. 1998, Fillmore et al. 2003 Background, Fillmore & Baker 2010)[7] is an online repository of lexical information that – thanks to Frame Semantics – structures the lexicon in a way that better reflects what we know about how humans organize information than traditional dictionaries. Lexical units are grouped according to the semantic frame that they evoke, and lexical entries appear alongside annotations of the corpus data that were used to create the frames.

Each frame in FrameNet is meant to denote a configuration of concepts that are related in such a way that to grasp one of them, a person must also understand the structure of which it is a part, i.e. the frame, its other components, and how they interrelate (1982: 111). For example, to fully understand the word *Tuesday*, one must have some notion of how weeks are divided into seven days, each of which have a different name, and so on. Words that denote any of the related concepts of a frame are said to evoke or belong to that frame; polysemous words evoke multiple frames (and thus represent multiple lexical units).

Organizing semantic information by frames allows linguists to analyze the English lexicon in a new way, and the sentence annotations allow patterns of realization to be studied more systematically. This reorganization of the lexicon has applications in many fields other than linguistics, including psychology and computer science. For these reasons, FrameNet has served as a blueprint for similar lexical resources in a variety of other languages (see Boas 2009b), which has created the opportunity for cross-linguistic semantic comparisons (see Lönneker-Rodman and Baker 2009).[8]

---

[6] Example taken from FrameNet's data for *roll.v* the Motion frame, accessible online.
[7] FrameNet is the product of Fillmore's early work and many years of collaboration with other researchers. In the interest of space, I cannot give them all their due credit here; please visit FrameNet's publications page for details about who has contributed to the project.
[8] This discussion of FrameNet's structure is fairly superficial, in that it does not go into the technical details of the database, its interface, or the xml format of the data files. For more information regarding such matters, see Baker et al. (2003).

As we explore the structure of data in FrameNet, let us use the `Grooming` frame as an example; the meaning it represents is already familiar. This frame represents speakers' background knowledge about the prototypical situations that involve grooming of the body, what kinds of participants are involved in such situations (e.g. someone who grooms, the body part being groomed, perhaps an instrument like a brush, etc.), and the real world relationships between these kinds of participants (i.e. the person grooming is using the brush to improve the state of the body part).

For example, English speakers, upon hearing the verb *shampoo*, use their knowledge of the prototypical grooming scenario to interpret what the word means in context; without this prior knowledge, the word would not be interpretable. `Grooming` is not particularly complex, and relates to two other frames in the database: the very general `Intentionally_affect` (with lexical units like *to do something with/to*), which it inherits some meaning from, and `Desirability`, which it uses. These are the only frame-to-frame relations identified in FrameNet for this particular example, but other frames may have different relations (e.g. "is causative of" or "perspective on"). Frame relations provide the lexicon with structure that is semantically motivated and allow FrameNet users easy access to related frames through the online interface. For detailed descriptions and motivation for each relation, see Baker et al. (2003: 286–287).

In the frame report for `Grooming`, as in any frame, there is first a general frame description in prose that gives an outline of the frame and what part each of the frame elements plays in it:

> In this frame, an Agent engages in personal body care by grooming either a Patient or a Body_part. An Instrument can be used in this process as well as a Medium.
> [Agent She] WASHED[Target] [Patient the baby].

FrameNet also provides short definitions for all frame elements typically together with annotated example sentences as well as a list of lexical units that evoke the frame. For `Grooming`, these are: *ablution.n, bathe.v, brush [hair].v, brush [teeth].v, cleanse.v, comb.v, facial.n, file.v, floss.v, groom.v, lave.v, manicure.n, manicure.v, moisturize.v, pedicure.n, plait.v, pluck.v, shampoo.v, shave.v, shower.v, soap.v, wash.v,* and *wax.v*.[9]

FrameNet provides for each LU a lexical entry reports, which is structured as follows: First, the frame of the LU is identified at the top, and then a brief definition is given, followed by a table that lists frame elements that appear with

---

[9] The letter appended at the end of the lexical unit indicates the part of speech (all nouns and verbs in this case, but the database does contain other parts of speech as well).

that lexical unit and how they are realized in annotated corpus sentences. There is also a table showing the valence patterns of annotated sentences, i.e. which frame elements are realized together and their grammatical roles in the sentences when they co-occur (for details, see Boas 2017 and Ruppenhofer et al. 2017).[10]

4.3 Enter the G-FOL (German Frame-Semantic Online Lexicon)

While FrameNet is a resource for professional linguists and software developers, the German Frame-Semantic Online Lexicon (G-FOL; Boas and Dux 2013, Boas et al. 2016; coerll.utexas.edu/frames) was developed specifically for learners of German who speak American English. This resource began with the data from FrameNet and adapted it to the German language and to the intended audience. Considerations such as those discussed in Section 2 above guided decisions about which LUs are included, and while annotated sentences are still featured prominently, other features are also included, all aimed at helping learners acquire the content more easily (see Lorenz et al. 2020). In short, the resource provides a kind of explicit instruction that learners can access outside the classroom, saving precious instructional time for interaction and language use.[11] Figure 1 shows the interface of the G-FOL website, which aims to presents information in a way that is not too crowded; users click to reveal details about particular LUs.

In G-FOL, frames are chosen because they contain a number of LUs that typically appear in first or second year textbooks. G-FOL is not aimed at complete beginners, partly because it assumes some knowledge of basic grammar and vocabulary (e.g. pronouns, articles, parts of speech).[12] G-FOL researchers typically base the G-FOL frames on FrameNet frames, and, if necessary, rewrite parts

---

10 FrameNet has been used as the basis for several similar resources in other languages, including Spanish (Subirats 2009), Japanese (Ohara 2009), German (Boas 2001, 2005b, 2013; Burchardt et al. 2009, Schmidt 2009), Portuguese (Salomão 2009), French (Pitel 2009; Schmidt 2009), and Swedish (Borin et al. 2009). For these resources, the frames from English FrameNet were re-used, and new frames were added where necessary (for methodology, see Boas 2002, 2009).

11 The G-FOL project was developed in collaboration with the Center for Open Educational Resources and Language Learning (COERLL) at the University of Texas at Austin and supported by funds from Title VI grants P229A140005 and P229A180003 from the U.S. Department of Education.

12 Infrequently, multiple FrameNet frames may be combined when realized in the G-FOL. This is because FrameNet prefers to split senses as much as possible, whereas the G-FOL wants to provide students with a cohesive semantic field. This is done with extreme caution and only when the sets of frame elements are compatible and the frame meanings fit together well enough to maintain a clear frame definition.

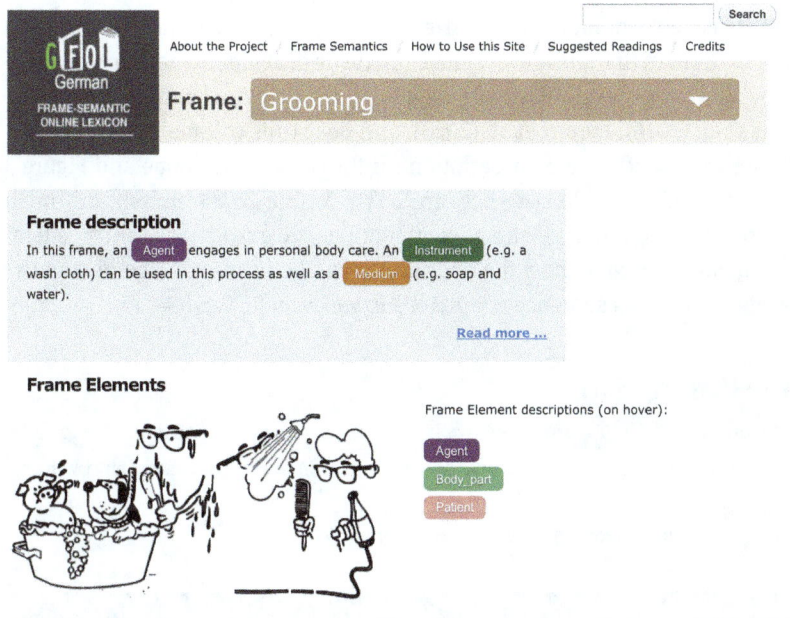

Figure 1: G-FOL webpage for the Grooming frame, retrievable at http://coerll.utexas.edu/frames/frames/grooming.

of them to make them more learner friendly (i.e. clear, concise and simple) and relevant to German (if there are any cross-linguistic differences that warrant mentioning at the frame level). For more details on the workflow underlying G-FOL, see Boas et al. (2016), Lorenz et al. (2020), and Boas (this volume).

Figure 2 shows the frame description for the Grooming frame and Figure 3 shows annotated example sentences in G-FOL for *die Zähne putzen*, 'to brush teeth.' The identified frame element combinations are encoded as sentence templates that show learners how the lexical unit can be used in the context of the frame. Figure 4 shows sentence templates for *waschen*, 'to wash.'

Frame description

In this frame, an Agent engages in personal body care. An Instrument (e.g. a wash cloth) can be used in this process as well as a Medium (e.g. soap and water).

Figure 2: Frame definition for the G-FOL Grooming frame.

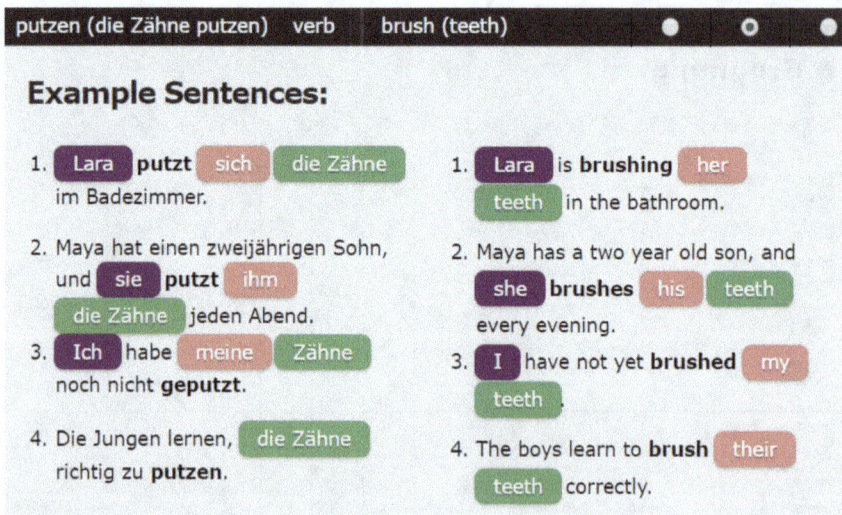

Figure 3: Annotated example sentences for *die Zähne putzen*, 'to brush teeth,' in the Grooming frame.

While compiling examples and templates, G-FOL researchers make note of alternate forms (e.g. plurals for nouns, irregular forms for verbs, comparative and superlative forms for adjectives) and write concise prose descriptions of the meanings and usage for each LU. In the simplest of cases it will read "Used like its English equivalent," but whenever the German LU does not precisely match,

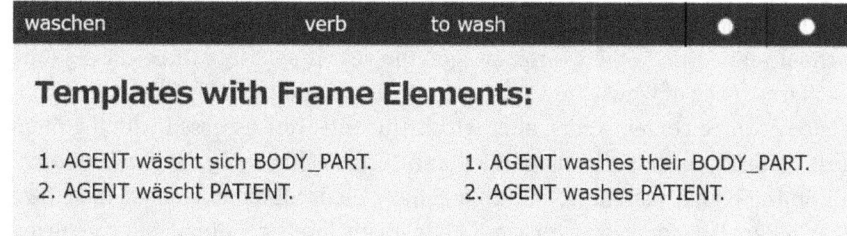

Figure 4: Sentence templates for *waschen* in the G-FOL `Grooming` frame.

learners can read the details section to learn all they need to know in order to properly use it in discourse.

This is where cross-linguistic differences, culture-specific information, collocations, etc. are presented and explained in prose with reference to examples and comparisons to English. Sometimes researchers find that particular grammatical structures appear frequently across a frame (e.g. German reflexive verbs for the `Grooming` frame), and will add a grammar note for that topic that will be linked in the database to each lexical unit for which it is relevant. Grammar topics that are relevant to individual lexical units are mentioned in the details section along with a link to that topic in a corresponding open grammar resource (Grimm Grammar; http://coerll.utexas.edu/gg/gr/index.html).

After other team members reviewed and edited the frame content, everything is published on the website and users can freely access it. The G-FOL currently covers over 350 LUs in 20 frames, and is continuously expanding (as of November 2021). Eventually, coverage will extend to more complex frames and linguistic concepts beyond first and second year German instruction.

5 How to build a curriculum around the G-FOL

Textbooks typically combine vocabulary content, grammar content, activities, readings, etc. into themed chapters. The decision of when to incorporate grammatical structures is sometimes arbitrary (e.g. past tense – it goes with just about any topic), and chapter length varies significantly between textbooks. When using the G-FOL as the basis for a second year German curriculum, it is up to the instructor to sequence frames in a way that makes sense and pair them with authentic language materials to engage students and help them navigate communicative situations in the target language.

This section describes how second year German was taught with the G-FOL as primary course material (a grammar book was used periodically to supplement instruction) at Southern Oregon University in the 2017–2018 and 2018–2019 school years. Due to the quarter system, the year is split into three classes (one per term), each of which are 10 weeks long (not including finals). Each term consisted of three content units, after which students were assessed with a written test of tasks in multiple modalities and formats (listening, reading, writing, fill-in-the-blank, matching, multiple choice, etc.). Students created their own vocabulary lists for weekly quizzes (20 linguistic forms per quiz), and completed various activities in and outside of class to develop their communication skills and practice the new forms.

5.1 Principles of the teaching approach

Every unit in the curriculum revolves around a set of frames and topics that combine in a way that makes sense conceptually. Grammar and vocabulary are presented as tools for expressing meaning, without separating them explicitly. Sometimes texts or films are used to build cohesion between frames that may otherwise seem disconnected (e.g. a film was used to incorporate the frames `Desire`, `Arguing` and `Fighting`). Within each unit, the frame under consideration provides students with a context to rely on when they are practicing new forms. This way, new forms (grammatical structures in particular) are practiced within a confined conceptual space, which allows students to focus their attention rather than trying to apply the structure to a variety of disparate contexts.

In addition to the context of the frame, authentic texts and videos that instantiate the frame are used in activities so that learners can apply their knowledge to real-world situations while practicing comprehension. Cross-linguistic differences in meaning and use are taught explicitly within each frame, and relevant cultural variations are also explicitly conveyed to students. This gives them a head start on the acquisition process by helping them understand the pattern of difference between English and German so that they can identify it when they encounter it.

Throughout the year, high frequency frames, lexical units and constructions are reinforced through review and practice in a variety of contexts. For example, the first term begins with the familiar frames `Sleep`, `Eating & Drinking`, and `Exercise`, which affords students the opportunity to review content from the first year (after a summer typically devoid of the German language) while adjusting to the structure and philosophy of the G-FOL. In that first unit, the basic tenses, cases and word order are reviewed as well. This entrenches those forms and builds a strong foundation for learners as they build on their German knowledge throughout the year, and as new concepts are introduced, they are linked to those with which students are already familiar. The content decisions made by G-FOL creators ensure that vocabulary included in the frames is not uncommon or esoteric, and because learners direct their own learning by deciding what items to include on their weekly quizzes, the task of content selection for vocabulary is already taken care of for the instructor. Only frames and grammatical constructions require attention in this manner.

5.2 Sample G-FOL curriculum

Tables 1–3 show a breakdown of the curriculum by term, each of which are divided into three units. Each unit contains themes (often frames; shown without bullet points) that provide context for lessons and learning activities. Grammar, vocabulary and culture topics that pair with the theme are listed beneath it. All frame names are capitalized and in bold. Topics with new content are marked with an asterisk (some may have already been introduced briefly or partially, but the asterisk indicates that the current unit introduces new information on the topic). This curriculum plan has been revised based on two years of implementation.

Table 1: Curriculum overview for fall quarter (German 201). This is the first class of three in the second year German sequence.

	Unit 1	Unit 2	Unit 3
German 201	**Sleep*** – personal pronouns – nominative case – present tense – irregular verbs – separable prefix verbs – conversational past tense **Eating & Drinking*** – noun genders – articles – *der-/ein-* words* – accusative case – word order – coordinating conjunctions **Exercise*** – days and times – adverbs of frequency – free time activities, sports – infinitive clauses	**Personal Relationship*** – family – possessive pronouns – dative case – genitive case* – *etwas machen lassen* construction ('to have something done [by another person]') **Grooming*** – daily activities – times and days – reflexive verbs (dative and accusative reflexives) **Cleaning*** – separable prefix verbs (present and past) – accusative case – simple past tense* – house/rooms/furniture	**Causation*** – accusative case – imperative – coordinating and subordinating conjunctions – modal verbs (present) *Text: short story** – reading strategies* – simple past tense* – word order – basic summarization – simple reactions

The first unit in German 201 is a review and expansion of content learned in the first year. The Sleep frame serves as a simple introduction to the G-FOL; all students can communicate about sleeping already (although most benefit from a reminder of the irregular conjugations of *schlafen*, 'to sleep'), and generally find the frame easy to grasp and its vocabulary interesting because it expands their conceptualization of a sleep scenario in unexpected ways (e.g. *in Ohnmacht fallen*, 'to lose consciousness;' *etwas ausschlafen*, 'to sleep something off;' *sich ausschlafen*, 'to sleep in'). The Eating & Drinking frame is also known to students, and affords them the opportunity to review food vocabulary while also engaging in conversations where they can competently communicate. The Exercise frame gives them similar opportunities to review and regain their confidence in the language after a summer off.

In terms of grammar, this unit guides students through a review of the basics. With verbs, for example, the Sleep frame contains mostly intransitive verbs, so students focus on the nominative case (for grammatical subjects), previously learned irregular forms (e.g. *er schläft*, 'he sleeps'), and word order (conjugated verb second, separable prefix at the end of the clause if applicable). Eating & Drinking is full of transitive verbs, so accusative case becomes a focus of instruction and practice while continuing to practice proper sentence structure, expanding the focus on word order to sentence structure with coordinating conjunctions. In the activity shown in Figure 5, students link the frame elements of Eating & Drinking to their typical grammatical roles in the sentence, then practice identifying the cases in sentences that evoke the frame. For this activity, students focus on the grammatical cases within the unified context of the frame. Building the activity on frame elements contextualizes the sentences within the frame even though they describe differing situations.

At the end of the unit, Exercise is characterized by a mixture of lexical units with similarities to English and some with strong cross-linguistic differences. While *spielen* ('to play') is used with organized sport games as in English, and *machen* ('to do') is used with non-game sports activities such as Yoga (also like English), the translation equivalent of *to play sports* is *Sport machen* (lit. 'to make sports'). Students struggle to implement this lexical unit in their discourse, despite having learned it in the previous year. To complicate matters, this German expression can also be translated as *to exercise* (*Sport*, 'exercise;' *Sport machen*, 'to exercise;' *eine Sportart [z.B. Basketball]*, 'a sport, a kind of exercise [e.g. basketball]'). By progressing through these frames in the first unit, students familiarize themselves with the G-FOL and learn to rely on it for explicit information regarding how to use each lexical unit. They can begin by reviewing and working at their level, then they transition to expanding their knowledge of the topics covered and improving their grammatical and discourse skills.

> **Nominativ und Akkusativ:**
>
> Im Eating & Drinking Frame, was ist normalerweise Nominativ und was ist Akkusativ?
>
> Ingestor: __Nominative__   Ingestibles: __Akkusative__
>
> Markieren Sie die Nomen mit N für Nominativ und A für Akkusativ.
>
> 1. Ich (N) esse drei Mahlzeiten (A) am Tag.
> 2. Lea und Klaus (N) haben das Mahl (A) zubereitet. — ist
> 3. Mein Lieblingsgericht (N) ist Currywurst.
> 4. Moritz (N) hatte einen Hamburger, Pommes, und Salat (A) zum Mittagessen.
> 5. Carla (A→N?) macht ihre Hausaufgaben (N?) beim Mittagessen.
> 6. Ich (N) frühstücke nie.

Figure 5: Student-completed activity from the Eating & Drinking frame. The first question asks which grammatical cases (nominative for subjects, accusative for direct objects) are typically associated with the two frame elements of this frame. Then students identify those cases in each sentence (all evoke the Eating & Drinking frame in different ways).

The themes in Unit 2 also expand topics covered in the first year, but they incorporate more completely new forms, such as the construction *etwas machen lassen* ('to have/get something done'), which is used to indicate that someone else is doing the activity for you, rather than you doing it yourself. This construction first appears in the Personal Relationship frame with *sich scheiden lassen* ('to have oneself divorced') and is strengthened in the Grooming frame with *sich die Haare schneiden lassen* ('to have one's hair cut').

The Personal Relationship frame reminds students of cross-linguistic and cultural differences of *Freund* ('friend'), such as its double meaning of 'male friend' and 'boyfriend,' or that it is reserved for one's close friends, and is not applied to just anyone in one's social circle (in contrast to English where acquaintances or coworkers can be referred to as friends). It also expands the notion of personal relationships from a focus on family and friends to a broader range of interpersonal experiences. Some of these are well suited to telling stories about the different stages a relationship can go through, for example: *sich befreunden* ('to befriend'), *anmachen* ('to hit on'), *Fernbeziehung* ('long-distance relationship'), *mit jemandem zusammen sein* ('to date,' literally 'to be together with someone'), *sich verlieben* ('to fall in love'), *sich verloben* ('to get engaged'), *heiraten* ('to marry'), and *sich scheiden lassen* ('to get divorced').

For the activity in Figure 6, students are tasked with narrating a brief story that describes the development of a relationship as shown in the pictures. By providing milepost events in the relationship, students are free to be creative, inserting details where they see fit. This student, for example, did not want to end the story with heartbreak, and so added that the man died after the couple was divorced, and the woman remarried. Despite errors in grammatical accuracy, the student found ways to incorporate much of the desired vocabulary, integrate it with known concepts (e.g. having *zwei Kinder*, 'two children'), and creatively fill in the gaps between events from the pictures to make a fuller narrative.

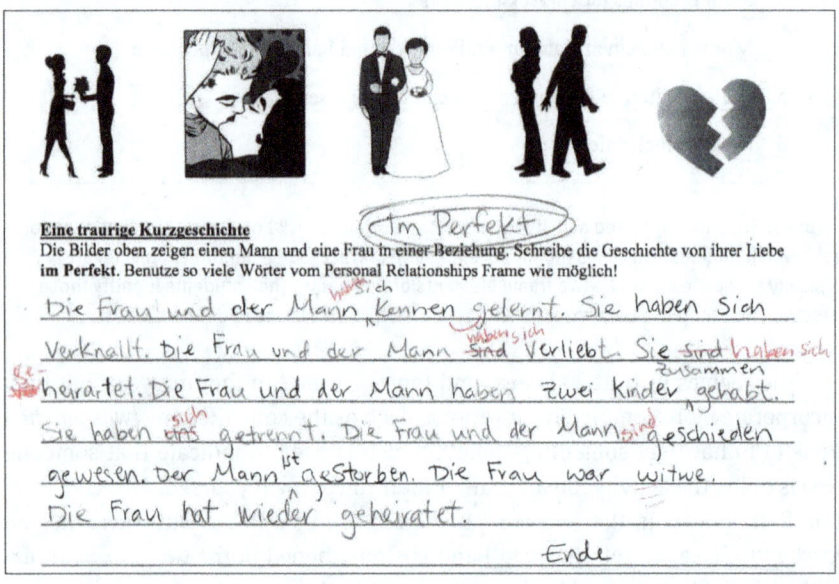

Figure 6: Sample activity for the `Personal Relationship` frame, completed by a student (includes corrections). The title and instructions read: "A Sad Story – The pictures above show a man and a woman in a relationship. Write the story of their love in present perfect tense (conversational past tense). Use as many words from the `Personal Relationship` frame as possible!".

The second frame in Unit 2, `Grooming`, is largely a review, and thus does not take up as much class time as other frames. At this point, however, students have likely not yet mastered the difference between accusative and dative reflexives in German, so the opportunity to practice is valuable. The real benefit in placing the `Grooming` frame here is to use it as a springboard to the `Cleaning` frame, which involves some of the same vocabulary and concepts (e.g. *waschen* 'to wash;' using an instrument such as a brush to help clean something) in a fundamentally different kind of situation. Classroom conversations can include concepts from the

Personal Relationship frame (e.g. sharing housework with a *Mitbewohner*, 'roommate,' or family members) and provide a context for reviewing vocabulary about the home, furniture or rooms covered in the first year of instruction.

Finally, Unit 3 introduces the Causation frame, whose lexical units are almost all new to students. After introducing the frame, students briefly practice new forms before reading a short story (the longest text they have encountered thus far) about a private detective investigating a case. While working with the text, students use vocabulary from Causation and eventually use the written past tense (simple past, imperfect) to describe events from the story. This unit may seem sparse compared to the others, but this is not the case. Much effort and class time is required for learning to read in the L2, practicing writing in the proper form of past tense and developing their summarizing skills.

Over the course of the term, students review and reinforce a great deal of familiar content and use it as a basis for adding new skills and topics to their repertoire. New concepts appear repeatedly, in a variety of contexts (frames), to aid acquisition and afford practice opportunities.

The fall quarter ends just before winter break, so when students return in German 202 (see curriculum overview in Table 2), they begin with discussing and writing about their experiences away from the university. This is a good opportunity to reinforce learned vocabulary and personalize their discourse while also allowing students to build relationships and rapport (making the classroom atmosphere more comfortable and encouraging speaking). The curriculum for German 202 builds in complexity much like in 201; the first frame, Buying & Selling, is filled with familiar concepts, and students have a wide knowledge of goods that could be bought or sold, so it is a great context for studying a more difficult grammar topic: dative. The dative articles are reviewed and used in the ditransitive construction, mentioned in Section 1. This construction's meaning involves transfer, and is used to convey a recipient in Buying & Selling, for example with *kaufen* ('to buy'), as in *ich kaufe meiner Mutter ein Geschenk* ('I'm buying my mother a present'). The familiarity of the other lexical items makes it easy to focus on grammatical forms/accuracy, and shopping makes for a good cultural topic so that authentic texts and videos can be used in learning activities.

The second unit is cohesive (Education, followed by Work) and particularly relevant to students. Mock job interviews are an entertaining way to try out new lexical units in discourse. Passive voice fits well with these frames (courses are taught, employees are hired and fired, etc.), as does subjunctive II (Konjunktiv II), the mood used for hypotheticals in German (students talk/write about their dream jobs, or what they would do if they didn't have to work to earn money).

Lastly, in Unit 3, the film *Goodbye, Lenin!* provides content to discuss with relation to the frames Deciding and Experiencing Emotion. The main character in the film makes several unorthodox decisions and the movie is emotionally charged, so students have plenty to work with. Grammatical concepts involve adjectives because they abound in Experiencing Emotion (e.g. *traurig*, 'sad;' *glücklich*, 'happy;' and *wütend*, 'angry'), while students continue to practice recently learned concepts (e.g. passive voice, Personal Relationship frame) and use the lexical items in the frames in combination with familiar grammatical structures (e.g. inseparable prefixes and infinitive clauses for Deciding vocabulary).

Table 2: Curriculum overview for winter quarter (German 202). This is the second class of three in the second year German sequence.

	Unit 1	Unit 2	Unit 3
German 202	winter vacation – holidays, traditions, gifts – conversational past tense – ditransitive construction* Buying & Selling* – noun morphology for grammatical gender* – stores and businesses* – home furnishings, clothing – shopping destinations* – KaDeWe (culture lesson)* – simple past tense – genitive case – dative case – ditransitive construction	Education* – passive voice (present)* – school system in Germany* – educational funding, BAföG* – academic subjects – subjunctive II (hypotheticals) – genitive prepositions* Work* – professions – job advertisements* – job interviews* – dative prepositions – two-way prepositions (acc./dat.)* – passive voice (past)* – civil service (culture lesson)* – modal verbs (past) <u>Text: short story</u>* simple past tense Causation	Deciding* – inseparable prefix verbs – reflexive verbs – subordinating conjunctions – word order – infinitive clauses – passive voice Experiencing Emotion* – expressing *to like* in German – comparative/superlative – adjectives (word order) – adjective endings* – adjectives from participles* <u>Film: Goodbye, Lenin!</u>* – subjunctive II (hypotheticals) – Personal Relationship

In order to provide continuity with the previous term, and to make use of the experiences students have over spring break as topics in discourse, the beginning of German 203 in the spring quarter includes activities that recall the frames

Experiencing Emotion and Work. The rest of Unit 1 is organized around the theme technology and media, which fits well with the fairly diverse frames explored: Desire, Thinking: Familiarity and Thinking: Opinion. Because students are at their most advanced stage yet, this quarter's curriculum is more advanced and complex. Unit 1 includes new vocabulary about technology and the media (little was covered on this topic in the first year; only a few basic words), some review of previous grammatical structures (e.g. conjunctions) and new grammar (e.g. relative clauses). This seems like a lot, but it is planned strategically. Much of the new technical vocabulary is similar to English (e.g. *bloggen*, 'to blog'), and the new grammar, while difficult, uses the same syntactic structure as the known form that was just reviewed (subordinating conjunctions and relative clauses both have a key word at the beginning of the dependent clause and place the conjugated verb at the end of the clause).

In Unit 2, the complexity remains as content shifts toward culture, retaining the Thinking: Opinion frame and expanding it to other kinds of thinking. Students practice expressing their opinions as they compare and contrast the cultures of German speaking countries with their own. Finally, the content is brought back down to a more personal, relatable level in Unit 3 to leave students in a fun and memorable way at the end of the year. After a brief introduction to the Desire, Arguing and Fighting frames (all of which include a small number of lexical units), students learn vocabulary relevant to the film *der Geilste Tag*, about two men with terminal illnesses who decide to go in search of the perfect day and have all kinds of interesting experiences along the way. Because the main characters are often at odds, and are on a mission to do the things they always wanted to do, these three frames fit very well with film discussions, summaries and critiques.

The curriculum outlined here begins with very basic concepts, to solidify them, and grows in complexity throughout the year. Students are provided with the tools they need to become proficient at speaking, listening, writing and reading about the themes covered in the course, and practice scenarios of real world interactions as well (e.g. a job interview). At each step, repetition and focus on form are built into instruction. New concepts are not taught in isolation, but rather on the foundation laid by related concepts already familiar to students. The next section discusses more specific aspects of teaching frames and constructions using the G-FOL.

Table 3: Curriculum overview for spring quarter (German 203). This is the last class of three in the second year German sequence.

	Unit 1	Unit 2	Unit 3
German 203	spring vacation – simple and conversational past tenses – free time activities, travel – **Experiencing Emotion** – **Work** technology and media* – **Desire*** – modal verbs – subjunctive II of modals – subordinating conjunctions – word order – **Thinking: Familiarity*** – *wissen/kennen*, 'to know'* – **Thinking: Opinion*** – relative pronouns/clauses* – infinitive clauses	news and media, politics* – **Thinking: Opinion** – **Thinking: Pondering*** – Der Spiegel (culture lesson)* – German political parties* – relative pronouns/clauses – German, Swiss and Austrian governments* – subjunctive II (hypotheticals) – other subordinating conjunctions (more complex meanings)* – word order (more difficult)* – comparative/superlative – <u>Text: short story*</u>	**Desire** – modal verbs (past) – word order **Arguing** – accusative prepositions – da- and wo- compounds* **Fighting** – accusative case *Film: der Geilste Tag** – summarizing plot – sentence connecting adverbs (e.g. *danach*, 'after that')

6 Teaching with frames and constructions

At the beginning of the year, it is imperative that students get to know the G-FOL website and what it has to offer. There are resources to assist students on the website itself (see "How to Use this Site" tab), including an overview video that explains the organization and the Frame Semantic approach, and an infographic for quick reference that describes what all the different bubbles next to a lexical unit will reveal when clicked. Students benefit from an in-class demonstration in the beginning, and later reminders of what different types of information the site has to offer (e.g. sentence templates, alternate forms).

When introducing a frame, students should explore the website on their own to familiarize themselves with the LUs and which ones require extra effort to use properly. To accomplish this, students complete an activity like that shown in Figure 7, which takes students from their own mental representation of the scenario described by the frame to their existing knowledge of lexical units that might evoke it, and finally to the G-FOL frame itself so that they can compare their ideas to those in the G-FOL frame, discover what frame elements are central to its meaning, get an overview of the LUs in the frame, and even begin to use some of them in sentences.

GFOL Activity
Eating & Drinking Frame
coerll.utexas.edu/frames

Exploring the Eating & Drinking Frame
Introductory Activity for the German Frame Semantic Online Lexicon

It is recommended that you watch the Intro to the GFOL video at http://coerll.utexas.edu/frames/how-to-use before completing this activity.

Part I. Brainstorm

1. When you think of the concepts *eating* and *drinking*, what kind of scenario do you imagine? Describe it in your own words.

   _____

   _____

   _____

   _____

2. What people or other kinds of participants are involved in a general eating and drinking scenario?

   _____

3. Do you think the concepts *eating* and *drinking* would be expressed in roughly the same ways in German as in English? Why or why not?

   _____

   _____

4. Make a list of any German words or expressions you know whose meaning directly refers to this scenario.

   _____   _____   _____

   _____   _____   _____

Figure 7a. Introductory activity for the Eating & Drinking frame, page 1. Available in the G-FOL's Google Drive folder for teaching materials (http://goo.gl/XSqiwU), no password required.

GFOL Activity
Eating & Drinking Frame
coerll.utexas.edu/frames

Part II. Exploring the GFOL Site
Open the Eating & Drinking frame on the GFOL website
(http://coerll.utexas.edu/frames/frames/eating-and-drinking). Read the frame description and
look at the frame elements. Hover over each frame element to read its description.

5. What similarities do you see between the frame description and your description of the scenario from question (1)? What is different?

_____

_____

_____

6. Do your participants from (2) match the frame elements? Do the frame element descriptions match your expectations of the participant's role in the scenario? Note any differences.

_____

_____

7. How many of your words/expressions from (4) appear as LUs in the Sleep frame?*

    _____ out of _____

   Remember, only the most common, practical words and expressions are included on the website, so if your word/expression doesn't appear there, that doesn't necessarily mean it's not part of the frame! Consult your instructor if you would like to know more about a particular word/expression.

8. Select three LUs from the Eating & Drinking frame that you would like to use in sentences. Write a short narrative using all three LUs (do not write three unrelated sentences).

_____

_____

_____

_____

9. Consider the LUs you chose for (8). Would you say there are significant usage differences between German and English for these LUs? If yes, explain.

_____

_____

Figure 7b. Introductory activity for the Eating & Drinking frame, page 2.

Similar activities can be used as homework to introduce other simple frames, but more focused activities are helpful with complex frames, because they are better suited for explicit instruction during class time. The activity in Figure 8 tasks students with deciding whether each LU listed is very close to English in meaning/use or whether it has significant cross-linguistic differences. To complete the task, students must look at entries for each LU. When they finish the activity, students have a list of words that they should pay special attention to, and a subsequent activity could involve elaborating on the differences students identified. To have students focus on the different forms associated with some of these, they could work in pairs to select the best of multiple translations for a sentence in English, where some of the poorer translations are word-for-word while the best one reflects the nuances of the German meaning and usage patterns.

A. G-FOL Vokabeln: Personal Relationships Frame. (20 Punkte)

1) *For each word in the box below, decide whether there are significant differences in meaning and use between German and English, or whether the word means pretty much the same thing as the English word (that is, it is used in the same types of contexts). List the words in the space provided.* **Tipp:** Du musst die GFOL Webseite besuchen!

der Mann / die Frau	sich scheiden lassen	der Kumpel
der Partner / die Partnerin	Schluß machen	befreundet sein (mit)
der Single	verlobt	der Freund / die Freundin
der Junggeselle	die Verlobung	der Bekannte / die Bekannte
die Ehe	verheiratet	der Geliebte / die Geliebte

For extra practice, write the English word too!

Very similar meanings in German and English: Significant cross-linguistic meaning differences:

_____   _____ der Mann / die Frau

_____   _____

_____   _____

Figure 8: Vocabulary activity for the `Personal Relationship` frame: sorting lexical units by similarity in meaning and use to English.

For any substantial differences in meaning and use between English and German, it is important that the difference be mentioned explicitly in instruction. Most instructors would likely do so if the difference became apparent during class, no matter their approach, but the G-FOL makes it easier to anticipate where students will have problems and get out ahead of those issues. Instructors can go over more minor differences in meaning and use, or they can simply assign students an activity that requires them to explore particular entries in the G-FOL and analyze some of the examples listed there to draw their own conclusions.

It is important to note that in this approach, vocabulary, grammar, and usage are taught concurrently, and often refer to cultural norms and concepts. This matches the nature of language use in that we are constantly combining our knowledge of all aspects of a language when we communicate. Instructors should provide some authentic cultural materials (videos, songs, texts, etc.) paired with form-focused activities to engage students as they practice their language skills. The pre-reading activity shown in Figure 9 focuses on vocabulary from the Education frame to help students approach an article from the German government concerning how funding for higher education is allocated to students.

Pre-reading Activity

Education Frame
Frame-evoking LUs (in-class)

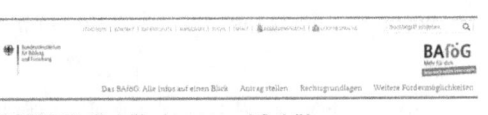

BAföG für Schülerinnen und Schüler

BAföG – das ist nicht nur etwas für Studierende. Das BAföG ist eine finanzielle Unterstützung, mit der man eine Ausbildung ergreifen kann, die den eigenen Neigungen entspricht, auch wenn die Eltern sie nicht finanzieren können.

Vor dem Lesen: Welche Worte evozieren den Bildung Frame? Suchen Sie sie im Text und unterstreichen Sie alle solche Worte, die Sie finden.

Lesen Sie den Text und beantworten Sie folgende Fragen:

1. Was ist der Unterschied zwischen „Schüllerinnen und Schüler" und „Studierende"?

2. Was ist das Hauptthema oder Hauptaussage des Artikels?

3. Was ist das BAföG?

Text adapted from:
https://www.xn--bafg-7qa.de/588.php

260.000 Schülerinnen und Schüler, die eine berufliche oder weiterführende Schule in Deutschland besuchen, finanzieren laut Statistischem Bundesamt ihre Schulzeit mit einer Förderung durch das BAföG. Dank der Förderung können sie ganz unabhängig von der finanziellen Situation ihrer Eltern einen Bildungsweg einschlagen, der es ihnen erlaubt, persönliche und berufliche Ziele zu erreichen.

Schülerinnen und Schüler, die einen berufsqualifizierenden Abschluss oder einen weiterführenden Schulabschluss erreichen wollen, können BAföG beziehen. Für Schülerinnen und Schüler an allgemeinbildenden Schulen gilt das aber nur ab Klasse 10 und wenn eine Unterbringung außerhalb des Elternhauses ausbildungsbedingt notwendig ist. Das ist zum Beispiel dann der Fall, wenn man den angestrebten Schulabschluss nicht in der Nähe des Elternhauses machen kann.

Figure 9: Pre-reading activity for the Education frame.

Figure 10 shows how a scene from a movie can be examined more closely to facilitate recall of vocabulary in the Experiencing Emotion frame. At designated parts of the conversation (noted by the numbers), students are asked to speculate about how the main character is feeling.

One of the most useful aspects of teaching with frames is that similar words can be distinguished from one another, and students begin to understand (without simply relying on English glosses) why to choose one word over another

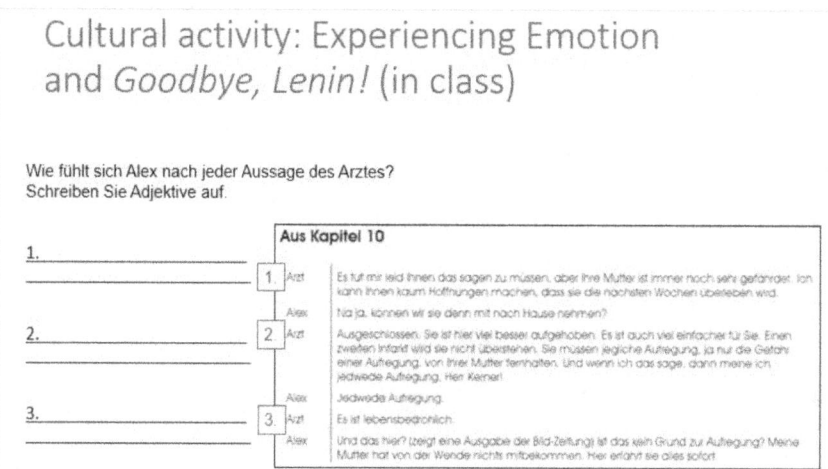

Figure 10: Activity for the Experiencing Emotion frame using the transcript for an important scene in the film.

when they describe similar situations. Activities in which students describe similarities and differences between near synonyms can be a useful way to review the vocabulary in a frame. Because students must explicitly state the differences in their own words, they are more likely to remember them later. In Figure 11, a student selected the synonyms (three to four synonyms from each frame: Sleep, Eating & Drinking and Exercise), then described important similarities and differences.

Another advantage to teaching with frames is that contextualizing students' language use is much simpler. A picture or other visual aid can serve to provide all the context necessary to ground student discourse in a specific set of circumstances, while the frame narrows the focus to a particular aspect of the situation. Figure 12, for example, shows how students can practice using new vocabulary to make statements about a predefined scenario that shows which items/entities fill which roles in the frame. This way, the student must attend to their language closely, as both the instructor and student can see exactly who is doing what. For example, in sentence (2), the student identifies each participant with their frame element role (in German, even though *Käufer* ['buyer'] is not listed in the G-FOL frame; only *Verkäufer* ['seller'] is). This shows that the student was acutely aware of the relationship of each entity to the opposing notions of *kaufen* ('to buy') and *verkaufen* ('to sell').

Synonymgruppen finden. Wählen Sie 3-4 Synonyme von jedem Frame und notieren Sie die Unterschiede und Ähnlichkeiten. Denken Sie an Bedeutung UND Gebrauch (*use*)!

Schlaf	Essen & Trinken	Sport
ausschlafen: means to sleep in, it can be used with a reflexive where schlafen cannot be. It is a verb.	Essen: Means food or to eat, it is a noun and a verb.	Sport treiben: It is a construction, to exercise or to work out. It is a phrase, not just a word.
Schlafen: the general word for sleep. You can use it as a regular verb to talk about sleeping: when, why, how long, etc.	Fressen: different from eating because it usually refers to an animal eating.	Die Fitnessübung: a noun that means exercise.
Schläfrig is an adj. & it means sleepy. It is different from schlafen because it is describing what you are.	Frühstücken: similar to eating but it means to eat breakfast, or to "Breakfast in general."	trainieren: to train, which is a verb, and is the act of exercising.
They all have to do w/ sleep and the act of sleeping.	Essen is probably used most often, frühstücken less often, and fressen only for animals eating. Fressen can also be used in reference a derogatory, "chowing down."	They all have to do with exercise, but they all have differing meanings.

Figure 11: Sample review activity for Unit 1 of German 201 (fall quarter).

7 Benefits of this approach

Students greatly benefit from using the G-FOL. Not only is the resource freely available online and ever-expanding to new topics, but it also allows them to learn vocabulary, grammar and culture concurrently, just as those concepts intertwine in the real world. The lack of division between grammar and vocabulary makes grammar more relevant because it is seen as necessary for communication, while the frames help students see relationships that influence grammatical patterns. The necessary inclusion of cultural information in lexical unit entries fosters cross-cultural understanding and intercultural competence. Bennett (2009) stresses the importance of intercultural competence today, and claims that engagement with the differences – plentiful in this approach – is key to its development. More recently, Lorenz et al. (2020) investigated beginning and intermediate L2 learners' impressions of working with G-FOL to learn new vocabulary. They show that both beginning and intermediate learners value G-FOL's highly contextualized learning and that both groups of learners feel confident in using the new vocabulary items because of the organization and categorization of the G-FOL site.

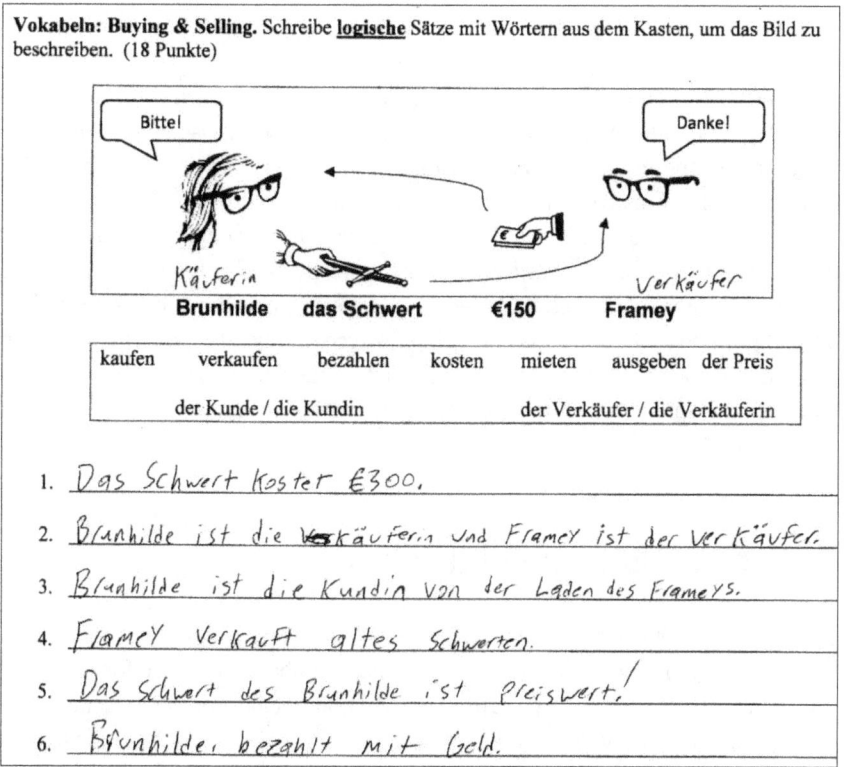

Figure 12: Sentence writing task for the Buying & Selling frame, completed by a student.

By frequently reviewing familiar forms and building on strong foundational knowledge, this approach provides a less effort-intensive way to teach new concepts. Rather than inserting grammar here and there where it seems necessary (as some traditional textbooks seem to do), grammar concepts are taught as they are relevant to the theme at hand, and are always connected to existing knowledge when introduced. This is better because research has shown it is easier to extend known forms to new contexts than to learn completely new forms (Bogaards 2001).

The G-FOL provides explicit instruction and examples for all LUs so that students do not need to rely on instructors to explain every cross-linguistic difference in meaning and use. Rose (2005) found that learners who were explicitly taught about pragmatics outperformed those who were merely exposed to pragmatic features. Detailed information about meaning and use of lexical units is a service to both teachers and learners. While particularly challenging forms will certainly be discussed in class, the lesser differences can be left for students to discover on their own, saving class time while still providing a path to successful acquisition and use.

The nature of the G-FOL content fosters a balanced approach of inductive and deductive grammar instruction,[13] in which students are exposed to grammatical structures in the many examples contained within the frame, and also receive explicit grammar instruction for the most common structures.

The downside to using the G-FOL in the second year curriculum is the lack of activities to accompany the frames. This is slowly becoming less of a problem as more and more of the activities used at SOU over the past two years are posted online. Finding authentic texts and videos to accompany the resource can also be challenging. Lastly, there are not (yet) enough frames on the website currently to cover all the topics one would typically encounter in the first two years of German instruction.

8 Conclusions and outlook

The German Frame-semantic Online Lexicon (G-FOL) is a useful resource for intermediate German learners. It provides information about linguistic forms that is unavailable in other teaching materials and impractical to present in class. The frames it contains provide a context for any learning activity and thus help to contextualize any grammatical construction. Sections 5 and 6 showed how strategies for overcoming language acquisition challenges discussed in Section 2 can be implemented using a frame-based approach. In addition to promoting proficiency in using vocabulary and grammatical structures, the frame-based approach to teaching language fosters intercultural competence by allowing students to engage with the differences between the L1 and L2 cultures, and the incorporation of authentic texts and videos enriches students' learning experience.

As the G-FOL continues to expand its content, this approach could be extended beyond the second year of instruction. Instructors will have more and more freedom to choose which frames they would like to cover in their courses. This is especially valuable to instructors of German because open resources beyond the first year of instruction are scarce. Eventually, Frame-Semantic Online Lexica may also be created for other languages, allowing this approach to extend beyond the German classroom as well.

---

[13] See Herron & Tomasello (1992) for evidence supporting a balance of inductive and deductive approaches to grammar instruction.

References

Atkins, Sue, Michael Rundell and Hiroaki Sato. 2003. The Contribution of FrameNet to Practical Lexicography. *International Journal of Lexicography* 16. 333–357.

Baker, Collin F., Charles J. Fillmore, and Beau Cronin. 2003. The Structure of the FrameNet Database. *International Journal of Lexicography* 16. 281–296.

Baker, Collin F., Charles J. Fillmore and John B. Lowe. 1998. The Berkeley FrameNet Project. In: *ACL '98/COLING '98: 36th Annual Meeting of the Association for Computational Linguistics and 17th International Conference on Computational Linguistics*. Montreal, Canada. 86–90.

Bennett, Janet M. 2009. Transformative training: Designing programs for culture learning. In Michael A. Moodian (ed.), *Contemporary leadership and intercultural competence: Exploring the cross-cultural dynamics within organizations*, 95–110. Thousand Oaks, CA: Sage.

Boas, Hans C. 2001. Frame Semantics as a framework for describing polysemy and syntactic structures of English and German motion verbs in contrastive computational lexicography. In: Paul Rayson, Andrew Wilson, Tony McEnery, Andrew Hardie, and Shereen Khoja (eds.), *Proceedings of Corpus Linguistics 2001*. Lancaster, U.K. 64–73

Boas, Hans C. 2002. Bilingual FrameNet Dictionaries for Machine Translation. In: Manuel González Rodríguez and Carmen Paz Suárez Araujo (eds.), *Proceedings of the Third International Conference on Language Resources and Evaluation IV*. Las Palmas, Spain. 1364–1371.

Boas, Hans C. 2005a. From Theory to Practice: Frame Semantics and the Design of FrameNet. In: Stefan Langer and Daniel Schnorbusch (eds.), *Semantik im Lexikon*, 129–159. Tübingen: Gunter Narr Verlag.

Boas, Hans C. 2005b. Semantic Frames as Interlingual Representations for Multilingual Lexical Databases.*International Journal of Lexicography* 18 (4). 445–478.

Boas, Hans C. 2009a. Recent trends in multilingual computational lexicography. In: Hans C. Boas (ed.), *Multilingual FrameNets in Computational Lexicography: Methods and Applications*, 1–26. New York: de Gruyter.

Boas, Hans C. (ed.) 2009b. *Multilingual FrameNets in Computational Lexicography: Methods and Applications*. New York: Mouton de Gruyter.

Boas, Hans C. 2013. Wie viel Wissen steckt in Wörterbüchern? Eine frame-semantische Perspektive. *Zeitschrift für Angewandte Linguistik* 57. 75–97.

Boas, Hans C. 2017. Computational Resources: FrameNet and Constructicon. In Barbara Dancygier (ed.), *The Cambridge Handbook of Cognitive Linguistics*, 549–573. Cambridge: Cambridge University Press.

Boas, Hans C. This volume. From Construction Grammar to Pedagogical Construction Grammar. In: Hans C. Boas (ed.), *Directions for Pedagogical Construction Grammar: Learning and teaching (with) constructions*. Berlin/Boston: De Gruyter.

Boas, Hans C. and Ryan Dux. 2013. Semantic frames for foreign language education: Towards a German frame-based dictionary. Special issue on Frame Semantics and its technological applications. *Veredas On-line* 17 (1). 82–100.

Boas, Hans C., Ryan Dux and Alexander Ziem. 2016. Frames and constructions in an online learner's dictionary of German. In: Sabine De Knop, and Gaëtanelle Gilquin (eds.), *Applied Construction Grammar*, 303–326. Boston: de Gruyter.

Boas, Hans C. & Ivan A. Sag (eds.) 2012. *Sign-based Construction Grammar*. Stanford: CSLI Publications.

Bogaards, Paul. 2001. Lexical units and the learning of foreign language vocabulary. *Studies in Second Language Acquisition* 23. 321–343.

Borin, Lars, Dana Dannélls, Markus Forsberg, Maria Toporowska Gronostaj, Dimitrios Kokkinakis. 2009. Thinking Green: Toward Swedish FrameNet++. *Proceedings of FrameNet Masterclass*, University of Milan.

Burchardt, Aljoscha, Katrin Erk, Anette Frank, Andrea Kowalski, Sebastian Padó, and Manfred Pinkal. 2009. Using FrameNet for the semantic analysis of German: Annotation, representation, and automation. In: Hans C. Boas (ed.), *Multilingual FrameNets in computational lexicography: Methods and applications*, 209–241. New York: de Gruyter.

Croft, William. 2001. *Radical Construction Grammar: Syntactic Theory in Typological Perspective*. Oxford: Oxford University Press.

Crossley, Scott A., Nicholas Subtirelu, and Tom Salsbury. 2013. Frequency effects or context effects in second language word learning. *Studies in Second Language Acquisition* 35. 727–755.

Ellis, Nick C. 1997. Vocabulary acquisition: Word structure, collocation, word-class, and meaning. In: Norbert Schmitt and Michael McCarthy (eds.), *Vocabulary: description, acquisition and pedagogy*, 122–139. Cambridge: Cambridge University Press.

Ellis, Nick C. 2002. Frequency effects in language processing: A review with implications for theories of implicit and explicit language acquisition. *Studies in Second Language Acquisition* 24. 143–188.

Ellis, Nick C. 2007. The Weak-Interface, Consciousness, and Form-focussed instruction: Mind the Doors. In: Sandra Fotos and Hossein Nassaji (eds.), *Form Focused Instruction and Teacher Education: Studies in Honour of Rod Ellis*, 17–33. Oxford: Oxford University Press.

Ellis, Nick C. 2009. Optimizing the input: Frequency and Sampling in Usage-based and Form-focussed Learning. In Michael H. Long and Catherine J. Doughty (eds.), *Handbook of Language Teaching*, 139–158. Oxford: Blackwell.

Ellis, Nick C. 2019. Essentials of a Theory of Language Cognition. *The Modern Language Journal* 103. 39–60.

Fillmore, Charles J. 1968. The case for case. In: Emmon Bach and Robert Harms (eds.), *Universals in Linguistic Theory*, 1–88. New York: Holt, Rinehart, and Winston.

Fillmore, Charles J. 1975. An alternative to checklist theories of meaning. *Papers from the First Annual Meeting of the Berkeley Linguistics Society*. 123–132.

Fillmore, Charles J. 1982. Frame Semantics. *Linguistics in the Morning Calm*, 111–137. Seoul: Hanshin.

Fillmore, Charles J. 1985. Frames and the Semantics of Understanding. *Quaderni di Semantica* 6. 222–254.

Fillmore, Charles J., and Beryl T. Atkins. 1992. Towards a frame-based organization of the lexicon: The semantics of RISK and its neighbors. In: Adrienne Lehrer and Eva Feder Kittay (eds.), *Frames, Fields, and Contrasts: New Essays in Semantics and Lexical Organization*, 75–102. Hillsdale, NJ: Erlbaum.

Fillmore, Charles J., Christopher R. Johnson, and Miriam R. L. Petruck. 2003. Background to FrameNet. *International Journal of Lexicography* 16 (3). 235–251.

Fillmore, Charles J., Miriam R. L. Petruck, Josef Ruppenhofer, and Abby Wright. 2003. FrameNet in Action: The Case of Attaching. *International Journal of Lexicography* 16 (3). 297–332.

Fillmore, Charles J., and Collin Baker. 2010. A frames approach to semantic analysis. In: Bernd Heine, and Heiko Narrog (eds.), *The Oxford Handbook of Linguistic Analysis*, 313–339. New York: The Oxford University Press.

Fujii, Noriko. 2005. Learning from learner discourse: Rethinking grammar instruction. *Japanese Language and Literature* 39 (2). 291–337.

Goldberg, Adele E. 1995. *Constructions: A construction grammar approach to argument structure*. Chicago: University of Chicago Press.

Hamavandy, Mehraban and Mohammad Golshan. 2015. Differential Potential of SLA Output Tasks versus Input-based Teaching of English Grammar: A Comparative Study. *Theory and Practice in Language Studies* 5 (10). 2083–2090.

Hanks, Patrick. 2000. Do Word Meanings Exist? *Computers and the Humanities* 34. 205–215.

Herron, Carol, and Michael Tomasello. 1992. Acquiring grammatical structures by guided induction. *The French Review* 65. 708–718.

Hidalgo, Encarnación, Luis Quereda and Juan Santana (eds.). 2007. *Corpora in the Foreign Language Classroom: Selected papers from the Sixth International Conference on Teaching and Language Corpora (TaLC 6). University of Granada, Spain, 4–7 July 2004*. Leiden: BRILL.

Holme, Randal. 2012. Cognitive Linguistics and the Second Language Classroom. *TESOL Quarterly* 46 (1). 6–29.

Jiang, Nan. 2020. Semantic Development and L2 Vocabulary Teaching. In: Peter Ecke and Susanne Rott (eds.), *AAUSC 2018 Volume: Understanding Vocabulary Learning and Teaching: Implications for Language Program Development*, 10–27. Boston: Cengage.

Jung, Eulho, Christine Bauer, and Allan Heaps. 2017. Strategic Implementation of Open Educational Resources in Higher Education Institutions. *Educational Technology* 57 (2) 78–84.

Kim, YouJin. 2011. The Role of Task-Induced Involvement and Learner Proficiency in L2 Vocabulary Acquisition. *Language Learning* 61. 100–140.

Langacker, Ronald W. 1987. *Foundations of Cognitive Grammar: Theoretical prerequisites*. Stanford: Stanford University Press.

Langacker, Ronald W. 2013. *Essentials of Cognitive Grammar*. Oxford: Oxford University Press.

Laufer, Batia and I. S. Paul Nation. 2012. Vocabulary. In: Susan M. Gass and Alison Mackey (eds.), *The Routledge Handbook of Second Language Acquisition*, 163–176. New York: Routledge.

Laufer, Batia and Bella Rozovski-Roitblat. 2015. Retention of new words: Quantity of encounters, quality of task, and degree of knowledge. *Language Teaching Research* 19 (6). 687–711.

Liddicoat, Anthony, and Scarino, Angela. 2013. *Intercultural Language Teaching and Learning*. Malden, MA: Wiley-Blackwell.

Lin, Ming Huei, and Joa-Ying Lin Lee. 2015. Data-Driven Learning: Changing the Teaching of Grammar in EFL Classes. *ELT Journal* 69 (3). 264–74.

Lönneker-Rodman, Birte and Collin F. Baker. 2009. The FrameNet model and its applications. *Natural Language Engineering* 15. 415–453.

Lorenz, Alexander, Crane, Cori, Benjamins, John, and Hans C. Boas. 2020. L2 German Learners' Perceptions and Use of an Online Semantic Frame-Based Dictionary. *Die Unterrichtspraxis/Teaching German* 53.2, 191–209.

Nation, I. S. Paul. 2001. *Learning vocabulary in another language*. New York: Cambridge University Press.

Nation, I. S. Paul. 2013. My Ideal Vocabulary Teaching Course. In: John Macalister and I. S. Paul Nation (eds.), *Language Curriculum Design: Concepts and Approaches in Action Around the World*, 49–62. New York: Routledge.

Neary-Sundquist, Colleen A. 2015. Aspects of Vocabulary Knowledge in German Textbooks. *Foreign Language Annals* 48. 68–81.

Norris, John M., and Lourdes Ortega. 2000. Effectiveness of L2 instruction: A research synthesis and quantitative meta-analysis. *Language Learning* 50. 417–528.

Ohara, Kyoko. 2009. Frame-based contrastive lexical semantics in Japanese FrameNet: The case of *risk* and *kakeru*. In: Hans C. Boas (ed.), *Multilingual FrameNets in computational lexicography: Methods and applications*, 163–182. New York: de Gruyter.

Omaggio Hadley, Alice. 1993. *Teaching Language in Context*. Boston, MA: Heinle & Heinle.

Petruck, Miriam R. L. 1996. Frame Semantics. In: Jef Verschueren, Jan-Ola Östman, Jan Blommaert, and Chris Bulcaen (eds.), *Handbook of Pragmatics*, 1–13. Philadelphia: John Benjamins.

Pitel, Guillaume. 2009. Cross-lingual labeling of semantic predicates and roles: A low-resource method based on bilingual L(atent) S(emantic) A(nalysis). In: Hans C. Boas (ed.), *Multilingual FrameNets in computational lexicography: Methods and applications*, 245–286. New York: de Gruyter.

Rankin, Jamie. 2020. *der | die | das*: Integrating Vocabulary Acquisition Research into an L2 German Curriculum. In: Peter Ecke and Susanne Rott (eds.), *AAUSC 2018 Volume: Understanding Vocabulary Learning and Teaching: Implications for Language Program Development*, 10–27. Boston: Cengage.

Redouane, Rabia. 2011. Assessing instructional methods in L2 French vocabulary acquisition: Guessing-from-context method versus a word-list method. *Economics, Management, and Financial Markets* 6 (2). 710–725.

Robinson, Peter, Alison Mackey, Susan M. Gass, and Richard Schmidt. 2012. Attention and awareness in second language acquisition. In: Susan M. Gass and Alison Mackey (eds.), *The Routledge Handbook of Second Language Acquisition*, 247–267. New York: Routledge.

Rose, Kenneth R. 2005. On the effects of instruction in second language pragmatics. *System* 33(3). 385–399.

Ruppenhofer, Josef, Hans C. Boas, and Collin F. Baker. 2017. FrameNet. In: Pedro A. Fuertes-Olivera (ed.), *The Routledge Handbook of Lexicography*, 383–398. New York: Routledge.

Salomão, Margarida. 2009. FrameNet Brasil: um trabalho em progresso. *Calidoscópio* 7(3). 171–182.

Schmidt, Thomas. 2009. The Kicktionary – A Multilingual Lexical Resource of Football Language. In: Hans C. Boas (ed.), *Multilingual FrameNets in computational lexicography: Methods and applications*, 101–134. New York: de Gruyter.

Schmitt, Norbert. 2008. Review Article: Instructed Second Language Vocabulary Learning. *Language Teaching Research* 12 (3). 329–363.

Shehadeh, Ali and Christine A. Coombe (eds.) 2012. *Task-Based Language Teaching in Foreign Language Contexts: Research and Implementation*. Philadelphia: John Benjamins.

Smart, Jonathan. 2014. The Role of Guided Induction in Paper-Based Data-Driven Learning. *ReCALL: The Journal of EUROCALL* 26 (2). 184–201

Subirats, Carlos. 2009. Spanish FrameNet: A frame-semantic analysis of the Spanish lexicon. In: Hans C.Boas (ed.), *Multilingual FrameNets in computational lexicography: Methods and applications*, 135–162. New York: de Gruyter.

Shintani, Natsuko. 2012. Input-based tasks and the acquisition of vocabulary and grammar: A process-product study. *Language Teaching Research* 16 (2). 253–279.

Tsai, Kuei-Ju. 2019. Corpora and Dictionaries as Learning Aids: Inductive Versus Deductive Approaches to Constructing Vocabulary Knowledge. *Computer Assisted Language Learning* 32 (8). 805–826.

Willis, Martin and Yoshie Ohashi. A model of L2 vocabulary learning and retention. *Language Learning Journal* 40 (1). 125–137.

James Law
Frame-based metonymy in teaching L2 vocabulary

1 Introduction

A major organizing principle in any language is the network of conceptual relations used by speakers of that language. Metaphors and metonymies are foundational to the way people structure their thoughts and express them in language, and each culture and language uses its own unique set of these relations (Lakoff & Johnson 1980, Kövecses 2005). However, traditional foreign-language instruction rarely includes any mention of these relations and how they are used in the target culture. In this paper, I argue that the teaching of culture-based conceptual relations can be supported by a frame-based approach to L2 vocabulary. I illustrate this approach with a sample L2 French lesson on metonymy within the Communication frame, restructuring material from an existing popular French textbook. The aim of the paper is to propose the integration of conceptual relations into foreign language teaching and to exemplify how this can be accomplished by instructors within the broader movement of frame-based language pedagogy.

1.1 L2 Metonymy

Metaphors and metonymies are sometimes culturally specific (Kövecses 2005). However, even when a learner's native language and target language make use of the same metaphor or metonymy, learners may need pedagogical intervention to use figurative language appropriately in their L2. The metonymy THE PLACE FOR THE INSTITUTION is found in many cultures. However, a native English-speaking learner of French who readily understands 'the White House' in the headline in (1a) as referring to the U.S. Executive Branch may not necessarily understand *l'Élysée* (the Élysée Palace, the official residence of the French president) in (1b) as referring to the department of the French presidency.

(1) a. White House condemns Turkey's tariffs on U.S. imports
                                                      (*Reuters*, August 15, 2018)

b. *Violences sur un manifestant : l'Elysée annonce avoir « mis fin à toute collaboration » avec un gendarme réserviste*
'Violence against a demonstrator: The Élysée announces it has "ended all association" with a reserve officer' (*Le Monde*, July 19, 2018)

An understanding of the word *Élysée* includes not just a familiarity with the Élysée Palace, but also a knowledge of its metonymic association as used especially in news genres. This is because even when similar metonymic patterns are found across cultures, the ways in which those patterns are exploited in language can be highly culture-specific (Musson & Tietze 2004: 1306). Although the same metonymy, THE PLACE FOR THE INSTITUTION, is used in both English and French, the ability to interpret and produce native-like metonymic expressions like those in (1) depends on a rich understanding of the target culture's politics, genre conventions and grammatical constructions. An uninformed transfer of the conceptual relation THE PLACE FOR THE INSTITUTION could lead to usage that is not native-like, such as the use of 'the Capitol' to refer to the U.S. Congress or the full place name *le palais de l'Élysée* to refer to the French presidency, rather than the shortened *l'Élysée*. Pedagogical instruction in the conceptual relations used in a particular language, whether shared or not by other languages, therefore has a role in developing L2 competence.

1.2 Frame-based pedagogy

A pedagogical approach to metonymy can be situated within a frame-based approach to language instruction. Frame Semantics (Fillmore 1982, 1985) views word meaning as fitting into a broader network of concepts. In order to understand the meaning of a word, one must understand the frame evoked by the word, namely the background of experiences, beliefs, and concepts underlying the meaning profiled by the word. For example, the word *sell* only has meaning within the frame of commercial transactions and cannot be understood without an understanding of frame elements like PURCHASER, SELLER, PRODUCT, and PRICE.

This view of meaning has inspired recent attempts to move beyond a traditional approach to vocabulary teaching where target words are organized either by theme or by inflectional class and are presented with simple L1 glosses to indicate their meaning. In a frame-based foreign language pedagogy, the basic unit of instruction is not the word but the frame; words are introduced as tools to talk about a particular frame in the L2 (Atzler 2011, Boas et al. 2016).

Frame-based foreign language pedagogy has seen little practical application in the literature, although it has been advocated as potentially useful by several researchers in Frame Semantics (Fillmore 1985: 223–224; Petruck 1996: 12; Boas 2001: 72). Atzler (2011) found that frame-based instruction in German vocabulary provided greater enjoyment to learners than traditional memorization while yielding statistically similar outcomes for retention and culturally appropriate usage. Boas and Dux (2013), however, found that learners using a frame-based dictionary were significantly more aware of grammatical, semantic and pragmatic differences between English and German vocabulary related to personal relationships than learners using a traditional dictionary (see also Lorenz et al. 2020). While the research is not yet conclusive on the outcomes of frame-based pedagogy, it is a promising new approach to vocabulary teaching. This paper aims to demonstrate a further possible advantage of frame-based language pedagogy, namely that it facilitates the teaching of metonymy to L2 learners.

Within a frames approach, metonymy is based on a contiguity relation between elements of the same frame (Koch 1999). Concepts like PLACE and INSTITUTION can be considered contiguous when they belong to the same frame, such as the EXECUTIVE BRANCH frame. Within this frame as it applies to U.S. government, a single linguistic expression, *White House*, always provides the source for this metonymy. For other metonymic patterns, the source element may be evoked by any number of linguistic expressions. For instance, in the Purpose frame, the MEANS or action taken to achieve a goal can metonymically stand in place of the AGENT who desires the goal. This MEANS FOR AGENT metonymy is seen in (2b), where although *surgery* cannot desire a goal, it can index *the surgeon*, referred to directly in (2a), who desires a goal and performs surgery to achieve it.

(2) a. The surgeon's goal was to remove the blood clot.
    b. The goal of surgery was to remove the blood clot.

An understanding of metonymy therefore relies on an understanding of the concept behind frames, namely that when we refer to ideas and situations, we evoke a number of entities that participate in them. These entities may share a relationship where one can index the other. When instruction is centered around frames, metonymies can be easily integrated into the curriculum.

1.3 Outline and data

A frame-based approach to language instruction is a radical departure from the methods of foreign language pedagogy used in most schools and universities today. I elaborate on this approach and why it might be beneficial in teaching vocabulary in the following section. I then provide some further discussion of how metonymy might feature in a frame-based pedagogical approach, and why it is an important concept to teach to language learners. I follow these discussions with the presentation of a practical example of a frame-based first-year university French lesson that includes a common metonymic pattern. The sample lesson begins with the introduction of the Communication frame and MEDIUM FOR SPEAKER metonymy within that frame and continues with a number of in-class activities, assignments, and assessments. This lesson is designed to illustrate the principles discussed in this paper and to hopefully inspire more attempts at frame-based foreign language pedagogy.

The sample lesson contributed by this paper is a revision of a section from the French textbook *Français interactif* (Kelton, Guilloteau, & Blyth 2017). I retained the theme, some of the vocabulary, and pre- and post-class readings from *Français interactif*. I added supplemental vocabulary evoking the target frame from the ASFALDA French FrameNet (Candito et al. 2014). In addition, I developed new in-class activities to replace those from the textbook. This work is meant to illustrate how instructors can modify material from standard language textbooks to create frame-based lessons that include metonymy.

2 A frame-based approach to vocabulary teaching

Approaches to teaching L2 vocabulary are varied, and rather than attempt to provide a full review, I will contrast a frame-based approach with the most common trends across the various approaches that are commonly used in L2 classrooms. With respect to several issues involved in vocabulary teaching, an approach built on Frame Semantics diverges from regular practice. In considering some of these issues, the perspective shift that a frame-based approach presents will become clearer.

The first issue is the question of motivation. Why should new vocabulary items be introduced? The standard reasoning goes that depending on their language goals, learners must set a threshold of frequency and learn the words with higher frequency than that threshold, beginning with the most frequent words (Nation 2001). A learner wishing to achieve native-like fluency must acquire the vocabulary of a native speaker. This reasoning suggests that learners should be introduced to a word simply because it is a word that native speakers use with some level of frequency. It does not directly consider the meaning of words.

In a curriculum based around word frequency, the starting point is a list of the most frequent words, which are then grouped according to some schema and introduced incrementally. Of course, highly frequent words are often closed-class words, and in practice it may be only open-class content words that are introduced based on frequency, while function words such as articles and prepositions are introduced more slowly as the associated grammar concepts are taught. In a frame-based approach, the starting point is not words but frames. Vocabulary items are selected for study based on their usefulness in communicating about a particular frame, which may be partially determined by their frequency. A word is included in a learner's inventory not because it has a high frequency, but because its meaning is relevant to the meanings the learner wishes to express.

Once a selection of vocabulary for a curriculum has been made, traditional approaches are faced with the task of organizing the presentation of that vocabulary. The most common schema is a grouping of vocabulary items that fall into certain semantic categories, such as food, hobbies, and modes of transportation. Words are also often grouped by part of speech, with prepositions presented separately from nouns, for example. In languages with inflectional classes, these may also be an organizing principle. For instance, in Spanish it is common to present so-called '-ar', '-er', and '-ir' verbs together, with a similar pattern common in French teaching (Hulstijn 1995). Although these groupings may be intuitive, Tinkham (1997) finds that they are counterproductive to learning. Concurrent presentation of words with similar semantic and syntactic properties (e.g. *knife, fork, spoon*) can cause interference, where learners confuse vocabulary items and have difficulty separating them in memory. In Tinkham's study, vocabulary retention was more effective with unrelated sets of vocabulary items than with semantic clusters.

However, the presentation of unrelated vocabulary based on frequency is not necessarily the solution. Tinkham finds that concurrent presentation of words belonging to a 'thematic cluster', i.e. words of the same frame but with varied syntactic and semantic properties (e.g. *frog, pond, hop, swim, green, slippery*), was for most learners the most effective method for acquiring vocabulary and generally avoided the problems associated with interference. A frame-based organization of vocabulary aims to help learners to create lexical associations between related words while minimizing interference by presenting a mix of words with different properties.

The simplest and most common way to indicate the meaning of L2 vocabulary is with L1 translations. This results in two problems. First, learners may rely exclusively on the L1 translation to assign meaning to the L2 word, unaware of differences in meaning that may exist. Second, for polysemous words, learners may erroneously transfer the range of meanings of the L1 word onto the L2 word (Tanaka & Abe 1984, Morimoto & Loewen 2007). The frame-based approach avoids the first problem by indicating word meaning by reference to a culturally-specific frame, rather than to an L1 translation equivalent.

For example, if the Spanish word *pan* is presented as equivalent to English *bread*, learners may miss the culture-specific differences in prototypical referents for these words. Instead presenting learners with a background of information about cuisine within a particular Spanish-speaking culture before associating *pan* with a particular element of that frame may encourage a more accurate representation of the meaning of that word. Boas and Dux (2013) associate frame-based presentation of vocabulary meaning with 'rich instruction' as advocated by Nation (2001) where cultural details are included along with vocabulary. As for the issue of polysemy, a frame-based approach links vocabulary words directly to their meaning rather than indirectly by way of an L1 word which may also have other meanings. This does not present the same potential for incorrect transfer of multiple meanings from L1 to L2 that an approach based on translations does.

Assessment of vocabulary can treat vocabulary as a discrete construct which is tested on its own, or as an embedded construct within a broader skill that is being assessed (Read & Chapelle 2001). This is the difference between a dedicated 'vocabulary test' and a more open-ended assessment such as a writing task where vocabulary knowledge is essential to success in the task but is not the explicit object of assessment. While discrete assessment of vocabulary may have a place in a frame-based pedagogy, the approach treats frames, not words, as the basic unit of instruction. Assessment is therefore directed towards learners' ability to communicate within a frame, not toward their knowledge of words. A frame-based approach to vocabulary instruction favors embedded assessment of vocabulary knowledge, where vocabulary knowledge is a secondary construct in support of competence at performing communicative tasks.

3 Teaching L2 metonymy

Metonymy has several communicative functions, which motivate its incorporation into an L2 instructional curriculum. It is not limited to poetic styles but is pervasive in everyday language (Jodłowiec & Piskorska 2015). It allows a speaker to shift focus, referring to an entity by using the word for a related concept, which may change the emphasized attributes or perspective by which the referent is viewed (Langacker 2008: 69). This can play an impersonalizing role similar to the passive voice (Rundblad 2007). This is the case in example (2) above, where the use of *surgery* in place of *surgeon* shifts focus away from the agent.

Metonymy may be used to humorous effect or for subjective expression (Feyaerts & Brône 2005). Reference to a person using a salient physical attribute may serve this purpose, e.g. *the mustache over there*. Musson and Tietze (2004) discuss how THE PLACE FOR THE INSTITUTION metonymy is used to negotiate power and social status, with place names being imbued with social meaning according to the institutions located there. Metonymy is also quite often a simpler way to refer to something than literal reference (Falkum et al. 2017). In the classic example from Lakoff and Johnson (1980), servers at a restaurant refer to a customer as *the ham sandwich*. In this context, referring to customers by their order is more practical and convenient than any other method, including longer expressions such as *the man who ordered the ham sandwich*. Because metonymy is used for so many purposes in everyday speech, it is surprising that L2 learners are so rarely provided with authentic input containing metonymy in order to incorporate native-like use of it into their own production.

If metonymy is to be incorporated into a frame-based L2 pedagogy, FrameNet can provide a starting point for identifying metonymic patterns. The Berkeley FrameNet is a lexical database of English containing descriptions of 1,224 frames (http://framenet.icsi.berkeley.edu/fndrupal/). Each frame description contains a definition, a list of frame elements and relations with other frames, and a list of words and phrases ('lexical units' or LU's) that evoke the frame. For each LU, FrameNet provides a collection of sentences from corpora with the frame elements annotated and a valency description indicating the possible syntactic configurations of frame elements with the LU (Fillmore et al. 2003, Ruppenhofer et al. 2017). For example, the lexical entry of the LU *put on*, as in *John put on his jacket*, indicates that it evokes the Dressing frame and that the subject of *put on* instantiates the WEARER while the object instantiates the CLOTHING.

Many frame descriptions also include one or more CoreSets. These are "groups of [frame elements that] seem to act like sets, in that the presence of any member of the set is sufficient to satisfy a semantic valence of the predicator" (Ruppenhofer et al. 2016: 25). In the Purpose frame discussed earlier, AGENT and MEANS are members of a CoreSet. In (2a), the AGENT is instantiated, while in (2b) the MEANS is instantiated. Either one of them can fill the same valence of the target LU 'goal'. Although not all CoreSets involve an alternation that could be considered metonymic, some such as the alternation of MEANS and AGENT in the PURPOSE frame do have a metonymic basis. That is, the same situation can be described literally using one frame element or figuratively using another that indexes it. CoreSets can therefore serve as a resource in identifying metonymic patterns that might be useful for language learners.

Several FrameNet projects exist for other languages.[1] The ASFALDA French FrameNet (Candito et al. 2014) has the same goal and theoretical foundation as the Berkeley English FrameNet, although it only contains descriptions of 105 frames and 1,109 LU's as of its 1.3 release (sites.google.com/site/anrasfalda/). There are also some differences in methodology between the English and French FrameNets such as the type of syntactic annotation used and the order in which frames are analyzed (Djemaa et al. 2016), but these differences are not relevant to the present paper. Both FrameNets include CoreSets for frames that allow alternation between two frame elements, some of which are metonymic.

In incorporating metonymy into an L2 curriculum, there is a risk of overwhelming learners with metalinguistic information. Frame-based pedagogy uses the concept of frames to present vocabulary in a way that is beneficial to learners, but it is not designed to make language learners into experts on Frame Semantics. While the term 'frame' is likely to be helpful for learners, more technical terms such as 'frame element', 'CoreSet', or 'lexical unit' may distract from the goal of language learning.

The term 'metonymy' could help learners to better understand, remember, and identify examples of the concept. In a frame-based curriculum, it would therefore be worth the time to explain the terms 'frame' and 'metonymy' to learners. However, metonymy and frame-based pedagogy can inform the approach to certain topics even within an otherwise traditional curriculum. It is possible to teach L2 metonymy without the added complexity of introducing new metalinguistic terms, and this may be preferable for certain learners, instructors, or contexts. In the following sample lesson, I therefore demonstrate an approach, which draws learner attention to metonymy within a frame without using any terminology with which learners would not already be familiar. The lesson could easily be adapted to include these terms if students are introduced to them.

4 Sample lesson

The lesson described here is intended for a second-semester French course at the university level. Although the coverage of frames within the French FrameNet would not be enough for an entire beginning French course, it contains many of the frames required for beginning learners. The French FrameNet could there-

---

[1] The Berkeley FrameNet website provides links to FrameNet projects in French, Chinese, Portuguese, German, Spanish, Japanese, Swedish, and Korean: framenet.icsi.berkeley.edu/fndrupal/framenets_in_other_languages.

fore serve as a resource in building frame-based French lessons and identifying metonymic patterns to include in instruction. Of the 105 frames described in the French FrameNet, 63 contain frame element CoreSets. Some broader patterns can be found in these CoreSets across frames. The frames in the French FrameNet are grouped into four notional domains: Causality, Cognitive Positions, Verbal Communication, and Commercial Transactions. Within the Verbal Communication domain, 24 frames contain a frame element CoreSet where MEDIUM can stand for another frame element (SPEAKER, COGNIZER, COMPLAINER, PERSUADER, or COMMUNICATOR, according to the frame). These other frame elements are specific to each frame, but the pattern is similar across all of them in that the MEDIUM can stand for a kind of speaker or agent. An example of the metonymy licensed by these frame element CoreSets is shown in (3).

(3) a. **The mayor** praised the firefighters' bravery in a press release.
　　b. **The press release** praised the firefighters' bravery.

Communication involves the conveying of information between communicators. While a MEDIUM of communication, such as a press release, does not itself create a MESSAGE to communicate an idea, it can metonymically stand for the communicator who does. This MEDIUM FOR SPEAKER metonymy is widespread in both English and French, but as discussed earlier, this does not necessarily mean that native English speakers will be automatically comfortable using it in L2 French. Exposure to MEDIUM FOR SPEAKER metonymy in L2 input, and noticing of that metonymy, would prepare learners to use it in more native-like ways.

One of the most common verbs of communication in French, and therefore one which is crucial for learners to acquire, is *dire* 'say'. The traditional approach to teaching French verbs such as *dire* is seen in the textbook *Français interactif* 'Interactive French', an open introductory French textbook developed by the Center for Open Educational Resources and Language Learning (Kelton, Guilloteau, & Blyth 2017). Although *Français interactif* is innovative in its open publication and its use of a mix of native and non-native speaker models, it generally employs the same approach to verbs found in many other modern language textbooks.

Although much of the vocabulary in *Français interactif* is introduced thematically, the presentation of *dire* is motivated by a structuralist approach. *Dire* is presented alongside other verbs of the same inflectional class: *lire* 'read', *écrire* 'write', *conduire* 'drive', and *décrire* 'describe'. These verbs have no obvious semantic connection, making it difficult to develop a lesson introducing these verbs with a consistent theme. This grouping is even less ideal because it is only a loose inflectional class, with several irregularities. These verbs have the same inflectional pattern in their singular present-tense forms, but the patterns vary in the plural forms, e.g. *vous dites* 'you (plural) say', *vous écrivez* 'you (plural) write', *vous conduisez* 'you (plural) drive'. There are also irregularities in other tenses, such as in the past participles *dit* 'said' and *lu* 'read'.

Français interactif, like many modern textbooks, aims for a communicative language teaching approach in which learning is task-based. That is, learning is centered on acquiring forms in order to accomplish a real-world communicative task such as ordering at a restaurant. However, since there is no semantic connection between the verbs of the *-ire* class, it is difficult to find a communicative task that requires learners to use these forms together. *Français interactif* therefore relies on activities that are less communicative and more restrictive and artificial for practicing these verbs. In what follows, I present my revision of this section of *Français interactif* that restructures it as a frame-based lesson and accordingly uses more authentic communicative tasks. This example lesson is illustrative of the type of modifications instructors wishing to adopt a more frame-based pedagogical approach could make to their own materials, regardless of the particular language they teach or textbook they use.

In *Français interactif*, *dire* is introduced in chapter 9, which has the theme of "Media and Communication". Vocabulary relevant to this theme that is introduced in the chapter centers around various forms of media such as television, newspapers, and films. This theme already suits a frame-based approach where *dire* is introduced alongside other verbs from frames of communication. In the French FrameNet, *dire* can evoke three different frames in the Verbal Communication domain: Encoding, Request, and Statement-Manner-Noise. These three frames represent slightly different meanings of *dire*, represented by examples in (4), but for pedagogical purposes can be collapsed with other frames of the Verbal Communication domain into a more general Communication frame. All three of these frames include the frame element CoreSet {MEDIUM, SPEAKER} in their descriptions.

(4) a. *Pour le **dire** autrement : vous voulez supprimer le chômage ?* (ENCODING)
'To phrase it differently: you want to suppress unemployment?'
b. *M. Dubois **dit** aux employés de travailler dur.* (REQUEST)
'Mr. Dubois tells the employees to work hard.'
c. *Paul a **dit** "J'aimerais aller à la piscine".* (STATEMENT-MANNER-NOISE)
'Paul said "I'd like to go to the swimming-pool".'

In a frame-based lesson, the point of departure is to select a frame, in turn requiring the introduction of new vocabulary relevant to the frame. Of the frames in the Verbal Communication domain of the French FrameNet, 24 have frame element CoreSets that indicate the possibility of MEDIUM FOR SPEAKER metonymy. These

24 frames are evoked by 464 unique words or phrases. I narrowed down this list of vocabulary to the most frequent words of each grammatical category, consulting frequency data from Lexique 3.80 (New et al. 2001, lexique.org). The list of LU's that evoke these frames consists of mostly verbs, with some nouns. I supplemented these with additional vocabulary already present in chapter 9 of *Français interactif* to assemble the list of target vocabulary shown in Table 1.

Table 1: *Target vocabulary from the French FrameNet (bold) and* Français interactif.

Verbs	Nouns	Adjectives
dire 'say'	*une série* 'series'	*amusant(e)* 'funny'
écrire 'write'	*une émission* 'show'	*effrayant(e)* 'scary'
parler 'speak'	**un(e) journaliste** 'journalist'	*ennuyeux/ennuyeuse* 'boring'
demander 'ask'	*les infos* 'news'	*triste* 'sad'
rappeler 'remimd'	*un journal* newspaper	
reconter 'tell'	*un magazine* 'magazine'	
répondre 'respond'	*un site* 'website'	
expliquer 'explain'	**un rapport** 'report'	
présenter 'prsent'	**un discours** 'speech'	
accepter 'accept'	*une demande* 'request'	
recommander 'recommand'	*une promesse* 'promise'	
	un conseil 'advice'	

The sample lesson prepares learners to engage with the `Communication` frame by discussing the messages expressed by speakers and media. Acquisition of the target vocabulary is not itself the primary goal of the lesson, but the target vocabulary features prominently in the provided input and can be useful to learners in the completion of the tasks. Tasks progress from structured, mechanical activities to more open-ended tasks where learners are required to create with the language. I situated the lesson within the chapter's theme of Media and Communication, and the tasks reinforce the vocabulary related to this theme, which is found throughout the chapter. I also incorporate the cast of cartoon characters who serve as mascots throughout *Français interactif* into several tasks, exemplifying how frame-based lessons can be adapted to fit within an existing curriculum.

In the following subsections, I briefly describe the parts of the lesson, including at-home work completed before class, the series of tasks to be completed in class, homework assigned after class, and a suggestion for assessment. I include illustrative examples from tasks within the text, and complete activities can be found in the appendix.

4.1 Before class

Within *Français interactif*, learners in chapter 9 are already familiar with the conjugation paradigms for all the verbs in the target vocabulary list except for *dire* 'say' and *écrire* 'write'. Rather than creating a new pre-class assignment, I retain the standard assignment suggested for use with *Français interactif*. Before class, learners become familiar with these verbs by completing the appropriate assignment in the open resource Tex's French Grammar (http://laits.utexas.edu/tex/gr/virr11.html), which is a companion to *Français interactif*. This assignment presents the verbs and their conjugations in the present tense, followed by two mechanical tasks. In the first, learners insert appropriately inflected verbs into cloze sentences. In the second, they listen to recordings of sentences and determine if the verb is singular or plural.

4.2 In-class

The tasks described in this section are intended for a roughly 50-minute class period. The first task asks learners to observe patterns in sentences that evoke COMMUNICATION frames, such as (5). These sentences and the others in the appendix are taken from the French FrameNet's annotated examples. The target words that evoke the frame are bolded.

(5) a. La **demande** des journalistes a été rejetée.
'The journalists' **request** was rejected.'
b. Un livre **raconte** également cette histoire.
'A book also **tells** this story.'

Learners are first asked to direct their observations to the frame evoked by these sentences, and to notice that the same frame can be evoked by words of different grammatical categories: *The words in bold all have to do with* **communication**. *English has many verbs which denote different ways of communicating, like 'tell', 'ask', 'present', and 'explain'. Which of the bolded words in these sentences are verbs of communication? What does each mean? English also has nouns which refer to types of communication, like 'a report', 'a request', and 'a promise'. Which of the bolded words in these sentences are nouns of communication? What does each mean?*

Learners are then asked to consider the frame elements that are instantiated in these sentences: *When talking about communication, there is always a communicator who creates or conveys a message. Who or what are the communicators in these sentences? Which sentences describe a person or group of people communi-*

cating a message? Which sentences describe an institution or organization communicating a message? Which sentences describe a document or piece of information communicating a message?

The possibility of medium for speaker metonymy is then made explicit as learners observe the sentences in (6).

(6) a. Les Misérables, *par Victor Hugo, raconte l'histoire de Jean Valjean.*
 '*Les Misérables*, by Victor Hugo, tells the story of Jean Valjean.'
 b. *Victor Hugo raconte l'histoire de Jean Valjean dans son roman* Les Misérables.
 'Victor Hugo tells the story of Jean Valjean in his novel *Les Misérables*.'

Learners are asked to consider and discuss the communicative functions of metonymy: *What is the difference in meaning between these two sentences? Why might a person choose to say one of these sentences over the other?* Note that these instructions intentionally do not include the words *frame* or *metonymy* to demonstrate how these concepts can be taught without introducing new metalinguistic vocabulary. Instructors who do wish to use these terms could provide them along with definitions after students have discussed these questions.

The remainder of the lesson provides opportunities for students to manipulate the vocabulary, progressing from mechanical to open-ended meaningful tasks. Metonymy is found throughout the input and the mechanical activities lead students to instantiate alternately the SPEAKER and the MEDIUM. This scaffolding prepares them to use MEDIUM FOR SPEAKER metonymy in the open-ended activities if they choose to do so.

The first task is a mechanical review of the conjugation of target verbs, in the context of sentences like those in (7) that variously instantiate SPEAKER or MEDIUM.

(7) a. *Cet article (parler) d'un nouveau film qui est au cinéma.*
 'This article (talk) about a new movie that's in theaters.'
 b. *Les actrices (dire) « bonsoir » au réalisateur.*
 'The actresses (say) "good evening" to the director.'

The next task addresses the syntactic valency patterns that each target verb allows, specifically reviewing the complementizers and prepositions that must be inserted before the complements of these verbs in some constructions: *Pour chaque phrase, décidez s'il faut ajouter 'que', 'de', 'si', ou rien* ('For each sentence, decide if you need to add 'that', 'about', 'if', or nothing'). The task uses cloze sentences such as (8).

(8) *Ce livre dit que les jeunes envoient plus de textos que les adultes.*
 'This book says that young people send more text messages than adults.'

After these mechanical, grammar-focused tasks comes a somewhat more meaningful task. Learners are asked to match a subject, instantiating either the SPEAKER or the MEDIUM, with a MESSAGE from a 'message bank', conjugating the verb and adding any necessary complementizers or prepositions in order to create a logical sentence. For instance, the beginning of the sentence *Le journal (dire)* 'The newspaper (say)' would be matched with the message *le président a signé un accord avec le Japon* 'the president signed an agreement with Japan', while *Tammy (expliquer)* 'Tammy (explain)' would match with *elle est végétarienne* 'she is a vegetarian'.

The fourth task is even more open-ended. Learners are prompted with a situation involving Tex, the cartoon armadillo mascot of *Français interactif*: *Tex is trying to decide if he wants to see a new movie at the theater tonight. For each quote below, tell Tex what you read or heard. What do you recommend to Tex that he should do tonight?* The example in (9) illustrates what learners do with each quote.

(9) Quote: Joe-Bob: « *J'aime le nouveau film de James Bond.* »
              'Joe-Bob: "I like the new James Bond movie"'
     You say: « *Tex, Joe-Bob recommande le nouveau film de James Bond.* »
              "Tex, Joe-Bob recommends the new James Bond movie."

The scenario of Tex seeking recommendations for activities provides a motivation for learners to report the MESSAGES of various SPEAKERS and MEDIUMS. The task contains similar quotes from other characters as well as from media such as movie schedules and news headlines. For some quotes, learners are provided with both a SPEAKER and a MEDIUM, e.g. a movie critic writing in the newspaper, and can therefore choose which frame element to instantiate in the sentence they produce.

The final in-class activity is the most open-ended. Learners are placed into groups of three, and each group member receives a different source related to a French television series called *Clem*. The first source is a synopsis of the series from the website *Allociné*. The second is an excerpt of a review of season 3 of *Clem* written for the weekly magazine *L'Obs* by columnist Marcus Dupont-Besnard. The third is a collection of tweets and reviews written by *Clem* viewers, some positive and some negative, with many reacting to the season 3 finale. These are also provided in the appendix. Because each group member reads a different source, the task creates an info gap where learners must report the MESSAGE of their source using the vocabulary from the lesson. In doing so, they are prompted by these questions, which can be given in French: *What is the source that you read? What did this source say about the TV series* Clem? *Compare your source with those of your classmates. Are there any similarities or differences of opinion? According to the sources, what kind of show is* Clem? *Can you think of any similar American shows? Would you be interested in watching* Clem?

4.3 After class

Learners read a short cultural note from *Français interactif* about radio stations in France (Kelton, Guilloteau, & Blyth 2017: 225) and write a short paragraph in French explaining in their own words what the cultural note said. This provides them with further opportunities to use MEDIUM FOR SPEAKER metonymy.

4.4 Assessment

One possible form of assessment would be to add a task similar in structure to task 4 from the lesson to the regular chapter 9 assessment. Learners can be presented with quotes from multiple sources, and for each quote must explain what the source says, using a mix of *dire* 'say' and at least two other verbs like *expliquer* 'explain', *demander* 'ask', or *répondre* 'respond'. Performance on this task can be assessed in terms of the logic of the verb choice and the grammatical correctness of the sentence. MEDIUM FOR SPEAKER metonymy could be required for some sentences, or learners could be left to choose whether or not to use metonymy.

5 Discussion

5.1 Contributions of a frame-based pedagogy

The sample lesson presented here illustrates some fundamental differences between frame-based L2 pedagogy and traditional communicative language teaching. The lesson on Communication frames replaces a traditional lesson on verbs of the *dire* inflectional class. Both lessons contain *dire* 'say' and *écrire* 'write' as target vocabulary, but the frame-based lesson includes other target vocabulary based on semantic relatedness, while the traditional lesson includes other target vocabulary based on structural similarity. Frequency plays a role in vocabulary selection for both lessons, but in the frame-based lesson it is secondary to the relevance and usefulness of vocabulary to the target frame.

The topic of the sample lesson is a semantic frame, not a morphosyntactic rule or a cluster of vocabulary with similar semantic and syntactic properties. This means that vocabulary words of multiple grammatical categories are taught together, because they are used together when evoking this frame. Although the frame-based lesson contains explicit grammar instruction and mechanical tasks focused on morphosyntactic structure, these are in the service of developing communicative competence in the target frame. Just as much attention is paid to semantic structure, including frame elements and metonymic relations.

Although a frame-based approach differs in many fundamental respects from traditional L2 pedagogy, it is compatible with many widely accepted principles behind communicative language teaching (see Brandl 2008). The sample lesson incorporates a task-based design where structured, mechanical activities provide scaffolding for more open-ended communicative tasks. Principles of frame-based pedagogy can also be used to inform specific lessons within an otherwise traditional curriculum, if necessary. A frame-based approach reinforces the cultural and semantic themes that typically define the organization of beginning language textbooks, which clash with the structuralist organization that is often maintained on a lower level. Frame-based pedagogy is consistent with the principle that L2 instruction should be guided by meaning in language, not formal structure.

A frame-based pedagogical approach allows for the simple incorporation of metonymy, which despite its prevalence in language is generally left out of L2 teaching. When learners are trained to recognize frame elements, they can be taught to observe when one frame element metonymically stands for another. Although explicit metalinguistic instruction may be useful, the sample lesson demonstrates that attention can be directed to these patterns even when time does not permit the introduction of terms such as *frame element* and *metonymy*. As learners become aware of these patterns and notice them in input, they can begin to use metonymy in their own language production. This can help them to become more creative and native-like in their L2 usage.

According to how the lesson is intended to be situated within *Français interactif*, the target vocabulary contains two verbs, *dire* and *écrire*, for which learners do not yet know the present-tense conjugation paradigm. The sample lesson proposes explicit grammar instruction to be read by learners as online homework prior to the lesson, along with mechanical drills for practice. This is the standard approach for verbs in *Français interactif*, although for some other grammatical concepts these exercises are preceded by inductive discovery tasks where learners make assumptions about grammatical principles by examining example sentences before confirming their observations. Although *Français interactif* favors an explicit approach to grammar, a variety of approaches are possible for introducing verbal morphology. Whatever the specific approach, the 'before class' assignment should prepare learners with a familiarity with the morphology of the target vocabulary. In class, learners continue to manipulate the vocabulary morphologically as additional practice, but providing this introduction prior to the lesson allows more time to be reserved for instruction in the semantic properties of the frame.

In contrast with the explicit morphological instruction before class, in-class instruction about `Communication` frames takes an inductive approach. Learners examine authentic input, sentences found in corpora that evoke these frames. They are guided in their observation by questions, which prompt them to notice the semantic similarity among these sentences. All of the sentences deal with a MESSAGE that is communicated between parties. It would be possible to introduce the frame explicity, presenting learners with a frame definition and a list of frame elements. Indeed, exploration of the frame description on FrameNet could be a useful way for learners to confirm their observations and fill gaps in their understanding. However, learners can first develop an understanding of the frame by noticing these semantic elements in authentic data. Using an inductive approach, learners can discover many important aspects of frame structure even if they have received no formal instruction in the principles and terminology of Frame Semantics.

From the question prompts in the sample lesson, learners discover that frames can be evoked by a variety of different words, including words of different grammatical categories. They will notice that individual words from the target vocabulary have quite different meanings, e.g. *dire* 'say' and *demander* 'ask', but that these meanings all share a core similarity relating to communication. From this, they may gain some understanding of frame relations, i.e. that the target vocabulary words evoke a variety of different frames, but that these frames are all children of a more general parent frame. The questions also prompt learners to notice the common roles in the frame that are filled in each sentence, encouraging an implicit understanding of frame elements. In the case of SPEAKER, this understanding may even benefit from the lack of a metalinguistic label. As the questions point out, the SPEAKER may be instantiated by a person or by an impersonal or collective entity such as *l'assemblée* 'the council' or *Wall Street*. In this respect, the label SPEAKER could be misleading for some learners. If learners intuit the frame elements from examining data, they may come away with a better understanding of the frame than if they had simply read the frame description.

The observation stage also helps learners to develop an understanding of metonymy based on what they see in the data. The questions prompt learners to notice how SPEAKER and MEDIUM can occupy the same slot in many constructions. Further than this, learners are asked to speculate about the motivation to focus on either SPEAKER or MEDIUM. Here, learners must draw on their own experience with metonymy in their L1. Because the observation occurs in class, instructors can guide learners in considering additional reasons why speakers use metonymy. Reflecting on these motivations develops learners' metalinguistic literacy. Metonymy becomes a linguistic feature that learners can interpret to make inferences about the motivations, attitudes, and priorities of interlocutors. It also provides them with reasons to use metonymy in their own L2 production, along with a sense of when it is and is not appropriate.

5.2 Progression of tasks in the sample frame-based lesson

I now review the series of tasks involved in the sample lesson after this initial observation stage and discuss how each of these reinforce the goal of building competence in dealing with the Communication frame and using MEDIUM FOR SPEAKER metonymy in French. The sequence is illustrated for reference in Table 2.

Table 2:. Summary of lesson tasks.

Task	Example
1. Conjugate verbs in context	See (7)
2. Provide post-verbal complementizers and prepositions	See (8)
3. Connect speakers and messages	Match *Tammy (expliquer)* 'Tammy (explain)' with *elle est végétarienne* 'she's a vegetarian' to create *Tammy explique qu'elle est végétarienne* 'Tammy explains that she's a vegetarian'.
4. Report messages to a third party	See (9)
5. Info gap sharing the messages of sources on a single topic	*La critique que j'ai lue recommande la série.* 'The review I read recommends the show.'
Post-class: Summarize the message of a reading	*La note culturelle explique qu'il y a des stations de radio publiques et privées en France.* 'The cultural note explains that there are public and private radio stations in France.'

In the first three tasks, learners primarily manipulate forms to become comfortable using the target vocabulary. Some of the input for these tasks contains metonymy, but while learners are practicing with forms, they are not given the freedom to choose which frame elements to instantiate. Instructors may wish to point out instances of metonymy in the input, continuing the task of inductive observation.

The first task is controlled and mechanical. The only information learners must extract from the input in order to complete the task is the number and person of the subject, so that they can correctly conjugate the verb. Similarly, for the second task, learners must examine the input enough to determine the identity of the verb and the syntactic type of the complement phrase, and based on that information must decide whether a complementizer or preposition is necessary to head the complement. The input sentences in both tasks make use of a variety of target vocabulary and are primarily centered around the themes of the chapter and lesson, media and communication.

The third task is controlled but meaningful. Learners must pair each subject and verb with a logical complement. They must therefore understand the meaning of the phrases in the prompts and in the message bank in order to complete the task. For the subjects containing proper names, learners who have used *Français interactif* are already familiar with the characters and their relationships. This may help them to pair, for example, *Tex (raconter)* 'Tex (tell)' with *l'histoire de comment il a rencontré Tammy* 'the story of how he met Tammy', because they know that the characters of Tex and Tammy are a couple. The prior tasks, which have a simpler focus on form, provide scaffolding for this task, preparing learners to manipulate forms while paying more attention to meaning. This task in turn provides scaffolding for the fourth task where learners have more freedom in how they construct their answers.

In the fourth task, learners are provided with constituents instantiating the necessary frame elements: SPEAKER and/or MEDIUM, and MESSAGE. They are free to select a frame-evoking target vocabulary word to link these elements together. However, they must pay attention to meaning as they do so, because a verb like *demander* 'ask' would not be appropriate if the MESSAGE is not a question. In some cases, learners are provided with both a SPEAKER and a MEDIUM, and in these cases, they can choose to instantiate the SPEAKER or to make use of MEDIUM FOR SPEAKER metonymy.

The fifth task has the same structure but is more open-ended. The MESSAGES are longer, so learners must paraphrase them in reporting their contents to their partners. All three sources can be referred to with either their SPEAKER or their MEDIUM, giving learners flexibility in the choice to use metonymy. The use of authentic, online materials also presents challenges and opportunities for learners to explore questions of genre and style. The first two sources, a promotional summary and a professional critic's review, are written clearly but may contain some advanced vocabulary and expressions that learners have not encountered before. The third source, a collection of tweets and an amateur review, contains non-standard orthography, abbreviations, emoji, and colloquial language. However, it is shorter and uses simpler vocabulary, putting it at a similar level of difficulty as the first two sources. Time permitting, the stylistic differences in the three sources can serve as a point of class discussion.

The post-lesson homework assignment reinforces for learners the everyday usefulness of the Communication frame, which is used whenever they report a MESSAGE. By summarizing what they read about French radio, they use vocabulary from the chapter about media and communication, and they also use MEDIUM FOR SPEAKER metonymy within the Communication frame (e.g. *La note culturelle explique que* ... 'The cultural note explains that ...').

Having completed two in-class tasks and one at-home task where they use the COMMUNICATION frame to report the MESSAGE contained in some quote or source, learners are prepared for an assessment targeting the same skill. Depending on the format of assessments within the curriculum and the range of material to cover, this assessment can be more controlled as in Task 4 or more open-ended as in Task 5 or the homework assignment. Either way, the assessment targets communicative competence within the Communication frame, not just knowledge about vocabulary or grammar.

The sample lesson illustrates two principles. First, that a frame-based pedagogical approach can be built into an existing curriculum, adjusting vocabulary selection and task design to situate frames as the basic unit of instruction, but otherwise maintaining many elements found in traditional L2 instruction. Second, that metonymies can be taught to beginning learners inductively by prompting observation of their use. The adoption of frame-based pedagogy and the inclusion of metonymy in L2 instruction need not be a radical upheaval. These principles can be incorporated into current pedagogical practice by adjusting existing lessons and curricula. Frame-based language pedagogy is still a new enterprise, and empirical research is needed to assess the success of such an approach on learner outcomes.

6 Conclusion

Although metaphor and metonymy are generally recognized to play a fundamental role in the semantic structure of all languages, their acceptance in linguistic theory has not led to their incorporation into L2 pedagogical practice. This can perhaps be attributed to a misplaced assumption that learners will recognize and use metaphor and metonymy on their own, without being taught. However, each language and culture has its own unique patterns of metaphor and metonymy.

Even universal conceptual relations are manifested linguistically in ways specific to each language. Empirical research is required to determine to what extent learners transfer metaphors and metonymies from L1 to L2, and how easily they adopt metaphorical and metonymic patterns that may be unique to the L2.

This paper has described and illustrated how instruction in metonymy can be incorporated into L2 pedagogy in a practical way. Whether such instruction would be successful in helping learners to understand L2 metonymies and use them in their own language production is a question left to future research. Pedagogical approaches to L2 metaphor are a separate challenge, which may also benefit from a frame-based paradigm. As language pedagogy continues to become more meaning-centered, these conceptual relations merit greater consideration in future approaches to L2 instruction.

References

Atzler, Judith Kerstin. 2011. *Twist in the List: Frame Semantics as Vocabulary Teaching and Learning Tool*. Austin, TX: UT doctoral dissertation.
Boas, Hans C. 2001. Semantics as a framework for describing polysemy and syntactic structures of English and German motion verbs in contrastive computational lexicography. In *Proceedings of Corpus Linguistics* (pp. 64–73). Lancaster, UK: Technical Papers.
Boas, Hans C. & Ryan Dux. 2013. Semantic Frames for Foreign Language Education: Towards a German frame-based dictionary. *Veredas On-Line*, *17*(1), 82–100.
Boas, Hans C., Ryan Dux & Alexander Ziem. 2016. Frames and constructions in an online learner's dictionary of German. In Sabine De Knop & Gaetanelle Guilquin (Eds.), *Applied Construction Grammar* (pp. 303–326). Berlin/Boston: De Gruyter.
Brandl, Klaus. 2008. *Communicative language teaching in action: Putting principles to work*. Upper Saddle River, NJ: Pearson Prentice Hall.
Candito, Marie, Pascal Amsili, Lucie Barque, Farah Benamara, Chalendar de Gael, Marianne Djemaa, Pauline Haas, Richard Huyghe, Yvette Yannick Mathieu, Philippe Muller, Benoît Sagot & Laure Vieu. 2014. Developing a French FrameNet: Methodology and First results. *Proceedings of the 9th Edition of the Language, Resources and Evaluation Conference (LREC 2014)*. 1372–1379.
Djemaa, Marianne, Marie Candito, Philippe Muller, & Laure Vieu. 2016. Corpus annotation within the French FrameNet: a domain-by-domain methodology. In *Proceedings of LREC 2016* (pp. 3794–3801). Portoroz, Slovenia, May 2016.
Falkum, Ingrid L., Marta Recasens & Eve V. Clark. 2017. "The moustache sits down first": On the acquisition of metonymy. *Journal of Child Language*. 44(1). 87–119.
Feyaerts, Kurt & Geert Brône. 2005. Expressivity and Metonymic Inferencing : Stylistic Variation in Nonliterary Language Use. *Style*. 39(1). 12–36.
Fillmore, Charles J. 1982. Frame semantics. In L. S. of Korea (Ed.), *Linguistics in the morning calm* (pp. 111–137). Seoul: Hanshin.
Fillmore, Charles J. 1985. Frames and the Semantics of Understanding. *Quaderni Di Semantica*. 6(2). 222–254.

Fillmore, Charles J., Christopher R. Johnson & Miriam R. L. Petruck. 2003. Background to FrameNet. *International Journal of Lexicography*. 16(3). 235–250.

Hulstijn, Jan H. 1995. Not all grammar rules are equal: Giving grammar instruction its proper place in foreign language teaching. In R. Schmidt (Ed.), *Attention and Awareness in Foreign Language Learning* (pp. 359–386). Honolulu: University of Hawai'i Press.

Jodłowiec, Maria & Agnieszka Piskorska. 2015. Metonymy revisited: Towards a new relevance-theoretic account. *Intercultural Pragmatics*. 12(2). 161–187.

Kelton, Karen, Nancy Guilloteau & Carl S. Blyth. 2017. *Français interactif* (3rd edn.). Austin, TX: Center for Open Educational Resources and Language Learning (COERLL).

Koch, Peter. 1999. Frame and Contiguity: On the Cognitive Bases of Metonymy and Certain Types of Word Formation. In K.-U. Panther & G. Radden (Eds.), *Metonymy in Language and Thought* (pp. 139–167). Amsterdam/Philadelphia: Benjamins.

Kövecses, Zoltán. 2005. *Metaphor in culture : Universality and variation*. New York: Cambridge University Press.

Lakoff, George & Mark Johnson. 1980. *Metaphors we live by*. Chicago: University of Chicago Press.

Langacker, Ronald W. 2008. *Cognitive Grammar: A Basic Introduction*. New York: Oxford University Press.

Lorenz, Alexander, Cori Crane, John Benjamin, & Hans C. Boas. 2020. L2 German Learners' Perceptions and Use of an Online Semantic Frame-Based Dictionary. *Die Unterrichtspraxis/ Teaching German* 53(2). 191–209.

Morimoto, Shun & Shawn Loewen. 2007. A comparison of the effects of image-schema-based instruction and translation-based instruction on the acquisition of L2 polysemous words. *Language Teaching Research*. 11(3). 347–372.

Musson, Gill & Susanne Tietze. 2004. Places and spaces: The role of metonymy in organizational talk. *Journal of Management Studies*. 41(8). 1301–1323.

Nation, Paul. 2001. *Learning Vocabulary in Another Language*. Cambridge: Cambridge University Press.

New, Boris, Christophe Pallier, Ludovic Ferrand & Rafael Matos. 2001. Une base de données lexicales du français contemporain sur internet: LEXIQUE. *L'Année Psychologique*. 101. 447–462.

Petruck, Miriam R. L. 1996. Frame Semantics. In Jef Verschueren, Jan-Ola Östman, Jan Blommaert, & Chris Bulcaen (Eds.), *Handbook of Pragmatics* (Vol. 23, pp. 1–13). Amsterdam/Philadelphia: Benjamins.

Read, John & Carl A. Chapelle. 2001. A framework for second language vocabulary assessment. *Language Testing*. 18(1). 1–32.

Rundblad, Gabriella. 2007. Impersonal, general, and social: The use of metonymy versus passive voice in medical discourse. *Written Communication*. 24(3). 250–277.

Ruppenhofer, Josef, Michael Ellsworth, Miriam R. L. Petruck, Christopher R. Johnson, Collin F. Baker & Jan Scheffczyk. 2016. FrameNet II: Extended theory and practice. FrameNet. Retrieved from https://framenet.icsi.berkeley.edu/fndrupal/the_book

Ruppenhofer, Josef, Boas, Hans C. & Baker, Collin F. 2017. FrameNet. In Pedro A. Fuertes-Olivera (ed.), *The Routledge Handbook of Lexicography* (pp. 383–398). New York: Routledge.

Tanaka, Shigenori, & Hajime Abe. 1984. Conditions on interlingual semantic transfer. In *TESOL – A Brave New World* (pp. 101–120).

Tinkham, Thomas. 1997. The effects of semantic and thematic clustering on the learning of second language vocabulary. 2. 138–163.

Appendix

Observation

1. *J'ai **dit** qu'on ne pouvait pas rechercher la qualité par la sélection.* 'I **said** that one cannot aim for quality through selection.'
2. *Volkswagen veut renforcer son réseau de distribution au Japon dans la région de Tokyo, **explique** le journal.* 'Volkswagen wants to reinforce its distribution network in Japan in the Tokyo region, **explains** the newspaper.'
3. *La **demande** des journalistes a été rejetée.* 'The journalists' **request** was rejected.'
4. *C'est pourquoi notre résolution **demande** la levée de cet embargo.* 'That's why our resolution **requests** the removal of this embargo.'
5. *Wall Street n'a pas réellement tenu ses **promesses**.* 'Wall Street has not really kept its **promises**.'
6. *Un livre **raconte** également cette histoire.* 'A book also **tells** this story.'
7. *En délibérant, l'assemblée a **accepté** la proposition du maire.* 'After deliberation, the council **accepted** the mayor's proposition.'
8. *Je voudrais donner un **conseil** au commissaire.* 'I would like to offer the commissioner some **advice**.'
9. *Un vieux proverbe asiatique **dit** qu' il vaut mieux enseigner comment attraper un poisson que de le donner.* 'An old Asian proverb **says** that it's better to teach a man to fish than to give him one.'

Task 1

1. *Les actrices (dire) « bonsoir » au réalisateur.* 'The actresses (say) "good evening" to the director.'
2. *L'université (dire) qu'un nouveau parking sera construit.* 'The university (say) that a new parking lot will be built.'
3. *Cet article (parler) d'un nouveau film qui est au cinéma.* 'This article (talk) about a new movie which is in theaters.'
4. *Qu'est-ce que tu (dire) de cette idée?* 'What do you (say) to this idea?'
5. *Mon proverbe préféré (dire) « Aime-toi et tu auras des amis ».* 'My favorite proverb (say) "Love yourself and you will have friends."'
6. *Les journalistes (expliquer) comment s'inscrire à voter.* 'The journalists (explain) how to register to vote.'

Task 2

1. *Les membres du club acceptent _que_ le budget est trop petit.* 'The club members accept that the budget is too small.'
2. *Nous disons ____ « bonjour » au professeur tous les jours.* 'We say __ "hello" to the teacher every day.'
3. *Ce livre dit _que_ les jeunes envoient plus de textos que les adultes.* 'This book says that young people send more text messages than adults.'
4. *Dans son article, Georges Dubois écrit _que_ la téléréalité est l'avenir de la télévision.* 'In his article, Georges Dubois writes that reality TV is the future of television.'
5. *J'ai demandé _si_ Faiza voulait venir avec nous au cinéma.* 'I asked if Faiza wanted to come to the movies with us.'
6. *Nous parlons souvent _de_ la politique française.* 'We often talk about

Task 3

1. *Le journal (dire)* . . . 'The newspaper (say) . . .'
2. *Tex (raconter)* . . . 'Tex (tell) . . .'
3. *Tammy (expliquer)* . . . 'Tammy (explain) . . .'
4. *Joe-Bob (demander)* . . . 'Joe-Bob (ask) . . .'
5. *Fiona et Corey (répondre)* . . . 'Fiona and Corey (respond) . . .'
6. *Le documentaire (présenter)* . . . 'The documentary (present) . . .'
   Banque de messages: Message bank
   la vie de Gérard Dépardieu 'the life of Gérard Dépardieu'
   l'histoire de comment il a rencontré Tammy 'the story of how he met Tammy'
   elle est végétarienne 'she is a vegetarian'
   le président a signé un accord avec le Japon 'the president signed an agreement with Japan'
   il y a un examen demain 'there is a test tomorrow'
   il y a des devoirs ce soir 'there is homework tonight'

Task 4

1. *Bette: « Est-ce que Tex est libre ce soir? Je voudrais aller au cinéma avec lui. »* 'Bette: "Is Tex free tonight? I'd like to go to the movies with him."'
2. *Edouard et Corey: « Le film avec Brad Pitt est un peu effrayant. »* 'Edouard and Corey: "The Brad Pitt movie is a little scary."'

3. *Un critique, dans le journal:* « *J'adore le nouveau film de super-héros! 3 étoiles!* » 'A critic in the newspaper: "I love the new superhero film! 3 stars!"'
4. *Le site web du cinéma:* « *Super-héros 2: Le Retour du Méchant 6h10, 8h25, 10h45 ; James Bond 5h50, 7h15, 9h30 ; Le Fantôme 8h30, 10h15 ; Le Couple Amoureux 6h30, 9h40* » 'The theater's website: "Superhero 2: Return of the Villain 6:10, 8:25, 10:45; James Bond 5:50, 7:15, 9:30; The Ghost 8:30, 10:15; The Couple in Love 6:30, 9:40"'
5. *Les infos:* « *Le public est furieux après que le cinéma décide d'augmenter le prix des billets* » 'The news: "Public furious after theater decides to increase ticket prices"'
6. *@BradPitt, sur Twitter:* « *Allez voir mon nouveau film le Fantôme, au cinéma ce week-end! C'est superbe! #Fantôme* » '@BradPitt, on Twitter: "Go see my new film The Ghost, in theaters this weekend! It's fantastic! #Ghost"'

Task 5

Source 1: www.allocine.fr/series/ficheserie_gen_cserie=8724.html (Accessed 8 Sep 2018)

A seize ans, Clem découvre qu'elle est enceinte déjà de quatorze semaines. N'ayant pas le choix, elle doit mener sa grossesse à terme. Son entourage, et surtout ses parents, vont s'efforcer de gérer au mieux la situation. Mais il n'est pas facile de rester cool lorsque l'on apprend que sa fille de seize ans va être maman. Et encore moins de préserver l'harmonie familiale.

Entre mauvaise foi, malentendus, rires et larmes, Clem et sa famille vont apprendre à gérer cette situation délicate, au plus près de la réalité, de l'émotion et du ton juste. Car si devenir maman à seize ans est une aventure difficile, faire face à la tourmente tout en ne cessant jamais d'être une famille n'est pas facile.

'At sixteen years old, Clem discovers that she is already fourteen weeks pregnant. Having no choice, she must carry her pregnancy to term. Those close to her, especially her parents, try to handle the situation as best they can. But it's not easy to stay cool when you learn your sixteen-year-old daughter is going to be a mom. And it's even harder to preserve harmony in the family.

Between bad faith, misunderstandings, laughter and tears, Clem and her family will learn to handle this delicate situation, as close as possible to reality, emotion and the right tone. Because if becoming a mom at sixteen is a difficult adventure, facing that upheaval while remaining a family is not easy.

Source 2: Excerpt from Dupont-Besnard, Marcus (13 Jan 2014). "Clem", la saison 4 sur TF1: une série un peu (trop) moraliste, mais divertissante. *L'Obs*. http://leplus.nouvelobs.com/contribution/1124612-clem-la-saison-4-sur-tf1-une-serie-un-peu-trop-moraliste-mais-divertissante.html (Accessed 8 Sep 2018)

"Clem", la saison 4 sur TF1: une série un peu (trop) moraliste, mais divertissante

La vie de Clémentine est dépeinte comme un tableau réaliste d'un destin qui a basculé en entraînant tout son entourage dans un tourbillon, aux conséquences bonnes et mauvaises, qui, elles-mêmes, ont des effets divers selon la façon dont elles sont abordées.

C'est une initiation à la vie et à ses imprévus, dans laquelle personne n'a tort ou raison puisque la série prend en compte l'existence individuelle de chacun, et sa place par rapport aux autres.

La série ne fait toutefois pas dans la philosophie, ce n'est pas un feuilleton pour réfléchir, mais pour se détendre. Et ce n'est pas un défaut. Finalement, c'est une série divertissante, drôle et tragique, sans le moindre surplus, la moindre once de gag ou de tracas superflu, pour un résultat très doux, voire tendre.

Lucie Lucas est parfaite dans son rôle de "Clem", avec des airs enfantins sous certaines expression et des traits de maturité d'autres fois; parallèlement, Victoria Abril est très gentiment tarée dans son rôle de mère.

'*Clem*, season 4 on TF1: a bit (too) moralistic, but entertaining

Clémentine's life is portrayed as the realistic portrait of a destiny which has come crashing down, sweeping up the whole family in a whirlwind, with both good and bad consequences with various effects depending on how they are faced.

It's an initiation to the mishaps of life, in which no one is wrong or right because the series takes into account each individual's existence, and his or her place with respect to others.

Nevertheless, the series does not deal with philosophy; you're not meant to reflect, but to relax. And this is not a fault. At the end of the day, it's an entertaining, funny, and tragic show, without excess, without an ounce of superfluous concerns or gags, for a result which is sweet, even tender.

Lucie Lucas is perfect in the role of 'Clem', at times childish and at others mature; likewise, Victoria Abril is delightfully crazy in the role of the mother.'

Source 3:

Tweet from @camiilledlr, 15 Apr 2013: *Le dernier #Clem de la saison 3 est magnifique* 'The last #Clem of season 3 is magnificent'

Tweet from @Alexbrown6992, 28 Oct 2016: *En fait Clem ils ont finit la saison 3 par un épisode triste et il ont recommencer la saison 4 par un épisode triste . . . #Clem* 'Actually Clem finished season 3 with a sad episode and started season 4 with a sad episode . . . #Clem'

Tweet from @ValoudelOM, 25 Jan 2018: *Moi perso j'addoorre #Clem j'ai même reçu pour mon anniv [celebration emoji] L'intégralité du coffret de la saison 1 à 7 [dancing emoji] #Vamos #Olé [dancing emoji]* 'Me personally I loooove #Clem I even got for my birthday [celebration emoji] The entire box set from seasons 1 to 7 [dancing emoji] #Vamos #Olé [dancing emoji]'

Review from Stéphane B., 19 Apr 2013, http://www.allocine.fr/series/ficheserie-8724/critiques/ (Accessed 8 Sep 2018): *Nul, ennuyant, du déjà vu! Il faudrait renouveler les séries françaises. Les acteurs sont si mauvais, tout est surjoué! qui peut encore regardee ca! vous voulez une série qui cartonne vous avez once upon a time, Lost, Heroes, frere scott, walking dead . . . mais pas ca! pas une serie française comme CLEM!* 'Lame, boring, same old thing! French shows need a redo. The actors are so bad, everything is overacted! who can still watch that! you want a successful show you've got once upon a time, Lost, Heroes, one tree hill, walking dead . . . but not that! not a French show like CLEM!'

Alexander Ziem, Anastasia Neumann-Schneider
Towards a FrameNet for linguistic terminology: Theoretical foundations, lexicographic practice, didactic potential

1 How to teach and learn linguistic terminology?

Teaching and learning linguistic terminology is anything but trivial.[1] Even though there is a plethora of both print and online dictionary resources (e.g., the "grammis" online terminology module[2]), prerequisites for understanding technical terms are often not taken into account, neither are relations between similar concepts addressed. One reason for this shortcoming is that dictionaries are usually organized in alphabetical order instead of grouping semantically related lemmas according to their conceptual similarity. Another reason is that meaning descriptions in dictionaries do not consider background knowledge structures ("frames") in which lexical meanings unfold. However, as the Berkeley FrameNet[3] project has demonstrated, such conceptual structures not only motivate lexical meanings but may also help understanding them better and more comprehensively. With this in mind, we developed LingTermNet,[4] an online repository of linguistic terminology methodologically based on FrameNet.

One aim of building such a repository was to meet the needs of bachelor students for well accessible explanations of technical terms specific to our curriculum. More concretely, the LingTermNet project hosted at the University of

---

[1] We would like to thank two anonymous reviewers as well as the editor of the volume Hans C. Boas for very helpful comments to an earlier version of this article. The usual disclaimer applies.
[2] The grammatical information system "grammis" provided by the "Institut für Deutsche Sprache" (https://grammis.ids-mannheim.de; last access: November 15, 2019) contains, among other components, a repository for terminology in the domain of linguistics (Suchowolec/Lang/Schneider 2018). Just like in most print dictionaries, terms are defined lemma-based. There are entries for terminological relations, including hyperonymy/hyponymy and holonyms/meronyms. Even though the approach is onomasiologic and even though it also provides information about relations between technical terms, the lexicon entries do not differ substantially from those in print dictionaries. Particularly, they do not comprise any information on conceptual background knowledge motivating the lexical meaning of the technical terms addressed. Also, semantic descriptions are not based on analyses of actual usages of the terms addressed (here: in the domain of linguistics).
[3] See: https://framenet.icsi.berkeley.edu, last access: June 17, 2019.
[4] See: "Linguistic Terminology Net", www.lingterm.net, last access: June 17, 2019.

https://doi.org/10.1515/9783110746723-011

Düsseldorf attempts to build a FrameNet-like repository that provides meanings of technical terms in the domain of linguistics, especially interactional linguistics. With a specific focus on application in academic teaching, the general aim of LingTermNet is to illuminate to what extent specialized terminology may be better described and illustrated by means of semantic frames.[5] The starting point of LingTermNet is the assumption that it is advantageous to approach technical terms with the help of frames because standard lexicographic approaches, in contrast to frame semantics, solely operate on the level of lemmas; they are thus limited to individual lexical meanings.

There are several good reasons to assume that a frame-semantic approach is superior. Based on the finding in neuroscience "that understanding is largely based on sensory and motor simulation with possibly a single convergence zone that affords the possibility to generalize across concepts that have similar semantic significance" (Faber 2011: 23), Faber comes to the following conclusions: (1) Technical terms should better be considered as integral parts of larger structures; (2) the knowledge acquisition process accelerates, if conceptual context is provided that indicates the extent to which "a concept is related to others in a dynamic structure that can streamline the action-environment interface" (Faber 2011: 24); (3) just like in FrameNet, non-hierarchical relations (defining purposes, goals, etc.) need to be treated on a par with taxonomic relations such as part-whole, hyponymy, etc.; and, finally, (4) it is important to acknowledge that knowledge domains are constrained "by the nature of their members" (Faber 2011: 24), an idea that is at the heart of frame semantics. On top of that, as Boas and Dux (2013) have argued, frame-based – rather than lemma-based – vocabulary learning and teaching turns out to be more efficient with respect to both the semantic and grammatical properties of lexical units:

> Students using the G-FOL [German Frame-based Online Lexicon, AZ&ANS] are more aware of the differences in grammar and meaning between German and English expressions of personal relationships than those students who do not use the G-FOL.   (Boas/Dux 2013: 95)

However, it still remains an open issue to what extent, and in which respects, frames are more suitable for vocabulary learning and teaching than traditional lemma-based methods. At least according to Atzler's empirical study on vocab-

---

[5] In academic teaching, LingTermNet serves to help preparing scientific literature in class. It also supports students in the process of writing a paper, and it assists students in using a term appropriately when analyzing authentic data such as transcripts. Finally, one of the advantages of the LingTermNet database is to provide an overview of potentially relevant technical terms; this, in turn, facilitates to envision the conceptual environment of the term addressed and thus enhances more comprehensive learning.

ulary learning (Atzler 2011), there seems to be no parameter in which a frame-based method leads to significantly better results (in the strict statistical sense).

In addition to frame-based approaches in the domain of L2, such as G-FOL (cf. Boas/Dux 2013, Ziem 2015, Boas/Dux/Ziem 2016), we would like to illustrate that frames are also of great benefit in the area of specialized terminology. The aim of the present paper is to introduce (a) the theoretical foundations, (b) the lexicographic implementations, and (c) the didactic potential of LingTermNet.

The paper is structured as follows. Section 2 introduces the theoretical background of the LingTermNet project, specifically the concept of semantic frames as developed and implemented in the Berkeley FrameNet project. The purpose of this section is (a) to explicate relevant frame-semantic concepts on which LingTermNet relies, (b) to illustrate the lexicographic procedure adopted from the Berkeley FrameNet project, and (c) to provide insights into the network in which each frame is embedded. For illustration, we present the so-called Communication frame;[6] our sample analysis of technical linguistic terms will build on this frame. In Section 3, we argue that meanings of technical terms can be taught and learned more efficiently with reference to (a) the frame evoked by the term and (b) the network structure of frames in which it ties in. To validate this hypothesis, we use linguistic terms from the domain of conversation analysis. Specifically, we show to what extent the Speaker_signal and Hearer_signal frames hook into the Signal_scenario frame. Given that meanings of technical terms are determined by the frames they evoke, we introduce the structure of frame entries as well as dictionary entries for each technical term. The definitions are compiled in recourse to the frames the technical terms evoke. Finally, Section 4 summarizes the results achieved and gives an outlook on future work.

2 Theoretical and lexicographic background

One of the major achievements of the Berkeley FrameNet project is to have lexicographically implemented fundamental insights of cognitive semantics on a large-scale basis.[7] For example, it is of great importance that linguistic units, most prominently 'words', do not carry meanings only by themselves, rather, their

---

[6] Following the usual conventions of FrameNet, we use the font Courier New for frame names and small caps for FE names.
[7] The following analyses are substantially based on data discussed in Neumann-Schneider/Ziem 2020. However, in the following we focus much more on (a) the overall scenario the addressed frames are embedded in and (b) the didactic potential of LingTermNet.

meanings arise through their manifold relationships to other linguistic units. As Fillmore, the founder of Frame Semantics, has put it:

> By the word 'frame' I have in mind any system of concepts related in such a way that to understand any of them you have to understand the whole structure in which it fits; when one of the things in such a structure is introduced into a text, or into a conversation, all of the others are automatically made available. (Fillmore 1982: 111)

In essence, this is in line with Saussure's (1916) concept of value ("valeur") which exposes the whereabouts of each linguistic sign in the network of relationships to other signs. If, following this view, the relationship of a linguistic sign to one of its neighbors changes, its linguistic value, including its semantic value, changes likewise. This fundamental assumption is at the heart of frame semantics as implemented in the Berkeley FrameNet project.

A frame provides the meaning skeleton that motivates the lexical meaning of a word. At the same time, a frame is related to other frames. The verb *to signal*, for example, evokes the `Communication` frame comprising a configuration of semantic roles, so-called frame elements (FEs) which define the situational setting in which communicative acts such as "signaling", "saying", "communicating", among others, take place. Frames are the empirical results of annotating the semantic and syntactic valence of lexical units; authentic corpus examples form the basis of the annotation. In this sense, frames, just like lexical meanings, are thus determined by the use of words.

It seems obvious that the semantic insights of frame semantics do not only apply to linguistic units of everyday vocabulary but also to specialized vocabulary in different technical domains. This means that also technical terms in the domain of linguistics can only be understood in the context of its relations to other technical terms and the semantic frame that motivates its meaning. The frame and the network structure in which it is embedded provide the prerequisites for understanding the technical term that evokes the frame.

Frames share essential characteristics with other concepts, such as word fields, ontologies and taxonomies; most importantly, all these concepts presuppose that the best way to approach the meaning(s) of lexical categories is to address the network structure in which the categories are embedded. However, frames also substantially differ from these concepts in that they suggest that lexical meaning can be described most adequately in terms of frames. Each frame consists of a specific configuration of frame elements (which come with specific semantic and syntactic constraints), and each frame is defined by the semantic relations it holds to other frames (for more details see Section 2.1). Also, from a didactic point of view, specifically in the context of this article, frames may prove to be helpful to the extent that they help both to impart and to acquire terminology in specialized domains (for the domain of molecular biology[8] cf. Dolbey 2009, for the domain of football[9] cf. Schmidt 2009, for the domain of environment[10] cf. Reimerink/Faber 2009).

The origin of Frame Semantics dates back to Fillmore's fundamental revision of his theory of case frames in the mid 1970ies (Fillmore 1975, 1976, 1977, among others; for an overview cf. Boas 2013, Ziem 2014a: 5–48, 2014b), finally resulting in the implementation of Frame Semantics in a large-scale lexicographic project called FrameNet (Fillmore/Atkins 1992, Fillmore/Johnson/Petruck 2003; for on overview Boas 2013). A frame is the result of multilayered annotations and lexicographic analyses. It motivates the use and meaning of semantically related lexemes. Building on the same methodology, the LingTermNet project attempts to lexicographically capture meanings of basic linguistic terminology, aiming at providing for each technical term its conceptual framework in which its lexical meaning(s) unfold(s). With a focus on frame semantic key concepts, Section 2.1 introduces the theoretical basics also relevant for the LingTermNet project. Section 2.2 singles out the relevance of the network structure in which each semantic frame fits in.

2.1 Frame Semantics: conceptual basics

The starting point of frame-semantic analyses are so-called lexical units (LUs). Following Cruse (1986: 23–24), an LU is defined as a word-meaning pair, i.e.

---

8 BioFrameNet investigates frames in the field of molecular biology. In concrete terms, it focuses on the way molecular biological processes are scientifically explained. Strictly speaking, in contrast to LingTermNet, BioFrameNet does not address lexicographic issues. Rather, the focus is on the syntactic and semantic embedding of technical terms; these embeddings are modelled with the help of frames.
9 Kicktionary is a contrastive lexicographic project addressing German, French and English technical terms in the domain of soccer. Conceptually, it differs from both FrameNet and LingTermNet in that lexical units are not only defined in terms of frames but also in terms of scenes. For example, the LE *foot* evokes the Body_Parts frame, which belongs to the scene "Actors" which includes further frames such as Team, Player and Ball.
10 EcoLexicon is a multilingual ontology for technical terms in the field of environment. It was developed on the basis of the frame-based terminology (Faber Benítez/Márquez Linares/Vega Expósito 2005). The focus here is not on frame elements as structural constituents of frames but on ontological relations between individual process-oriented terms. They are processed in the form of a visual thesaurus. Starting from the most abstract stage of a so-called environmental event, which has a relatively typical frame structure of superordinate conceptual roles such as AGENT, PROCESS and PATIENT, conceptual hierarchies and relations are that help classify the terms.

a lexical expression in one of its meanings. If a word is ambiguous, there are several LUs (word-meaning pairs). In the case of the verb *to signal*, for example, the Berkeley FrameNet distinguishes between two closely related meanings.[11] In one case, the verb *to signal* denotes a gesture-based, non-verbal communicative behavior (e.g. in *She signaled me that it is time to go*); here *signal* evokes the Gesture frame. However, the same verb *to signal* may also refer to linguistic actions (e.g., *They signal that they are ready to stand up to the right-wing majority*); here the verb evokes the Communication frame.

At the same time, different LUs, which in lexicographic analyses have proven to be semantically similar, evoke the same frame. In the case of the Communication frame, for example, this is true for the LUs *code word, communicate, communication, contact, convey, indicate, password, say, share, signal, speech*. The sentences in which these LUs occur are annotated with regard to the semantic roles they instantiate. The results obtained are the empirical basis for compiling frame entries. Semantic roles (FEs) are defined with respect to the frame in which they occur. Currently, based on more than 200,000 annotated sentences, Berkeley FrameNet comprises 13,640 LUs and 1,224 frames (June 17, 2019).

Each frame entry comprises a definition of the frame and its FEs, a list of frame-evoking LUs, as well as details and examples of the annotation. The documentation of the frame-to-frame relations also belongs to a frame entry. For illustration, we introduce the Communication frame in some detail.

In general, frames are defined on the basis of their FEs (Figure 1). Of particular relevance are core FEs since they are considered constitutive for a frame's meaning. For example, the Communication frame is characterized by four core FEs: COMMUNICATOR, MEDIUM, MESSAGE and TOPIC (see Figure 2).

> **Definition:**
>
> A Communicator conveys a Message to an Addressee; the Topic and Medium of the communication also may be expressed. This frame includes no specification of the method of communication (speech, writing, gesture, etc.). This frame and the frames that inherit the general Communication frame can add elaboration to the Medium in a variety of ways (*in French, on the radio program, in a letter*) or to the Manner of communication (*babble, rant, shout, whisper*). There are also frames related to Communication that either do not inherit all of the FEs of this frame or do not inherit them in a straightforward manner (such as Conversation, in which Communicator and Addressee alternate roles, and are often expressed by a single,

Figure 1: Definition of the Communication frame, excluding additional notes (https://framenet.icsi.berkeley.edu, last access: June 17, 2019).

---

[11] From a lexicographical point of view, it is more useful to split meanings first and, if necessary, to lump them later, than vice versa (cf. Atkins/Rundell 2008: 268).

Figure 1 shows the definition of the Communication frame in Berkeley FrameNet. Definitions are sometimes supplemented by additional notes on specific characteristics of the frame. In the case of the Communication frame, for example, there is additional information on the metaphorical use of communication verbs.

The frame definition is followed by a list of FEs of which each is usually defined and illustrated with recourse to an annotated example. FEs are the building blocks of a frame (Fillmore/Petruck 2003: 359). Figure 2 introduces the core FEs of the Communication frame.[12] In addition, this frame comprises eleven non-core FEs: ADDRESSEE, AMOUNT_OF_INFORMATION, DEPICTIVE, DURATION, FREQUENCY, MANNER, MEANS, PLACE, PURPOSE, QUOTE, TIME.

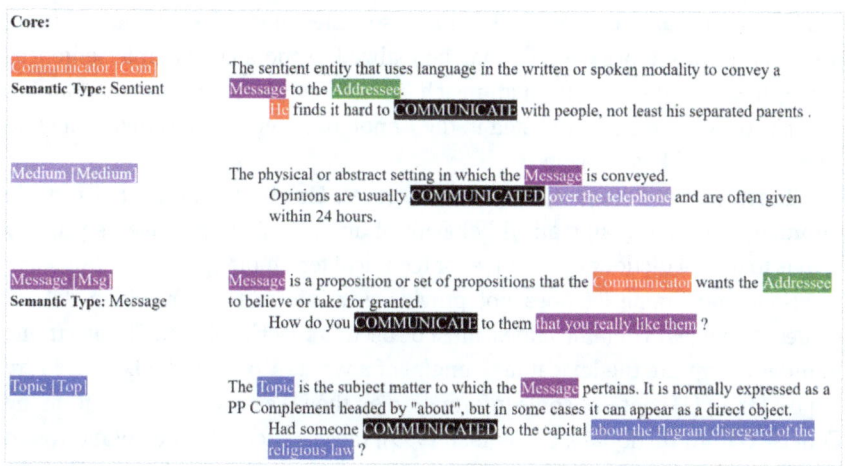

Figure 2: Core FEs of the Communication frame (https://framenet.icsi.berkeley.edu, last access: June 17, 2019).

The Communication frame provides the framework for the lexical meaning of each LU evoking this frame. For *to signal*, this means that some FEs are specified with default values while others have variable values or value ranges. Note that the verb *to signal* is polysemous since it has two distinct meanings, one evoking

---

12 Omissions of core FEs must be licensed by one of the following null instantiation mechanisms: (a) Definite null instantiations (DNI) are contextually licensed omissions in which the omitted element is accessible by context (e.g. in *I keep you posted* the MESSAGE is a DNI); (b) indefinite null instantiations (INI) concern the omission of the object in transitive verbs (e.g. *She is eating*); and (c) constructional null instantiations (CNI) refer to omissions of FEs licensed by a grammatical construction, for example, the omission of a grammatical subject in imperatives (e.g., *Don't do that!*).

the Communication frame, the other the Gesture frame. Thus, the verb *to signal* is split into two LUs, each connected to its own frame. The meaning of *signal* evoking the Gesture frame is characterized by the FE MEDIUM specified by the default value "non-verbal characters" while the same FE in the Communication frame is assigned the default values "linguistic characters". For both lexical meanings it applies that further FEs are specified by ranges of default value: AMOUNT_OF_INFORMATION, for example, is considered "low" for prototypical purposes and DURATION is "short".

The Berkeley FrameNet repository also provides a so-called Lexical Entry Report and an Annotation Report for each LU. A short definition of the LU is followed by a list of valence patterns, that is, configurations of FEs, in which the LU can be syntactically realized. This list also specifies in which grammatical functions and phrase types each FE may be realized. Annotated example sentences illustrate each valence pattern and each licensed syntactic realization of an FE. All annotated sentences are listed in the Annotation Report, preceded by a table summarizing all FEs attested.

In contrast to Berkeley FrameNet, however, LingTermNet does not provide information on the grammatical behavior of an LU. This is because its primary goal is to offer a dictionary resource for technical terminology.

Note that FrameNet does not provide any information on which default values, or ranges of default values, must be used to specify selected FEs of a frame in order to capture the lexical meaning(s) of a word. Although the Lexical Entry Report for an LU contains some information on the LU's meaning (taken from the Concise Oxford Dictionary, cf. Pearsall 1999), these indications are not motivated by the respective frame. In this respect, LingTermNet differs fundamentally from Berkeley FrameNet; we see great strength and benefit in defining lexical meanings as closely as possible to the frames that motivate them.

2.2 Identifying, elaborating and connecting frames

The identification procedure of frames and their FEs is based on a complex lexicographic procedure that essentially comprises three steps in the Berkeley FrameNet project (Baker/Fillmore/Lowe 1998: 88). Each step is implemented by a working group, with all participants assigned to at least one working group, sometimes in alternating roles: (a) the vanguard, (b) the annotators, and (c) the rearguard. In the LingTermNet project, just like in the German FrameNet and Constructicon project (www.german-framenet.de, last access: June 17, 2019), we stick to this division of labor whenever possible.

The aim of the first working group is to prepare the annotation of corpus examples. More specifically, the vanguard selects a set of words to be prioritized and to break them down into different meanings. This is done by using dictionaries and results of initial corpus searches (cf. Atkins et al. 2003: 335).

As explained above, the LU *to signal* is ambiguous since it evokes two frames. Based on the assumption that each meaning is motivated by its own frame, the task of the first working group is to check whether one or more of the LUs evoke frames that have already been created. If this is the case, it must be ensured that the corresponding LU actually matches the existing frame; this is done by pre-annotating corpus examples and analyzing the results obtained. If there is no matching frame, the vanguard needs to create a new frame provisionally. Next, the group members have to identify further LUs that potentially evoke the new frame. They are also responsible for compiling corpus examples and preparing them for annotation. This step is called "subcorporation" (Fillmore et al. 2003: 331). Finally, the vanguard creates a provisional frame definition as well as a provisional list of FEs. This should enable the second working group – the annotators – to annotate corpus data as efficiently as possible.

In the second phase, it is the job of the annotation working group to annotate corpus examples for each LU, the so-called "target" (Fillmore/Petruck 2003: 361) of annotation. To illustrate, in the following, we limit ourselves to the LU *signal* evoking the `Communication` frame; this frame is already available in the FrameNet repository. For annotation purposes, we have developed our own annotation tool that is tailored to the specific requirements of the LingTermNet and the German FrameNet and Constructicon project (cf. Ziem/Flick/Sandkühler 2019: Section 3.3). All instantiated FEs are annotated with regard to their grammatical function, their phrase type and the realized semantic roles (FEs). In LingTermNet, however, as already mentioned, we only annotate semantic roles since syntactic information is not relevant for the meaning and description of technical terms.

The third working group, the rearguard, essentially aims at critically checking the annotations and ensuring that they are consistent within a frame, i.e. across different LUs. If inconsistencies occur, this can result in the necessity to define the LUs more precisely, to add further FEs or to revise the list of FEs defined in the first phase. Although the three phases build on each other and are thus implemented consecutively, it often turns out to be necessary that each working phase is repeated. Once the annotations have been validated, a lexicon entry can be created for each LU. It is also the task of the rearguard, based on the annotation results, to extend the first frame sketch of the vanguard to a complete frame entry.

FrameNet also identifies and documents frame-to-frame relations in each frame entry. Fillmore and Baker (2010: 330) mention seven types of frame-to-frame relations that can be divided into three groups: (1) generalization relations ("Inheritance", "Perspective_on", "Using"), (2) event structure relations ("Subframe", "Precedes") (3) systematic relations ("Causative_of", "Inchoative_of"). In Ruppenhofer et al. (2016: 73–79), this classification is supplemented by the relation "See_also". In the FrameNet database, we even find a total of twelve relation types.

For example, the Communication frame evoked by the LU *to signal* is connected to a large number of frames: It inherits information from the Cause_to_perceive frame and also from other six frames, such as the Gesture frame. At the same time, it is in a Using relation ("Uses") to the Information frame. A total of 33 frames use information from the Communication frame ("Is Used by").

Frame-to-frame relations make evident that frames are not isolated units but rather integrated into a complex network (i.e. a FrameNet). The semantic similarity between the LU *to signal* evoking the Communication frame and the LU *to signal* evoking the Gesture frame is, to a large extent, motivated by the relationship of these frames. The Communication frame is related to the Gesture frame by an inheritance link, i.e. it inherits its FEs from the latter. The fact that the Communication frame, in turn, inherits information from the Cause_to_perceive frame reflects the intentional act that is inherent in both variants of meaning.

Frames evoked by technical terms also exhibit a complex network of relationships. Since technical terms may coincide with (metaphorically used) words of everyday vocabulary, such as *Schritt* ('step'), *Gesprächsschritt* ('conversation step'), or they may be derived from them, such as in the case of *Eröffnungssignal* ('opening signal'), there is good reason to assume that such expressions, which are part of technical terms (here: *Gesprächsschritt* 'conversation step' and *Eröffnungssignal* 'opening signal'), are related to those frames in FrameNet that are evoked by the corresponding expressions in everyday vocabulary (here: *Schritt* 'step', *Signal* 'signal'). For example, it would be plausible to assume that in LingTermNet the Speaker_signal frame, which is evoked, among others, by the LU *Eröffnungssignal* ('opening signal'), is related by an inheritance link to the Communication frame in FrameNet. At the same time, the FEs COMMUNICATOR, MESSAGE and ADDRESSEE of the parent frame Communication are inherited to the Speaker_signal frame; within this frame, they become specified, yielding the FEs SPEAKER, HINT and HEARER.

In the remainder of this paper, we discuss the details of the Speaker_signal, Signal_scenario, and Hearer_signal frames. With the help of these frames, we introduce the design and structure of the LingTermNet repository.

3 Building a FrameNet for linguistic terminology: implementation and didactic application

Having introduced the conceptual basics of Frame Semantics, we are now in the position to turn to the LingTermNet repository. In Section 3.1, using the `Speaker_signal` frame for illustration, we explain the lexicographic procedure of compiling frame entries for LingTermNet. In this context, we also introduce our annotation guidelines and the technical tools used. Section 3.2 provides insights into the structure of the LingTermNet repository; in addition to a general overview, frame entries are presented and explained. In this and the following paragraphs, we also highlight the didactic potential of using the repository by discussing the relevance of different entry types for academic teaching and learning. Based on the `Speaker_signal`, `Hearer_signal`, and the `Signal_scenario` frame and with a specific focus on the didactic usability of frame-to-frame relations, Section 3.3 draws the attention to the network structure in which each frame is embedded. Finally, Section 3.4 introduces the dictionary-like repository of LU entries, including its potential uses for academic teaching and learning purposes.

3.1 The lexicographic procedure in LingTermNet

In general, lexicographic working processes start with the fictitious assumption of both stable and homogenous word meanings across usage events. The same goes for LingTermNet. However, we consider it an advantage that the subject of investigation are technical terms rather than everyday vocabulary. Regardless of varying strands of research, all LUs addressed in LingTermNet belong to a well-established terminological inventory of basic linguistic terms. Surely, we can expect, depending on the approach, that there will be definitional deviations on a small scale, but on the abstract level of FEs these deviations are neutralized.

The workflow in the LingTermNet project is based on the three-phase workflow in the Berkeley FrameNet project as outlined in Section 2.2. In the LingTermNet project, the first objective is to design a frame sketch. This is followed by (a) the identification of potential FEEs (frame-evoking elements, i.e. LUs), (b) the compilation of corpus examples, and (c) the annotation of FEs. On the basis of the annotated data, the created frame sketch is extended to cover a complete frame entry. This workflow is usually not linear, but circular, because after first annotations it may be necessary to modify or extend the selected annotation categories (FEs) and/or the selection of the LUs.

In the following, using the example of the aforementioned `Speaker_signal` frame, we briefly outline three relevant lexicographic work stages in LingTermNet, i.e. (a) the development of a frame sketch and collection of corpus examples, (b) the annotation of corpus examples and (c) the compilation of entries.

Although LingTermNet, unlike Berkeley FrameNet, does not focus on basic everyday vocabulary but on technical terms in the realm of linguistics, the first phase also begins with creating a list of relevant LUs. Since LingTermNet primarily addresses first-year students, the selection of the LUs was initially guided by their relevance for the curriculum. A first focus was on technical terms in the domain of conversation analysis. An extension to technical linguistic terms in syntax and semantics is currently taking place.

Based on a review of selected linguistics literature (including current introductory textbooks such as Henne/Rehbock 2001, Brinker/Sager 2006, Schwitalla 2006, Deppermann 2008, Gülich/Mondada 2008, Mroczynski 2014), we compiled the following list of LUs potentially evoking the `Speaker_signal` frame: *Rückversicherungssignal* ('reassurance signal'), *Tag Question* ('tag question'), *Diskontinuitätsmarker* ('discontinuity marker'), *Diskursmarker* ('discourse marker'), *Eröffnungssignal* ('opening signal'), *Gliederungssignal* ('structuring signal'), *Schlusssignal* ('closing signal'), and *Sprechersignal* ('signal of speaker'). The closely related terms *Gesprächsschrittbeanspruchendes Signal* ('turn-claiming signal'), *Backchannel* ('back channel'), *Hörersignal* ('signal of listener'), and *Rezeptionssignal* ('reception signal') are also relevant according to the literature, but can be identified as listener-related conversation signals. In LingTermNet, they evoke the `Hearer_signal` frame (cf. Section 3.3). As already mentioned in Section 2.2, the `Communication` frame in FrameNet is the parent frame for the `Speaker_signal` frame discussed here. Thus, it can serve as the basis for a first sketch of the `Speaker_signal` frame. Specifically, the FEs of the `Communication` frame can be re-used and adapted to the more specific semantics of the new frame. As a result, the `Speaker_signal` frame includes the frame element SPEAKER, who conveys discourse-organizing HINTS to a HEARER.

To prepare the annotation process, the vanguard provides a set of corpus examples for each potential LU evoking the frame.[13] For the step of subcorporation, we use current technical literature in the domain of linguistics (with the exception of encyclopedias and introductory literature since they usually include metalinguistic information, including explicit definitions, which is of little help). (1) illustrates a corpus example for the LU *structuring signal*.

---

[13] Corpus compilation takes place both via bibliographic searches in libraries and online, in particular via Google Scholar.

(1) **Gliederungssignale** werden von den Sprechern verwendet, um den Aufbau ihres Diskurses zu markieren. (Barme 2012: 37)
('Structuring signals are used by speakers in order to highlight the structure of their discourse')

The second work phase consists of annotating corpus examples for each LU. Previously defined FEs are used for annotation. (2) exemplifies annotations of the corpus example introduced above; each annotation is indicated by indices.

(2) [**Gliederungs**]$_{HINT}$**signale** [werden]$_{SUPPORT}$ [von den Sprechern]$_{SPEAKER}$ [verwendet]$_{SUPPORT}$, [um den Aufbau ihres Diskurses zu markieren]$_{PURPOSE}$. (Barme 2012: 37)
('Structuring signals are used by speakers in order to highlight the structure of their discourse')

LingTermNet uses the same graphical representations for annotations as Berkeley FrameNet. For a better recognition, annotated FEs are highlighted in color both in the annotation report and in the frame entry. In line with Berkeley FrameNet, we doubt that it is helpful to assume a fixed set of semantic roles defined independently of a frame. Rather, we take the view that FEs are specifically tailored to the frame they instantiate. Thus, the name of a FE should reflect its function in the frame as precisely as possible.

The FEs HINT and SPEAKER annotated in (2) are already included in the frame sketch, and they are also represented in the related `Communication` frame. Both FEs have the status of core FEs since they are semantically constitutive for the frame. Non-core FEs, such as in (2) PURPOSE, are usually identified in the course of annotation. They address further lexically relevant meaning facets of the LU respectively the frame.

Methodically, the annotation of technical terms in LingTermNet is based on annotation principles established in FrameNet (cf. Ruppenhofer et al. 2016). However, in contrast to FrameNet, LingTermNet only annotates nouns as targets, simply because our linguistic target domains merely include nominal units. Another difference concerns the annotation categories. While FrameNet annotates not only semantic roles (FEs) but also phrase structures of realized FEs and their grammatical functions, LingTermNet exclusively annotates FEs. Licensed syntactic realizations of FEs can be neglected due to the lexicographical and didactic orientation of LingTermNet. In contrast to FrameNet, we do not annotate null instantiations. In what follows, we briefly explain our main annotation guidelines.

In LingTermNet, annotations are limited to linguistic units that syntactically depend on the target expression. Table 1 provides an overview of these units, each illustrated by an example.

Table 1: Annotated units in LingTermNet.

Annotated unit	Example[14]
Determinative compounds (annotation of determinans if the LU instantiates the determinatum)	Das „Gut" des Sachbearbeiters ist hier keine bewertende Äußerung, sondern ein themenbeendendes [**Gliederungs**]$_{HINT}$ **signal**. (Becker-Mrotzek 2001: 1516) ('The 'Gut' of the case worker is not an evaluative utterance but a topic-finishing structuring signal.')
Left-adjacent attributes	Das „Gut" des Sachbearbeiters ist hier keine bewertende Äußerung, sondern ein [themenbeendendes]$_{EFFECT}$ **Gliederungssignal**. (Becker-Mrotzek 2001: 1516) ('The 'Gut' of the case worker is not an evaluative utterance but a topic-finishing structuring signal.')
Right-adjacent attributes	Da wir die Unterscheidung von **Gliederungssignalen** [am Anfang eines Satzes]$_{POSITION}$ und Gliederungssignalen am Ende eines Satzes (...) für fragwürdig halten (...). (Radtke 1994: 289) ('Since we consider the distinction of structuring signals at the beginning of a sentence and structuring signals at the end of a sentence dubious ... ')
Target LUs as annotated units	Particle frame:[15] Die Konsensfähigkeit dokumentieren sowohl der Inhalt der Äußerung als auch die Verwendung der [**Partikel**]$_{FUNCTION\_WORD}$ *ja*. (Hagemann 2009: 168) ('The ability to reach consensus reflects the content of the utterance as well as the use of the particle *ja*.')
Copula constructions (if the LU is the predicate, and the annotated phrase coincides with the referring expression)	[Das „Gut" des Sachbearbeiters]$_{EXAMPLE}$ ist hier keine bewertende Äußerung, sondern ein themenbeendendes **Gliederungssignal**. (Becker-Mrotzek 2001: 1516) ('The 'ok' of the case worker is not an evaluative utterance but a topic-finishing structuring signal.')

---

14 To illustrate the annotation categories addressed here, corpus examples were annotated only with regard to the category presented. All annotations are documented in the Annotation Report; cf.: http://gsw.phil.hhu.de/diskurslinguistik/index.php?title=Annotationsreport_Gliederungssignal (last access: June 17, 2019).
15 Since there is no annotation of this kind in the Speaker_signal frame, we take an example from the Particle frame. The full frame entry is documented in the online repository: www.lingterm.net (last access: June 17, 2019).

Table 1 (continued)

Annotated unit	Example[14]
Support verb constructions[16]	**Gliederungssignale** [werden]$_{\text{SUPPORT}}$ [von den Sprechern]$_{\text{SPEAKER}}$ [verwendet]$_{\text{SUPPORT}}$ [um den Aufbau ihres Diskurses zu markieren]$_{\text{PURPOSE}}$. (Barme 2012: 37) ('Structuring signals are used by speakers in order to highlight the structure of their discourse.')

The final work phase ('rearguard') focuses on compiling dictionary entries. The entries are based on the frame sketch and analyses of annotated corpus examples. On the technical side, the compilation process is currently supported by a so-called 'MediaWikiSuite', a software programmed for LingTermNet that serves as an interface to the publicly accessible MediaWiki. At the same time, LingTermNet is part of the German FrameNet and Constructicon project (www.german-framenet.de; last access: November 15, 2019). In order to allow the broadest possible use of the terminology repository, including establishing interfaces with German FrameNet, we consider converting LingTermNet to a structured database and thus fully integrating it in the infrastructure of the German FrameNet and constructicon.

3.2 LingTermNet as a didactic resource: the bipartite structure of the repository

LingTermNet consists of two types of entries designed for different levels of learning. On the one hand, the frame entries provide technical background knowledge on a more abstract and therefore demanding level. The lexical entries for technical terms, on the other hand, are beginner-friendly. Here, definitions are lemma-based just like in conventional dictionaries. Hence, LingTermNet consists of two dictionary-like resources. Both are related to each other in such a way that entries in the frame-based dictionary form the basis for lemma-based entries.

---

16 We consider this annotated example an instance of a support verb construction because "the support changes the profiled point-of-view of the frame-evoking noun" (Ruppenhofer et al. 2016: 44); cf. *Gliederungssignal verwenden* ('use structuring device') vs. *Gliederungssignal empfangen* ('receive a structuring device'). Generally, support verb constructions address deverbal LUs in noun-verb combinations in which the frame-evoking potential of the analyzed target expression is semantically stronger than the frame-evoking potential of the verb. In such cases the verb is annotated as 'support verb'. At the same time, those units which syntactically depend on the support verb are annotated as FEs of the target.

For users of LingTermNet, there are two options to determine the meaning(s) of technical terms. On the one hand, it is possible to look up a lemma in the alphabetical index like in conventional dictionaries. On the other hand, the term can also be searched in the LU index. Here, the LUs are also sorted alphabetically, while each LU gives access to the background frame, which motivates the LU's meaning.

For laymen and students who do not search for specific meanings of technical terms but want to deepen their knowledge of a linguistic domain across LUs, there is also the possibility to access frame entries either via the frame index or via the overview of domains covered in LingTermNet. This overview includes both frames and LUs clustered in terms of the linguistic domain to which they belong. Finally, it is possible to select a frame via a dynamic frame-network structure displaying all frames and relations holding between them. Depending on the focus of interest and prior knowledge, LingTermNet offers various options for acquiring specialist knowledge.

Frame entries feature all components mentioned in the previous sections, notably FEs, LUs, Annotation Reports and information on frame-to-frame relations. Each entry starts with a definition of the frame. In the definition, all core FEs of the frame (and, if required, also some of the non-core FEs) are related to each other. If the frame is closely related to a frame in Berkeley FrameNet, correlations are listed wherever possible. In (3) we see the frame entry for the Speaker_signal frame.

(3) In this frame, a SPEAKER conveys discourse-organizing HINTS to a HEARER. The frame describes the perspective of the SPEAKER; it inherits information from the non-perspectivized Signal_scenario frame which can be considered a more general frame superordinated to the Speaker_signal and Hearer_signal frame.

The Speaker_signal frame resembles the Communication frame in Berkeley FrameNet. Specifically, core FEs of the latter are adopted and specified in the Speaker_signal frame.

The Speaker_signal frame subsumes a total of 13 FEs, each of which is defined and illustrated by annotations in a table following the frame definition. To illustrate, Table 2 presents three FEs and their definitions.[17]

---

[17] Other FEs not mentioned here include WAY_OF_REALIZATION, POSITION, PURPOSE, EFFECT, PLACE_OF_APPEARANCE, FREQUENCY, QUANTITY, LANGUAGE, SUBTYPE, EXAMPLE.

Table 2: Selected FEs of the Speaker_signal frame.

FE	Definition & annotated example
SPEAKER (core FE)	The person who conveys the signal. Ex. *[Sprecher]*_{SPEAKER}*signale können vom Sprecher gesetzte Segmentierungen sein.* (*'Signals of the speakers could represent segmentations realized by the speaker.'*)
HINT (core FE)	The Discourse-organizing message which is conveyed along with the signal. Ex. *Das Erkennen von textsortenspezifischen Invarianten und [Gliederungs]*_{HINT}*signalen im Text macht solche Texte durchsichtiger und transparenter.* (*'Recognizing text genre specific invariants and structuring signals in texts makes these texts more transparent and intelligible.'*)
HEARER (non-core)	The Person to whom the signal is addressed. Ex. *[Bei neurotischen Versuchspersonen]*_{HEARER} *[benutzt]*_{Support} *der Sprecher zudem signifikant mehr **Sprechersignale** als bei gesunden.* (*'In case of neurotic test subjects the speaker also uses significantly more speaker signals than in case of healthy subjects.'*)

This way, learners are offered not only a comprehensive explanation of each FE but, at the same time, they get acquainted with authentic linguistic realizations of the FEs in scientific texts. A frame entry also comprises a list of frame-evoking LUs including hyperlinks to the LU entries (cf. Section 3.4) as well as hyperlinks to the Annotation Reports of each LU. In the case of the Speaker_signal frame, for example, the LU list includes *signal of speaker, structuring signal, discourse marker, discontinuity marker, reassurance signal, tag question, opening signal,* and *closing signal*). The Annotation Reports provide all annotated corpus examples, a short definition, and a table with information on the number of annotated FEs for each LU. LingTermNet allows seeing at a glance which FEs are particularly relevant for an LU and how they have been implemented in the analyzed literature.

Finally, a frame entry contains information on frame-to-frame relations as well as a visualization of these relations. This graphic representation is dynamic in that all nodes can be re-arranged freely so that interactive learning is made possible. The types of relation are displayed by mouse-over function. A left click on a node hides indirectly related frames, and a right click takes the user to the entry for the respective frame.

3.3 Didactic usability of networks of frames in LingTermNet

In LingTermNet, each frame is embedded in a rich network of frames ('frame net'). The frames are connected by links that define the nature of the relations. For example, in Figure 3 the `Speaker_signal` frame is related to the `Signal_scenario` frame by a perspective-on relation (cf. Ruppenhofer et al. 2016: 75). Thus, the latter frame represents the superordinate frame.

LingTermNet supports not only network-based learning of technical terms, it also facilitates easy access to tacit knowledge in that frame entries reflect relevant background structures of the whole (linguistic) domain to which the LU and its frame belong. Consider, for example, the embedding network structure of the `Speaker_signal` frame (Figure 3). This frame holds (a) a Perspective_on relation ('Perspektive_auf') to the `Signal_scenario` ('Signal_Szenario') frame, (b) a See_also ('Bezug_auf') relation to the `Conversation_particle` ('Gesprächspartikel') frame, and (c) a Uses ('Verwendet') relation to the `Hedge_expression` ('Vagheitsausdruck') frame.

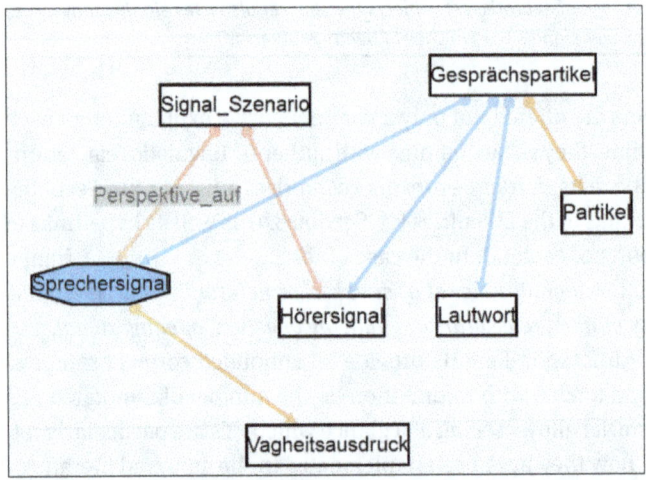

Figure 3: Embedding network structure of the `Speaker_signal` ('Sprechersignal') frame.

The `Signal_scenario` frame is a frame, which is neutral in terms of perspective. It is characterized by a SPEAKER and a HEARER who both convey communicative HINTS to each other. These hints help organize the discourse whereas neither the perspective of the SPEAKER nor that of the HEARER is in the foreground. The `Signal_scenario` frame provides background knowledge relevant for the Speaker_signal and `Hearer_signal` frames. Specifically, these frames inherit core FEs from the more general `Signal_scenario` frame but differ with regard to some non-core FEs. While the

Speaker_signal frame is evoked by LUs such as *tag question*, *discourse marker*, and *opening signal*, the LUs *turn-claiming signal*, *back channel*, *signal of listener* and *reception signal*, evoke the Hearer_signal frame. In analogy to the Speaker_signal frame, the Hearer_signal frame is defined as an event in which a HEARER conveys discourse-organizing HINTS to a SPEAKER, to whose utterance he refers.

In the domain of conversation analysis, it is crucial for students and other learners to conceptually distinguish these two perspectives and to use the technical terms correctly when analyzing spoken discourse. The frame-semantic structure of LingTermNet enables users to identify conceptual structures across LUs and even across frames. With the help of a so-called frame grapher that visualizes frame-to-frame relations, these structures become accessible more comprehensively. With one click, learners can also move, for example, from the Hearer_signal frame to the Speaker_signal frame and vice versa. They learn that there are both speaker-related and listener-related signals in the realm of conversation signals. Even though both are captured in different frame entries, they are motivated by the same superordinate background frame: the non-perspectivized Signal_scenario frame.

The domain of turn-taking exemplifies the relevance of frame-to-frame relations in some detail. It is characteristic for this domain that frames are predominately related by part-whole links; in LingTermNet this link is called Subordinated_of ('Untergeordnet_von') (cf. Figure 4). The predominance of this relation reflects the fact that turns are integral parts of turn-taking processes and, in addition, that turn-constructional units (TCUs), as well as transition relevance places (TRPs), are both integral parts of turns. Note that each of these concepts – turn, turn-taking, TCU, and TRP – constitute an own frame because these frames differ in terms of their FEs.

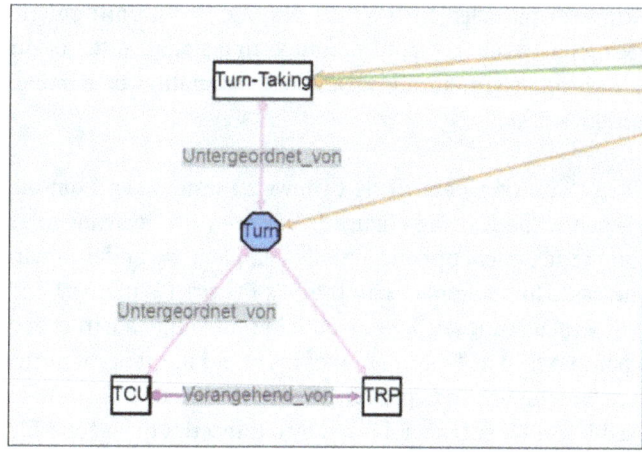

Figure 4: The Turn frame and its neighbors visualized by the frame grapher.

The TCU frame is related to the TRP frame in such a way that the first precedes ('Vorangehend_von') the latter (cf. Figure 4). This linking reflects general background knowledge about the domain, here especially that a TRP always takes place at the end of a TCU within a turn. Before learners deal with individual technical terms in the field of turn-taking, frame-to-frame relations help them to realize important insights across frames. Generally, by means of the frame-based access structure and visualized relations between frames, LingTermNet offers its users the possibility to recognize and acquire background knowledge of technical terms at a higher level of abstraction.

3.4 Compiling lexical entries for technical terms

In contrast to frame entries, LU entries offer definitions of individual LUs (technical terms). Crucially, since each definition is based on its corresponding frame entry, it is also validated by lexicographically evaluated corpus data. To align each LU entry with its corresponding frame as closely as possible, we ensure that core FEs find their way into the LU definitions. For example, the LU entry for *structuring signal* ('Gliederungssignal') comprises the core FEs SPEAKER ('Sprecher') and HINT ('Hinweis'). In the definitions of LUs, these elements, along with others, are highlighted in bold, as shown in (4).

(4) A *structuring signal* is a phenomenon of **spoken language** and describes a signal conveyed by a **speaker** to a **hearer** in order to provide a **hint** as of how **the content of his or her utterance is structured**. The structuring signal may be **linguistic** (e.g. particles such as *no*, *yes*, etc.) or **paralinguistic** (e.g. pitch courses, pauses, etc.) in nature. Structuring signals often occur in combination with other structuring means (e.g. salutation or naming, appeals for attention, etc.).

In (4), the FEs SPEAKER ('Sprecher') and HINT ('Hinweis') were taken from the `Speaker_signal` frame without being changed. However, if a relevant FE is considered too abstract or technical or conceptually complex, we prefer to paraphrase it. This is the case, for example, with the FEs EFFECT ('Wirkung') and WAY_OF_REALIZATION ('Realisierungsart'). Since both FEs are rather abstract and complex, the first is paraphrased as "the content of his or her utterance is structured" and the latter as "linguistic" and "paralinguistic".

If useful and possible, an LU entry is followed by a transcript or a sound file that illustrates the technical term. Figure 5 shows a transcript exemplifying structuring signals in an authentic conversation.

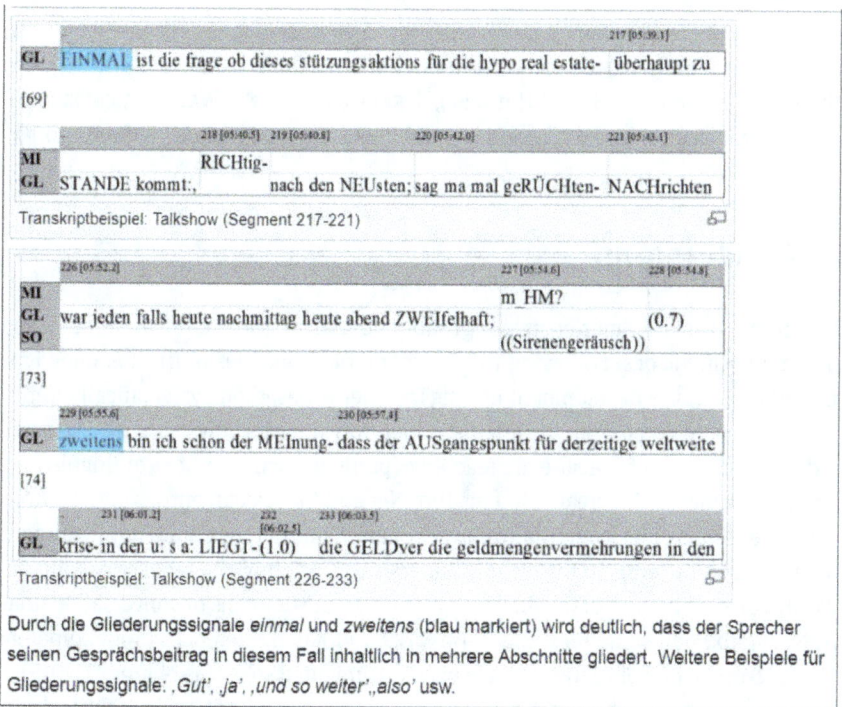

Figure 5: Transcript exemplifying *structuring signal* ('Gliederungssignal').

Sound and transcript examples not only help to identify the described phenomena in authentic texts. They also make it possible to learn how the phenomena occur in authentic texts. For convenience, in the transcripts the phenomena are highlighted in color. Each transcript is complemented by a brief explanation of the technical term in the context of the transcript.[18]

In the last section of each LU entry, we first find a list of conceptually related technical terms, each hyperlinked to the LU entry. In the case of *structuring signal*, this list includes *discontinuity marker, discourse marker, opening signal, reassurance signal, closing signal, signal of speaker*, and *tag question*. This list encourages more comprehensive learning. Instead of learning each technical term in isolation, a network of closely related terms may be addressed and acquired.

---

[18] In Figure 5, the bottom three lines constitute this part. They can be translated into English as follows: "The structuring signals 'once' and 'secondly' (marked in blue) indicate that the speaker divides his or her contribution into several sections. Further examples for structuring signals are 'good', 'yes', 'and so on', and 'so', among others."

Finally, the last section of an LU entry provides a list of those FEs that have been used here for defining the technical term. For *structuring signal*, this list includes SPEAKER ('Sprecher'), HINT ('Hinweis'), HEARER ('HÖRER'), WAY_OF_REALIZATION ('Realisierungsart'), EFFECT ('Wirkung'), and PLACE_OF_OCCURENCE ('Auftretensort').

4 Conclusions

LingTermNet is a FrameNet-style repository specializing in technical terms in the domain of linguistics. Following the lexicographic principles of the Berkeley FrameNet project, the development of LingTermNet is based on systematically annotated sentences taken from the linguistic literature. LingTermNet aims at serving as a didactic resource for academic teaching (particularly in the field of linguistics). Both the frame entries created in LingTermNet and the lexicon entries derived from them are results of lexicographic analyses of authentic corpus data. They document actual use of the terms in the technical literature. Currently, the repository contains 245 linguistic terms, most of which originate from the domains of conversation analysis, syntax, and semantics. Based on 3,729 annotated references (approximately 15 per term), a total of 72 frames have been documented so far (as of June 17, 2019).

A major goal of the LingTermNet project is to document basic technical terminology in the domains of conversation analysis, grammar, semantics, and pragmatics. It aims to illuminate the prerequisites for understanding technical terms and to make these prerequisites available as an online resource. The starting point of the project is the assumption that conceptual background knowledge can be systematically identified and modeled using semantic frames. To achieve these goals, we adopted the same three-step annotation procedure ('vanguard', 'annotators', 'rearguard') as practiced in the Berkeley FrameNet project.

In many ways, LingTermNet may help supporting the teaching and learning of technical terms in the domain of linguistics. In addition, LingTermNet can be used as a reference resource. Definitions of technical terms are didactically prepared and made accessible to learners. By using a traditional lemma-based access structure, learners can access definitions of technical terms as well as descriptive transcripts and sound examples. As an add-on, the frame-based access structure allows advanced students, teachers, and researchers to recognize and capture conceptual prerequisites of technical terms as well as conceptual commonalities and differences between technical terms. Frames specifically help to illuminate conceptual relationships between technical terms across lexemes and even across sub-domains.

In the near future, we plan to scale up and cover basic linguistic terminology relevant for the curriculum in the Bachelor's and Master's programs as comprehensively as possible and to implement it in curriculum development. For conversation analysis, this goal will soon be achieved, but the domains of syntax, morphology, and semantics still have gaps, while technical terms in the domain of pragmatics have not yet been addressed at all. In the final phase of the project, we aim at filling these gaps.

References

Aitchison, Jean. 1994. *Words in the Mind: An Introduction to the Mental Lexicon*. Oxford: Blackwell.
Atkins, Beryl T. S. & Michael Rundell. 2008. *The Oxford guide to practical lexicography*. Oxford: Oxford Univ. Press.
Atkins, Beryl T. S., Michael Rundell & Hiroaki Sato. 2003. The contribution of FrameNet to practical lexicography. *International Journal of Lexicography* 16, 333–357.
Atzler, Judith K. 2011. *Twist in the list: Frame Semantics as a vocabulary teaching and learning tool*. Austin (Texas): The University of Texas at Austin.
Baker, Collin F., Charles J. Fillmore & John B. Lowe. *1998*. The Berkeley FrameNet Project. *Proceedings of the 17th International Conference on Computational Linguistics* 1, 86–90.
Boas, Hans C. 2013. Wie viel Wissen steckt in Wörterbüchern? Eine frame-semantische Perspektive. *Zeitschrift für Angewandte Linguistik* 57, 75–97.
Boas, Hans C & Ryan Dux. 2013. Semantic Frames for Foreign Language Education: Towards a German frame-based dictionary. *Veredas: Frame Semantics and Its Technological Applications* 17 (1), 82–100.
Boas, Hans C., Ryan Dux & Alexander Ziem. 2016. Frames and Constructions in a German-English online learner's dictionary. In: Sabine de Knop & Gaëtanelle Gilquin (eds.), *Constructionist Approaches to Second Language Acquisi-tion and Foreign Language Teaching*, 303–326. Berlin/New York: De Gruyter Mouton.
Brinker, Klaus & Sven F. Sager. 2006. *Linguistische Gesprächsanalyse. Eine Einführung*. Berlin: Schmidt.
Cruse, David A. 1986. *Lexical semantics*. Cambridge: Cambridge Univ. Press.
Deppermann, Arnulf. 2008. *Gespräche analysieren. Eine Einführung*. Wiesbaden: VS Verlag für Sozialwissenschaften.
Dolbey, Andrew E. 2009. *BioFrameNet: a FrameNet Extension to the Domain of Molecular Biology*. Dissertation. Berkeley.
Faber, Pamela. 2011. The dynamics of specialized knowledge representation: Simulational reconstruction or the perception–action interface. *Terminology. International Journal of Theoretical and Applied Issues in Specialized Communication* 17 (1), 9–29
Faber Benítez, Pamela, Carlos Márquez Linares & Miguel Vega Expósito. 2005. Framing Terminology: A Process-Oriented Approach. *Meta* 50 (4), doi: https://doi.org/10.7202/019916ar.
Fillmore, Charles J. 1975. An alternative to checklist theories of meaning. In: Cathy Cogen, Henry Thompson, Graham Thurgood, Kenneth Whistler & James Wright (eds.), 123–131. *Proceedings of the first annual meeting of the Berkeley Linguistics Society*. Berkeley: Berkeley Linguistics Society.
Fillmore, Charles J. 1976. The need for a frame semantics within linguistics. *Statistical Methods in Linguistics* 12, 5–29.

Fillmore, Charles J. 1977. Scenes-and-frames semantics. In: Antonio Zampolli (ed.), *Linguistic Structures Processing* vol 5, 55–81. Amsterdam/New York/Oxford: North-Holland.
Fillmore, Charles J. 1982. Frame Semantics. In: Linguistics in the morning calm. Selected Papers from SICOL 1981. Seoul, 111–137.
Fillmore, Charles J. & Miriam R. L. Petruck. 2003. FrameNet Glossary. *International Journal of Lexicography* 16, 359–361.
Fillmore, Charles J. & Beryl T. S. Atkins. 1992. Toward a Frame-based Lexicon: The Semantics of RISK and its Neighbors. In: Adrienne Lehrer & Eva F. Kittay (eds.), *Frames, Fields and Contrasts: New Essays in Semantic and Lexical Organization*, 75–102. Hillsdale, New Jersey: Erlbaum.
Fillmore, Charles J. & Collin Baker. 2010. A Frames Approach to Semantic Analysis. In: Bernd Heine & Heiko Narrog (eds.), *The Oxford Handbook of Linguistic Analysis*, 313–339. Oxford: Oxford Univ. Press.
Fillmore, Charles J., Christopher R. Johnson & Miriam R. L. Petruck. 2003. Background To FrameNet. *International Journal of Lexicography* 16, 235–250.
Fillmore, Charles J., Miriam R. L. Petruck, Josef Ruppenhofer & Abby Wright. 2003. FrameNet in Action: The Case of Attaching. In: International *Journal of Lexicography* 16, 297–332.
Gülich, Elisabet & Lorenza Mondada. 2008. *Konversationsanalyse. Eine Einführung am Beispiel des Französischen*. Tübingen: Niemeyer (Romanistische Arbeitshefte).
Henne, Helmut & Helmut Rehbock. 2001. *Einführung in die Gesprächsanalyse*. Berlin/New York: De Gruyter.
Lönneker-Rodman, Birte & Alexander Ziem. 2018. Frames als Repräsentationsformat in modernen Terminologie-Systemen. In: Alexander Ziem, Lars Inderelst & Detmer Wulf (eds.), *Frame-Theorien interdisziplinär. Modelle, Anwendungsfelder, Methoden*, 251–288. Düsseldorf: dup (Proceedings in Language and Cognition).
Mroczynski, Robert. 2014. *Gesprächslinguistik. Eine Einführung*. Tübingen: Narr Francke Attempto.
Neumann-Schneider, Anastasia & Alexander Ziem. 2020. LingTermNet: Konzeption und Entwicklung eines FrameNet für linguistische Fachterminologie. In: Christian Lang, Roman Schneider, Horst Schwinn & Angelika Wöllstein (eds.), Grammatik und Terminologie. Beiträge zur ars grammatica 2017, 105–128. Tübingen: Narr.
Pearsall, Judy (ed.). 1999. *The Concise Oxford Dictionary. ed. 10*, Oxford: Oxford Univ. Press.
Reimerink, Arianne & Pamela Faber. 2009. EcoLexicon: A frame-based knowledge base for the environment. In: Jiří Hřebíček, Jindřichův Hradec, Emil Pelikán, Ondřej Mírovský, Werner Pilmmann, Ivan Holoubek & Rudolf Legat (eds.), *Towards eEnvironment (Challenges of SEIS and SISE: Integrating Environmental Knowledge in Europe)*. Brno: Masaryk University.
Rosch, Eleanor. 1977. Human Categorization. In: Neil Warren (ed.), *Studies in Crosscultural Psychology*, 1–49. London/New York/San Francisco: Academic Press.
Ruppenhofer, Josef, Michael Ellsworth, Miriam R. L. Petruck, Christopher R. Johnson, Collin F. Baker & Jan Scheffczyk. 2016. *FrameNet II: Extended Theory and Practice*. Berkeley: International Computer Science Institute.
Saussure, Ferdinand de. 1916. *Cours de linguistique générale*. Lausanne, Paris: Payot.
Schmidt, Thomas. 2009. The Kicktionary – a multilingual lexical resource of foot-ball language. In: Hans C. Boas, Hans (ed.), *Multilingual FrameNets in computational lexicography: Methods and applications*, 101–132. Berlin/New York: De Gruyter Mouton.
Schwitalla, Johannes. 2006. *Gesprochenes Deutsch. Eine Einführung*. Berlin: Schmidt.
Suchowolec, Karolina, Christian Lang & Roman Schneider. 2018. An empirically validated, onomasiologically structured, and linguistically motivated online terminology.

Re-designing scientific resources on German grammar. *International Journal on Digital Libraries*. Berlin/ Heidelberg,1–16, DOI: doi.org/10.1007/s00799-018-0254-x.
Ziem, Alexander. 2014a. *Frames of Understanding in Text and Discourse: Theoretical Foundations and Descriptive Applications*. (= Human Cognitive Processing 48) Amsterdam/Philadelphia: Benjamins.
Ziem, Alexander. 2014b. Von der Kasusgrammatik zum FrameNet: Frames, Konstruktionen und die Idee eines Konstruktikons. In: Alexander Ziem & Alexander Lasch (eds.), *Grammatik als Netzwerk von Konstruktionen? Sprachwissen im Fokus in der Konstruktionsgrammatik*, 263–290. Berlin/New York: De Gruyter Mouton.
Ziem, Alexander. 2015. Fußball für Anfänger: Sieben Thesen zur Konzeption eines elektronischen Wörterbuches für den Sprachunterricht. In: Joachim Born, & Thomas Gloning (eds.), *Sport, Sprache, Kommunikation, Medien: Interdisziplinäre Perspektiven* (= Linguistische Untersuchungen 8), 381–410. Gießen: Gießener Elektronische Bibliothek.
Ziem, Alexander, Johanna Flick & Phillip Sandkühler. 2019. The German Constructicon Project: Framework, Methodology, Resources. *Lexicographica* 35 (1), 15–40.

Sources of corpus examples

Barme, Stefan. 2012. *Gesprochenes Französisch*. Berlin/Boston: De Gruyter.
Becker-Mrotzek, Michael. 2001. Gespräche in Ämtern und Behörden. In: Klaus Brinker, Gerd Antos, Wolfgang Heinemann & Sven F. Sager (eds.), *Text- und Gesprächslinguistik*. (= Band des Handbuches für Sprach- und Kommunikationswissenschaft, HSK 16, Halbband. 2), 1505–1525. Berlin/New York: De Gruyter.
Hagemann, Jörg. 2009. Tag questions als Evidenzmarker. Formulierungsdynamik, sequentielle Struktur und Funktionen redezuginterner tags. *Gesprächsforschung*. Online-Zeitschrift zur verbalen Interaktion 10, 145–176.
Radtke, Edgar. 1994. *Gesprochenes Französisch und Sprachgeschichte. Zur Rekonstruktion der Gesprächskonstitution in Dialogen französischer Sprachlehrbücher des 17. Jahrhunderts unter besonderer Berücksichtigung der italienischen Adaptionen*. Tübingen: Niemeyer.

Author Index

Achard, M. 4, 20
Atkins, B.T.S. 9, 10, 201, 277, 337, 338, 341
Atzler, J. 306, 334, 335

Baayen, H. 57, 58
Baker, C. 10, 11, 278, 340
Beavers, J. 220
Behrens, H. 217
Bergs, A. 90
Berthele, R. 220, 227
Bertoldi, A. 13
Boas, H.C. 4, 6, 7, 8, 9, 10, 11, 12, 13, 15, 16, 18, 22, 25, 89–91, 139, 181, 187, 200–201, 267, 277, 278, 280, 282, 306, 307, 310, 334, 335, 337
Bolinger, D. 125
Booij, G. 8, 167
Busse, D. 9
Butler, C. 6
Bybee, J. 47, 65, 84

Cappelle, B. 5, 79, 80, 189
Chomsky, N. 6
Croft, W. 7, 8, 89, 139
Cruse, A. 337

Dabrowska 99, 105, 114
De Cock, S. 74
De Knop. S. 4, 20, 73, 123, 127, 181, 182, 217, 225, 235, 258
Diessel, H. 6, 76
Diewald, G. 90
Dirven, R. 217, 258
Divjak, D. 161
Dobrovol'skij, D. 132, 133
Dolbey, A. 13
Dux, R. 4, 6, 22, 26, 200, 201, 267, 280, 307, 310, 334, 335

Ellis, N. 3, 5, 52, 62, 63, 64, 66, 161, 180, 223, 266, 268, 269, 274
Engelberg, S. 135

Fellbaum, C. 10
Fillmore, C.J. 6, 8, 9, 10, 11, 13, 15, 16, 18, 76, 179, 185, 186, 187, 188, 201, 277, 278, 336, 337, 340, 341
Finkbeiner, R. 123
Fischer, K. 76, 90
Francis, G. 188, 195, 199, 207
Fried, M. 75

Gilquin, G. 4, 20, 73, 74, 76, 80, 82, 83, 84, 89, 181, 182, 199
Goldberg, A. 6, 7, 8, 21, 48, 65, 74, 76, 79, 97, 125, 126, 127, 179, 183, 189, 266, 277
Gonzalvez-Garcia, F. 6, 27
Granger, S. 83, 98, 110
Gries, S.T. 3, 21, 49, 50, 57, 66, 76, 149, 161

Herbst, T. 4, 5, 8, 20, 21, 97, 110, 115, 116, 185, 186
Hilpert, M. 84
Höder, S. 6
Hoffmann, T. 6
Holme, R. 3, 4, 181, 182, 183, 184, 191, 198, 209, 210, 265
Hunston, S. 188, 195, 199, 207

Jacobs, J. 123, 126, 128, 133
Janda, L. 162, 179
Jurafsky, D. 179

Kay, P. 6, 76, 179

Lakoff, G. 6, 61, 305
Lambrecht, K. 76
Langacker, R. 6, 47, 51, 52, 98, 116, 183, 266, 310
Lee-Goldman, R. 16, 187
Lorenz, A. 4, 27, 200, 280, 282, 298, 307
Lowe, J.B. 340
Lyngfelt, B. 16, 18, 78, 179, 186, 210, 280

Madlener, K. 5, 103, 217, 222, 228, 249, 253, 256, 257
Michaelis, L. 6, 76, 188
Mollica, F. 4, 182

Nation, I.S.P. 87, 271, 272, 273, 275, 308, 310
Nesset, T. 163, 164
Neumann-Schneider, A. 335
Nikiforidou, K. 90

Ohara, K. 187
Östman, J.-O. 75

Patten, A. 4, 189, 190
Perek, F. 4, 189, 190
Petruck, M. 10, 16, 187, 277, 307, 341
Proost, C. 135

Römer, U. 62, 63, 66, 161, 180
Ruppenhofer, J. 10, 12, 13, 188, 204, 210, 280, 311, 345, 347, 350

Sag, I. 6, 277
Sambre, P. 76
Schmidt, T. 13, 280, 337
Sinclair, J. 97, 98, 184
Slobin, D. 216, 220, 223, 225, 243
Stubbs, M. 89
Subirats, C. 280
Swan, M. 192, 194, 195, 196, 198

Talmy, L. 123, 128, 167, 219, 220, 225
Tomassello, M. 21, 76, 180, 216
Torrent, T. 13
Traugott, E. 135
Trousdale, G. 6

Uhrig, P. 185

Willems, K. 128
Wulff, S. 3, 21, 49, 161

Ziem, A. 4, 6, 7, 9, 139, 187, 200, 201, 335, 337, 341

Subject Index

Adjusted frequency 57
Advanced learner discourse 272
Allostruction 80
American National Corpus 10
Analogy 126
Annotation 16
Antonym 168
Applied Construction Grammar 5, 13, 73, 89
Aspectual prefix 164, 167
Assessment 106, 310
Association 64
Authentic language 181, 195
Authentic speech 85
Author recognition test 109
Automaticity, degree of 81

Berkeley Construction Grammar 6, 13
Bigram 79
British National Corpus 10, 56

Case Grammar 6, 9
Center for Open Educational Resources and Language Learning (COERLL) 22, 276, 280
Chunk 28, 274
Cloze procedure 184
COBUILD Grammar Patterns 29, 185, 188, 190, 202, 209
Cognateness 274
Cognitive commitment 61
Cognitive Construction Grammar 6, 91
Cognitive linguistics 265
Cognitive restructuring 258
Collinear frequency 59
Collocation 28, 97, 99, 112, 114, 115, 273
Collostructional analysis 80
Communicative
– approach 181, 196
– breakdown 86
– function 194
– language teaching 320
– task 314
Conceptual slot 234

Constructicon 13, 78, 179, 191, 199, 202
Construction 6, 7, 266
– Argument structure 18
– Autonomous 127
– Caused-motion 242
– Ditransitive 8, 76, 266
– Gapping 16
– Imperative 64
– Intransitive motion 76
– *Let alone* 16, 76
– Light verb 77
– Localization 249
– Mad magazine 76
– Meaningful 18
– Metaphorical 172
– Non-directional 174
– Negation 76
– Nominal extraposition 76
– Phonological 80
– Phrasal verb 76
– Phraseme 132
– Right-node-raising 16
– Schematic 76, 116, 127, 131
– Semi-idiomatic 18
– Spontaneous motion 249
– Subject-auxiliary-inversion 8
– Subject-predicate 16, 18
– Support verb 347
– Transitive 76
– Valency 28
– Verb-free 136
– *Way* 8, 18
– *Way*_manner 18, 19
– Weather 164
– WXDY 76
Constructional
– complexity 222, 226, 231, 233, 236, 249, 255
– network 211, 226
– preference 226, 236, 237, 257, 258
– repertoire 226, 257
Constructionalization 51
Constructional meaning 208

Construction Element 16
Constructional Approaches to Language
    Pedagogy (CALP) 3, 4, 91
Construction Grammar (CxG) 6, 74
Construction grammar syllabus 196
Context availability 53
Context of usage 62
Contextual distinctiveness 53, 54, 63
Contextual diversity 55, 58
Contextualized learning 298
Contingency 64
Conversation analysis 351
Core 7
Correlation coefficient 105
Corrective feedback 87
Corpus of Contemporary American English
    (COCA) 79
Cultural information 298

Data driven learning 271
Datenbank Gesprochenes Deutsch (DGD)
    123
Deductive grammar instruction 300
Dialogic Construction Grammar 86
Dialogic syntax 86
Diasystematic Construction Grammar 6
Digitales Wörterbuch der Deutschen Sprache
    (DWDS) 22, 30
Directive speech act, 123
Discourse marker 83, 85
Discovery learning 191
Disfluency 79
Dispersion 55, 62, 63
– Measure 57
Distribution
– Posterior 53
– Prior 53

Encoding preference 232, 236
English 23, 224, 225, 226, 236, 240, 256,
    295, 306
English as a second language 182
English lexicon project 58
Entrenchment 52, 56, 60, 61, 81, 83, 216
– Principle 127
Entropy 64, 65
Erlangen Valency PatternBank 185

Explicit instruction 269
Exposure 104, 274

Family resemblance 135
Fan effect 65
Foreign learner dictionary 97
Foreign Language Learning (FLL) 5, 6, 10,
    28, 99
Foreign Language Teaching (FLT) 5, 6, 10,
    28, 115
Formulaic expression 184
Frame-based language pedagogy 305, 307,
    310, 320, 324
Frame Element (FE) 11, 16, 277, 339, 343
– Core 11
Frame-evoking element (FEE) 343
FrameNet 10, 13, 18, 179, 185, 186, 187, 188,
    200, 202, 209, 278, 311, 333, 336
Frame Semantics 6, 8, 185, 200, 265, 277,
    292, 306, 308, 336, 343
Frame-to-frame relation 189, 195, 204, 342,
    343
French 224, 305, 306, 312, 313, 314
French FrameNet 314
Frequency 5, 15, 24, 47, 52, 58, 60, 61, 77,
    161, 165, 190, 271, 274, 308, 309, 314,
    319
Frequency of occurrence 51

German 23, 25, 26, 224, 225, 226, 236, 240,
    256, 295
German Frame-based Online Lexicon
    (G-FOL) 22, 24, 25, 27, 28, 29, 35, 201,
    265, 276, 277, 280, 286, 291, 334
Global utterance complexity 232
Glottal replacement 80
Goal-over-source principle 128
Grammar instruction 191
Grammatical function 12, 16
Grammaticalization 51
Grammaticography 15, 16
Grammis 333
Guided induction 271, 275

Homonym 268
Homophone 268
Human forgetting curve 63

Idiom 266
Illocutionary force 124
Illocutionary speech act 139
Implicit grammar instruction 270
Inductive grammar teaching 275, 300
Inductive learning 199
Information
– condensation 224, 235
– density 217, 230, 257
– focus 216, 219, 236, 256
– locus 216, 219, 236, 256
– packaging 230
– reduction 235
Input-based instruction 273
Input engineering 181
Instructional manipulation 87
Instructional model 267
Intercultural competence 267, 300
Interlanguage restructuring 255
Italian 26, 145, 146, 224

Kicktionary 337
Korean 221

Language chunking 82
Language pedagogy 181
Learned attention 223, 230, 257
Learner speech 78, 80
Learning activities 285
Lexical
– access 55, 60
– association 309
– decision task 52
– entry report 12
– processing 54
– substitution 198
– unit (LU) 9, 10, 13, 187, 193, 266, 277, 280, 337
– variation 53
Lexicalization pattern 217, 236
Lexicogrammatical continuum 98
Lexicographic procedure 335
Lexicon 18
Lexicon-syntax continuum 98
Linear regression model 57
LingTermNet 334, 335, 337, 340, 343, 352

Linguistic relativity 221
Localization 236
Log transformation 57

Meaning group 188
Metalinguistic literacy 322
Metaphor 305
Metonymy 305, 311, 313, 322, 323, 324
Mini-construction 23, 24, 25
Multiword expression 83, 274

Naming latencies 60
Native speaker 5
Native speech 78
Network 154
– of constructions 6, 116
N-gram 79, 82
Norming data 60
Null hypothesis 51
Null Instantiation 13, 339

Paraphrase 86
Pedagogical Construction Grammar (PCxG) 4, 5, 8, 20, 21, 22, 24
Pedagogical intervention 305
Pathbreaker 183
Path complexity 250
Pattern 188, 199
– Preference 237
Peripheral representative 137
Periphery 7
Phonological similarity 84
Phrase type 12
Phraseological unit 111
Phraseology 181
Phraseoschablonen 133
Polysemy 310
Prediction error 66
Predictor
– Frequency 59
– Morphological 59
– Word-level 59
Priming 62
– Effects 150
Principle of No Synonymy 125
Productivity 8, 199

Profile
- Constructional 161, 171, 172, 177
- Grammatical 161, 174
Projectionist approach 126
Psychological reality 181

Rank correlation 57
Reduction effect 84
Register 77
- Difference 123
Relative entropy 53
Relative frequency 49
Reaction time 52, 57
Response time 52
Response time latency 53
Resting activation level 62
Rules of correct usage 195
Russian 25, 26, 161, 163, 166, 167, 177, 225, 256
Russian National Corpus 162, 165

Satellite-framed language 123, 167
Schematicity 90
Semantic frame
- Activity 206, 208
- Activity_ongoing 207
- Activity_start 206, 208
- Activity_stop 207, 208
- Arguing 284, 291
- Arriving 206
- Being_located 15, fn 22
- Buying and selling 289
- Causation 289
- Cause_impact 27
- Cause_motion 27
- Choosing 27
- Cleaning 288
- Commercial_transaction 9
- Commitment 27
- Deciding 27, 290
- Desirability 12, 279
- Desire 27, 291
- Dressing 311
- Drinking 30, 284
- Eating 30, 284
- Education 289
- Exercise 28, 284
- Experienceer_focused_emotion 27
- Fighting 284, 291
- Giving 8
- Gizmo, 15, fn 22
- Giving_birth 13, fn 22
- Grooming 11, 12, 22, 23, 29, 279, 287, 288
- Intentionally_affect 12, 279
- Leadership 27
- Motion 277
- Path_shape 27
- Personal relationship 287, 289, 290
- Purpose 311
- Self_motion 8, 27
- Sleep 265, 284
- State_continue 207
- Temperature 15, fn 22
- Thinking: Familiarity 291
- Thinking: Opinion 291
- Transition_to_a_situation 206
- Transition_to_a_state 206, 207, 208
- Work 289, 291
Semantic
- role 9
- transfer 245
- variable 56
Sentence template 23
Sequence of potential acquisition 86
S-framed language 220, 256
Sign-Based Construction Grammar 6
Sketch Engine 123, 131
Slot-filler complexity 228
Spanish 27, 224
Spatial language 216
Spoken corpora 73
Spoken language 73
Spontaneous motion 253
Statistical complexity 66
Strategic input 161, 165, 177
Structural priming 127, 149, 153
Stylistic sensitivity 76
Syntactic coding 228
Syntax 18
Syntax-lexicon continuum 8

Target vocabulary 315
Task effect 244
Tertium comparationis 139

Thinking for speaking 216, 223
Translation equivalent 269, 286
Two-way preposition 141
Type frequency 58, 65
Type-token ratio 65
Typological bootstrapping 216, 221

Unlearning 257

Valence pattern 12, 110
Valence table 12, 18
Valency Theory 6
Verb
– Aspectual 203
– Generic lexical 254
– Light 183
– Manner 238, 254
– Non-directional 166
– Phrasal 205
– Semantically rich 238, 254
– Unidirectional 166
Verbless directive 124, 126, 128, 133
V-framed language 220
Vocabulary
– Acquisition 200, 269
– learning 21
– metalinguistic 317
– prefixed 168
– retention 309
– simplex 168
– size 60

Word frequency 54
Words-that-go-together test 99
Written language bias 74, 75

Zipfian frequency distribution 55

www.ingramcontent.com/pod-product-compliance
Lightning Source LLC
Chambersburg PA
CBHW061930220426
43662CB00012B/1855